Florentine Political Writings from Petrarch to Machiavelli

Florentine Political Writings from Petrarch to Machiavelli

EDITED BY

Mark Jurdjevic,
Natasha Piano,
and
John P. McCormick

PENN

UNIVERSITY OF PENNSYLVANIA PRESS

PHILADELPHIA

A volume in the Haney Foundation Series, established in 1961
with the generous support of Dr. John Louis Haney.

Published by
University of Pennsylvania Press
Philadelphia, Pennsylvania 19104–4112
www.upenn.edu/pennpress

Printed in the United States of America on acid-free paper

1 3 5 7 9 10 8 6 4 2

A catalogue record for this book is available
from the Library of Congress.

978-0-8122-2432-0

In Memory of Ronald G. Witt

I think something has been true and is true
in this city more than in any other; the men
of Florence especially enjoy perfect freedom
and are the greatest enemies of tyrants.
—Leonardo Bruni

Contents

PART III. ON FLORENCE
BETWEEN REPUBLIC AND PRINCIPATE

Introduction

MARK JURDJEVIC

Dante famously pathologized the incessant mutability of Florentine culture as a bedridden sick woman vainly attempting to ease her pain by constantly shifting position. Students of political culture, however, have been drawn to medieval and Renaissance Florence precisely because of what the medieval poet condemned as a tragic deviation from the pacific and timeless ideal of universal Christian monarchy. From our perspective, the city's conflicts add up to more than the sum of their parts. In the intensity of Florentine factionalism and the frequent alterations in its political institutions lay a larger inquiry—more experiential and improvised than theoretical—into the nature of political legitimacy and the relationship between authority and its social context.[1] In this respect, Florence was both exceptional and typical of Renaissance political culture. As Dante rightly observed, Florentine political life was particularly unstable, but throughout Italy the emergence of communes and city-states in the collapse of papal and imperial power led to similar experiments in political legitimacy, constitutional configurations, and competing bids for power from newly empowered urban classes.

This volume provides a selection of political texts—largely but not exclusively Florentine—that illustrates the language, conceptual vocabulary, and issues at stake in Florentine political culture at key moments in its development. The volume opens in the mid-fourteenth century with the letter of Petrarch (Francesco Petrarca) to Francesco da Carrara, the ruler of Padua, on the nature and duties of the ideal prince. A quintessential example of the widespread mirror-for-princes genre (*speculum principis*) by the most influential humanist of his day, Petrarch's advice to the lord of Padua demonstrates how late medieval Italians argued for the advantages and legitimacy of princely rule. Two texts by the early humanist Coluccio Salutati and the jurist Bartolus of Sassoferrato further explore the nature of monarchical government through an analysis of tyranny, monarchy's corrupt counterpart. Texts by two leading fifteenth-century humanists, the Florentine chancellors Leonardo Bruni and Poggio Bracciolini, celebrate the republican constitutions of Florence and Venice in a context of increasing aristocratic domination of politics. Their texts demonstrate the way in which humanism's emphasis on unity and consensus added a veneer of classical gravitas first to oligarchical rule in Florence and then to outright control of the city by the Medici family.[2] Not all humanists deployed their learning on behalf of those in power, however. *De libertate*, a text by Alamanno Rinuccini, demonstrates how classical ideas—in particular an exhortation to a life of Platonic withdrawal and contemplation—could become a bitter form of protest against the degree to which the Medici had subverted republican self-rule in Florence. Fifteen years after Rinuccini lamented the corruption of Florentine government, the French king Charles VIII invaded Italy, triggering a half century of peninsular warfare between Spain, France, and the Holy Roman Empire that permanently altered the political context in Florence and Italy.

The remainder of the texts in this volume—none by humanists, strictly speaking, but by thinkers nevertheless deeply immersed in the literature of antiquity and inconceivable without the Florentine humanist setting—were all composed in this context of heightened instability and all directly or indirectly address its implications. The first text is a constitutional proposal for the Florentine government by the Dominican friar Girolamo Savonarola, the most accomplished theologian of his day and consequently widely admired in the city's humanist circles in spite of his fiery sermons expounding on the immorality of pagan writers. Savonarola's treatise robustly championed a more popular and inclusive variety of republicanism that had distant precedents in Florentine history but had been more recently undermined in the fifteenth century by the Florentine elite and the rise of the Medici. Like Rinuccini, Savonarola's treatise had a subtext that associated the Medici family, who had been ousted from the city in 1494, with tyranny. The next text, written by the Florentine *ottimate* Paolo Vettori, addressed the Medici family at the moment of their triumphant return to Florence in 1512, advocating that they adopt a de facto princely regime based on force. The remaining texts were all written by the two greatest political theorists of the Renaissance, Niccolò Machiavelli and Francesco Guicciardini. The texts selected (several of which are translated into English for the first time) are all formally prescriptive: constitutional recommendations for the ideal configuration of the republic and for the stable integration of Medici power within it, technical analyses of electoral techniques and procedures, and complex mechanisms for harmoniously integrating the city's competing social groups. They reveal a lesser-known aspect of the two thinkers' intellectual preoccupations, both famous for other writings—Machiavelli of course for *The Prince* and *Discourses on Livy* and Guicciardini for his monumental history of Italy. Here we see them less as the grand sages of Renaissance political thought engaged in timeless dialogue with the canon and more as political artisans, intensely working on the technical aspects of Florentine politics, fine-tuning the city's constitution with tools furnished by their experience and sharpened by their formidable intellects.

What these texts do not reveal, and hence part of their appeal, is the larger theoretical normative understanding of political authority elsewhere in Europe to which they were the exception. In Europe of the Middle Ages, political authority was fundamentally linked to the notion of universal monarchy. Because a single omnipotent God ruled over the universe, it followed in principle that a single divine figure should rule over Europe's peoples, conceptualized not as members of different nations but as common members of Christendom.[3] Of course no such central authority ever existed, but the theory of universal monarchy was supple enough to subsume and legitimate Europe's complex political chessboard. In principle, power on earth in both spiritual and temporal affairs belonged to the pope, who, as God's chief vicar on earth, enjoyed supernatural legitimacy. Primarily preoccupied with spiritual matters (in theory if not fact), the popes deputized emperors to wield the temporal sword on their behalf and administer justice in worldly matters. The emperors in turn granted authority to lesser monarchs, who in turn granted authority to lesser princes. As a result, all rulers in Europe outside of Italy in this period were local variations on a universal ideal, and they occupied rungs in an ascending ladder of authority that ultimately led, through kings, emperors, and popes, to God. Admittedly, this neat hierarchy was never more than theoretical, but as a shared theory it had considerable power to condition the language through which politics was conducted. We see this in the degree to which scholastic political thought overwhelmingly focused on monarchy, its prerogatives and limits, and its relationship to the church, also conceived as a monarchical structure.[4]

In the early Middle Ages, the political units of the Italian peninsula fit relatively clearly into the prevailing political schema. In the south, the Kingdom of Naples was a natural monarchy much like those north of the Alps, and the myriad city-states that dotted central and northern Italy were all theoretically subject to either pope or emperor. Many towns were supervised or ruled outright by papal or imperial vicars, and up and down the peninsula Guelf (pro-papal) and Ghibelline (pro-imperial) parties vied for power.[5] Even as late as the sixteenth century vestiges of the luster of an imperial lineage remained: ambitious families who already wielded de facto power over their city, such as the Medici in Florence or the Sforza in Milan, sought out imperial investiture to suggest, however notionally, that their rule fit into Europe's schema.[6] The fact that these families valued theoretical imperial investiture long after they had already established themselves in power without making any reference to it whatsoever demonstrates the pan-European durability of the model of universal monarchy.

By the thirteenth century, occasional requests for investiture notwithstanding, the political landscape in Italy had changed in ways that required the creation of new versions of political legitimacy. The long and costly struggle for supremacy between the papacy and the empire left the two major powers increasingly bankrupt and unable to press their claims to the loyalty and obedience of Italy's increasingly wealthy cities. As a result Italy's many self-governing towns rejected their papal or imperial overlords and declared themselves autonomous and sovereign in their own right, removing themselves in the process from universal monarchy's accepted chain of hierarchy. To articulate their new status in language required the fashioning of a new political vocabulary and novel arguments about how and why political communities come into existence. In that new vocabulary and those novel arguments lay the origins of Renaissance political thought and the underlying conceptual framework for the texts presented in this volume.

Initially, most of the central and northern Italian cities developed along republican and popular lines. In a fortuitous stroke of good timing, the thirteenth-century discovery and translation of Aristotle's *Politics* added intellectual ballast to the fledgling communal regimes. For Aristotle, the city was the quintessential unit of political life, and his political theory correspondingly began with humanity's natural instinct to gather together in political communities in pursuit of the common good. Urban Italians of the fourteenth century, living in socially complex communes organized around greater and lesser guilds, found a number of Aristotelian arguments congenial, particularly his definition of a citizen as one who alternately rules and is ruled; his account of distributive justice—the notion that wealth and status should be distributed according to merit; and his defense of the mixed constitution—the notion that an ideal government combines elements of the governments of the one, the few, and the many.[7] Further, Aristotle's theory was in significant ways applied from close study of the actual constitutions of the myriad Greek city-states of his day; the applied orientation appealed to the practically oriented merchant culture of the burgeoning communes as much as the numerous parallels between the Italian and ancient city-state systems.[8]

With a few major and important exceptions—particularly Florence, the subject of this volume—the experiment in communal government did not endure. In most cases, Italy's urban communities succumbed to one-man, or signorial (lordly, from *signore*) rule. Conflict within the cities' aristocracies, civil wars, external conflicts, and aristocratic hostility to periodic bids for power from the laboring classes all combined to create instabilities that fatally undermined communal regimes in Ferrara, Mantua, Verona, Milan, and elsewhere. Stability became a paramount priority for strife-ridden cities dominated by merchant elites who privileged commercial over martial values, and it usually came with the constitutional price of one-man rule. In some cases, mercenary captains installed themselves as lords of the cities they were hired to defend; in other cases, despots emerged out of the city's judicial institutions, such as the captain of the people; and in others, powerful families outmaneuvered their elite competitors to claim control.[9] As Machiavelli observed in *The Prince*, such new princes were products of conflicts between popular and elite groups and tended to arise as the champion of the people against the nobles or vice versa. In one respect, the monarchical form of government ubiquitous throughout Europe had returned. But these new self-styled and self-appointed princes, much like the communes they supplanted, could not defend their legitimacy in transalpine universalist language and were compelled to seek new justifications for their power. They found that justification through the reinvention of the mirror-for-princes tradition, a venerable genre of political counsel for monarchs dating from antiquity that was particularly dominant during the Middle Ages.[10]

The prevailing genre could not be applied without alteration, however, because the axioms on which it prescribed the conduct of ideal princes were fundamentally linked to and compatible with larger ubiquitous assumptions about universal monarchy (unsurprising, given that many were based on Thomas Aquinas's *On Kingship*). We see this clearly in one of the quintessential medieval Italian examples of the genre, the *De regimine principum* (*On the Government of Princes*) by Giles of Rome (Egidio Colonna, also known as Egidio Romano). Giles's arguments in favor of monarchical rule hinged critically on the institution's religious universality: "Just as all the universe is directed by one ruler, God, who is a separate and pure intellect, all things which are in a person, if they are properly to be governed, must be governed by intellect and reason. If, therefore, the government of the whole universe is assimilated to the government which ought to be in one person, since the city is part of the universe, much more should the government of the whole city be reserved to one house."[11] It followed from this deduction that the chief responsibility of a monarch as a key mediator between God and individual was not the pursuit of power, wealth, or glory, but the inculcation of Christian ethics, both as an example to his subjects and in order to discharge his own fundamentally religious duties. Giles's assumptions and language spoke immediately to established rulers occupying clear rungs in the feudal ladder of authority and obligation but offered little to the new princes of Italy intent on asserting their independence from any higher authority.

In another stroke of intellectual good timing, much like the rediscovery of Aristotle that coincided with the rise of the independent communes, the new princes of Italy capitalized on and benefited from the increasingly dominant intellectual movement of Renaissance humanism and its glorification of classical antiquity, particularly its praise of glory won by virtuous individuals.[12] Although the humanist movement had initially begun in private writings and poetry that were far removed from the political arena, by the late fourteenth century humanists had become essential figures in Italian political culture, whether as notaries and speechwriters in chanceries or as court intellectuals and tutors to the children of princes. Humanists in search of patronage deployed their classical learning and their pens to normalize and exalt the rule of the Aragonese monarchs in Naples, the Visconti and Sforza dukes in Milan, and the peninsula's many petty despotisms, such the Este family in Ferrara, the Gonzaga in Mantua (see Petrarch's letter in this volume), and the Bentivogli in Bologna.

Humanists at princely courts all produced texts that followed the structure and form of the mirror-for-princes tradition but replaced the Christian interpretation of authority with antiquity's exaltation of the glory achieved by individuals of exceptional virtue. In Milan, Giovanni Manzini and Antonio Loschi portrayed Giangaleazzo's rise to power as the triumph of virtue over fortune by a prince skilled equally in arms and letters.[13] In Naples humanists such as Lorenzo Valla and Giuniano Maio celebrated Alfonso V's classicization of the city's layout and architecture, the abundance of classical scholars attracted by his learning and the patronage his court offered, and his practical pursuit of the city's common good, such as the founding of a public school and plague hospital and the renovation of the city's ports.[14] In Petrarch's text from this volume, we see him urging the lord of Carrara to engage in similar practically oriented public-improvement projects. Petrarch drew on Cicero, Seneca, and Roman historians to portray society as a family and the ideal ruler as a loving benevolent father, a recurring humanist analogy that we will see in Florence accompanied the rise of elite oligarchy. In all these texts, rulers derived their legitimacy from their own exceptional virtue, defined according to classical secular values such as glory, magnificence, and liberality, not from royal blood in their veins that established their role in God's providential plan.

The experiments in communal government did not fail everywhere, however. Of those that survived, Venice, a city-state and territorial power with a commercial empire in the eastern Mediterranean, was the only major power to maintain a relatively unchanging republican constitution without interruption until its conquest by Napoleon in the final years of the eighteenth century. Venetians saw their government as the perfect realization of the mixed constitution championed by Aristotle, Polybius, Cicero, and other ancient authorities. The Venetian government combined elements of rule by the one, the few, and the many by distributing power respectively between the princely figure of the doge (a chief magistrate elected for life), an aristocratic Senate, and a popular Great Council. Consistent with ancient theory, Venetians valued the mixed constitution because its harmonious fusion benefited from the advantages of each form of government—the stability of monarchy, prudence of aristocracy, and moderation of democracy—and was uniquely effective at preventing the corresponding corruption associated with each—tyranny, oligarchy, and anarchy.[15] They attributed the longevity of their regime to its perfectly designed balance.

Although politically empowered Venetians cherished the notion that their government balanced its power via the one, the few, and the many, in practice Venice was an aristocratic republic dominated by a closed caste of nobles. The Venetian doge, elected for life, may have possessed considerable symbolic influence but in practice was largely a figurehead compelled to operate through and with the consent of the major Venetian councils: the Great Council, the Senate, and the Ten.[16] The constitutional constraints on his power were such that "ducal influence," as Robert Finlay put it, "was covert and subtle."[17] Nor was the Great Council a meaningful representation of "the many." It is true that it was the largest and hence most inclusive of Venetian councils and membership in it confirmed patrician status, but a law—known as the *serrata*, or closing—passed in 1297 stipulated that membership would henceforth be restricted to families of the then-sitting council. As a consequence, only two hundred families, approximately, possessed rights to full active citizenship. Their system, as perceived by them and abroad, was indisputably successful: the government was wealthy, stable, and a major peninsular and maritime power.

Contemporaries nevertheless understood who was in charge in Venice in spite of its rhetoric of harmony and balance. As the Florentine ottimate Francesco Vettori observed, somewhat ironically given that he himself advocated for a narrow aristocratic republic in Florence: "Is it not tyrannical that three thousand aristocrats rule over one hundred thousand popolani who have no hope becoming aristocrats themselves?"[18] But—pointed observations notwithstanding—the fact that their success was the product of a regime that limited power to a small caste of noble families only heightened its appeal in the eyes of elites in other republics. This was nowhere more true than in Florence, whose elites frequently praised Venetian government in principle and advocated the actual adoption of similar institutions (as the texts by Poggio Bracciolini, Francesco Guicciardini, and Niccolò Machiavelli in this volume demonstrate).[19] The political preferences of the Florentine elite saw Venetian-style institutions as the best way to inoculate their power from aggression from below and above: popular bids for power by the city's lesser families and princely bids for power from the Medici family.

Venetian stability and longevity did not reflect, as the Venetians were uniquely proud to recognize, the other peninsular experiments in republican government. Florence, Venice's only republican rival in terms of wealth and power, was as famous for division, constitutional change, and factional conflict as the Venetians were famous for their opposites.[20] Between the thirteenth and sixteenth centuries, advocates of rule by the one (whether the brief tyranny of Walter of Brienne in the fourteenth century or the rise of the Medici in the fifteenth), the few (the oligarchical period led by the Albizzi family), and the many (whether the radical Ciompi revolt of wool workers in 1378 or the more moderate Second Republic of Machiavelli's day) fought many fierce battles for control of the city, and each form, for a time at least, had moments of triumph. Each triumphant group altered the city's constitution to their advantage, and hence the form of the government itself remained a fundamentally unsettled question (as the documents by Vettori, Machiavelli, and Guicciardini in this volume demonstrate so clearly) until the abolition of the republic in 1532 by the Medici family, who installed themselves as dukes of a princely state.

In spite of the relatively frequent alterations to the city's constitution, there were a few durable features that persisted either throughout or for much of the city's history. The Florentine government distributed power through a network of councils and committees in which the duration of memberships was usually limited to brief intervals (two or three months). The *signoria*, the city's chief executive council and center of power, consisted of nine priors, one of whom, the standard bearer of justice (*gonfaloniere di giustizia*), led the committee and therefore enjoyed elevated status and wielded additional powers (and for a brief period, 1502–12, was elected for life rather than for the standard two-month term). The composition of the Signoria, in keeping with the principles of guild government on which the government was based, was meant to represent the constituent parts of the city: each of the city's four major neighborhoods elected two priors to the committee. The priors were advised by two councils, the Sixteen Standard Bearers and the Twelve Good Men, and by informal standing committees of ex-priors. The Council of the People and the Council of the Commune were the government's major legislative bodies, though their power was limited to approving or vetoing proposals originating in the Signoria and its advisory colleges—they could not initiate legislation.[21] The two other major committees were the Ten of War, which conducted diplomacy and military matters, and the widely feared Eight of Public Safety (*otto di guardia e balìa*), which investigated and punished political crimes. After the expulsion of the Medici family in 1494, the government added a major popular element in the form of a socially inclusive Great Council with the primary responsibility of appointing the city's many lesser magistracies and political offices (and which Machiavelli's texts in this volume demonstrate remained a controversial and symbolically charged institution for years afterward).

The nomenclature of the government's most important offices and institutions—the captain of the people, standard bearer of justice, Councils of the Commune and the People, for example—reflects the influential role played by the laboring classes and the guild community during the early years of the commune's development. As their political vocabulary suggests, Florentine guild republicanism of the fourteenth century was the product of the middle and working classes (known as the *popolo*) and was a self-conscious and substantial competitor to the oligarchic power of the city's elite families. Unlike in Venice, where those families managed to restrict political citizenship to themselves, in Florence political participation was a function of membership in the city's guilds, which, however much dominated by elite families, included a broad and multitudinous range of the city's social classes (over a third of the city's adult male population).[22] In 1293, a popular regime led by Giano della Bella passed the Ordinances of Justice that, among other popular initiatives like banning the city's magnate class from holding office, established the government as a sovereign federation of guilds, each an autonomous institution in its own right that protected and promoted the interests of its members. Given the multiplicity of the city's guilds and their centrality to the Florentine economy, this vision of government recognized the inherent legitimacy of multiple competing and conflicting class interests. And given that its concept of government structure was modeled explicitly on guild structure, it championed similar values: the key words of guild republicanism were accountability, delegation, representation, and consent. Classically inclined Florentines viewed the system as the manifestation of the principle of Roman law *quod omnes tangit*: that which touches all must be approved by all. This brand of guild republicanism was fiercely, frequently, and often successfully contested by Florence's great families, but it was particularly influential during the 1250s, 1290s, 1340s, and 1370s (culminating in the 1378 Ciompi revolt, an uprising of the city's wool workers).[23]

As much as the political vocabulary of the major political institutions might imply a government with an inherently popular predisposition, the city's inner circle of elite families, wealthy, old, and as powerful as they were large, championed an altogether different vision of politics that ultimately triumphed over its guild rival. If the many imagined the political community in horizontal, fraternal terms—a band of brothers, separate and equal—the few, Florence's elite families, imagined the political community in vertical, patriarchal terms—a family governed by a benevolent patriarch who ruled wisely but firmly.[24] Their vision of politics grew organically out of the informality and privacy of their patronage politics and the degree to which their wealth and connections made them naturally less dependent on public institutions to promote their interests. As Giovanni Cavalcanti, describing one such period of oligarchical rule, put it: "the commune was being governed more at dinners and in studies than in the palace."[25] They worked first and foremost through the familial institutions of relatives, friends, and neighbors (*parenti, amici, vicini*) to create, cultivate, and expand reciprocal relationships of obligation and dependence. When cultivated on an adequately large scale, these networks of personal and family bonds of friendship and marriage became neighborhood-based factions that were shadow political parties, though defined less in the modern sense of a common ideology or advocacy of particular policies and more in terms of a commitment to mutual promotion and advantage. Well-organized and disciplined factional networks were capable of controlling the city's politics and bending its laws to their will, in some cases by directly putting their members in the government's key offices and in others by simply manipulating officeholders whose private lives were sufficiently entangled in their patronage network to make them vulnerable to informal pressure.[26] The key words of patronage politics were loyalty, obligation, deference, and protection.

Regimes of the few built on such foundations prevailed at numerous moments in Florentine history, but none was as successful, long lasting, or as fondly recalled within the city's aristocratic houses as the Albizzi oligarchy that ruled Florence from the late fourteenth century to 1434 (though we see that Machiavelli, in his *Discursus* included in this volume, pointedly disputed such views). This regime came to power in the aftermath of the Ciompi revolt of 1378, which attempted to broaden the guild system and hence establish a considerably more inclusive range of politically active citizens. Benefiting in part from the temporary unity within the city's normally fractious and mutually suspicious elite caused by the Ciompi revolt and in part from the skilled and muscular leadership of Maso and Rinaldo degli Albizzi, the Albizzean oligarchy maintained a firm grasp on the government and controlled the city's domestic and foreign policy until they were outmaneuvered and ousted by Cosimo de' Medici in 1434.

As a result of its success, most advocates of a narrow, aristocratic government throughout the fifteenth and sixteenth centuries pointed to the Albizzi oligarchy as an undisputed example of the virtues of rule by the few. For example, in the 1460s the patrician Niccolò Soderini declared that "only those who had governed prior to 1433 knew how to govern."[27] In 1500, Luca della Robbia declared that Florence during the Albizzi era was ruled by citizens "who were not inferior to the most wise and celebrated Romans of antiquity."[28] But the regime's most influential and intellectually formidable champion was Francesco Guicciardini, who declared in his *History of Florence*: "Florence was successful both at home and abroad: at home, because it remained free, united, and governed by well-to-do, good, and capable men; abroad, because it defended itself against powerful enemies and greatly expanded its dominion. Florentine successes were so great that this government is deservedly said to be the wisest, the most glorious, and the happiest that our city had had for a long time."[29] As Guicciardini's texts in this volume reveal, however, as much as he esteemed the Albizzi oligarchy, he shared Machiavelli's view that any regime whose power relied on informal and private methods was flawed. He wished to see an aristocratic republic in Florence in which the elite's leadership was formal, public, and constitutionally mandated.

In the 1430s, the Albizzi regime began to face increasing competition by a faction led by Cosimo de' Medici, who, after a brief period of exile in 1433, outmaneuvered them the following year, seizing control of the government and banishing the Albizzi and their allies. The Medici family—Cosimo, his son Piero, and grandson Lorenzo the Magnificent—informally ruled Florence for sixty years. They left the city's formal republican constitution intact, wielding power from behind the scenes using a combination of traditional but aggressive patronage politics and manipulation of the political process and the city's electoral system.

Owing to the immense wealth of the Medici bank, Cosimo was able to build the largest and most effective patronage network in the city's history. The family's correspondence from these years reveals the vast extent of their patronage: they assisted clients with payment of taxes and appointments to political office, brokered marriage alliances, and arranged political introductions and a broad array of other favors.[30] In addition to political patronage, Cosimo was a major patron of artists such as Donatello and intellectuals such as Niccolò Niccoli and Marsilio Ficino, whose works naturally portrayed Cosimo and the Medici in the best possible light.[31] In architecture, the scale and ambition of his patronage was colossal. As a Florentine contemporary of Cosimo put it: "Cosimo himself, a most famous man, builds now private homes, now sacred buildings, now monasteries, inside and outside the city, at such expense that they seem to equal the magnificence of ancient kings and emperors."[32] Cosimo's patronage enabled him not only to wield an effective political machine, but also to create the kind of propaganda that masked the rough edges of his politics with the lofty notion that the family's conspicuousness in the city's political life reflected their pursuit of the common good, a sentiment expressed in the city's bestowal on him of the title *pater patriae* upon his death in 1464.[33]

In addition to patronage, Cosimo and Lorenzo also maintained their power through careful manipulation and modification of the city's political institutions.[34] They frequently relied on *balìe*, special emergency councils with the power to override the city's larger, and hence more difficult to control, legislative bodies such as the Councils of the People and the Commune. They also established new councils—Cosimo created the Council of One Hundred and his grandson Lorenzo the Council of Seventy—designed to enhance the family's control of the appointments process and military and diplomatic matters. They deftly exploited a clause in the city's electoral policy whereby, during periods of immediate crisis, the standard electoral procedure in which the names of appointees to office were drawn randomly from bags containing name tickets of eligible candidates (Coluccio Salutati, an author from this volume, served as chief notary of the *tratte*, the office in charge of preparing the lists of names) could be suspended and replaced by a system of direct appointment by officials known as *accoppiatori*. In a particularly adroit maneuver, while restricting key offices to party loyalists, Cosimo's regime at the same time dramatically expanded the ranks of candidates eligible for office and widely distributed those lesser offices, creating the appearance that the government was becoming broader and more inclusive and granting a measure of pride to many Florentines for whom eligibility alone conferred status and prestige. As one astute observer put it: "many were elected to office but few to government."[35] The combination of these techniques ensured that the family's shadow government steered the city's politics between 1434 and 1494 without any overt assault on the city's cherished republican tradition (though there were several moments of concerted opposition made possible, according to Machiavelli's constitutional assessment in this volume, by the limitations of their system of informal control).

The period between 1380 and 1494 that saw aristocratic domination of Florentine politics and the increasing restriction of power around the Medici family and their allies coincided with the rise of humanism as the dominant intellectual trend in Italy and the establishment of Florence as its center of gravity. The humanist movement itself had begun in the 1260s with the Latin poems of Lovato dei Lovati in Padua, roughly contemporaneous with the emergence of the communes from the power of popes and emperors. Humanism remained a largely poetic genre that circulated in the private writings of Lovato and his circle until Albertino Mussato's *Historia augusta*, which extended the application of ancient Latin into prose composition and historical narrative. In the later fourteenth century the movement centered around Petrarch, who wrote classically inflected Latin texts in a variety of genres. Although he did apply his learning to political questions, such as his letter to the Roman revolutionary Cola di Rienzo, praised by Petrarch as "the young Brutus," and his letter to Francesco da Carrara from this volume, Petrarch more often preferred Christian and contemplative themes that shifted humanism's emphasis away from the communal secular themes of Lovato and Mussato. From Petrarch, the torch of humanist learning was passed to his admiring correspondent, the Florentine chancellor Coluccio Salutati, who created a circle of exceptional humanist scholars in Florence, among them the future chancellors Leonardo Bruni and Poggio Bracciolini (whose writings in praise of the Florentine and Venetian constitutions are included in this volume). By 1427, when Bruni was appointed chancellor of Florence, humanism had become the dominant intellectual movement in Italy and Florence its epicenter, in part owing to the success of Bruni himself, who was a best-selling author.[36]

Humanism also became the dominant language for the Florentine establishment during the periods of aristocratic and Medicean hegemony, as the texts in this volume demonstrate. By its nature, given that it drew heavily on the cultures of ancient Greece and Rome and their estimation of the duties of citizenship and patriotism, humanism appealed to the elites of Italian city-states and Florentines in particular, who saw clear parallels between their lives as merchants and politicians and the values championed by humanism. In the fifteenth century, intellectuals such as Leonardo Bruni and Matteo Palmieri argued for the superiority of the active life of the engaged citizen over a life of scholarly and Christian withdrawal advocated by the influential Petrarch, who was shocked and disappointed to learn that Cicero had been a politician deeply invested in the Roman politics of his day. In keeping with the pragmatic orientation of Italian political thought, Poggio Bracciolini's dialogue *On Avarice* (*De avaritia*) inverted the traditional Christian critique of wealth as an obstacle to virtue (a critique shared by Roman Stoicism) by contextualizing the question in terms of the day-to-day realities and necessities of the city-state.[37] Republics, the avaricious interlocutor proclaimed, rely for their existence, well-being, and prosperity on avaricious men: Because "money is necessary as the sinews that maintain the state . . . it seems to be preferable to have many avaricious men who we can depend on in times of difficulty like a stronghold or a citadel."³⁸ Although *De avaritia* was a dialogue that elaborated the dangers of wealth in equal detail, it is hard to imagine that Poggio's audience of Florentine bankers and cloth merchants would not have identified with the text's frequent proclamations that abundant wealth was a vehicle for the expression of civic virtue and patriotism. Leon Battista Alberti's *On the Family* (*Della famiglia*) drew on classical examples to elaborate the duties and values of the patrician *pater familias*, providing a Florentine example of a peninsular-wide humanist genre that portrayed the state as a family and implicitly argued that it should be ruled as fathers ruled their families—with benevolent, stern, and fundamentally incontestable authority.³⁹

These kinds of arguments spoke directly to the lived experience of the Florentine political community. We see striking evidence of this in the degree to which Florentines—politicians, not humanists—at the *consulte e pratiche* (advisory deliberations of former priors) began increasingly to defend their policy proposals in terms of classical precedents and parallels.⁴⁰

Many humanists worked in the chanceries of republican and princely governments and wrote explicitly political texts, applying their expertise in classical culture in support of their governments' ideological and diplomatic needs. As chancellor of the Florentine republic, Coluccio Salutati was one of the first and most successful humanists to demonstrate the political utility of mastery of ancient rhetoric and classical culture. Giangaleazzo Visconti, the duke of Milan and frequent target of Salutati's diplomatic correspondence during Milan's long conflict with Florence, testified to Salutati's power when he was reported to have declared that "one letter of Salutati was worth a troop of horses."⁴¹ Leonardo Bruni's *Panegyric to the City of Florence* (*Laudatio florentinae urbis*) and *Oration for the Funeral of Nanni Strozzi* (*Oratio in funere Ioannis Stroze*)—both reprinted here—celebrated Florence's culture of liberty and equality and defended Florence's increasing acquisition of territory in Tuscany by arguing that, as a state founded by the Romans, Florence was uniquely entitled to wield imperial power.⁴² In Milan, court humanists ennobled Visconti rule and territorial ambition through texts such as Antonio Loschi's *Achilles*, an epic that personified the Visconti as the forces of order triumphing over fortune, the chief cause of Italy's factional divisions.⁴³ In Naples, humanists such as Giuniano Maio, Giovanni Brancati, and Francesco Bandini praised the city's Aragonese rulers, much as Petrarch had praised Carrara rule in Padua, in terms of their commitment to justice and the city's material well-being.⁴⁴

The political thought of the Florentine humanists from the first half of the fifteenth century—often referred to as civic humanism, a term coined by the German scholar Hans Baron—has been the subject of considerable debate and controversy since Baron published *The Crisis of the Early Italian Renaissance* in 1955, one of the most influential twentieth-century contributions to Renaissance historiography.[45] In their celebration of the active life and Florence's republican institutions, Baron saw a self-conscious and sustained defense of protodemocratic values: individualism, citizenship, political participation, and collective self-rule. Further, civic humanism as Baron saw it was no theoretical construct of ivory-tower intellectuals but the product of citizen-scholars intensely invested in the defining political struggle of the Florentine republic in their day: the imminent threat of conquest by Giangaleazzo Visconti. Humanism prior to Florence's war of self-defense against Milanese expansion may have been fully committed to the recovery of ancient culture, but it did so while privileging the traditional Christian ideal of the withdrawn, contemplative life. While doing diplomatic intellectual battle against the Visconti, Florentine humanists, such as the chancellors Coluccio Salutati and Leonardo Bruni (most critically, in Baron's interpretation), were pushed to articulate the moral righteousness of the Florentine cause. The more they gazed on Visconti tyranny the more clearly they saw the values of the Florentine cause—equality of all citizens before the law, free access to political positions, and freedom of speech—and the more squarely they resituated humanism from the quiet solitude of the scholar's study to the civic loci of city hall and marketplace. Because Florence was one of the few remaining self-governing republics in Renaissance Italy and absolute monarchy was ascendant virtually everywhere else in Europe, Baron saw Florentine civic humanism as a vital moment in the survival and transmission of the democratic culture of antiquity to modernity, a point of considerable significance for a Jewish Weimar intellectual displaced from his homeland by the rise of anti-Semitic fascism.[46]

Like all great theses, Baron's interpretation of fifteenth-century Florentine humanism generated abundant controversy and criticism.[47] On some issues, such as the chronology of key texts and their genesis relative to Florence's wars with Milan, Baron's arguments proved durable, but on a number of other issues the "Baron thesis," as it came to be known, required considerable revision or qualification, such that its relevance now is less the historical accuracy of its various claims and more the degree to which it has become a vehicle for exploring many of the competing claims about the significance of Florentine humanism. Some scholars, Quentin Skinner chief among them, have concurred with the "civic" dimension of Florentine humanism but disputed its genesis as a result of Florence's triumph over Visconti Milan in 1402. Skinner instead situates Florentine civic writing of the fifteenth century as one chapter in a much longer tradition of medieval city-state political literature evident in texts such as the *Livres du trésor* by thirteenth-century Guelf (and guardian to the young Dante) Brunetto Latini.[48] Some scholars have argued that many Florentine humanists trumpeted Florentine cultural affinity with Roman traditions of republican freedom precisely to provide propagandistic ballast to Florence's predatory subjugation of smaller and formerly independent Tuscan cities.[49] Others have disputed altogether any meaningful connection between the political content of Florentine humanist texts and their political environment. As professional rhetoricians trained to argue both sides of an issue, *in utraque parte*, the apparently republican sentiments of Bruni and others were not sincerely held convictions but temporary postures of contextual convenience, evident in Bruni's—Baron's most important republican ideologue—continuation as chancellor of Florence and lifelong tax exemption after Cosimo de' Medici's rise to power and subversion of the republic.[50] For some of these debates we can see in the texts reprinted here the validity of both sides and hence the degree to which students of these writings and the culture that generated them must decide for themselves. Take the key text at the center of Baron's thesis, Bruni's *Panegyric to the City of Florence*: it boldly and clearly praises freedom in terms of free access to political office and equality before the law, indisputably significant and rare in a Italian context of rising princely and oligarchic power and a European context of increasingly ambitious absolutist monarchies; but his idealization of Florence as the defender of freedom abroad is directly contradicted by the text's triumphant imperialism.

Less immediately evident in the texts themselves is the degree to which their target may not have been the external threat of conquest by foreign princes, as John Najemy has forcefully argued, but rather Florence's internal rival to the aristocratic and Medicean oligarchies: the guild republicanism of the thirteenth and fourteenth centuries.[51] The elite regimes that dominated Florentine politics during the efflorescence of civic humanism, even at moments of their most intense internal rivalry, shared a distaste for the corporate principles and language of guild republicanism. They particularly rejected its view of politics as a locus of healthy and legitimate competition between different social classes and social groups, each pursuing their specific interests, for the simple reason that popular movements of the city's middle and lower classes had in the past periodically wrested control of the city's politics from them in the name of those guild principles. Civic humanism, the political language that superseded guild republicanism, privileged consensus, concord, unity, and harmony, all values that made it difficult for those on the political perimeter to contest the authority of those at the center.

The case of Leonardo Bruni, as always, is illuminating. As Najemy has demonstrated, Leonardo Bruni's otherwise laudatory *Life of Dante* quietly shifted the blame for the poet's permanent banishment to Dante himself for criticizing those in power: "Dante could not maintain his resolve to wait for favor, but rose up in his proud spirit and began to speak ill of those who were ruling the land. . . . Dante entirely lost all hope, since he himself had closed the way of a change of favor by having spoken and written against the citizens who were governing the republic."[52] Bruni also played an instrumental role in promoting the familial vision of politics that took patriarchal authority for granted. He concluded his summary of Florence's primary political institutions with a vision of paternal benevolence: "under these magistracies this city has been governed with such diligence and competence that one could not find better discipline even in a household ruled by a solicitous father. As a result, no one has suffered any harm, and no one has ever had to alienate property except when he wanted to."[53] So long as civic humanism's vision of politics prevailed, there were no words in the political lexicon to express legitimate dissent or loyal opposition, as Alamanno Rinuccini's bitter exhortation to a life of contemplative withdrawal from this volume reveals.

After sixty years of Medicean hegemony, the political landscape in Florence changed dramatically in 1494 when the French king, Charles VIII, invaded Italy to press his claim to the Kingdom of Naples. Upon his arrival in Tuscany at the head of a forty-thousand-strong army, he was met by Piero de' Medici, who had acceded to the position of *primus inter pares* in the Florentine government following the death of his father, Lorenzo the Magnificent, in 1492. Lacking his father's charisma and political cunning, Piero soon learned the degree to which he had alienated a powerful faction of the city's elite families. Capitalizing on the widespread outrage caused by Piero's surrender of Florentine fortresses in Sarzana, Pisa, and Livorno and a sizeable Florentine payoff to the French king, Piero's enemies expelled him from the city and seized control of the government, thereby restoring the reality of Florentine republicanism. The anti-Medicean conspirators were all members of powerful elite families resentful of the subordinate role they had played to the Medici over the course of the fifteenth century, hence their desire to reestablish the Florentine government along the aristocratic lines of the Albizzi regime that preceded the Medici—still elite, still narrow, and still conservative, just no Medici. But, as most revolutionaries discover, unintended consequences are difficult to foresee and more difficult still to overcome.[54]

The republic that they ushered in quickly became more socially inclusive than they had intended, resulting in a popular regime that had to contend with opposition from many of the disgruntled aristocrats who had expelled Piero and from Medici sympathizers who agitated for the family's return. The unexpected popular orientation of the new regime was largely the result of the sudden intervention of the prophetic Dominican friar Girolamo Savonarola, under whose influence a new Great Council was created that elected officials to all major government offices and committees (except for the Signoria) and approved or rejected all legislation, and whose numbers and social composition were unprecedentedly large (though the city's working classes were still excluded).[55] Associated as it was with Savonarola and the religious fervor he inspired in his followers, the Great Council was considered not only the popular anchor of the new regime but also a sacral institution with more enhanced status than the other purely secular committees and councils (and that remained at the center of Florentine constitutional experiments in the sixteenth century, as the texts by Machiavelli and Guicciardini in this volume clearly demonstrate).[56] Although the Savonarolans were only one of several factions in this period (there was also a powerful anti-Savonarolan faction, the angry ones or *arrabbiati*, a Medicean faction, the grays or *bigi*, so-called because their unpopularity compelled them to operate in the shadows, and others) Savonarola exerted an outsized impact on politics between 1494 and 1498 (evident also in his constitutional treatise from this volume).[57] Although Savonarola was burned at the stake as a heretic in 1498, the movement that he created continued to influence Florentine politics in subsequent decades and particularly the city's adoption of institutions inspired by the Venetian republic that Savonarola had forcefully and publicly praised in his advocacy for a Great Council. The most significant Venetian-inspired institution adopted by the Florentines was their creation of a lifetime standard bearer of justice (*gonfaloniere a vita*), an attempt to add an element of long-term continuity that the Florentines identified with the Venetian office of the doge, an innovation particularly supported by the Florentine elite who felt that a lifetime standard bearer would increase aristocratic influence in general.[58] They were disappointed in that expectation, however: Piero Soderini, the only person to hold the office, maintained a position of relative neutrality until 1512, when a Spanish army toppled the republic and returned the Medici to power.

The year 1512 was a crucial one in the lives of Niccolò Machiavelli and Francesco Guicciardini, the two greatest political thinkers of the Renaissance and with whom our volume concludes. For Machiavelli, it meant an immediate end to his political career and a period of humiliation and political ostracization. After his election as second chancellor in 1498 in the aftermath of Savonarola's execution, Machiavelli had become intensely involved in Florentine diplomacy as a de facto ambassador (owing to his middle-class status he held the title of secretary, rather than ambassador) on missions to the court of the king of France (Louis XII), Pope Alexander VI's illegitimate son (Cesare Borgia), Pope Julius II, and the Holy Roman Emperor (Maximilian I), among other lesser figures. A close ally of Piero Soderini, he was also entrusted by him with creating and training a militia force, the first nonmercenary Florentine fighting force since the origins of the commune in the High Middle Ages. When the Medici returned to Florence in 1512, Machiavelli was one of only two people immediately sacked from their posts in the chancery, the result in part of his close relationship with Piero Soderini, to whom the Medici were particularly hostile, in part because of his conspicuous role in the creation of the militia, and in part because the blunt, critical, and sometimes outright dismissive tone of his diplomatic correspondence with his aristocratic superiors in the Florentine government had generated powerful enemies. Shortly afterward, his name was implicated (most likely without his knowledge) in a conspiracy against the Medici, who as a result had him arrested, tortured, and then confined to the Florentine countryside. Forcibly evicted from political life, Machiavelli reinvented himself as a political philosopher, writing *The Prince* and the *Discourses on Livy*, his two most famous works of political theory.[59]

For Guicciardini, 1512 marked a beginning rather than an end. The republic appointed him its ambassador to the Spanish court of Ferdinand of Aragon. Shortly afterward, the Medici returned to Florence by force of arms and abolished the Great Council, leading Guicciardini to write the first of several treatises on the ideal Florentine constitution. Although the treatises differed from each other in terms of specific details and recommendations, they all generally argued for a classical mixed government in which the Medici were figureheads, the people were represented by a Great Council, and an aristocratic Senate of distinguished families held a preponderance of power. After two years serving in the Florentine government, Pope Leo X (Giovanni de' Medici) appointed Guicciardini governor of Modena and Reggio, followed by his appointment as president of the Romagna by Pope Clement VII (Giulio de' Medici). Between 1514 and 1527, when an imperial army sacked Rome and a republican uprising in Florence evicted the Medici for a second time, Guicciardini occupied some of the most powerful positions in the papal government, including a post as lieutenant-general of the papal army.

Machiavelli and Guicciardini, who became good friends, shared a number of political convictions and intellectual affinities. They both desired to see Florence ruled by a republican government, although Guicciardini, always the more cautious and prudent of the two, expressed that sentiment privately whereas Machiavelli expressed it openly. Their ideal governments were both variations on the ancient mixed constitution, though with admittedly substantial institutional differences. Their preference for the mixed constitution was doubtless the product of their fascination with antiquity and the larger humanist belief that the solutions to the problems of the present could be found in ancient examples. Yet they were also both sharp critics of many cherished assumptions of humanism, particularly humanism's positive conception of human nature. By contrast, Machiavelli and Guicciardini both believed that people were self-serving, shortsighted, and irredeemably corrupt, an axiom evident in all their political writings. However much they used the Renaissance language of virtue and admired the Roman values of duty and patriotism, they both offered political thought premised on the ubiquity and legitimacy of self-interest. And, by the 1520s at least, they were both in the unusual position of proposing constitutional models for the Florentine government even while working for the Medici, the republic's most existential threat (and who finally abolished the republic altogether in 1532).

On the issue of class and class conflict, however, their common ground gave way. The Guicciardini family were one of Florence's most distinguished and oldest houses, and as a result Guicciardini always approached Florentine politics as an entitled insider who respected the status quo of elite dominance. The Machiavelli family not only were middle class but had been politically ostracized in the fifteenth century. As a result, Machiavelli always approached Florentine politics with an outsider's sense of distance and popular mistrust of elite claims to wisdom and prudence.[60] Machiavelli built that outlook into the heart of his two major works of political thought, *The Prince* and the *Discourses*. In *The Prince*, he argued that the chief enemy of any new prince was the aristocracy that claimed to serve him; a wise prince, he declared, should build alliances with the people to subdue the natural arrogance and ambitions of the aristocracy. In the *Discourses* he made the more shocking argument that the class conflict in Rome between the plebs and the nobles was precisely what made the republic a mighty expansionist empire. In pursuit of those arguments, he frequently defended the people's capacity for rationality, judgment, and moderation (assumptions also at work in the principles of guild republicanism). However much he agreed with Machiavelli on many issues, Guicciardini never accepted Machiavelli's argument about the benefits of class conflict. As a proud member of the Florentine patrician class's most inner circle, he maintained their traditional belief in the irrationality and immoderation of the people—conflict with them could never have beneficial results.[61] While he did believe the people had a role to play in politics, as his constitutional proposals reveal, he always made an aristocratic Senate the fulcrum of the state.

Their paths began to cross in the 1520s in a context of Florentine constitutional reform that generated their technocratic constitutional proposals included in this volume. However much the future of Florence seemed inextricably tied to the Medici, especially given their power base in Rome, the family was uncertain about the best way to integrate their power with the city's constitution and whether their rule should be discreet and indirect, as Cosimo and Lorenzo had ruled in the fifteenth century, or overt and outright. The death of Lorenzo de' Medici (grandson of Lorenzo the Magnificent), the family's presumptive ruler of Florence, in 1519 had thrown these questions into sharp relief. Lorenzo's brief period in Florence had been controversial and resented. His brother Giuliano did not have the trust of the family's inner circle: they deemed him excessively prone to compromise and conciliation, traits ill suited to the hostile context in Florence. His cousin Cardinal Giulio de' Medici (the future pope Clement VII) had Roman responsibilities that prevented him from spending enough time in Florence to rule it himself. As a result, the family began to solicit proposals from its following, which now— after considerable effort—included Machiavelli, about how to reform the city's government in a way that ensured the family's primacy in the least controversial and most stable manner.

Both thinkers are best known for other writings: Machiavelli for *The Prince* and the *Discourses on Livy* and Guicciardini for his political reflections and his history of the Italian wars. The texts included here demonstrate a different side of their thinking, less universal and abstract and more technical and applied. However, because the self-image of both men unambiguously prioritized active political engagement over literary activity, these texts also reveal them at work on what mattered most to them—Florentine politics and the republican question.

They also reveal, frankly and openly, what the civic humanists tended to conceal: the experimental and mutable nature of all regimes, institutions, and political procedures. In praising the timeless perfection of the Florentine and Venetian constitutions, Bruni and Poggio implicitly portrayed politics as something resolved. Machiavelli and Guicciardini, on the other hand—whether analyzing electoral procedures in Lucca or debating the relative merits of sortition and election—exposed politics as a permanent work in progress that demands ongoing modification, reevaluation, and reimagining. In that sense, they are an apt illustration of the larger improvised nature of Renaissance politics and political thought that this volume explores; and as the two indisputably most penetrating intellects of the era, they are also a fitting conclusion.

This volume offers readers an opportunity for a more sustained encounter with the languages and arguments generated by the political developments discussed above than available in other collections of texts in English translation. In pursuit of that goal, it is simultaneously narrower and broader than other collections.

Whereas the main goal of many Renaissance readers is to present the multi-faceted intellectual preoccupations of humanist writing, this volume focuses exclusively on formally political texts. Readers will not find here similar examples of humanist-inflected history and poetry available in Renée Neu Watkins's *Humanism and Liberty* nor similar examples of humanist-inflected philosophy and private correspondence available in Ronald G. Witt and Benjamin Kohl's *The Earthly Republic*. Our volume is also narrower than the only other collection of purely political Renaissance texts in English translation, Jill Kraye's *Cambridge Translations of Renaissance Philosophical Texts*, volume 2, *Political Philosophy*. With brief selections from English, Spanish, French, and northern European texts, Kraye's volume provides a pan-European sampling of nineteen authors, whereas this volume offers fewer authors (ten) but full-length texts focused predominantly on Florence and Tuscany. Readers of this volume will instead enter into leisurely discussions of political legitimacy, characteristics of tyrannical rule, constitutional assessments of regimes, and detailed analyses of the mechanics and implications of voting and representation in communal regimes.

In spite of its narrow thematic focus, however, this volume presents a broader vision of politics than available in other editions. Because its ten authors and nineteen writings span roughly two hundred years, it is an ideal vehicle to gauge issues of continuity and change. Rather than presenting Renaissance political thought as a static set of arguments, it shows instead the degree to which political thought was more a common cluster of topics undergoing a continual state of modification and revision and the degree to which those common topics could be made to serve radically divergent political purposes.

This volume also expands the scope of humanist political writing by explicitly connecting it with the sixteenth-century "realist" turn most influentially exemplified by Niccolò Machiavelli and Francesco Guicciardini. Readers here have an opportunity to appreciate the degree to which the two greatest political thinkers of the Renaissance deployed many of the same major categories of analysis as their predecessors. In keeping with the volume's overall theme of improvisation and experimentation, readers will not encounter the most famous texts by Machiavelli (*The Prince* and *Discourses on Livy*) and Guicciardini (*Ricordi* and *Dialogue on the Government of Florence*). In addition to their ready availability in other editions and online, those texts do not as forcefully and bluntly reveal the degree to which Renaissance political thought, however often expressed in the language of classicizing idealism, could be productively applied to pressing and immediate technical political questions. This volume offers lesser-known texts by Machiavelli and Guicciardini, several of which are translated into English for the first time, that show them deploying the Renaissance political imagination to work through issues of electoral technology, the right balance of power to different social groups, and other practical issues of political stability.[62]

PART I

On Monarchy
and Tyranny

Chapter 1

_____

PETRARCH

How a Ruler Ought to Govern His State

(1373)

Born in Arezzo, Tuscany, and raised in Avignon, France, Francesco Petrarca (Petrarch) (1304–74) was a leading figure—indeed, perhaps the father—of Italian humanism. A prodigiously prolific composer of romantic poetry and scholar of Latin letters, and promoter of Italian culture, Petrarch undertook intellectual efforts that are said to have bridged the medieval Christian and the modern secular world. His writings revived the importance of pagan authors such as Cicero, Virgil, and Seneca for contemporary readers, while he continued to engage substantively with Christian authorities like St. Augustine. Petrarch's greatest works include the poetry collection *Canzoniere*; his unfinished compendium of profiles of exemplary Italian statesmen, *De viris illustribus*; *De vita solitaria*, which praises the contemplative life; and the unfinished epic *Africa*, devoted to the exploits of the ancient Roman general Scipio Africanus. Late in life Petrarch composed "How a Ruler Ought to Govern His State," dedicated to his patron, Lord Francesco da Carrara of Padua. A paradigmatic example of the widespread mirror-for-princes genre (*speculum principis*), Petrarch's advice epistle demonstrates how late medieval Italians understood good government under princely rule.

The text is a reprint of Francesco Petrarch, "How a Ruler Ought to Govern His State," trans. B. G. Kohl, in B. G. Kohl and R. G. Witt, eds., *The Earthly Republic: Italian Humanists on Government and Society* (Philadelphia: University of Pennsylvania Press, 1978), 35–78.

———— ❋ ————

How a Ruler Ought to Govern His State

For a long time now, distinguished sir, I have been meaning to write to you. And you have, in your usual way, gently reproved me, so that I am now aware that I have omitted your name from among the names of the many great men and men of middle rank to whom I have addressed letters. This omission is especially disgraceful when I consider the patronage that I have received from you and your father. Indeed, it would be an enormous act of ingratitude if I should let myself forget the thanks and affection that I should always hold for you. Therefore, I have decided to write to you even though I am still undecided where I ought to begin and on what topic. This indecision does not derive from the lack of a suitable subject matter, but rather from a perplexing abundance of material, so that I feel like a traveler poised at a crossroads. On the one hand, your great and constant generosity compels me to tender you my deepest thanks. Indeed, it is a time-honored custom to give thanks to friends and especially to princes for their gifts, and I have done so to you many times. On the other hand, you have so daily and continually laden me with gifts and honors that I, weighted down with the number and magnitude of your gifts, cannot ever hope to repay you adequately with mere words. Rather, I think that it would be better to pass over such generosity in respectful silence than to try and repay it with inadequate words.

So I leave aside this matter of gratitude and turn to the vast and easy task of singing your praises. Now and again it has been the custom of many men to praise princes (and indeed I have done so myself occasionally), not in order to gain favors from those who are praised as much as to pay homage to the truth and to spur the prince on to greatness with the very stimulus of praise to a generous mind, which is a spur more powerful than anything else. For in these matters of giving praise I find nothing more offensive than adulation or an inconstant attitude. There are those indeed who would praise unworthy men and there are others who, having praised their subjects, promptly begin to vituperate them with an incredible turn of mind. I know of nothing more dishonorable, more base, than this. And in this matter so especially notorious was Cicero (whom I esteem and admire more than any other ancient author) that I feel almost compelled to hate him. Cicero did this to many people, but, most significantly, he ladened and honored Julius Caesar with a wealth of praise and then subjected Caesar to insults and abuse. Read Cicero's letters to his brother Quintus, in which everything said there about Caesar is friendly and complimentary. But then turn to his letters to Atticus, in which you first will find mixed feelings toward Caesar and finally even hatred and reproach. Read Cicero's orations, spoken before Caesar alone or before him when he was present in the Senate; so great are these praises of Caesar that they seem unmerited by any mortal and beyond the capacity of a mortal genius to compose. But read further in the book *On Duties* and in the Philippic orations and you will find expressions of hatred equal to the former affection and base abuse comparable to earlier praise. What makes these great changes in Cicero's attitude even worse is that Cicero gave Caesar nothing but praise while he was alive and nothing but vituperation after he was dead. I would have been able to tolerate this much more easily if Cicero had criticized Caesar when he was alive and praised him after he was dead, because usually death either diminishes or extinguishes altogether hatred and envy. However, Julius Caesar had a companion in this situation (as he did in many things) in the person of his nephew and adopted son Caesar Augustus, who was inferior to Julius Caesar in his military prowess but surely superior in his ability to rule. Cicero, likewise, at first praised Augustus immoderately, but then he began to criticize him strongly while still alive and even wrote fierce censures of him.[1] I am reluctant to speak thus of a man whom I esteem so much, but truth is stronger than admiration. I regret that it must be this way, but it is. And I do not doubt that if Cicero were present he would answer me easily with his overpowering eloquence, but the truth is not altered by mere words.

I think I shall never turn with a diseased mind from praise to vituperation. Now, as I return to my theme, this occurred to me at the very outset of my discussion with you: While true virtue does not reject merited glory, glory should follow it even if virtue is unwilling, just as the shadow follows the body. I said to myself: This man, you can easily see, prefers to be criticized rather than praised, and it is easier to acquire favor with him by finding fault than by giving him due praise. What, therefore, shall I do? What course shall I take? A man whom I do not hesitate to praise I would not fear to criticize if he would be as fine a subject for criticism as for praise. I confess that it is the condition of mortals that no one is entirely above reproach. A person who has a few small defects can be called perfect and very good. Therefore, give thanks to God who made you what you are, so that if your detractor and your praiser were of equal ability the praiser would naturally be more eloquent. This is like the case of the two farmers who are of equal ability and energy; the one who has the luck to own the more fertile land will appear to be the better farmer. Likewise, in the case of two ship captains equal in every other way, he will be the more fortunate who sails on more tranquil seas and is propelled by more favorable breezes.

But after I had decided to criticize you and selected this topic for my epistolary discussion, I had found nothing in you worthy of blame except for that one thing concerning which I had a private discussion with you some time ago. If in this matter you will be so kind as to pay heed to my humble and faithful advice, there is scarcely any doubt that you will soon derive healthy nourishment for mind and body and for the greatness of your present fame and future glory. So I will express it to you with the same words that Crastinus used with Caesar on the battlefield of Thessaly: "You will thank me either dead or alive."[2] I shall not speak of this any more. For what is the use of words to those who already understand and know? You know what I want, and I ought not to want, nor am I able to want, anything but your good. I do not doubt that you know this.

Since things are this way, I feel that I am relieved from telling at this point the long story that, as I have said, is not in the least pleasant for you and, in any case, is well known to everyone. I am referring to the fact that in the very flower of your young manhood you were deprived of your worthy and magnanimous father, by whose example and erudition you were able to learn everything that is noble and magnificent.[3] At the time when it seemed especially fitting for you to have your own mentor, you took up the reins of government and, with the city of Padua under your control, overcame the difficulties created by your youth. You ruled with such competence and such maturity that no rumor, no hint of rebellion, disturbed the city in that time of great change. Next, after a short time, you transformed into a large surplus the enormous deficit that debts to foreign powers had left in your treasury. And now the years and experience in government have so matured you that you are esteemed as an outstanding lord, not only by your own citizens but also by the lords of many other cities, who hold you up as a model. As a result, I have often heard neighboring peoples express the wish that they could be governed by you and nurture envy for your subjects. You have never devoted yourself to either the arrogance of pompous display or to the idleness of pleasure, but you have devoted yourself to just rule so that everyone acknowledges that you are peaceful without being feckless and dignified without being prideful. As a result, modesty coexists with magnanimity in your character. You are thus full of dignity. Although, because of your incredible humanity, you permit easy access to yourself even to the most humble, still one of your most outstanding acts is to have at the same time contracted for your daughters very advantageous marriages with noble families in distant lands.[4] And you have been, above all other rulers, a lover of public order and peace—a peace that was never thought possible by the citizen-body when Padua was ruled by a communal regime or by any of your family, no matter how long they held the power-you alone constructed many strong fortresses at suitable points along the Paduan frontiers. Thus you acted in every way so that the citizens felt free and secure with you as a ruler, and no innocent blood was spilled. You also have pacified all your neighbors either by fear or by love or by admiration for your excellence, so that for many years now you have ruled a flourishing state with serene tranquility and in continual peace. But at last that adversary of the human race, that enemy of peace [the Devil], suddenly stirred up a dangerous war with that power you never feared. Consequently, although you still loved peace, you fought with Venice bravely and with great determination over a long time, even though you lacked the aid from allies that you had hoped for. And when it seemed most advantageous to do so, you skillfully concluded peace so that at one stroke you won twofold praise both for your bravery and your political wisdom.[5]

From these facts and from many others I shall omit, you have been viewed as vastly superior to all other rulers of your state and to all rulers of other cities, not only in the judgment of your own subjects but indeed in the opinion of the whole world as well.

But praising you in detail when the facts speak so clearly for themselves would be only a pleasant exercise, and it is a useless chore to try and criticize you. Besides, because of the lack of material my speech would end in unbecoming silence as soon as I began to talk. So I shall tell you what I have decided to speak about, a topic which I am sure is well known to you even without any further elaboration but which may be sometimes useful even to someone like yourself who has already been made aware of it. For even though the mind has grasped something well and learned it thoroughly and used that knowledge frequently, it can recall that thing when stimulated by another and, urged on by another's words, it follows more readily a path it would still take by itself. I shall discuss, therefore, something that almost everyone knows but that people often neglect, namely, what should be the character of a man to whom the task of governing a state has been entrusted. I am not unaware that such a subject could easily fill many volumes, and that I am content to write only one letter. Yet for some people a single word is more useful than a long speech is for others, and, moreover, the quality of the mind of the listener is much more important than the eloquence of the writer, whoever he may be. Indeed, let me repeat what I have often said: There must be within you a tiny spark that can be increased by fanning and will eventually burst into flame. Without this one will have only fanned dead ashes for no good purpose. I hope (or indeed I am certain) that in you there are not just faint embers but bright and burning coals or even an excellent flame of virtue and an able mind that is accustomed to utilize all it hears. I can recall how much one letter—a great one because it was the product of a great mind, namely the letter from Marcus Brutus to Marcus Tullius Cicero—stimulated you to excellence, so that for a long time you could scarcely speak of anything else.[6] And I often used to say to myself about you: If he were not such a true friend of virtue he would never have been stimulated so strongly by such a brief, though admittedly excellent, piece of writing. Moreover, it has often been a great source of pleasure to me that I had procured this letter for you, and thus rescued from oblivion and neglect a letter that had been previously lost for a long time.

But before I begin to discuss this subject that I have just proposed, I wish to recall for you a passage from Cicero that, I suspect, is not unknown to you. Surely a man like yourself, who wants to be a good ruler, will listen eagerly to this passage as soon as you know that a good ruler is as dear to God as the state itself is dear to God. Here, therefore, is the passage from the sixth book of *On the Commonwealth*: "But, Africanus, be assured of this, so that you may be even more eager to defend the commonwealth: all these who have preserved, aided or enlarged their fatherland have a special place prepared for them in the heavens, where they may enjoy an eternal life of happiness. For nothing of all that is done on earth is more pleasing to that supreme god who rules the whole universe in justice, which is called the State. Their rulers and preservers come from heaven and to that place they return."[7]

Moreover, it is imagined that this conversation took place in Heaven. Who, therefore, could be so completely hardhearted, so opposed to excellence, and so contemptuous of true happiness that he would not seek out the task of governing and strive after such rewards? For although it is a pagan who speaks, yet his thought is not opposed to Christian truth or religious belief, even though our way of thinking and theirs are quite different when it comes to such doctrines as the creation of man and the soul.

But now at last I shall do what I have promised, and I shall discuss those things that the lord of a state ought to do. And I want you to look at yourself in this letter as though you were gazing in a mirror. If you see yourself in what I am describing (as no doubt you will quite often), enjoy it. And may you become every day more devoted and more faithful to God, who has bestowed upon us every good and perfect gift and virtue; and may you, albeit with enormous effort, overcome every difficulty and rise to that degree of holiness beyond which you cannot at the present moment ascend. On the other hand, if sometimes you feel that it is difficult for you to meet the standards I describe, I advise you to put your hands to your face and polish the countenance of your great reputation written there, so that you might become more attractive, and certainly more illustrious, as a result of this experience.

The first quality is that a lord should be friendly, never terrifying, to the good citizens, even though it is inevitable that he be terrifying to evil citizens if he is to be a friend to justice. "For he does not carry a sword without good cause, since he is a minister of God," as the Apostle says.[8] Now nothing is more foolish, nothing is more destructive to the stability of the state, than to wish to be dreaded by everyone. Many princes, both in antiquity and in modern times, have wanted nothing more than to be feared and have believed that nothing is more useful than fear and cruelty in maintaining their power. Concerning this belief we have an example in the case of the barbaric emperor named Maximinus.[9] In fact, nothing is farther from the truth than these opinions; rather, it is much more advantageous to be loved than to be feared, unless we are speaking of the way in which a devoted child fears a good father. Any other kind of fear is diametrically opposed to what a ruler should desire. Rulers in general want to reign for a long time and to lead their lives in security, but to be feared is opposed to both of these desires, and to be loved is consistent with both. Fear is opposed both to longevity in office and security in life; goodwill favors both, and this affirmation is supported by that opinion that one can hear from Cicero (or from the mouth of a Cicero who is speaking the truth). He says: "Of all things, none is better adapted to secure influence and hold it fast than is love, and nothing is more foreign to that end than is fear."[10] And a little further on he states: "Fear is but a poor safeguard of lasting power, while affection, on the other hand, may be trusted to keep it safe forever."[11] Since you know well that this matter was important to Cicero, let me cite another passage: "To be a citizen dear to all, to deserve well of the State, to be praised, courted, loved is glorious; but to be feared and an object of hatred is invidious, detestable, and proof of weakness and corruption."[12]

Now it does not seem necessary to speak of security since there can be no one so stupid and ignorant of politics that he does not know that opinion is criticized by certain men affirming that security is always threatened and ultimately destroyed by fear. This fear is in subjects and not in the ruler, so that it is their security, not his, that is endangered. To which I answer with the famous words directed by Laberius, a Roman knight noted for his wisdom and learning, to Julius Caesar: "He who is feared by many must himself fear many in turn."[13] That this opinion might be more convincing, let me reinforce it with another similar statement by Cicero, whom I have often named: "Furthermore, those who wish to be feared must inevitably be afraid of those whom they intimidate."[14] He borrowed the essence of this idea, which we should not be ashamed to embrace, from Ennius: "Whom they fear, they hate. And whoever one hates, one hopes to see dead."[15] And I add that whatever one wants, one desires to become. What strong passions urge many to accomplish can scarcely be forestalled.

Now, although the truth of the matter is as I have just sketched, there still are those who say: "They may hate me, provided they fear me." This was the speech that Euripides gave to that cruel tyrant Atreus.[16] Daily did Caligula, who was certainly no more merciful than Atreus, say and practice this idea, which was beneficial neither to its creator nor to his followers.[17] In this last category many people have wanted to place even Julius Caesar. This would certainly be strange if true; for although Julius Caesar did, to be sure, have an enormous appetite for empire and glory, I would say too enormous, still he did everything with mildness and mercy, with munificence and an incredible generosity, so that he would be loved rather than feared. For example, he kept nothing for himself from the booty won in his numerous victories and military commands, except for the very faculty to lavish gifts on others, and to this the most authoritative writers give witness. Indeed, Julius Caesar was so prone to be merciful to others that Cicero himself wrote that Caesar was accustomed to forget nothing except past injuries.[18] It is indeed a splendid kind of revenge to pardon past wrongs; to forget them altogether is more splendid still. What is most amazing is that this quality was noted as Caesar's most noble trait by Cicero, who had as often viewed him as an enemy as seen him as a friend. Do you want more examples? I shall remain silent concerning Caesar's other excellent qualities, but I must say that he was endowed with many more virtues than anyone else, although they were not sufficiently acknowledged.

Indeed, he was cut down by those very men upon whom he had heaped wealth and honors. On these men he had bestowed the privileges that came to him from his victories, and he had forgiven every one of his hostile acts and injuries. But neither his generosity nor his mercy aided Caesar in the end. So it was with good reason that at his funeral this verse of Pacuvius was sung:

> That ever I, unhappy man, should save
> Wretches, who thus have brought me to the grave.[19]

In this case it can be asked what were the causes that brought about this hatred, since the conspiracy against Caesar was surely not lacking in hatred. I myself can find no cause except a certain insolence and haughtiness of bearing that raised Caesar above the customs of his country because he enjoyed unwarranted honors and usurped extraordinary dignities.[20] Rome was not yet ready to endure the imperial pride that was so much increased by Caesar's successors, that compared to them Caesar seems to be the very soul of humility. If then even Julius Caesar was not protected by his power and wealth from the hatred of the many, it is an important question to ask in what ways are the love of one's subjects to be sought. Since hatred is the cause of ruin, so love is the cause of the contrary of ruin. The former casts one down, the latter protects a ruler.

What I can say is that the nature of public love is the same as private love. Seneca says: "I shall show you a love potion that is made without medicines, without herbs, without the incantations of any poison-maker. If you want to be loved, love."[21] There it is. Although many other things could be said, this saying is the summation of everything. What is the need for magical arts, what for any reward or labor? Love is free; it is sought out by love alone. And who can be found with such a steely heart that he would not want to return an honorable love? "Honorable" I say, for a dishonorable love is not love at all, but rather hatred hidden under the guise of love. Now to return love to someone who loves basely is to do nothing other than to compound one crime with another and to become a part of another person's disgraceful deceit. On this topic I shall, therefore, speak no more, but let us return to the theme of honorable love of others.

Indeed, from the discussion of this topic nothing but immense and honorable pleasure ought to come to you since you are so beloved by your subjects that you seem to them to be not a lord over citizens but the "father of your country." In fact this was the title of almost all of the emperors of antiquity; some of them bore the name justly, but others carried it so injustly that nothing more perverse can be conceived. Both Caesar Augustus and Nero were called "father of his country." The first was a true father, the second was an enemy of both his country and of religion. But this title really does belong to you. There is no one among your citizens (that is, among those who really seek the peace and well-being of Padua) who looks upon you otherwise, who thinks of you as anything other than as a father. But you have to continue to strive so that you merit this dignity; it endures forever because of your noble efforts. I hope that, urged and encouraged, you will continue to rule as you already willingly have ruled for a long time. You should know, moreover, that to merit this kind of esteem you must always render justice and treat your citizens with goodwill. Do you really want to be a father to your citizens? Then you must want for your subjects what you want for your own children. I am not saying that you must love each of your subjects as much as you do one of your own children, but you should love each subject in the same way you do your child. For God, the supreme lawgiver, did not say: "Love your neighbor as much as you love yourself," but "as yourself."²² This means love sincerely, without deceit, without seeking advantages or rewards, and in a spirit of pure love and freely-given goodwill. I am, moreover, of the opinion (without disputing the opinions of others) that you ought to love not each individual citizen but the whole citizen body at the same time, not so much as you love a child or a parent, but as you love yourself. Whereas in the case of individuals there are individual feelings for each one, in the case of the state all feelings are involved. Therefore, you ought to love your citizens as you do your children, or rather (if I may put it this way) as a member of your own body or as a part of your soul. For the state is one body and you are its heart. Moreover, this act is to be manifested by kind words, especially in righteous actions, and above all (as I was already saying) with justice and devotion to duty. For who could not love someone who has always pleasant, just, helpful, and always showed himself to be a friend? And if we add to these fine qualities the material benefits that good lords are accustomed to bestow on their subjects, then surely there develops an incredible fund of goodwill among the citizens that will serve as a firm and handsome foundation for a lasting government.

So put away arms, bodyguards, mercenaries, bugles, and trumpets, and use all these things only against the enemy because with your citizens your love is sufficient. As Cicero says: "The prince ought to be surrounded not with arms, but with the love and goodwill of his subjects."²³ And I reckon as citizens those who desire the preservation of the state and not those who are always trying to change things, for these should be thought of not as citizens but as rebels and public enemies. These considerations call to mind that well known saying of Augustus: "Whoever does not wish to disturb the present state of the city is a good citizen and a good man."²⁴ Therefore, I have no doubt that whoever desires the opposite should be viewed as evil and not worthy to bear the name of citizen and enjoy the community of good men. In any case, in these matters your own nature has always guided you well, so that you have already gained both the citizens' love and goodwill. These qualities are, indeed, not just a path to glory, but even a road to salvation. As the good father said to his fine son Scipio Africanus: "Love justice and duty, which are very important in regard to parents and kinsmen, and most of all, to your native country. Such a life is the road to heaven."[25] What lover of heaven would not love the road by which he may ascend to Heaven?

Now there are innumerable examples of the fact that arms will not defend evil and unjust leaders from the wrath of their oppressed subjects. It will suffice to adduce here only the most interesting and notorious instances. What use to Caligula were his German bodyguards even though they hastened to his defense?[26] In extreme danger, Nero was informed that the soldiers had deserted their posts and his guards had fled.[27] But no cohorts of soldiers were necessary for Augustus, Vespasian, and Titus. Consider the death of Augustus: at his death bed you do not find armed bodyguards but rather friendly subjects, and, in conversation with friends amidst the embraces of his beloved wife, Augustus did not expire and die but rather was almost lulled to sleep.[28] Afterwards his remains were laid to rest with more honors than owed a human being, and his memory was cherished. Vespasian, who believed that it was not proper for an emperor to die standing up, expired held off the floor in the hands of his many friends.[29] Afterwards his son Titus met a premature but peaceful death with innumerable expressions of gratitude. As a result, Titus's death was viewed (as Suetonius says) as more of a tragedy for mankind than for himself.[30] Indeed, unless I am mistaken, all those princes who pass their lives in governing a state ought to consider and remember the following: the death of good princes is for them tranquil and happy while it is terrifying and dangerous for their subjects. For evil princes precisely the opposite is true. In that same city of Rome, where (as I have just mentioned) many emperors have died in complete peace and contentment and have had their names recalled by everyone with honor and admiration—in that city Domitian, the brother of Titus, was killed, and the Senate itself applauded his demise, besmirching his reputation (as I have seen written) with bitter denunciations and calumnies.[31] Further, the Senate decreed that his statues be taken down and destroyed, that his name be cancelled from inscriptions, and that the very memory of him be obliterated. Likewise, Galba's very head was detached, stuck on a spear, and carried about by camp followers and servant boys through the encampments hostile to him to the jeers and horror of all.[32] Vitellius was cut down with many blows on the Scala Gemonia in the Forum and hacked into many pieces. Finally, his remains were dragged around on a hook and thrown into the Tiber.[33]

I shall pass over examples of many others who met their end in horrible ways. But does not this vast difference in manner of death surely follow from a vast difference in manner of living? For this reason that very wise emperor Marcus Aurelius, who joined to the difficult task of governing an empire the name and learning of a philosopher, after he had discussed the fall of many emperors who preceded him, concluded by saying that each emperor met the death that was consistent with his manner of life. He predicted that he himself would be among those who died peacefully.[34] Indeed, his prediction came true. Now since this was the opinion of a great and wise personage, and since every wise man agrees that one should live as decently and well as possible in order to gain—besides the many other benefits from leading a good life—the additional benefit of dying well. Surely it is not too great a task to spend all the preceding years well for a worthy final hour, although, according to the best opinion, this passage into eternity requires only a moment. And we should not wonder at this. Nor should we be surprised since we enter an immense city through a narrow gate, and we penetrate the vast reaches of the sea in a tiny ship. Likewise, through that brief passage of death we enter into an eternity, and just as the soul is when death takes it, so it endures for all time.

Now I shall speak of justice, the very important and noble function that is to give to each person his due so that no one is punished without good reason. Even when there is a good reason for punishment you should incline to mercy, following the example of Our Heavenly Judge and Eternal King. For no one of us is immune from sin and all of us are weak by our very nature, so there is no one of us who does not need mercy. Hence, one who wishes to be just must also be merciful. Therefore, although mercy and justice seem, at first glance, to be opposites, they are in fact inseparably linked. Indeed, it is as St. Ambrose says so perceptively in his book *On the Death of the Emperor Theodosius*: "Justice is nothing other than mercy, and mercy is the same as justice."[35] Thus, the two qualities are not merely linked; they are one. Now this is not to say that you should let go scot-free murderers, traitors, poisoners, and other such miscreants, so that by being merciful to a few criminals you are actually harming the vast majority of your subjects. What I am suggesting is that you ought to be merciful to those who have gone astray a little and who have lapsed momentarily if it can be done without encouraging their example. But otherwise remember that too much mercy and indiscriminate leniency can lead to a greater cruelty.

Now, after justice, the best way to earn the affection of your citizenry is generosity. Even if the head of a state cannot benefit individual subjects, he may at least benefit the entire population. There is hardly anyone who esteems someone from whom he does not expect either private or public benefaction. Of course, I am speaking of that esteem in which princes are held; among friends and equals there is a different kind of love, which is sufficient in itself, neither asking for favors nor expecting them. In the sphere of public beneficence there is the restoration of temples and public buildings for which Caesar Augustus, above all others, is to be praised. Livy named him rightly "the builder and restorer of all temples."[36] Similarly, Suetonius says: "He boasted, not without cause, that he found a city of brick and left one of marble."[37] Just as important is the construction of the walls of the city, which gave fame to the name of Aurelian, otherwise a cruel and bloody emperor. In the less than six years during which he ruled, this emperor enlarged the walls of the city of Rome to their present dimensions. As a result, the historian Flavius

Vopiscus, following, I believe, the system of measures of antiquity, was prompted
to say: "The circumference of the walls was now nearly fifty miles."[38] But you, sir,
have been relieved of the task of wall-building thanks to the great industry of your
forebears. In fact, I do not know a city in all of Italy, or even all of Europe, that is
ringed with walls more handsome than Padua's.

But the ancients were, I believe, as much concerned with the construction of
highways as with the erection of walls. While walls give safety in time of war, roads
are a very useful addition in peacetime. The chief difference between the two is
this: walls last for a long time because of their great size, whereas roads are soon
destroyed because of the continual traffic in men and horses and, above all, the
traffic in those heavy Tartarean carts, which I strongly wish that Erichthonius had
never invented.[39] These carts not only damage the streets, the foundation of buildings, and the peace of those living in them, but they also disturb the thoughts of
those wanting to meditate on the good. Therefore, I ask you to turn your attention
to the streets of Padua, which have for a long time been neglected and broken up
and which, with their silent deformity, call out for your assistance. I think that you
will want to tackle this difficult task, not just because you are responsible for the
city and its inhabitants. I know that the beauty of Padua and the wellbeing of its
citizens ought to be—as they are—close to your heart, but the repair of the streets
is in your own interest as well. For I have never known anyone—and I am not only
speaking here of princes but of every sort of men—except perhaps your own dear
father, who liked to ride on horseback, as you do, into every part of his country for
such long stretches of time. I am not criticizing this habit of yours since your first
duty and care is clearly the good government of Padua, and the presence of a good
prince is always pleasing to faithful citizens; but you ought to take care that what
you do so eagerly you also do safely. Hence you should remove all danger and
difficulties from this horseback-riding and turn it into an agreeable and pleasant
recreation.

Entrust, therefore, the repair of Padua's streets to some good man who is dedicated to your own welfare and that of the city. And don't be afraid that by appointing
a well-known and noble man to this seemingly vile job you are inflicting harm on
him. To an honest and upright citizen no duty that results in benefit to his country
can ever seem base. History provides an example of this truth. There was in Thebes
a very brave and learned man named Epaminondas, who was—if we count virtue
alone and not just good luck, which often raises up the unworthy—the leading
man, or at least one of the leading men, of Greece. Now this man, about whom it
has been written truly that with him the glory of Thebes was born and with him
it died, was opposed by his fellow citizens—such evils often occur in democratic
states—who appointed him to the job of street cleaner, which was in Thebes
regarded as the dirtiest job of all.[40] The citizens hoped thereby that they would
diminish the glory and good reputation attached to this man. But Epaminondas

did not respond to this punishment with force, or even with a harsh word. Rather, he readily accepted the task assigned to him and said: "I shall undertake this task not with the idea that an indignity has been visited upon me as a result of this job, but rather that it has brought me dignity so that in my hands something very noble will be created out of a task that has always been viewed as base and ignoble." And soon, indeed, the job gained such a good reputation under his splendid administration that a task which has previously been despised, even by the lowliest of the plebs, now became a post sought after even by the most illustrious citizens.[41] Now I hope you will entrust this same task to some industrious and honest citizen of Padua and that you soon will see that many compete for this job, and thus, aided by the zeal of the citizens, the old homeland will be made good as new.

Now I am going to write concerning a matter that seems almost ridiculous and that I have already discussed with you one day recently when you came to visit me in my study at Arqua, an honor that you have paid me often, even though I am unworthy of such visits. Moreover, the very subject of the discussion stood before your very eyes. Indeed, Padua is a fine city on account of the noble lineage of its leading families, the fertility of its site, and its ancient origins that go back many centuries before the founding of Rome itself. Moreover, Padua is furnished with a good university, fine clergy and outstanding religious celebrities, and truly impressive shrines, including the churches of the bishop Prosdocimo, the friar Anthony, and the virgin martyr Justina. What I think is not insignificant—nor should you—I add immediately: that the City has you as lord and protector. Finally it is celebrated in some verses by Vergil.[42] This city, I say, so outstanding in its many glories, is being transformed—with you looking on and not stopping it, as you easily could—into a horrid and ugly pasture by rampaging herds of pigs! Everywhere one turns one can hear their ugly grunts and see them digging with their snouts. A filthy spectacle, a sad noise! These are evils that we have already borne for a long time, and those who came to Padua are amazed and scandalized by them. This state of affairs is repulsive to all who meet it and even worse for those who come on horseback, for whom the free-roaming pigs are always a nuisance and sometimes even a danger because an encounter with these stinking and intractable animals will frighten a horse and even throw its rider. Now I recall that the last time I spoke with you concerning this matter you said that there was an ancient statute that carried with it a heavy penalty that anyone could seize the pigs found roaming freely in the streets.[43] But who does not know that, just as men grow old, so do all human creations? Even the Roman laws fell into disuse and, if it were not for the fact that they have been studied assiduously in the schools, they would now be quite forgotten. So what do you think is the fate of municipal statutes? So that this old law may be applied again, let us have it drawn up again and announced publicly by the town crier with the same, or even a heavier, fine attached to it. Then send out some officials who will remove the wandering pigs so that these urban herders will discover at their own expense that they cannot flout what the law forbids anyone to do. Let those who own pigs keep them on a farm and those who don't have a farm keep their pigs shut up inside their houses. Those who don't even own a house should still not be allowed to spoil the homes of other citizens and the beauty of Padua. Nor should these pig owners think that at will, without hindrance from law, they can convert the famous city of Padua into a pigsty! Now some might think this is a frivolous matter, but I don't think it is either frivolous or unimportant. On the contrary, the task of restoring Padua to its former noble majesty consists not so much in large projects as in small details. Partly, of course, these latter concern the task of governing the city, but you must also pay attention to the decorum of the city so that the eyes have their share of the common joy, the citizens are proud of and revel in the improved aspect of the city, and strangers feel that they are not entering a mere village but a real city. This is what you can do for Padua, and if you do it, I think you will have done something worthy of yourself. But concerning this subject I have already said more than enough.

From this issue there arises still another matter; after you have repaired the streets both within the city and leading away from Padua; I hope that you will undertake with every effort the draining of the marshes and bogs which lie near the city. In this way you will be able to improve the already beautiful countryside surrounding the city and to restore to their true worth the farms of the famous Euganean Hills, pitted with bogs that are already rich in the fruits of Minerva and Bacchus, so that the cultivation of the grains of Ceres, prevented now because of the foul, boggy ponds, can be restored.[44] With this project you will be able to combine utility with beauty, and thus, with a single act, you will gain multiple praise. Undertake this project, I beg you, and you will gain that kind of glory which all your forebears never enjoyed because they did not think of such projects or were afraid to undertake them. Good God will assist you in this noble undertaking. Nature will help you too, because almost all the bogs are situated in the higher altitudes, making it a very easy matter to drain the swamps by letting the water flow to lower ground, into the nearby rivers, and thence into the sea. As a result, the present generation will enjoy more fertile fields, a more handsome countryside, a healthier and more pleasing climate. And future generations will, because of this one project, always remember your name. Although I have often been irritated when those who love laziness and leisure say that such a project would be impossible, I know from my own common sense, and from the judgment of the inhabitants of the Euganean Hills, that such an undertaking is not only possible but even very easy. So put your hand to this task, my generous lord; if you willingly undertake this project, then surely a happy outcome will result. And you should not consider this sort of project unworthy of your dignity for none other than Julius Caesar took pride in such tasks. Concerning this point, Suetonius writes that a little before he died Caesar planned to drain the Pontine Marshes and to dig a canal across the isthmus on which Corinth is situated so that seaborne trade to the north and east could be expedited.[45] I would wish that you were in a position to undertake similar monumental projects. But the marshes I'm talking about are not far away, as are the Pontine Marshes; they are nearby, right under your very eyes. So give the orders to clean and drain these fetid marshes while your health and strength are good and age not too far advanced. Now I don't want to laugh, but lest you think I am prepared to offer nothing but words toward the completion of this project, I intend to offer you my little purse for part of the expenses, even though I am not a citizen of Padua. What should a lord contribute? What ought we to expect of a private person? If perhaps one wants to know exactly what I will contribute, the answer will be known in due time. For now I will give you the same answer that the freedman gave once to Augustus: "On my part, I will give to you, lord, what seems to you proper to my new status."[46] But as to the repair of the streets, which I mentioned earlier, you ought to do this before other projects since that project is fairly easy and clearly more honorable. I have heard that at one time public funds were appropriated for such projects so that these tasks could be completed without any additional taxes on the citizen-body and without reducing the communal treasury or your own private wealth.

Indeed, I do not deny, nor am I ignorant of, the fact that the lord of a city ought to take every precaution to avoid useless and superfluous expenditures. In this way he will not exhaust the treasury and have nothing left for necessary expenditures. Therefore, a lord should spend nothing and do nothing whatsoever that does not further the beauty and good order of the city over which he rules. To put it briefly, he ought to act as a careful guardian of the state, not as its lord. Such was the advice that the Philosopher gave at great length in his *Politics*, advice that is found to be very useful and clearly consistent with justice.[47] Rulers who act otherwise are to be judged as thieves rather than as defenders and preservers of the state. One should always remember that saying of the Emperor Hadrian, who was speaking I know not whether more as a prince or a citizen. In either case, Elius Spartianus wrote concerning him: "He discussed policy frequently both in the Assembly and in the Senate. Thus he seemed to run the government of Rome as though he knew that it was not part of his own private property but belonged to the people.[48] Thus, I repeat, he did everything so that he could render account of his spending to anyone, and it is clear that he had to give account, if not to men, at least to God. Similarly, it was very proper that on his deathbed Augustus rendered account of his rule to the Senate.[49] Likewise, whoever has led a good and honorable life—no matter what is his social station—or has acted in such a way that he weighed every possibility and, even if answerable to no one, he could still give full and honest account of his actions to anyone. In this action consists the definition of duty (as Cicero gives it): "Duty is the thing that one cannot neglect without neglecting virtue itself."[50] Why is it important that you have no one to whom to

account since your soul must answer to itself and its conscience, which, if dissatisfied, leaves you sad and unhappy? Granted, he was not one of the best of princes,
but the promise of Tiberius given in the Senate, full of generous trust, deservedly
was praised as excellent: "I will see to it that you will always have an accounting
of my actions and words."[51] Thus he did more than we asked for, for he gave not
just an accounting of his actions but of the words. Concerning the moderation
that rulers ought to display in their programs of public works, we may consider
the example of the Emperor Vespasian. Although that emperor undertook very
generously to make certain public improvements, still, when a workman wanted
to transport some very large columns to the Capitoline at little cost, Vespasian
thanked the man for the fair offer but would not allow the work to be done. He
said: "Let me provide bread instead to my poor plebs."[52] Such is the righteous and
laudable preoccupation of a good prince: to reduce the hunger of the plebs with
every effort and to procure for his subjects plentiful foodstuffs and make happiness
their honest companion. In this context that saying of the Emperor Marcus Aurelius
is very appropriate: "When stuffed with food, no people are happier than the
Romans."[53] This opinion can be applied to all nations: a people are always driven
to despair more from a lack of foodstuffs than from a deficiency in moral qualities.
Thus, the happiness of every nation consists more in the well-being of the body
than of the spirit.

From these concerns, however, derives not just the happiness of the people,
but the security of the ruling class as well. For no one is more terrifying than a
starving commoner of whom it has been said: "the hungry pleb knows no fear."[54]
Indeed, there are not just ancient examples but contemporary ones, especially
from recent events in the city of Rome, which bear out this saying.[55] In this matter
the prudence of Julius Caesar is especially to be praised. During both his Gallic
and German wars he was always very intent on providing foodstuffs, and so, returning to Rome, was quick to send ships to seek grain from fertile islands for the
precise purpose of meeting the needs of the Roman people. No less concerned
was Caesar Augustus, of whom it is written that when grain was in short supply
he used to distribute it at a very low price and sometimes gave it virtually free to
the Roman people, one by one.[56] For this sort of policy a prince is really worthy of
praise, for this policy is motivated by a true love of country and a desire to gain
adulation so that the people will bear their taxes more happily, suffer more willingly,
and bear hardships more readily. Such a love Augustus showed clearly when he
alleviated the hunger of the Roman people (as I have said) by selling grain at a
very low price or dispensing it free. But the same Augustus silenced complaints
over the scarcity of wine with a stinging and somber reply, making it apparent that
he had not provided the grain out of a desire to curry favor with the people but to
provide for the well-being and health of his subjects. For he told them that for the
needs of thirsty men the city of Rome had plenty of aqueducts, which had just

been built by his brother-in-law Marcus Agrippa, and that, moreover, there was always the Tiber flowing past the city walls.[57] There is, to tell the truth, a vast difference between grain and wine: the former is certainly a necessity of life, while the latter is often harmful to it. Of course, wine is more pleasant than bread to the people who often seek what gives pleasure more than what is good for them. But, indeed, the good and prudent prince does not pay heed so much to what is pleasureful as to what is beneficial.

Now this concern over the grain supply is so much a part of a prince's duty that even evil and feckless leaders cannot avoid it altogether. Hence, good princes ought to be especially diligent in seeing that grain is provided. It is true that from such preoccupations you have been released by God and by nature since the regions over which you rule are so fertile that you are far more accustomed to selling a surplus of grain from your district to others than to importing grain. Nonetheless, I would advise you that even in time of good harvests you should prepare yourself for scarcity, so that you may predict by cautious consideration not what is available now but what the future may hold, thus protecting yourself and your state from unexpected changes of fortune.

Until now I don't know whether I have spoken too much or too little concerning those things that a prince ought to do. Surely that indulgence in banquets and circus games and the exhibiting of wild and exotic animals is useless; these things may provide a brief delight and momentary pleasure to the eyes, but indeed they hold nothing honorable or worthy for the eyes of a good prince. Hence, I would recommend that a good prince avoid these things even though they are adjudged pleasing by the insane and vulgar mob. In this instance I cannot bring myself to admire the policy of the ancient Roman leaders who, even though they recognized the vanity of these things, staged these vulgar games in order to curry favor with the people, and thus depleted the treasury and diverted the money for other than intended uses. But if I were to speak of leaders who had lapsed in their own time into these sorts of errors and narrated the flights of madness of each one, my discussion would surely soon become disorganized and not at all germane to my topic. Therefore, I return at once to the main subject.

Now when a ruler has decreed that his people are to be burdened with some new tax, which he will never want to do unless in times of public need, he should make all understand that he is struggling with necessity and does it against his will. In short, he should argue that, except for the fact that events compelled him to levy the tax, he would gladly have done without it. It will also redound to his good reputation if he will have contributed some of his own money to the new tax. Thus he will show that he, the head of the people, is but one among them, and at the same time he will demonstrate his great moderation. This is exactly what the Roman Senate did during the Second Punic War, following the advice of the consul Valerius Laevinus, and this act has been remembered with great admiration by many generations.[58] However high it is, the exaction will always be judged lighter and milder. Although it was not spoken by a good prince, yet let us not forget the excellent advice he is said to have written to provincial officials who recommended burdening the provinces with new taxes: "Good shepherds ought to shear their sheep but not skin them."[59] And if such a saying applied to Roman provinces, should it not also apply to one's homeland? Because I wish you to be compared only with the best and most outstanding of princes, I beg you to imitate this policy and follow the example of those just words and deeds which have merited great praise. When your tax collectors, therefore, offer you hope of large profits follow the example of Antoninus Pius, of whom it is written that he was never pleased by any income gained at the expense of his provincial subjects.[60] How much less should you want to cause any harm to your own subjects? Similarly, Constantius uttered a laudable sentiment: "I would rather have the public wealth distributed among my subjects than closed up in my treasury."[61] Now his policy has two rationales. First of all, it is better for riches to be held and enjoyed by many than by one person, and second it is more useful for private citizens to earn money from their own industry. What is a treasury but an inert and useless mass of metal heaped up on account of greed? Who cannot see that the wealth of the citizens is also the wealth of the prince? And it is *vice versa*, as Lucan writes: "The poverty of a servant is harmful not to the servant, but to the master."[62]

And there are other even easier ways of gaining your subjects' affections—ways that are, I admit, difficult for a haughty prince but in those cases where the prince's temperament tends toward humane behavior these methods are easy and pleasant. For instance you have a tale that is told as follows: "Hadrian liked to visit twice or three times a day the sick, now of the equestrian order, now of the class of freedmen. These he revived with consolation, and he raised up their spirits with encouraging words. He always invited some of them to dine at his own table."[63] Now who can there be with such a terrible disposition that he would not be moved by such solicitous acts by his lord? And no one is more well endowed with these qualities than you are. Hence all you have to do is to follow your own good instincts and everything you want will come to you. So be compassionate to those who are suffering from sickness or some other misadventure, and, if you can, you ought to give them some help. But I do not doubt that you already act in this way. For who except a barbarian would remain unmoved when exhorted to help those whom he loves?

Furthermore, just as the love of the people is gained more easily by mercy and generosity than by any other quality, so, conversely, nothing is more guaranteed to provoke a people's hatred than cruelty and greed. If you compare the two evils you will see that while cruelty is harsher, greed is much more common. Cruelty is harsher but it only afflicts a few people, while greed is not so harsh but it affects everyone. Innumerable tyrants and princes have been undone by these two vices and made themselves hated and maligned through the centuries. But it is not necessary to speak with you concerning the vice of cruelty at any length because you are not merely a stranger to it but positively opposed to it. Thus I would judge that nothing would be more difficult for a merciful person such as yourself to commit, or even to consider committing, a cruel act against someone else. Cruelty is the quality of an ignoble, capricious, and treacherous person—someone quite different from yourself—a person quick to wreak vengeance when the possibility is offered. This vice is foreign to human nature and especially alien to the dignity of a prince, whose power to mete out vengeance is sufficient revenge. For this reason that short saying of Hadrian has been admired for a long time. Speaking to one who had been his mortal enemy when he was a private citizen and who now, seeing Hadrian emperor, was justly afraid and awaited all kinds of punishment, Hadrian said with a placid brow: "You have escaped."[64] But no more about this need be said, except that it seems to me that humanity is the high expression of human nature. Without this a person is not only not good but, indeed, cannot even be called a man.

It is more difficult, however, to banish greed completely from one's character. What person is there who does not lust after something? But I beg and beseech you that since, by God's grace, you have the means of leading a magnificent style of life, you will always hold a lustful appetite in check. Greed is insatiable, inexhaustible, and infinite, and whoever is governed by greed loses his own property while he desires that of another. Do you, perhaps, wonder at this opinion? This much is certain: whoever desires something very much and does not get it often forgets what he already has. Thus inattentive persons lose their way, and, intent on riches, they do not perceive immediate dangers; indeed, I don't think a mortal life can suffer an evil greater than this one. You ought not say to yourself what so many others do: "I am all right for the moment, but what is going to become of me later on?" Isn't this worrying about what is going to happen many years hence rather silly when no one knows what the next hour may bring? Leave aside these useless preoccupations, for it is written: "Abandon yourself to the care of the Lord and He will nourish you, and He will never let the righteous be shaken."[65] Why do you waver? Why do you fear? Why do you worry? Don't you know that the Lord cares for you? You have a good shepherd; He will never fail you, He will never desert you. Again, it is written: "Reveal your needs and go to the Lord and place your trust in Him, and He will care for you."[66] Now some may say that this is good advice for monks but not for princes. Such a critic does not understand, however, that princes ought to adhere to God and love and put their trust in Him because they have received more great benefits from Him. It is a kind of ingratitude to expect only a little from Him who has given you so much. God is the one who has nurtured you from infancy and who will care for you until the last. God will never abandon hope in you whom He did not abandon even when you could not hope in Him; indeed, even while you were growing larger in your mother's womb.

Once you have overcome this difficult evil of greed, I shall show you another sort of greed that is generous and above reproach; you must lust after the treasure of virtue and win the fame of outstanding glory. This is a property that moths and rust cannot corrupt, nor can thieves steal it in the night.[67] Now, except in the case of war (as has recently happened to you)[68] or in the event of some unavoidable difficulty, you should avoid anyone who wants his lord to take over property at the expense of others. Indeed, such urgings are the practice of almost all courtiers. Hence, you should view persons who advise such a policy as the enemies of your good reputation and mortal soul. Such evil courtiers arouse their lords so that as they steal and pillage the property of others, thus earning the hatred of their subjects and this iniquitous kind of men so oppresses the people and deceives their lords that they bring to ruin both their lords and themselves. Concerning such matters, there is that true and famous saying of Marius Maximus—as Elius Lampridius records it in his history of the Emperor Alexander—and these are his very words: "The state in which the ruler is evil is happier and almost more secure than the one in which he has evil friends; for, indeed, one evil man can be made better by many righteous men, but in no way can many evil men be held in check by one man, however righteous he may be."[69] Hence, this Alexander was a good prince, for, besides his own innate virtues of character, he also had, as the same historian writes, friends "who were upright and respected, never spiteful, or thieving, or seditious, or cunning, or leagued together for evil, or hateful to the righteous, or lustful, or cruel, or deceivers of their prince, or mockers, or desirous of hoodwinking him like a fool. But, on the contrary, they were upright, revered, temperate, pious, fond of their prince, men who neither mocked him themselves not wished him to become an object of mockery by others, who sold nothing, who lied in no matter, who falsified nothing, and who never tricked their lord so that he might love them."[70] So, according to this author, such are the friends whom a prince ought to want and seek out. The other type ought to be avoided like the plague by the prince and to be excluded from his circle as though they were public enemies. These courtiers are the masters of evil arts who have never known and always hated good morals. Moreover, these men are eager to teach the greedy ways they so like to their own princes, so that if the princes are persuaded to follow their evil ways, they can be transformed into the worst of men. For if greed is an evil in the private citizen, how much worse is it in princes?

Just as a prince has such a capacity for harming, and just as contempt for base things is a very fine quality in a prince, so a prince's greed and desire for treasure and riches is very ugly. Not without good reason, that very wise emperor Marcus Aurelius (whom I have had occasion to mention earlier) used to say: "In an emperor avarice is the most grievous of all evils."[71] For this failing alone did Pertinax and Galba suffer on account of their cruelty. Therefore, all those who love virtue and wish to have a good reputation should avoid and despise the evil of greed. But, most of all, princes should avoid greed because they are the leaders of men and in their care has been placed vast sums and much property as well as the state itself. And if they will administer their governments properly, they are certain to consider wealth foul corruption and obtain the treasures that are most prized, namely, an easy and clear conscience and the love of God and of their fellow men. Those who follow their own desires will only come to ruin, for they will never satisfy their insatiable desires and they will surely earn the hatred of God and of men. Both the consensus of the wise and experience itself—that infallible mistress of truth—teach that greed for wealth is never extinguished but only grows stronger. Concerning this question the best advice was given by Epicurus, who said that to become rich one did not need to increase his property but rather to curb his own desires.[72] Hence it is obvious that those things that are called riches are not really riches, for if they were, they would really make one rich, but they do not. In fact, all the treasure under the sun will not make one rich. Rather, consider the brief and modest axiom that in abandoning greed we approach nature more closely.

Indeed, there are many ways of acquiring money (as Aristotle points out in the *Economics*),[73] and to these the courtiers of the princes of our own age have added innumerable other methods. Consequently, the Philosopher now seems to have been quite unlearned in these matters. But these talents ought to be despised and condemned by a good prince, just as he ought to hate anything instituted for mere expediency to the detriment of justice. Rather, he ought to keep in mind that precept of the most learned and wisest of men: Nothing can be useful that is not at the same time just and honorable.[74] In the case of some courtiers, when they are good no one could be better (but this is very rare), and when they are bad nothing could be worse (and this is often the case); on this subject you have had my final thoughts. No, not really my thoughts but those of the emperor Diocletian, for although Diocletian was very harsh in his persecutions of the practitioners of Christianity, still he may be considered among the outstanding emperors. Here are his words, written down, unless I am mistaken, as they appear in a book on the life of the emperor Aurelius: "Four or five men gather together and devise a plan for deceiving the emperor, and so they tell him to what policies he ought to give his approval. Now the emperor, who is shut up in his palace, cannot know the truth. He is forced to believe only what these men tell him. He appoints as judges men who ought never to be appointed to that office and he removes from public office precisely those officials whom he ought to retain." What more can be said? As Diocletian himself was wont to say: "The favor of even a good and wise and righteous emperor is often sold."[75] When for these and other reasons he was finally persuaded to step down from the throne, he concluded: "There is nothing more difficult than to rule well."[76] And indeed it is so. Princes should not think that they can enjoy both happiness and ease in governing; perhaps they will find happiness, but I don't think that it will happen very often. If you don't believe me, just ask some prince who has had a great deal of experience in governing.

From this question I proceed to a topic concerning which I cannot warn or advise you enough, namely, never act in such a way so as to give control of the state to one of your courtiers and thus give Padua a lord other than yourself. History has seen many instances of princes who wanted to exalt their followers but who actually debased themselves and became contemptible and despised in the eyes of their subjects and ultimately were jeered at and reduced to poverty by the very men they had promoted. Because of such a disaster the emperor Claudius, who preceded Nero, was regarded as vile. He accorded many favors to his worthless freedmen, Posides, Felix, Narcissus, and Pallas, and gave them control over the provinces so that they despoiled the Empire and Claudius himself. At last he was reduced to begging from his former servants, now affluent. "Dependent on these men and their wives," Suetonius says, "Claudius acted more like a vile slave than an emperor."[77] Guided and compelled by such men, he acted very stupidly and very cruelly. The same mistake was made by the emperor Heliogabalus, who, to the grief of all good men, let those around him have great power and put everything up for sale, while dishonest friends made the emperor, as Lampridius says, "even more of a fool than he was naturally."[78] And Didius Julianus merits the same condemnation because he gave the power to rule to precisely those men whom he ought to have kept under his own authority.[79] Of course, there are always stupid and mediocre princes under whom such a state of affairs has to be tolerated. I know, however, that there is nothing mediocre about you, nothing that is not singular and outstanding. Indeed, you will not fulfill my hopes or those of many others unless you at least reach or even surpass the achievement of many good and outstanding rulers. And if you fail to achieve this I will not attribute it to a lack of natural ability but to the failure of your will.

But why should we talk only about lesser emperors when we can cite the example of such an outstanding man as the Emperor Marcus Aurelius over whom mere freedmen exercised at great deal of control?[80] Because of this sort of example, it is proper to warn fervently anyone like yourself, who proposes to excel and govern, that you should watch diligently and not permit yourself (as many outstanding princes have) to fall into this vice using the benevolent disposition (which you possess) as an excuse. Although it is well to imitate illustrious men, you should not follow their example in every particular. There is no one who does not occasionally make a mistake and thus fall short of his potential for excellence.

But you will say, and perhaps you have already said to yourself, that I am advising you to be ungrateful to your courtiers. If I did that, how then would I be allowed to enjoy the gifts that you have already bestowed on me? Would I really advise you to be niggardly? Never! Nothing is more wicked in a prince, more wicked in a man, than ingratitude. Every virtue has some distractors, every vice some defenders.

Only ingratitude never pleases anyone, and, conversely, gratitude displeases no one. But there are a great many things that you can bestow on those who merit rewards: horses, clothing, arms, plates, money, dwellings, land, and so forth. Follow, however, what is written in the Bible: "Do not bestow your honor on another."[81] I know well that you are ready to share cheerfully with your friends not only your own power but even your very life. But I beg you—not only for your own sake but for the sake of your country, which God gave you to govern. Nothing could be worse, nothing more harmful to the Paduan people, than to obey many chiefly unworthy men placed above them. At present all the citizens regard you as their lord, they all respect, admire, and even venerate you, and they look upon your courtiers not as rulers but as representatives who have been sent out to execute your orders. They see the courtiers as private persons with neither the dignity nor the power that you alone ought to possess. And there are other reasons why what I am saying is important; I myself have observed the unbelievable patience with which several citizen-bodies have suffered the rule of harsh and demanding lords who ruled alone. Conversely, I have seen a people become indignant and rebellious when more than one lord tried to command their respect and obedience. Indeed, unless I am entirely mistaken: we discussed this very subject when you did me the honor to visit me in my rustic retreat a year or so ago.

Now it would be superfluous for me to write you concerning the other type of friends, the ones who are not seeking your wealth but who respect and honor you for what you are. This topic is really unnecessary because you are among the most faithful and upright cultivators of friendship, and since Cicero has already discussed that topic in his elegant little book.[82] Putting all this into a few words, we can say that in human affairs nothing is sweeter than friendship, and, after virtue, nothing is more sacred. Those who rule over others by their power and ability especially have need of true friends who will stick with them through thick and thin. You should never ask a friend to do anything dishonorable, nor should you ever do anything dishonorable on behalf of a friend. But nothing honorable is to be denied to a friend. Now you ought to adopt this principle: Among friends everything ought to be held in common, all should act with one accord and by common consent; and what friends agree to ought never to be changed simply because of other expectations, fear, or some imminent danger. Each person ought to love his friend as himself and to overlook any difference in status or wealth. In short, seek to act as Pythagoras orders: "Several persons are gathered in one."[83] Likewise, the conditions of true friendship are expressed in Holy Scripture, where in the Acts of the Apostles it is written: "The company of those who believed and who loved one another in Christ was of one head and one soul, and no one of them, whatever he possessed, claimed it for his own use, and all their property was held in common."[84] If someone were to define friendship as being faithful and lovers in Christ, I certainly would not contradict him, because I do not believe there can be friendship, or any firm or stable relationship for that matter, except that Christ be the foundation. At the same time, however, I am in agreement with the opinion of the pagan philosophers that there can be no true friendship without there being at the same time true wisdom and virtue. In saying this I am not following those who say with a foolish sophistry that there never has been nor ever will be anyone called wise. I am not discussing here impossibilities, but I am content with what the human condition is capable of creating,[85] and surely we must number among these things the sort of friendship that I have just been talking about. Although it is true that we can actually name very few pairs of friends who knew a perfect and consummate friendship such as the younger Scipio and Laelius were famous for, still there has often been practiced among men a pleasant and fine sort of friendship. In this relationship there was never any fawning adulation, nor disparaging remarks, nor back-biting, and no discord or reproach. In fact, there was nothing in these friendships that did not lead to the pleasure and honor of the friends and to peace, harmony, and good fellowship. In these friendships there was nothing false, no dissembling, nothing duplicitous, but only what was pure, candid, and open. In these cases many things were held or done in common: advice, work, honors, wealth, talent, and even life itself. We know that such friendships have been frequent in history, and they have often, and rightly, been praised. But I have already spoken at length concerning these things, so it ought to be now an easy matter to distinguish a true friendship from a false one. For the time being enough has been said.

From here on I shall proceed without any preconceived plan and treat what I deem important, setting down with my pen whatever topic may come to mind. I would like to add another topic to those things that I have been discussing about fellowship and generosity toward a friend. The saying of Martial is especially true today: "Wealth is given to none but the rich."[86] Indeed, there are many crafty and cunning men who do get rich. Cicero has described the system by which you make many benefactions at interest and especially generous ones to those whom you are certain will return your benefactions manyfold.[87] But you, on the contrary, who never seek any reward from your gifts except to give benefits and obtain from this the happiness of a mind at peace with itself, act contrary to the habits of the greedy. Always make donations to the neediest and do not simply give away your own wealth; when you receive voluntary donations from the rich you should give them to the poor. You have in this matter the precedent of Alexander, who (as I have said) made exactly such benefactions when he was still an outstanding youth and prince.[88] Nor am I unaware that in what I have just been advising I may seem to be speaking against my own case. Although I am not so rich a man as to arouse envy, as the recipient of both your own generosity and that of your father, I lack nothing, a condition that in my view means the highest wealth. But when I gave this advice I was thinking neither of myself nor of others, but only of your own best interests.

Now there is another thing I want to discuss with you, something that ought to please you very much. I know, of course, that generosity is praised in a prince more than humility. Perhaps this is as it should be. But I really do think that both qualities are worthy of praise and that one quality does not necessarily exclude the other, as foolish men often think. For in this matter as in almost all things, the mob of men is mistaken. They call magnificence pride, and they consider humility to be timidity; both opinions are wrong. I would like you to be a prince who is humble at home among his own people and in prosperity while being magnanimous facing his enemies in adversity. In neither case is such a prince acting timidly or proudly. Indeed, it seems to me that humility is in the first rank of all the virtues. However, some stupid and blind rulers do not feel that they can be truly great lords unless they are swaggering and prideful beyond human dimensions. This is really just the idiocy of ignorant princes. Caligula, that vilest of emperors, was not content with the honors due him as a man; he wished to be worshipped as a god. Consequently he placed statues of himself in the temples so that he who was certainly unworthy to be revered as a god, would be worshiped and venerated. He even established his own temple where priests sacrificed victims before his golden effigy.[89] Caligula did many other things that he thought would bring him greater honor but that really only served to disclose his own stupidity. Is there anyone more evil, more monstrous than the emperor Commodus? Indeed, sacrifices were even made to this most evil son of an illustrious father, just as one would offer to a god. Statues in the form of Hercules were raised to Commodus, who certainly was not a god nor even really a man, but a cruel and ferocious beast.[90] Even Heliogabalus himself, that vilest of princes and of men began to be worshipped. All of these emperors merited being murdered on the spot and having their bodies thrown into the Tiber or into sewers.[91]

I must confess that I am reluctant to speak of these crimes and I am saddened and ashamed that these men so polluted with sins were our emperors. I have been discussing this matter, however not because I enjoy it but because the truth compels me to. In like manner, these northern barbarians of our own time ought to be less angry at me if, when I speak of them, I am moved by a desire to tell the truth more than by hatred.[92] For I do not hate men; I hate vice, and I hate it more (not less) in us Italians than in other people. Similarly, a farmer is bothered more by rocks, tares, and thistles on his own farm than he is by finding them in another man's field. Yet I must confess that I really cannot hear the vain boasting of that good-for-nothing northern people that is always ready to lie about its accomplishments and brag about what it thinks are its glorious achievements. But, lest I get into a new dispute with those who are not even present, I shall return to my topic.

After those bad emperors, Diocletian wanted to be worshipped like a god and encrusted his shoes as well as his clothing with gems. In this fashion he transformed the dress of Roman emperors into a new style,[93] a great novelty for a man otherwise serious and disciplined and one who finally abdicated his throne in order to enjoy a peaceful retirement. Hence, I can only think that this desire for pomp and circumstance derives not from a desire for true glory but from a weak mind. Now it often seems to base persons that when they have attained high office, they have reached heaven, so that losing their perspective they lose control. On the contrary, no earthly honor is of much importance to the truly magnanimous leader. He does not strive to seem more than he really is. For example, the greatest and best of emperors, Caesar Augustus, did not hanker after divine honors, nor did he allow himself to be worshipped.[94] Indeed, he did not want to be called "lord," even by his children or grandchildren. For he believed (as Suetonius says) that "the name of 'lord' ought always to be abhorred as a curse and an insult."[95] Hence he forbade the use of the term, and he reproved anyone who dared to use it with a threatening word, a look, or a gesture. Likewise, did Alexander—and I don't mean that king of the Macedons who surpassed everyone in vanity and pride and who, after he had conquered the Persians, was himself conquered by Persian customs. Then impelled by some madness, this Alexander came to want himself worshipped like a god and the son of a god following the Persian belief much to the harm of true religious practice. No, I am speaking of that other Alexander, the Roman emperor, whom we have often mentioned today, and who not only forbade the worship of himself but even enjoined that he be greeted in no other way than "Hello, Alexander."[96] If anyone dared to greet him with a bow of the head or any grand title, he either banished him from his presence or ridiculed him harshly with a loud guffaw.[97]

Now if I know you and your beliefs well (and after so many years I cannot help but know them), I have no doubt that you bear the title of "lord" more with patience than with pleasure. I have heard you say more than once, and really affirm it almost under oath, that the lordship of Padua was not a pleasure to you and that you would gladly relinquish it if it were not for the fear that an intruder might invade the city and place the Paduan people under oppressive rule and compel you unwillingly to live under a lord. Otherwise, I would much prefer that you were a free private citizen than a ruling lord, for then you could live of your own wealth and you could—as an important man free of the cares of governing—enjoy a quiet and profitable prime of life and, when it came, an honorable old age. From all this it is abundantly clear to me that you do not take pride in something unless you value it very highly. But since it is difficult to change a people's habits and to abolish longstanding customs, you should bear with the Paduan people and let them call you "lord" if they want to. After all, you can always speak of yourself as you see fitting and proper. Now I know that you never apply to yourself in speech or writing the name, "lord." Thus you reject the present usage of most other lords and princes. You sign your name at the bottom of your letters without any title; you never use the plural but always the singular form of address—and not just with superiors but with equals and inferiors as well. Even to me (and there is no one more humble), you never say "we" (as other lords do), but rather you say: "I wish this, I beg this, I order this." When I read these phrases in your letters I am pleased, and I say to myself that if this man really had an inflated opinion of himself his style of writing would show it too. Other princes wish to appear as more than one person, but they are not even one; in fact, they are nothing. You are doing in this instance a fine thing; unwittingly, and from your own sound instincts, you are imitating the great leaders of ancient Rome. Look at the letters of Julius Caesar and of Augustus (some of which you will find preserved in the works of Josephus and others in Suetonius) and you will never find "we" written there. You will never find "we wish" or "we command," but instead "I wish," "I command," and the like. Indeed, it is—just as you are accustomed to joke—that those who speak of themselves in the plural seem to be naming not just themselves but their wives, children, and servants as well. But you speak only in your own name, and it is you (and no one else) who commands and orders your followers. I have nothing but admiration for your character and your manner and your style of writing, practiced not only by the contemporary leaders I have mentioned but by almost all of the ancient Roman emperors as well. This we know from many letters found in many different books. I mention it in the hope that you will be proud of your style of address while other princes will be made ashamed of theirs, which they consider to be a mark of great status when, in fact, it is an obvious indication of their inferiority and timidity.

Further, to your modesty in speech there is joined another modesty, a modesty in dress that is obvious to everyone. Thus, one modest habit merits approval through the eyes of the beholder while the other comes through the ears, and both together convey through the intellect and the senses the impression of a very modest person and a complete gentleman. Many other lords display themselves before their subjects covered, and even laden down, with gold and finery[98]—rather like altars decorated for a high feast day—and they consider themselves very important merely because they are laden down with precious clothing. You, on the other hand, are content with modest dress, so that you prove to be a lord on account of neither costly clothing nor display but from the dignity of your manner and the authority of your bearing. This is a double good, just as the opposite is a double evil. Vulgar display is hateful in itself, and it often leads to the dangerous disease of imitation. Every people strives to imitate the deeds and habits of its prince. Hence, there is that very true saying that there is nothing more harmful to the state than the bad example of its prince. And in complete truth, the poet says: "The whole world follows the king's example."[99] There you have it: the bad habits of princes are dangerous not just to themselves but to everyone. Concerning this there is a very apposite passage in the third book of Cicero's *On the Laws*:

For it is not so mischievous that men of high position do evil—though this evil is bad enough in itself—as it is that these men have so many imitators. For if you will turn your thoughts back to history, you will see that the character or our most prominent men has been reproduced in the whole state; whatever change took place in the lives of the prominent men has also taken place in the whole people. And we can be much more confident of the soundness of this than of what so pleased our beloved Plato. He thought that the characteristics of a nation could be changed by changing the character of its music. But I believe that a transformation takes place in a nation's character when the habits and mode of living of its aristocracy are changed. For this reason, men of the upper class who do wrong are especially dangerous to the state, because they not only indulge in vicious practices themselves, but also infect the whole commonwealth with their vices, and not only because they are corrupt, but also because they corrupt, others and do more harm by their bad example than by their sin.[100]

So much for Cicero. Indeed, I myself, when I have been with you and others, used to say: "This prince will teach boasting to no one; he will lead no one into pompous ways." And I have often reflected upon what Livy wrote about Hannibal: "He was equal to all others in dress, he stood out only in arms and in horses."[101] However, this is not such great praise for a soldier in time of war, when, of necessity, all comforts must be excluded. You show modesty in times of peace and prosperity, which are the mothers of immoderation, and luxury. Therefore, when I consider your dress, the matter ought not to be compared with that of Hannibal, which I have just been describing, but with that of Augustus, under whose reign all kings and people enjoyed a universal peace. Concerning him it is written that he wore only clothes made at home by his wife, his sister, his daughter, and his granddaughters.[102]

Now there are many topics that I still might discuss if I did not fear that I might exhaust your patience (perhaps already wearied with all that I have said up to now). But there is one topic that I simply cannot pass over, a practice that will make princes both respected and venerated (and indeed on this theme you need no exhortation). In short, I appeal that you honor famous men and hold them in esteem and friendship. You are so eager to do this that you could not do otherwise (even if you wanted to)—your very nature would stop you—for a leader does nothing better than what he does following his own nature. Custom is a strong force, training is stronger still, nature is more so, but if all three are joined together it becomes the most effective. Now I view as outstanding those men who are set apart from the common herd of humanity by some singular quality; this could be outstanding justice or holiness (which these days is virtually nonexistent), or military skill and experience, or profound learning in literature and science. Although (as Cicero says in the first book of *On Duties*) "most people think that military science is more important than knowledge of government, their opinion is really quite mistaken."[103] He has pointed out many Greek and Roman leaders who were examples of this fact; Themistocles and Solon, Lysander and Lycurgus, and from the Romans, Gaius Marius and Marcus Scaurus, Gneus Pompeius and Quintus Catulus, the younger Scipio and Publius Nasica, and since Cicero wanted fame and glory for himself, he also added his own name to the list.[104] And indeed this judgment is not without justice, for I do not doubt that Anthony did no more for the good of Rome when he defeated Catiline on the field of battle than did Cicero himself when he exposed Catiline's horrible conspiracy to the Senate and threw the conspirators into prison.

Among those honored for their abilities in governing, the first place ought to go to learned men. And among these learned men, a major place should go to those whose knowledge in law is always very useful to the state. If, indeed, love of and devotion to justice is added to their knowledge of law, these citizens are (as Cicero puts it) "learned not just in the law, but in justice."[105] However, there are those who follow the law but do no justice, and these are unworthy to bear the name of the legal profession. For it is not enough simply to have knowledge; you must want to use it. A good lawyer adds good intentions to his legal knowledge. Indeed, there have been many lawyers who have added luster to ancient Rome and other places: Adrianus Julius Celsus, Salvius Julianus, Neratius Priscus, Antonius Scaevola, Severus Papinianus, Alexander Domitius Ulpianus, Fabius Sabinus, Julius Paulus, and many others.[106] And you too (as much as our own times permit) have by the patronage of your university added honor to your country. There are other kinds of learned men, some of whom you can depend on for advice and learned conversation, and (as Alexander used to say) invent literary tales.[107] One reads that Julius Caesar, in like fashion, used to confer Roman citizenship on doctors of medicine and on teachers of the liberal arts.[108] Now, among learned men there is no doubt that we ought to give preference to those who teach the knowledge of sacred things (or what we call theology), provided that these men have kept themselves free from any foolish sophistries.

That very wise emperor Augustus used to bestow patronage on learned men to encourage them to remain in Rome, and hope of such a reward stimulated others to study, for at that time Roman citizenship was a highly valued honor. Indeed, when St. Paul claimed that he was a Roman citizen, the tribune judging the case said to him: "I myself have at a high price obtained this status."[109] You, my great lord, do not have such rewards in your gift, but you can do this: you can give learned and distinguished men dedicated to honorable studies a place among your citizen-body. So be generous and kind to scholars, and Padua will be filled with learned men and its university restored to its ancient glory. Nothing entices outstanding men so much as the friendship and patronage of a prince. Caesar Augustus gathered together his famous troop of scholars and artists with his hospitality and patronage rather than with the power of his empire. He numbered among his friends Cicero in the beginning, and then Asinius Pollio, Valerius Messala, and Parius Geminus, all great orators, as well as Vergil and Horace, outstanding poets to whom he wrote personal letters. It was clear from these letters that the supreme ruler of the inhabited world treated these two rustics—one from Mantua, the other from Verona—not just as his equals but even as his superiors. By his example Augustus taught others that no ruler should be ashamed to enjoy the friendship of commoners who had been ennobled by their own genius and learning. Who could possibly be ashamed of such a friendship if the Emperor Augustus were not ashamed of it? Later on he was also friendly with Tucca and Varius of Cremona and with Ovid of Sulmona, though Augustus did eventually find Ovid unworthy and banished him from his court. And there were others, including Marcus Varro, perhaps the most learned of all, and the Paduan Titus Livy, the father of history who, if he were alive today, would be your fellow citizen. So at this one moment in history these and many others were gathered around Augustus so that he was made glorious as much by these illustrious men as by the conquests of all his Roman legions. Can the thirty-five tribes of Rome or her forty-four valorous legions really be compared to that one great man, Vergil, who so honored Augustus with his friendship? Vergil still lives by his fame; the others have long since perished. Indeed, learned men attracted by this famous imperial generosity came from Greece as well as from Italy. Now I am asking you: where can a talented and intelligent man be happier and lead a better life than under the benevolent gaze of a just and generous prince? I sincerely believe that if it were not for the bonds of your own generosity, a great many scholars who have come to Padua would soon leave. For my part, I praise and laud your patronage. Although soldiers can at times be useful to you and perform good services in time of war, it is only learned men who can provide the right advice at the right moment, and thus ensure the fame of your name. Moreover, they can show you the proper road to heaven, you can mount on the wings of their expert advice, and, if you get lost, you can find your way again by following their counsel.

But I have said enough, I fear even too much. At the beginning of this letter I had intended that I would exhort you, at its end, to correct the morals of your subjects. Yet I now think this would be an impossible task, for it is always difficult to change what had evolved out of custom. It cannot be done by force of law or by kings. Hence, I have changed my aim because it is always useless to attempt the impossible. However, there is one custom among the Paduan people that I cannot overlook. And I will not simply ask you, but I shall implore you, to correct this public evil with your own hand. Now don't say to me that this evil that I want you to correct is not unique to Padua but common to many other cities. This is a question of your own dignity, and just as you have been the beneficiary of many individual gifts, so that you now excel your contemporaries, Padua has received many gifts from you so that it excels all the neighboring cities.

Now you should certainly know, best of men, that it is written in the Old Testament: "Everyone dies."[110] The New Testament says: "It is established that every man dies once."[111] And among the pagan authors you find: "Death is certain, which day it will happen is uncertain."[112] Even if it were not written in any book, still death is certain, as our common nature tells us. Now I do not know whether it is because of human nature or from some longstanding custom that at the death of our close friends and relatives we can scarcely contain our grief and tears, and that our funeral services are often attended by wailings and lamentations. But I do know that scarcely ever has this propensity for public grief been so deep-rooted in other cities as it is in yours. Someone dies—and I do not care whether he is a noble or a commoner, the grief displayed by the commoners is certainly no less manifest, and perhaps more so, than that of the nobles, for the plebs are more apt to show their emotions and less likely to be moved by what is proper; as soon as he breathes his last, a great howling and torrent of tears begins. Now I am not asking you to forbid expressions of grief. This would be difficult and probably impossible, given human nature. But what Jeremiah says is true: "You should not bemoan the dead, nor bathe the corpse in tears."[113] As that great poet Euripides wrote in Crespontes: "Considering the evil of our present existence, we ought to lament at our birth and rejoice at our death."[114] But these philosophic opinions are not well known, and, in any case, the common people would find them unthinkable and strange.

Therefore, I will tell you what I am asking. Take an example: Some old dowager dies, and they carry her body into the streets and through the public squares accompanied by loud and indecent wailing so that someone who did not know what was happening could easily think that here was a madman on the loose or that the city was under enemy attack. Now, when the funeral cortege finally gets to the church, the horrible keening redoubles, and at the very spot where there ought to be hymns to Christ or devoted prayers for the soul of the deceased in a subdued voice or even silence, the walls resound with the lamentations of the mourners and the holy altars shake with the wailing of women. All this simply because a human being has died. This custom is contrary to any decent and honorable behavior and unworthy of any city under your rule. I wish you would have it changed. In fact, I am not just advising you, I am (if I may) begging you to do so. Order that wailing women should not be permitted to step outside their homes; and if some lamentation is necessary to the grieved, let them do it at home and do not let them disturb the public thoroughfares.

I have said to you perhaps more than I should, but less than I would like to say. And if it seems to you, illustrious sir, that I am mistaken in one place or another, I beg your pardon, and I ask you to consider only the good advice. May you rule your city long and happily. Farewell. Arqua, the 28th of November.

Chapter 2

COLUCCIO SALUTATI

On the Tyrant

(1400)

Like Petrarch, Coluccio Salutati (1331–1406) was a Tuscan native territorially dislocated because of his family's embroilment in the Guelf-Ghibelline conflicts of the time. Salutati studied in Bologna and held significant administrative appointments in Todi, Rome, and Lucca before becoming chancellor, or head of the bureaucracy, of Florence in 1374. Salutati put his classical learning to formidable use in diplomatic service to Florence during its bitter military conflicts with the pope and with the Visconti of Milan, out of which emerged the present text, "De Tyranno." In this essay Salutati defended Dante's decision to place Brutus and Cassius in hell for the crime of tyrannicide, an argument that required not only a defense of Julius Caesar's legitimacy but more abstract considerations on the nature of tyranny in general. A confidant of Petrarch and mentor to a successive wave of humanist literati (Poggio Bracciolini, Niccolò Niccoli, Leonardo Bruni, and Pier Paolo Vergerio), Salutati fostered a community of scholars who translated the texts of important ancient Greek authors, Plato and Aristotle foremost among them. The text is a reprint of Coluccio Salutati, "De Tyranno," in Ephraim Emerton, trans. and ed., *Humanism and Tyranny: Studies in the Italian Trecento* (Cambridge, Mass.: Harvard University Press, 1925), 70–118.

On the Tyrant

Coluccio, son of Piero, Chancellor of Florence, to Master Antonio of Aquila, student in Arts at Padua, Greeting!

A TREATISE ON TYRANTS
WITH AN INTRODUCTION

Since you ask of me a thing at once difficult to answer and yet worth knowing, I cannot refuse a reply, my learned friend—for such your letter shows you to be. It has always seemed to me fair to repay esteem with esteem and, if one can, to give a suitable reply to anyone who makes a reasonable inquiry. Indeed the very bond of human society, seeing that man is made for the sake of his fellow man and that, according to the divine ordinance it is not good for man to be alone as he was created, requires not merely that we show favor to those who ask it, but that, as far as we can, we anticipate those who do not ask. And this not only in things that have reference to our final end, to which we are bound by our common faith, but also in those which mark the good citizen or, more broadly, the good man. The race of men is bound together by religious faith, by common citizenship and by nature. The first has to do with our final salvation; the second with the civil order; the third with human relations and the perfecting of mankind. Since, then, your inquiry touches directly or indirectly upon each one of these I cannot and ought not to decline to answer it.

But first I must refer to the beginning of your letter, in which you compliment me far too highly. For, if we owe a reply to one who asks for it, so do we to one who gives us the material for a reply. You assume many fine things of me—I hardly know whether to say, out of politeness or out of ignorance. You speak too confidently of things that have come to you by common report, as if you had carefully investigated them. You praise me too much, nay, more than too much. You say that as a leader in each and every art worthy of the liberally educated man I am superabundantly equipped. You declare that I have won the praise of all men by singular talent, culture and refinement. To use your own words: besides my superior literary accomplishment I am a man devoted to giving pleasure to everyone; I spare myself no labor to give satisfaction to others, and on this you rest your hopes of a reply.

You say that I work for all, and that it makes little difference to me what class of men I address, provided only that I can be of service. You refer to certain letters of mine written to various scholars and containing things which they could not have learned from others or by themselves. You bring forward these things to give yourself greater confidence in the request you have to make.

I am truly sorry for your mistake in these matters; for I do feel that you have deceived yourself, taking "with Gallic lightness," as the saying is, things as proven which are only matters of hearsay, and praising me for what after all, even if it were in me, is not really my own. For what have I that has not been given to me, and gratis at that, not for my own merit, but by the grace of the bountiful Giver? I would rather have you give praise to Him who is the giver and the artificer, rather than to me the receiver and the mere tool of the craftsman's hand. Whatever I am, subject or accident, is His, whose work I am; to say it is mine would be the height of folly; to take praise for it would be unpardonable conceit. Wherefore I beg you henceforth to have done with this sort of thing and not to flatter my all too ready ear with such blandishments, lest I forget that what you praise is not my own but His who gave it.

Whoever says he has learned anything by his own zeal or diligence or reflection declares himself to be the primal cause, and what folly that is, you, a student in Arts, can judge for yourself. You shall never lead me into any such foolishness. I am the tool of the Master, not the efficient cause of the work or of the action. And yet, if we think of the work in so far as it depends upon our own will, we truly cooperate with God, and from this comes all our merit in the work, not as a reason for recompense, but as a measure of it. For, in so far as we fail in the perfection of an action, we depart from the eternal law, and failing to do as we ought we cripple the work and thus incur the penalty of that law.

Now then, praise me if you can, and pretend that is mine which you now see cannot come from me! If I have learning—or rather if you believe I have it, congratulate me that God has given it to me and pray that His grace may remain, lest if it were taken away my ignorance should be exposed. When you accuse many of selfishness, for the best of reasons, because they are unwilling to give instruction or, if they do give it address themselves only to the fortunate of this world neglecting the rest, you do well. They are indeed most worthy of reproof who, knowing, if they are not fools, that they have freely received the gift of God, try to bring under their own private control this favor of the universal cause, and what is worse, boast that they have gained by their own labor what they could never keep except by God's favor and what they see is denied to others who work far harder than they do.

But let them remain in their error, and let us follow the precept of the Mediator between God and man: "Freely ye have received; freely give!" When I see the lord of all things giving such gifts to men who are of themselves nothing, I could never wish to overlook any one in repayment for that talent which is mine. If majesty supreme has deigned to bestow some gift upon my insignificance, can I dare think it was given me to keep to myself and not rather through me to be shared with others? Or shall I look down upon my neighbor on account of his humble station or his modest fortune, when I consider how God has not scorned me, low as I am and so far below His supreme excellence? I will not disdain you or anyone, even were he as unknown to me as you are, who may desire to learn what I know, nor will I begrudge to anyone what has been given to me. If I shall find out the truth of the matter about which you inquire, you may rejoice with me; but if I shall disappoint your expectations ascribe it in part to my ignorance, but partly also to yourself for having greater hopes of me than experience shall have shown to be warranted. Enough of this.

[This apology, conventional as it is, is perfectly characteristic of the early Renaissance attitude toward all speculative subjects. Our author is proposing to express various opinions which might seem almost "radical" to the classes of Florentine society with which he desired to stand well and upon which he was dependent for the continuance of his honorable and profitable office. He anticipates possible criticism by disclaiming responsibility for his utterances. He is writing only to oblige a youthful inquirer, and indeed it is hardly he himself at all who speaks but the divine grace which has chosen him for its instrument.]

Now, coming to your inquiry: I will first give a definition of a tyrant, both as to the word and the thing itself, so that we may not be floating about in misunderstandings, and I will add also how many kinds of tyrants there are. In the second place, we will discuss whether it is lawful to kill a tyrant for any definable reason. Third, we will discourse upon the rule of Caesar and whether he can and ought to be considered a tyrant. Fourth, whether he was rightly or wrongly slain by his assailants, and finally, we shall prove that Dante, my divinely gifted fellow citizen, was right in placing these assailants in his lowest hell. When all this has been done I think you and all who raise similar questions will be satisfied. As to your final query, whether Antenor and Aeneas were traitors to their country, since this does not involve an argument, it will be enough if I make a note of what I could find about this in the ancient writers, and this I will try to do at the close of my treatise.

Chapter I
What a Tyrant Is, and Why He Is So Called

The word "tyrant" is of Greek origin and has the same meaning among both the Greeks and ourselves, in ancient times and now. For the word "tyros" is the same as "brave." Now, from the beginning, as Trogus testifies, every community was governed by kings, and these, as Justinus says, were raised to power, not through any arts of popularity, but by the well considered judgment of good citizens. Their special function was to defend the frontiers of the realm, to rule justly and to settle quarrels, if the innocence of the time should produce such, in accordance with that sense of equity which is implanted by nature in the human mind; and since these duties required bravery of mind and body, the most ancient Greeks and the primitive Italians called their kings "tyrants." From his function as ruler the king is called in Greek Basileus, for the verb *basileuo* in Greek is the same as *regno* in Latin. But then, as evil increased and kings began to rule oppressively [*superbe*][1] the name "tyrant" was confined to those who abused their power "tyrannically" [*per insolentiam imperii*]. On this point we have the witness of Vergil, greatest of poets. He says:

Gens, bello preclara jugis insedit Etruscis
Hanc multos florentem annos rex deinde superbo
Imperio et sevis tenuit Mecentius armis

                                        Aen. VIII, 480–482

and he adds, touching upon the idea of *superbia*

Quid memorem infandas cedes? quid facta tyranni?

                                        Aen. VIII, 483.

You notice that the person whom he first called "a haughty . . . king" is here called "tyrant," and previously he had said of his hero Aeneas, whom he everywhere describes as loyal [*pius*] and as a king:

Pars mihi pads erit dextram tetigisse tyranni

                                        Aen. VII, 266.

Thus much I have said as to the meaning of the word in order to dispose of the ignorant fancies of certain persons.

Now, to come to the definition of a tyrant, I propose a text from St. Gregory, who, in the twelfth book of his commentary upon Job, expounding these words: "and the number of the years of his tyranny is uncertain"[2] (Job, xv, 20) defines with divine accuracy not only the tyrant but also the various types of tyrant. He says: "Properly speaking a tyrant is one who rules a state without the forms of law [*non jure*], and then adds "but everyone who rules *superbe* [?autocratically] exercises a tyranny of his own sort. Sometimes a person may practice this in a state through an office which he has received, another in a province, another in a city, another in his own house, and another through concealed malignity, within his own heart. God does not ask how much evil a man does, but how much he would like to do. If outward power be lacking he is a tyrant at heart whose inner viciousness governs him; for, although he cannot injure his neighbors outwardly he inwardly desires to have the power to injure them." So far Gregory.

To dispose first of what he says as to the kinds of tyrants: In his most important chapter the tyrant appears under two forms, one in character, the other in action. If a man lacks power, and practices tyranny in his intentions from hidden baseness of quality, he presents the character but not the act. He is, properly speaking, a tyrant within himself, and this defect in the sight of God who trieth the hearts and reins is a serious one; for God considers not only what one is able to do, but still more what one desires to do.

As to this defect in man we say nothing at present. It may, however, properly be considered under three forms according to the types of government, the royal, the constitutional and the despotic. If one governs according to the standards of his own prudence and the dictates of his own will, freely and without laws or the limitations of any statutes or of any man, solely for the good of his subjects, this rule is a royal one. If one governs with an authority limited by laws which it is a crime to break, this is called a constitutional government. But that kind of government which is exercised over slaves and beasts, of which the aim is the preservation of property and the welfare of its owner, this the Greeks called a despotic rule. Its ultimate purpose is similar to that of the housefather.

Now in these several forms of government, the autocratic [*superbus*] ruler becomes a tyrant, and that is the meaning of those words of Gregory above quoted, if we consider them carefully. For he first describes the legitimate royal power in a state, then the constitutional in a province or a city and then the despotic in one's own house, each as being corrupted by *superbia*.

The government of a household is not opposed to a royal or a constitutional or a despotic one, but embraces all three. The father of a family governs his son royally through his affection for him, his wife constitutionally according to principles of law, but his slaves despotically as being his own property. The tyrant, however, although he is contrasted with all these, since it is his character to destroy laws, to carry himself haughtily toward his subjects and to consider his own welfare rather than theirs, yet comes nearer to the despotic government of a household as regards his main object, namely, to pursue what is specially profitable to himself and to increase his own wealth. As regards the action of his own will, on the other hand, he approaches more nearly a royal government.

The special quality of the tyrant is, that he does not rule according to law; and this may happen in either one of two ways: He may have seized upon a civil government which was not his own, or he may rule unjustly or, speaking more broadly, may pay no attention to the principles of right. Hear what a tyrant says of himself in the words of Seneca: "I will wield the sceptre which I have captured with the hand of a conqueror and will carry on everything without fear of the laws, etc.!" The words "captured sceptre" show the unlawfulness of his title, and the words "carry on everything without fear of the laws" show that corruption in administration which Gregory says is the mark of the tyrant: "one who governs without the law."

We conclude, therefore, that a tyrant is either one who usurps a government, having no legal title for his rule, or one who governs *superbe* or rules unjustly or does not observe law or equity; just as, on the other hand, he is a lawful prince upon whom the right to govern is conferred, who administers justice and maintains the laws.

Chapter II
Whether It Is Lawful to Kill a Tyrant

Now, to begin with the question of usurpers:—Who will deny that the people as a whole, or a majority of the citizens, or a part of the population of a town,—nay, even a single citizen may lawfully resist anyone who attacks the liberty of the people or usurps the government? For if, as those greatest of rulers, the emperors Diocletian and Maximian, writing to Theodorus, decreed, it is right for a lawful possessor in defence of property to which he has a faultless title to repel force by force *cum inculpatae tutelae moderatione*; and if, as Ulpian, the ablest of jurists, says, one may forcibly resist an armed assailant; and if according to Cassius it is a right of nature to oppose force with force, who can deny that any person whosoever may lawfully resist one who usurps the government of a city, a province or a kingdom?

It is, therefore, lawful to repel by force the assailant of an individual or of a piece of property and if he persist, to kill him, and shall we not have the right to prevent by force, even to the point of death, one who tries to seize the rule of a city, or kingly power or the government of a republic? Most unfair would the laws be—or rather no laws at all, if that which is permitted to private persons in case of danger or abuse were forbidden for the preservation of the liberty or the life of the community. Or if, as Ulpian bears witness, it is lawful to kill a nocturnal robber who defends himself with a weapon in such a way that the slayer could not have spared him without endangering his own person or property; if Arcadius, Theodosius and Honorius permitted the killing of common thieves and deserters from the army on the ground that the right of public execution for the sake of the peace of the community was permissible to everyone—as they wrote to Hadrian, a praetorian prefect; if Valentinian, Arcadius and Honorius granted to the people of the provinces the right of resistance against citizens or soldiers, so that night raiders in the fields or those who lay in wait on the public roads might be put down by any person with suitable punishment, even with the death they had prepared for others, on the principle that it was better to meet the evil beforehand than to punish it afterward, and that a crime which it would be too late to punish by the judgment of the praetors should [thus] be brought under a decree of the emperor—if, I say, all these things were permitted, who could so unfairly interpret the law or be so opposed to justice or such a determined enemy of the public weal as to think these same things were not lawful against those who should try to set up a tyranny?—and this so much the more as the public safety is more important than that of individuals.

A proof that this is true is found in the story of Servilius Ahala who murdered Spurius Melius, the richest man of his time, on suspicion of aiming at kingly power. In a time of scarcity at Rome, Melius had brought in grain from Etruria through the hired services of clients and foreigners and had distributed it freely to the people, a most evil precedent. Afterward, when L. Quinctius Cincinnatus was made Dictator, Melius was brought to justice and appealed to the people to rescue him from the Lictor; but Servilius Ahala, without waiting for a judgment, which might have been hindered by popular clamor, slew him on the spot. And this was not reckoned as a crime, but rather as a glorious deed. We have preserved a famous word of Cincinnatus the Dictator, when the murder of Melius was reported to him: "Well done, Servilius! The republic thrown into confusion is now set free!" Then calling an assembly of the people he made proclamation that Melius had been lawfully put to death and, by his authority as Dictator, he declared his goods forfeited to the state.

And why need I mention Publius Scipio Nasica who by his own action put down Tiberius Gracchus, grandson of the elder Africanus through his mother Cornelia? Gracchus had stirred up the people and had plotted to prolong his tribuneship, which he had used for purposes of agitation, into a second term, to the ruin of the state. In the midst of the uproar he raised his hand to his head as if he were seeking a kingly crown. The Consul made only a languid protest, but Scipio, calling upon all who would save the state to follow him, wrapped his toga about his left arm and, with the help of the chiefs of the nobility, succeeded in crushing Gracchus, who fleeing to the Capitol, was beaten to death with pieces of the benches and thrown unburied into the Tiber. Nor did this murder, though Nasica avoided a trial and punishment by claiming his privilege as an ambassador, lack a most distinguished apologist. The younger Africanus, in the course of his triumph after the capture of Numantia, was asked by Gnaeus Carbo, a defender of the uprising of Gracchus, what he thought of the killing of his relative and replied without hesitation that he thought he had been justly put to death.

Thus it always seemed to the Romans such a serious matter to usurp the government of the Republic that the mere suspicion of this crime deserved the severest punishment. They did not regard as a citizen at all, but rather as a public enemy any man who would set himself above the laws and above the Senate or who was believed to be aiming at kingly power. Upon this suspicion Marcus Manlius, who had once defended the Capitol against the Gauls with consummate bravery, charged with aspiring to a crown because he had used his private property to release debtors and redeem those who were enslaved for debt, was hurled from that same Tarpeian Rock from which he had repelled the Gallic assault. More than this: the Manlian clan determined by a memorable decree that henceforth no member of the family should bear the name of Marcus Manlius.

[The following *excursus* on the personality of Publius Scipio Nasica, while it has no bearing whatever upon Salutati's main argument, is a very interesting illustration of his method of historical criticism. Whatever we may think of his conclusions we cannot fail to recognize the general soundness of his principles, especially his unwillingness to accept any statement merely on the authority of a famous name. He uses his own mind with a freedom altogether modern, in marked contrast to the blind receptivity of the mediaeval chronicler, and he does not hesitate to make emendations of his own where he thinks they will serve to bring the statements of a classic author more nearly into harmony with common sense.]

But now to return to Gracchus: It seems to me to be decidedly doubtful which Scipio Nasica was the leader in that murder. For if, as Livy tells us, a son of that Gnaeus Scipio who was killed with his brother in Spain, a most honorable youth named Publius Scipio Nasica and declared by the Senate to be *vir optimus*, received the Mater Deorum summoned from Pessinus into a kind of adoption, which event took place before the elder Africanus crossed over to Libya in the time of the Second Punic War; and if we remember that fifty years intervened between the Second and Third Punic Wars, and that Carthage was destroyed in the fourth year after that interval, and finally that the Numantian War, after the close of which Tiberius Gracchus was killed, lasted fourteen years, a careful calculation of these periods shows that from the year in which Nasica played the host to the Goddess before the end of the Second Punic War to the close of the Numantian War was a period of sixty-eight years: namely, fifty years between the two Punic Wars, four for the duration of the second of these and fourteen during which the city of Numantia held out against the Roman people; and if now we add to these the time of the adolescence of Scipio Nasica and the years between the coming of the Mater Deorum and the end of the Second Punic War you will easily see that at the time when Tiberius Gracchus was put down this Scipio must have been more than ninety years old. But now, who would dare to say that a man of ninety would, as is recorded, suddenly have thrown his toga about his arm and made himself the leader and chief of young men in the murder of a man in the prime of manhood and backed by a crowd of the most powerful citizens? I am sure that the most violent critic could not force this conclusion, and I am equally sure that everyone would agree that it is strange enough to be readily classed among the improbabilities. Furthermore, if it were true, it would have been specially celebrated among the glories of old age, and it is incredible that so marked an example as this, the like of which could nowhere be found, should have been passed over in silence by all writers, especially by those who were concerned with the collection of all remarkable events.

I find, however, after the distinguished *pontifex* Nasica, another Publius Scipio Nasica. It is he who so closely resembled a certain Serapion, a dealer in cattle for sacrifice, that the tribune Curiatius dubbed him "Serapion" by way of a joke. Now I am fairly convinced that this man was the son of the elder Nasica. Perhaps there were others also whom the loss of records or similarity of names may have left in obscurity. For it is incredible that there can have been but one Nasica, since in that case, if it is true that Publius Scipio Nasica declared war on Jugurtha, king of the

Numidians, which event certainly happened A.U.C. 635, while the Second Punic War ended in A.U.C. 541, as Livy, greatest of historians, states, at which time Scipio Nasica, being then at the close of his adolescence, was declared to be *vir optimus*, it would appear that this Nasica had lived one hundred and fifteen years! And, what would be more than a miracle, he would have been ruling the state as Consul at that age! Since these things are not probable, I leave the decision open to all.

If they are pleased with what I have said let them be satisfied. If they agree with Valerius that there was only one Publius Scipio Nasica, let them call him "that most brilliant light of the Roman power, who declared war against Jugurtha, who received with consecrated hands the Idean Mother when she came over from her Phrygian home to the altars of Rome" and all the rest which that author collected in his chapter *de repulsis* in praise and characterization of the one Nasica—or rather annotated after it had been collected by someone else; for he did not carefully investigate every point himself. They may agree with Valerius and defend themselves with the authority of so great a writer; but I beg them to take into account the reckoning of time. If they cannot straighten this out let them rather say: "Valerius wrote thus and so" than say that what he wrote agrees with the truth of history. They ought rather to believe that the text of Valerius is corrupt than that he could fall into such a thoughtless error, a thing which should not happen to a man of such great learning.

While I was looking into these matters I discovered a clear case of error in regard to this same name in the chapter of Valerius *de mutatione morum ac fortunae*. In all the texts that I have examined Gnaeus Cornelius Scipio Nasica is said to have been captured by the Carthaginians at Lipara while commanding the Roman fleet as Consul, whereas we read most plainly in Seneca—called, I know not why, Florus—in Eutropius and in Orosius that not Scipio Nasica but Gn. Cornelius Asina was invited by Hannibal the elder to a conference and then with Punic treachery was made prisoner in the fifth year of the First Punic War. Now, since this is quite certain, I think someone must have changed the word Asina into Nasica, thinking, perhaps, that such an ugly [*deforme*] name would be a dishonor in so distinguished a family. If this person had only read in Macrobius, a most faithful recorder of antiquity, how Cornelius, having bought a piece of land in the market and his bondsmen being called upon for the payment, ordered on the spot as much money to be brought on an ass's back as was necessary to pay the debt, and that from that time on the cognomen "Asina" was given to the Cornelian family, not in derision but in admiration for this noble action, he would not have wondered at the name.

Still, you or anyone else may take this as you please. I am not asking anyone to put any more faith in me than he will. I want everyone to choose what seems true or probable to himself; but I am so sure of a corruption in the text that I have stricken out of my copy of Valerius the words Scipione Nasica and amended Asina as I believe was originally written. If in the chapter *de repulsis* where it reads: "Publius Scipio Nasica, that most brilliant light of the Roman power, who declared war against Jugurtha" we add: "son of him who received the Idean Mother etc.," those two words *filius ejus*, which the error of a scribe may have omitted, clear up our doubts completely.

But let us return to our subject. It has thus, I think, been sufficiently demonstrated, that anyone who sets up a tyranny may lawfully be resisted, not merely by a party of the people, but by an individual, and that such a monster may be put down by force, even to the point of murder. And this not only at the beginning of his tyranny, but afterward, even though time has elapsed in which the forces needed to repel the tyrant may have been collected at his expense. This principle is most learnedly laid down by Ulpian in reference to private cases. He says: "It is lawful not only to resist in defence of one's property, but, even if one be ejected therefrom, to eject the intruder, not after an interval but on the spot [*ex continenti*]," that is before he can turn to other matters. For Neratius interprets a "continuous action" as one in which some period of time [*mo(vi)mentum naturae*] may intervene. We have it also on the authority of Ulpian that, since it is lawful for a father, if he detects a daughter who is under his *potestas* in adultery in a house inhabited by him or by his son-in-law, to slay her on the spot [*in continenti*], he shall be held to have killed her on the spot even though some hours shall have intervened while she was being pursued and caught. Therefore it must be lawful to rise up against a usurper of civil power, and this not only at the moment of the usurpation but by continuous action and with preparations made, to go against him with armed forces.

But what shall we say if a usurper rules tyrannically, and yet no one resists him because the people are shamefully long-suffering and therefore his rule goes on for some time? Perchance this tacit consent and obedience—seeing that measures imposed by violence or terror do not, as the laws require, lose their force when resistance dies down, but by a certain law of their own may become purified by subsequent consent, express or implied, and may begin to work neither through violence nor terror—perchance, I say, this tacit consent and obedience may be of such sort that, unless a prior judgment of a superior authority declare the contrary, the tyrant may come to have the semblance of a lawful ruler.

[This is the first reference in the present treatise to a political condition which Salutati was able to take for granted, but which is by no means a matter of course to the modern reader. This is the distinction between self-governing communities and those which acknowledge an overlord (superior). . . . In theory every earthly rule—at least so far as Christian people were concerned—was subject to the overlordship of the Roman Emperor, except where, as in the case of the Roman Papacy, such overlordship was limited or abrogated by specific contract. The emperor was, in theory, the supreme arbiter in all cases of conflict of jurisdictions.

He was supposed to have about him a body of legal advisers through whom he could express his decisions. In practice, however, such exercise of oversovereignty was casual in the extreme. It occurred, if at all, not as the orderly working of a regular judicial system, but rather as a political action. The emperor or his representative entered as a party into the particular local controversy which called for his interference. If he had a strong enough following his decisions might, temporarily, be enforced. If not he lost his case and was likely to be treated with deserved contempt.

In many Italian communities imperial overlordship was to all intents and purposes nonexistent, or at most in a state of suspended animation. The situation then would be that described in the next paragraph of the treatise: "If the people acknowledge an overlord but are really without one because he does not rule but stays abroad." The same is true of papal or princely overlordship. The community might recognize it in theory, but in practice would insist on regulating its own affairs. Only under stress of political necessity would the community accept the definite action of the overlord as decisive. While, therefore, differences in this matter were differences of degree, their range was so great that Salutati could fairly speak of the Italian communities as divided into two classes, those which did, and those which did not, acknowledge an overlord. In the former case it seemed clear that if an apparent tyrant *ex defectu tituli* were recognized by the overlord, then his defect was ipso facto remedied and his title became legitimated. In the latter case his defect could be removed only by such conduct in office that the community would acquiesce in his usurpation, as the least evil in sight. Florence, as a persistently Guelph city, was the most important representative of the civitates of the second class, those claiming to "be sovereign, neither having nor recognizing any superior," and it was, of course, with Florentine problems that Salutati was especially concerned.]

When a state is torn by factions, civil strife with daily conflicts generally takes place, and sometimes to quiet this discord and out of weariness with the existing troubles a Signor is chosen. Sometimes through popular demonstration, without due deliberation or election a prince is set up. Sometimes one faction prevails in armed conflict, and supreme power is conferred upon one person and the government of the whole community is entrusted to him. Whether a person raised to power in any of these ways may attain a legitimate title may perhaps be questioned. On this point I think it should be said that if a people be sovereign, neither having nor recognizing any superior, the will of the majority gives validity to their action. And if, in a people having an overlord his confirmation ensues, then beyond all doubt the rule in question will be a lawful one. If, however, this consent be lacking, the people being without authority of its own, and if the person thus elected begins to govern without waiting for confirmation from the overlord, then he is a tyrant. On the other hand, if the people acknowledge an overlord, but are really without one because he does not rule but stays abroad, then perhaps the title may be good until the contrary be declared by the overlord.

But now, our chief problem is, whether it is lawful to rebel against a ruler who through arrogance [*superbia*] begins to abuse his power, even though he have a lawful and approved title. That he ought to be deposed and punished by an overlord I should suppose no one could doubt—provided only that it be done by regular legal process. Also, if the overlord or any other having authority shall judge him to be an enemy of the state, he may with impunity be driven out or killed. But a ruler deposed by a judicial sentence may not be banished or killed or injured without the approval of the overlord.

A community which recognizes no overlord may without doubt reject the rule of its executive. It may banish him or, for sufficient reason, may put him to death, as it sees fit. Thus the Roman people, on the motion of Lucius Junius Brutus, abolished the kingly power on account of the crimes of Tarquinius Superbus and his sons. So, on account of Virginia, who was dragged away by the wretch Claudius for his lust under pretence of possessing her as a slave, the rule of Decemvirs was done away, and the authors of the laws were themselves overthrown. Thus Nero, last of the Caesars, declared a public enemy by the Senate, was marked for death by assassins who were set upon him.

[At this point the argument begins to swing over to the other side of the main problem. Up to now Salutati has done his best to show the evil of all tyranny. The tyrant is "a plague to society" because he is a tyrant, because he governs "not according to law"—*non jure*. The beneficence of his rule does not alter the fundamental irregularity of his relation to the community. This being admitted it follows that his rule ought somehow to be controlled or eventually destroyed. But how? Historically speaking the answer has been a simple one. Tyrants have been "removed" by violent means, and Salutati goes on to illustrate using the famous defence of tyrannicide by John of Salisbury (d. 1180) as his text. Yet even here he finds room for a distinction. A tyrant may be removed, yes, but not "tyrannically." The violator of law may be resisted, but only by lawful action, and this may be either a decree of an overlord or a regular decision of the people.]

I will not dwell too long upon illustrations which can be gathered from Holy Writ as well as from pagan and Christian histories because, though an infinite number of murders of lawful kings and princes may be cited, these are not arguments to prove that the murder of kings or tyrants is not a crime. Let us, therefore, go on to the question. It is true as Aquinas quotes:

Ad generum Cereris sine caede ac vulnere pauci
descendant reges et sicca morte tyranni

Juvenal, Sat. X, 113–114

"Few kings descend to Ceres' son-in-law except by murder, and few tyrants by a bloodless death." But the frequency of these murders does not imply that they are or ought to be considered lawful. It is one thing to kill a man and quite another thing to kill him lawfully. So that the learned John of Salisbury in his book called—I know not why—"Policratus" [Policraticus], in which he declares that it is right to kill a tyrant and tries to prove this by a multitude of illustrations, seems to me to reach no result. His illustrations prove, not that the murder of tyrants is right, but that it is frequent. In his third book, having said that the murder of a tyrant is not only lawful but fair and just, he adds: "For he that taketh the sword shall perish by the sword." I wish he had carried out this reasoning and proved his point; but soon in his exposition he adds: "but it is understood that he 'takes the sword' who usurps it of his own motion, not he who receives the right to use it from an overlord." Here he seems vaguely to hint that it is lawful to slay a tyrant. At the close of this third book—not to quote the whole—he says: "If the charge of treason includes all oppressors, how much more the charge that a man suppresses the laws, which ought to govern even emperors? Certainly no one would avenge the murder of a public enemy, and anyone who should fail to oppose him would fail in his duty to himself and to the whole body politic."

In the eighth and last book he treats the same subject in several chapters and in great detail, giving a multitude of illustrations. Occasionally, however, he sets certain limits to the right of tyrannicide. In the eighteenth chapter, after citing many cases from history, he adds: "Because it has always been proper to flatter a tyrant, it has been proper also to deceive him and honorable to slay him if he could not otherwise be held in check." "We are not," he says, "speaking of tyrants in private life, but of such as oppress the state. For private persons can easily be controlled by the public laws, which govern the lives of all men. A priest, however, even though he plays the tyrant, may not be constrained by the temporal sword because of his sacramental character, unless perchance after being deprived of his office he may have stretched forth blood-stained hands against the Church of God."

But John of Salisbury says also in the twenty-first chapter: "History teaches us, however, that we should beware not to plot the ruin of one to whom we are bound by an obligation of loyalty or by an oath." You see, then, do you not, how far even this writer, great as his authority is, would go in restricting the licence of tyrannicide? He would not sanction laying violent hands upon a tyrant without due deliberation, nor would he think everyone authorized to decide whether a man be really a tyrant or not. So that, if you would proceed regularly, a sentence of the overlord must first be obtained if possible, or if there be no princely sovereignty, then a decree of the people must be waited for. A tyrant caught in adultery with a wife or a daughter may be slain as lawfully as any regular magistrate. For, though a tyrant is the worst plague that can infect the body politic, nevertheless no single person nor even several together may of their own motion without the authority of the overlord disturb a civil order lawfully established either by a decree of the people or through the obedience or the consent, express or implied, of the community. It would be a presumptuous, nay, a *superbum* act to rebel against a ruler while all the rest were willing to endure him, were he a Nero, an Ezzelino, a Phalaris or a Busiris. And though it may happen that the overthrow of the tyrant is approved by the people, though the highest felicity may be attained by those who are set free, though the greatest praise may be heaped upon the liberator or liberators, with undying renown, still if a valid procedure be lacking, the undertaking was not well advised.

True, a successful and fortunate crime passes for a virtuous deed. Yet in my opinion, just as he who destroys a tyrant in a lawful way is to be loaded with honors, so he who unlawfully slays a ruler deserves the severest penalty. For, though every man is under such obligation to the Fatherland that he ought to devote even his life to the welfare of the state, nevertheless no bond or obligation requires that even a thing useful to the community shall be accomplished by a crime. So great indeed is the force of law, of honor and the authority of the state that we are told by Cicero that when Pompilius as Imperator discharged the legion in which a son of Cato was serving, and the son in his zeal for the service remained in the army, his father wrote to Pompilius that if he wished to keep his son he ought to have him take a second military oath, because with the discharge of the legion he had fulfilled the obligation of his former oath and could not properly engage in combat with the enemy. And surely no one could claim that without a public commission, without a general or a commander he had the right to take up arms even to set his country free.

Let no one, therefore, take his soul in his own hand or make a reason out of his own will and so rise up against his lord, even though the lord be acting as a tyrant! This may be done only with the approval of an overlord or of the people, not through the impulse of an individual. Even a criminal, publicly convicted as worthy of death may not be executed by any and every one, but only by the edict of the prince and in the form prescribed by the laws of the state. Whoever sets these aside is a criminal. Enough as to our second proposition.

Chapter III
Concerning the Principate of Caesar, and Whether He Ought Properly to Be Regarded as a Tyrant

[It is in this third chapter that Salutati develops most clearly his sympathy with the idea of benevolent despotism. According to all his definitions Caesar was a tyrant. His title was defective. His power had been gained by violence and could be maintained only in the same way. And yet, out of the chaos of civil war he had brought order and a working administration of government. Salutati is convinced that things had come to such a pass that the rule of one man was inevitable. It was only a question whether this man should be Caesar or Pompey, and fortune gave the decision to Caesar. This result was then approved by every element of the population. Even the unstable judgment of Cicero inclined rather to the side of praise than of blame. And so our fourteenth-century political philosopher concludes that Caesar cannot properly be described as a tyrant. His *defectus tituli* was wiped out by his eminence *ex parte exercitii*.]

John of Salisbury, whom we mentioned in the previous chapter, makes many references to Caesar in the nineteenth chapter of his eighth book and expresses his opinion as follows: "Nevertheless, since he had seized upon the government by violence he was regarded as a tyrant and, with the approval of a majority of the Senate, was stabbed to death in the Capitol." Such is the view of "Policratus." Cicero also, who after Caesar's death spoke very freely against him, says in his treatise on *Duty:* "That saying of Ennius: 'No social bond is sacred; there is no loyalty in the state,' is now more clearly manifest; for when things are in such a condition that but few persons can rise to eminence there is generally so great rivalry that the bonds of society are with difficulty preserved." And he adds: "This has recently been shown by the rashness of Caesar who violated all laws, human and divine, for the sake of that dream of power which his mistaken judgment had conjured up."

Elsewhere, however, Cicero expressly calls Caesar a tyrant, which he does not do in the above passage, giving him here no name at all. In the second book of the *De Officiis* he says: "If heretofore we did not know that no power can stand against the hatred of many, this has of late become clear. Nor does the downfall of this tyrant alone, whom the state, held down by force, endured and even now that he is dead obeys, but the fate of other tyrants also shows how powerful the hatred of men is against this plague." I might also cite other passages in which this same Cicero pursuing too violently the memory of the dead Caesar, censures and condemns him. Without further reference to "Policratus," this Cicero of ours, according to the teaching of the Academy which he followed, took upon himself to speak too freely *ex tempore*, saying now this and now that and contradicting himself with the change of circumstances.

It may be that a careful examination of his writings would show far greater praise of Caesar than blame. In fact Cicero never attacks Caesar without at the same time praising him or somewhat modifying the violence of his invective. Before the civil wars he always professed friendship for him and received from him many favors for himself and his friends. Further, his brother Quintus Cicero served under Caesar in Gaul and was honored with the post of legate. Cicero himself wrote to the general Lentulus: "I must mention the divine generosity of

Caesar toward me and my brother. Whatever he may do I ought to support him, and now that he is in such great good fortune and has won such victories, even had he not done for us what he has, I think honor should be shown him."

That is the way Cicero spoke of Caesar before the civil wars. Writing to his brother Quintus he says: "You speak of Caesar's great affection for us; do you cherish this, and I will try to increase it in every way I can." When the civil wars began Cicero was always an advocate of peace, and Caesar showed himself readily inclined thereto, and I believe that if we had his speeches on the subject we should find him taking Caesar's part. But, in the course of the civil wars, as Cicero himself testifies, his sense of duty carried him into the party of Pompey. Notice what he writes on this point to M. Celius, who seems to have suspected that Cicero would go over to Caesar and to have written him to this effect, as we may judge from Cicero's reply: "Why you should suspect this from my former letters, as you say you do, I have no idea; for what was there in them but complaints of these [evil] times, which I am sure cause you as much anxiety as they do me?"

A little farther on he says: "I wonder that you should have brought up this matter, you who ought to know me too well to suppose that I am so imprudent as to turn from a well established cause to one that is failing and almost ruined, or so fickle as to throw away the favor of a most successful man after I had once gained it, to be untrue to myself and to throw myself into civil strife, from which I have ever held myself aloof." And again: "Even if this were so, I should never have thought of a departure [from Pompey] without your approval." Yet in many places he openly expresses the friendship he had with Caesar. We have still preserved intimate and cordial letters between them. Cicero often refers to Caesar's generosity and good qualities and says that he supported his cause in the Senate. Nowhere in his writings can you find any unfavorable criticism of Caesar except in regard to the principate and the civil wars. But what he thought about Pompey's army and the menace of a victory on his part and how greatly he suspected and dreaded the violence and cruelty of his troops is made clear in many passages.

From his words quoted above in regard to Caesar's principate, where he says that Caesar conceived this design through a "mistaken judgment," does he not thus free him from the chief accusation by ascribing to him a blunder rather than a crime? What is done through a fault is beyond comparison more serious than what happens through a mistake. And in that passage where he calls him a tyrant, does he not suppress the name of Caesar as if he feared to say in so many words what he was nevertheless trying to make everyone believe? In my opinion, as I think the whole matter over, as long as Caesar lived, Cicero was always heaping praises upon him, not only before the civil wars but after an end had been put to that struggle in five great triumphs. Read, if you please, his speeches in behalf of M. Marcellus and Q. Ligarius. Read also, I beg you, his letter to S. Sulpicius. Speaking of the restitution of Marcellus he says: "So glorious did that day appear to me that I seemed to see as it were the vision of a restored republic." In the speech in which he thanks Caesar for the restitution of Marcellus he says the same thing. Caesar was said to have boasted that he had lived long enough to pay the debt of nature and of glory, and Cicero replied: "the debt of nature perhaps, and I will add if you insist, the debt of glory, but, what is of the highest importance, not your debt to the Fatherland," as if this most ardent champion of liberty believed that the form of the state which Caesar represented inclined not to tyranny but to a republic.

Nor did he think that any different state of affairs would be produced by a victory of Pompey. Observe what he writes on this point to M. Marcellus: "First, to suit oneself to the times, that is, to make a virtue of necessity, is ever the part of a wise man. Later there is less trouble on this score, as for example at the present moment. One cannot, perhaps, speak out what one feels, but one is at perfect liberty to keep silence. Everything is reported to one man, and he follows his own opinion, not taking counsel even with his own partisans. And there would be no great difference if he whom we have followed were master of the state. Now can we suppose that a man who in the midst of war, when we were all exposed to the same dangers, acted upon his own opinion and that of certain most unwise counsellors, would be more complaisant in victory than when his fortunes were in doubt?"

After some further remarks to the same effect Cicero adds: "Civil war is deplorable in every way, but the worst part of it is the victory, which, even though it fall to the better party, renders them more cruel and less powerful, so that, even though they be not tyrannical by nature, they are forced to become so. The victor is obliged, even against his will, to do many things at the dictation of those through whom he gained his victory. Did you not see at the same time that I did, what a cruel victory that [of Pompey] would be?" Consider then, my worthy brother, what Cicero thought about the possible success of Pompey. In view of this it seems to me that it was the duty of those [two] most powerful chiefs of Rome not to engage in partisan warfare but to strive with all their might and with all their resources to prevent such a conflict and to avert civil war and bloodshed by lawful means.

The fact is, their struggle was not as to whether some one man should rule and be the supreme dictator of the state, but which of the two it should be. For not only were standards set against standards, eagles against eagles, weapons against weapons, all of the same kind, but on both sides were also equal disloyalty, equal fury and self-seeking, an equal desire to oppress the citizens, to set aside the laws and to think anything right which was pleasing and profitable to the victors. It was a fight, not to maintain the Republic, but to destroy it. "Which cause was the better, it is forbidden to know," says the poet. Now, when the citizens, divided into hostile camps, determined to settle by force which should rule, it came to pass by the will of God that Caesar conquered. No one will deny that he atoned for the horrors of civil strife, than which nothing can be more cruel, by his wonderful magnanimity.

For, as Cicero says: "He conquered, yet did not excite hatred in his good fortune, but rather allayed it by his leniency." Speaking of his geniality and his gentleness of nature the Man of Arpinum did not hesitate to say: "We saw thy victory decided by the fortune of war; thy sword we have never seen unsheathed within the City. The citizens whom we have lost perished in the heat of battle, not in the fury of victory; so that no one can doubt that Caesar if he could, would call many of them back from the realm below. In fact he is protecting as many of the hostile party as he can."

Who then can think the rule of a man of such a character, such sentiments and such deeds as these, ought to be called a tyranny? But you ask me to give it a name. Hear then what Seneca—whom some call Florus—says. In his compendium of Roman history, after describing Caesar's wars, he concludes as follows: "Here at last was an end of fighting, a bloodless peace, a war counterbalanced by clemency. No one was put to death by order of the commander except Afranius, to whom he had once before been sufficiently indulgent, Faustus Sulla—Pompey had taught him to be afraid of sons-in-law—and the daughter of Pompey together with her children by Sulla. In this case he was taking precautions for the future." So that, with the approval of the citizens, all kinds of honors were heaped upon this one man: statues around the temples, in the theatre a pointed crown, a raised seat in the Senate, a decorated gable for his house, his name given to a month of the year; besides these the titles of "Father of the Fatherland" and "Perpetual Dictator"; finally—whether by his own consent or not is uncertain—the insignia of royalty offered him publicly by Antony as Consul. Can a man raised to power constitution- ally and through his own merits, a man who showed such a humane spirit, not to his own partisans alone but also to his opponents because they were his fellow citizens—can he properly be called a tyrant? I do not see how this can be main- tained, unless indeed we are to pass judgment without clear definitions.

We may, therefore, conclude with this proposition: that Caesar was not a tyrant, seeing that he held his principate in a commonwealth, lawfully and not by abuse of law.

Chapter IV
Was the Murder of Julius Caesar Justified?

[If, then, Caesar was no tyrant the conclusion follows inevitably that his assas- sination was not justifiable. In working out this conclusion Salutati dwells especially upon the point that Caesar's rule was accepted by all classes, but more particularly by the very persons who took upon themselves the responsibility of the assassina- tion. They had no scruple in retaining the offices and honors which they had received from the Dictator. Most of all Salutati finds himself at odds with what he calls the "snarlings" of Cicero after Caesar's death. His summary of the political situation at the close of the civil wars prepares the way for an eloquent appreciation of Caesar's services to the state. He convicts Cicero out of his own mouth of playing fast and loose with the principles of a sound government, and he concludes with a glorification of monarchy as the nearest approach on earth to that single divine administration of the universe which is the model for all human political endeavor.]

Since, therefore, Caesar cannot properly be accounted a tyrant, seeing that he was raised by the gratitude of his fellow citizens to that height whence other princes, whom no one considers as tyrants, were carried on to the imperial succession, who can maintain that his murder was justified? Who will not say that his assailants, not lawfully, but by abuse of law, laid accursed hands upon the father of their country, the most righteous ruler on earth?—a crime, as Cicero declares, far more atrocious than the murder of one's own father! Think over what has been said above about tyrannicide and you will readily conclude that those senatorial conspirators had no justification for the murder of the Perpetual Dictator.

I think we should consider especially that the leading assassins of Caesar—Brutus, Cassius and other Romans—kept the praetorships, pontificates, quaestorships and other government offices which had been established by decrees of Caesar. Furthermore, that all the acts of the Dictator were confirmed by decrees of the Senate, and that everything he had done or even planned to do and for which he had drawn up written documents, remained in force. Who, then, can bear with patience to hear Cicero and others speaking against Caesar, when they and some whom the law of conquest had deprived of their honors as well as of their citizenship, received from Caesar restitution or new positions or confirmation of former ones as legitimately acquired.

What, I pray you, became of that devotion to the laws, that love of country, that hatred of the tyrant, when they were ready to accept as lawful, grants or confirmations made by him to citizens whom he had overcome? Search through all the histories and tell me, if you can, of one person who refused a favor from Caesar because he ruled unjustly or like a tyrant! Scipio Nasica and C. Figulus, called back, the one from Gaul the other from Corsica, resigned their consulates because on the motion of T. Gracchus, it was discovered that in the consular comitia the auspices had not been regularly taken. Camillus would not even return from his exile at Veii until he learned that all measures relating to his dictatorship had been legally carried out. Cincinnatus checked the Senate in its desire to prolong for a second term the consulate which he had completed, thus denying himself an honor forbidden by the law. And yet at that time no one pretended that a dictator, even though he were created irregularly and contrary to law, could not take valid action, and no one would have refused, even after the murder of such an one, honors which he had conferred.

This being so I marvel that Cicero—whom I admire—should have been so stirred to fury against the memory of the Dictator as to say, not only that he was justly slain, but that all good men either counselled his death or desired it in their hearts or approved it by their declarations. This statement he makes in his discussion with Antony in his second Philippic. Now, was the death of the Dictator pleasing to "all good men," when the Roman plebs returning from his funeral attacked the houses of Brutus and Cassius with torches and were with difficulty held in check, or was there not in the whole people a single "good man," my dear Cicero? Or was it with the favoring consent of all good men that the assailants of Caesar and their accomplices, after they had murdered him, seized upon the Capitol to protect themselves? Or, when the day was not long enough for the vast number of those who brought gifts to the funeral, was that a sign that his murder was pleasing to everyone? Or was the decree of the Senate conferring upon him all honors human and divine not a sign of the public devotion? And was it not a proof of affection rather than of hatred that matrons threw upon the funeral pile the ornaments they were wearing, together with the robes and amulets of their children, and legionaries and veterans gave the arms they had carried at the funeral service? Was not his tomb visited night after night by people of foreign nations as a token of the public grief? Who could say that subjects of the Roman Empire, always on the watch for their own advantage, would have shown such interest in the funeral of a tyrant hateful to all good men and thus have given offence to all these good people?

But, why bandy words with me, my dear Cicero? Why make conjectures as to the secrets of men's hearts, when the facts of the case proclaim the contrary? You will have to be a greater master of oratory than you are, Cicero, if you expect to make guess-work and mere words overcome the evidence of facts. The terror of the conspirators and their precautions in occupying the Capitol are not indications that the murder was approved by "all good men." Who can believe that all those good men who had experienced Caesar's generosity and had received from him the gift of their lives and honorable distinctions would, to a man, have proved so ungrateful that all would have desired and approved his death? If this were so I should insist that they deserved to be shut out from the generous favor of the chief of state and thrust into the vilest servitude.

For myself, in spite of the snarlings of Cicero and the rest in the fury of later civic strife, as I study the movement of events and their outcome, I have no doubt whatever that Caesar so won over his followers by kindness, his enemies by leniency and all by his prudence and magnanimity, that his murder was welcome to but very few. It was pleasing to all of the opposing faction not, in my judgment, because of their hatred of Caesar, but in the hope of recovering their positions and their honors, which, if he were to be chief, they saw would never be equal to those of the victorious party. I believe that the boldness of speech against Caesar was put on, not on account of hatred for the man, but out of zeal for liberty, so that through this example everyone should be deterred from aspiring to supreme power.

But why so many words? Does it not seem as if men and gods, the powers above and below, conspired to avenge the death of Caesar? Within three years every one of his assailants and the conspirators against him met violent deaths in various ways. It is especially to the credit of Octavius that he spared all the rest and contented himself with punishing those who were guilty of parricide. But you will say: "Were not his assailants aiming to secure the freedom of the state? Do we not owe to our country all that we are and all that we can do? And what greater, what more godlike service can we render to the Fatherland than to deliver it from the misery of servitude? So great, so excellent, so all-embracing a good is this that nothing else can or ought to be compared with it. Therefore Cassius and Brutus and Trebonius and the rest of the conspirators did what was becoming to great-hearted men and performed the greatest possible service to the state."

To this objection let that greatest of princes, the godlike Augustus, make answer. It is reported that when he was visiting the house of Cato out of respect for the memory of that great citizen, and the throng of flatterers present with one voice were criticizing Cato because he had been a too persistent partisan of Pompey, he said in his defence: "He who is unwilling to change the existing order of the state is a good citizen and a good man." In truth, so many misfortunes are wont to follow and so many scandals to be stirred up when such a change in the state is made that it is better to bear all ills rather than take the risks of change.

There never was anyone possessed of power so great or prudence so divine that a revolution could realize his [or its] true intention. In a great community there are varied talents, differences of judgment, a multitude of wills, and in laying the foundations of a constitution every man aims at his own honor and his own advantage. Nor is there a man who does not think it fitting that whatever he desires should come to him. So it happens, that before an agreement can be reached and the ambitions of all can be met, there will be many tumults, no end of contentions and countless plots with imminent peril. And this even though fighting may have ceased and no extreme bloodshed have been attempted—for if it comes to that, nothing more cruel and more ruinous can happen.

Therefore, to avoid these evils, the life of a man is to be spared—not merely the life of a Caesar, who practiced such leniency, as history shows, but that of a Sulla or of a Marius, who could not be satiated with the blood of their fellow citizens. I should like, then, if you please, my dear Cicero, to examine this argument with you for a moment. You saw the whole Roman body politic split into two parties and engaged in a conflict, not merely between fellow citizens, but between blood relations, or, to use a more familiar word, a worse than civil war. You saw Pompey conquered and overthrown; you saw Cato and others, the broken fragments of the defeated party, obstinately renewing the fight in Africa, beaten with equal slaughter; you saw the name and faction of Pompey in Spain renewed and touching a higher point of success than could have been hoped for the remnants of a conquered party; and then, just as fortune seemed to promise them the very height of prosperity, thrown down by a disaster not unlike those which befell the other attempts; you saw the laying down of arms, the end of civil war, and the exhausted Republic rising as if from the disease of mortal strife and resting peaceful and secure in the power of one chief.

Now answer me, Cicero, I pray you: What haven did you perceive for the ship of state so long tossed by storms except that the Republic should be brought under the control of one victor, as a check to the victorious party and for the safety of the defeated one? Tell me, had you forgotten the five years of Sulla's dictatorship, which, bloody as it was and fatal to almost every one of the vanquished was nevertheless in a way a prop to the Republic? What did you find lacking in the perpetual dictatorship of Caesar which the conquered could ask for? Was it not a protection to the defeated and a bridle upon the victors? His dictatorship ruined no one, but on the contrary preserved the lives and the fortunes of many. It was a protection to the timid, a restraint upon the cruel, safety for all and a glory to the chief. The public welfare increased daily, and already the conquerors and the conquered were being set upon an equal level of honor and service.

Do you remember, Cicero, what you yourself said: "By you alone, O Caesar, can all those interests be revived which you see overthrown by the fury of that inevitable war and now lying prostrate. The courts are to be reopened, credit restored, license repressed, a new generation brought into being. Whatever has gone to ruin is to be reestablished by stringent legislation. It was inevitable in the midst of so great a war, in such excitement of opinion and of arms that the exhausted republic, whatever the outcome of the conflict, should lose many of the adornments of its dignity and many guarantees of its stability and that both leaders should do many things while under arms which as civil magistrates they would have prohibited. All these wounds of the war are now to be healed by you, and there is no one but you who can heal them."

These are your own words, and they were far more than mere flattery. For who but Caesar could have cured those evils? The Senate, divided as it was into factions? The Equites? Or the populace or the *plebs* struggling in the same factional conflict, fighting between victors and vanquished, with interests not merely diverse but directly in opposition—how could they have accomplished the result? Believe me, you could have imagined no hope for the Republic that would have had a favorable outcome, except the clemency and justice of the conqueror. There might, perhaps, have been a chance for harmony if Caesar had not fallen a victim to the unjust violence of men. But the opportunity for this was lost through the fury of those friends of yours whom you laud to the skies as liberators of the city and the world, when they not merely opposed the only man who, according to your evidence, could apply the remedy, but by means of ingratitude, treachery and crime actually removed him.

Why, you yourself, Cicero, in defending the cause of your friend Plancius, said, with the approval, I believe, of all and in divinely appropriate language: "If I see a ship holding her course with favoring winds, not toward the harbor which I had formerly chosen, but towards another equally safe and tranquil, should I risk a fight against the storm rather than give way to it and seek safety first?" Such *was* your judgment. But now, when the ship of state, not with favoring winds, but tossed upon the billows of civil war, was nearing a harbor, not the one you had chosen, but one equally good or perhaps better, would you have had it pushed out again into the troubled sea of civil commotion? Imperial rule is a mighty monster, not easily guided or controlled at will. But, by the majesty of the everlasting God! Is there no such thing as a commonwealth under a single rule? Was there no commonwealth at Rome so long as it was under kings? Was there to be none after Caesar under the rule of one or another consecrated ruler? Is it not sound politics, approved by the judgment of all wise men, that the monarchy is to be preferred to all other forms of government, provided only that it be in the hands of a wise and good man? There is no greater liberty than obedience to the just commands of a virtuous prince. As there is no better or more divine rule than that of the universe under one God, so human sovereignty is the higher the more nearly it approaches that ideal. But nothing can be more like this than the rule of one man. For the government of many is nothing unless the multitude are united in one common sentiment, and unless one commands and the rest obey, there will be not one government but several.

Why, Cicero, should you condemn what you have learned from Aristotle? You know that among the kinds of government, various as well in their nature as in the order of time, considering the welfare of the subjects and the very nature of things, the monarchy has precedence of all the rest. It is a law of nature that since some are born to serve and others to rule, in order that equality may be preserved among all in due proportion, government should be in the hands of the better man.

If in your time, O Cicero, there had been one prince, there would never have been a civil war and such great disorder among you. You might, in fact you ought, to have learned from the devastations of the Sullan period and the party conflict which followed, that in order to remove these evils a monarch was needed, through whom the whole body politic should be guided in due order. In that political aristocracy of which you were so fond there could either have been no remedy at all for the ills of the state on account of the conflict of opinions, or it would have been accompanied by such difficulties and dangers as to be wholly unsuited to the times. This was clearly shown by experience after Caesar had been slain and the harmony of a single rule had been destroyed. Straightaway the civil strife broke out again, so that it was not merely useful but necessary to resort to a monarchical ruler in whose hands so many disturbances and such diversities of interest might be reconciled and harmonized through his justice and equity. If this had not been done by Octavius, never would the Roman fury have quieted down; never would there have been an end of evil days, and civil strife once begun again would have gone on to the final ruin of the very name of Rome. We read that Octavius seriously considered the plan of restoring the Republic, and I am persuaded that nothing could have turned him from that purpose except the conviction that everything would then fall back into confusion. The earlier agitation had not subsided, and the minds of citizens had not recovered from that terrible shock.

Referring to this, Vergil, speaking as always with divine genius, says:[3]

Pauca tamen suberunt priscae vestigia fraudis,
Quae tentare Thetim ratibus, quae cingere muris
Oppida, quae jubeant telluri infindere sulcos.
Some traces may remain of that old guile
Which bade men vex with ships the sacred sea,
Or circle towns with stone, or scar earth's breast
With furrows.

Trans. T. C. Williams

We must note that he says "fraud," not "error," and fraud implies wrongdoing, in which sense it is often found in Livy.

We may, therefore, conclude that the murderers of Caesar slew, not a tyrant but the father of his country, the lawful and benignant ruler of the world, and that they sinned against the state in the most serious and damnable way possible by kindling the rage and fury of civil war in a peaceful community. I am not blaming them for their proud spirit in refusing to tolerate a superior—or even an equal. I will not blame them for their ambition in hoping for honors and offices and desiring to be counted among the leaders of the Roman Senate and people. This was the glory they desired and worked for; but these are things not to be gained by parricide, by criminal practices, by pride and ambition. True glory is the offspring of true virtue and is found only in the reputation for true virtue.

So much for the fourth article of our program.

Chapter V
That Dante Was Right in Placing Brutus and Cassius in the Lowest Hell as Traitors of the Deepest Dye

[In this final chapter Salutati tries to strengthen his case by bringing in the evidence of a modern, who, after a period of comparative obscurity, had come into his own as the acknowledged interpreter of the finest national tradition. Dante's judgment upon the murderers of Caesar as types of the most depraved forms of treason seems to Salutati to confirm his own opinion as to the validity of Caesar's rule. Furthermore, this judgment of Dante is proved correct by the fate of the conspirators themselves, the divine judgment prefiguring the poet's fancy.]

Since then Caesar, as has been most abundantly proved, was not a tyrant by defect of title, seeing that a grateful country freely chose him for its prince, nor by reason of *superbia*, since he ruled with clemency and humanity, it is clear that his murder was a most accursed crime. Wherefore our own Dante in his description of the spiritual life, remembering that treason, which always breaks out through a breach of faith, is the gravest of all sins, placed traitors in his lowest hell, where also in the centre of the universe he put the three-headed Lucifer, distinguishing the three heads thus: The middle one he made red, that on the left the deepest black, the right-hand one a color between white and yellow, known as "pallor." Then Dante represented Judas, the betrayer of Christ, as caught by the head in the central jaws of the demon and wretchedly stuck there, with Brutus in the maw of the left head and Cassius of the right, caught by the legs and torn by the torture of this perpetual feast.[4]

All this is conceived by the supreme poet with a divine reasonableness. For he made those traitors equal in place and in person with the Lucifer who is punishing them. One of them had for a price betrayed the son of the eternal God, father and creator of all things; the others had murdered the father of their country, and Brutus even his own father, with the added crime of treason. Further, the poet so distinguished them by the heads in which they were tormented that the enormity of their offences was made clear, each by itself. The colors of the three heads may be referred to the effects produced in the minds of the criminals. The first is redness from the gnawings of conscience; the second pallor from fear of punishment; the third blackness from the stain of the offence itself.

These effects, though common to all sinners, are apportioned among these three in a peculiar sense. For Judas, plunged in the red head, which is the first, pays the penalty with his head in the jaws of Lucifer. In fact the word "Juda," as Jerome proves from the book of Philo, taken in the Hebrew sense means in Latin *laudatio* or *confessio*, and "Judas" therefore, "confessor" or "glorifier." Now, when he was overcome by remorse and returned the thirty pieces of silver, he said: "I have sinned and have betrayed innocent blood," the word of confession being *peccavi tradens* and the word of praise or glorification being *sanguinem justum*. And so he, being penitent, and having hanged himself with a cord, is punished by being plunged into the first head, the red one.

As to Cassius, it is said that, believing Brutus to be beaten and fearing to fall into the enemy's hands, he begged one of the bystanders to cut off his head. But history tells us that in that fight Brutus met the army of Octavius and drove it out of its camp beaten and destroyed; but Cassius, seeing horsemen hurrying back to occupy the camp, supposed they had taken flight and thinking it was all up with

Brutus, betook himself to a little hill, and there, his scout being too late in returning, took his own life. Therefore he is assigned by Dante to the pallid head.

Brutus, although victorious over Octavius, and though he learned at a late hour that his party had won a naval victory on the same day, when he saw that Cassius was beaten and learned of his death, perceiving that his own fortunes were declining and overcome by the baseness and treachery of his cause, begged one of his companions to pierce him in the side. Since, therefore, he was branded with the mark of an especially atrocious crime, being reputed to be the son of Caesar, Dante assigned him to the black head. That he was Caesar's son those may readily convince themselves who know that Caesar had had intercourse with the mother of Brutus and who read that at the moment of his death the Dictator, seeing Brutus rushing at him with drawn sword, cried out in Greek,—if I may express the Greek words in Latin letters,—*kai sy, teknon?* that is "Thou too, my son?" which is written in Greek thus: καί σύ, τέκνον. In the case of Brutus, besides the reason of his shameful conduct there is added a certain strange incident. It is historically recorded, that as he was working alone at night, after a light had been brought, a dark figure appeared to him, and in reply to his question: "Who art thou?" replied: "I am thy evil spirit!"

Dante, therefore, was right in assigning the black face to him. And who can criticize Dante for thrusting into the depths of hell and condemning to extreme punishment those abandoned men who sinned so grievously in treacherously murdering Caesar, the father of his country, while he was administering with such clemency the government which the Senate and people of Rome had conferred upon him in a desperate crisis to put an end to the evils of civil war? It was a reasonable idea to plunge Judas, Cassius and Brutus into the same place to which the prince of the world of demons, who through pride had rebelled against God his maker, was relegated in the plan of the poem. For Judas betrayed the God-man, and Cassius and Brutus treacherously slew Caesar, the image, as it were, of divinity in the rightfulness of his rule and in the multitude of favors which he had abundantly heaped upon them, thus destroying the republic and bereaving the Fatherland.

Finally, we may find sufficient authority for Dante in the words of Vergil, whom he chose for his guide and master. For among the very last of those whom Vergil places in the lowest hell he puts those

quique arma secuti
Impia nec veriti dominorum failere dextras

Aen. VI, 612.

"who took up arms disloyally and feared not to deceive the hand of their masters." Those who treat events with the art of the poet are wont to praise or blame men and their deeds according to the success of their undertakings. Thus Homer sets Achilles above Hector; Vergil prefers Aeneas to Maecentius and Turnus, and places Antony below Octavius and Pallas below Turnus. So all the rest try to show that the victors were better men than the vanquished. Why, then, should we expect our Dante to praise those whom defeat has laid low and whom the later good fortune of the victors has left in obscurity? Or why should we suppose that in his poem he would reinstate and declare worthy of praise those whom the strength of man has smitten and whom the will of God has shown by the arbitrament of war and the evidence of fortune to be not merely unfortunate but disloyal and criminal?

Further, since that most learned and Christian author saw from the logic of events—the most certain witness of the divine will—that God had decreed that all the affairs of men should be brought under the one single government of the Romans, was he not bound to place among the damned, as men working against the divine plan, those who tried in every possible way to oppose this order?

And so we may conclude that our Dante, in this matter as in others, made no mistake either theologically or morally, and still less poetically, in condemning Brutus and Cassius in the way he did—nay, not only that he made no mistake, but that without any question he rendered a just judgment.

It remains, finally, to dispose in a few words of the question you raise about Antenor and Aeneas. In the first place, those most ancient historians Dares Phrygius and Gnosius Dictys, state in no doubtful terms but plainly and clearly that those men negotiated with the Greeks to betray their country. For this reason I cannot blame Guido de Columna Messana, who follows these authors, for branding both with the mark of treason. It is my belief that [later] when the Romans had prospered and the Julian family had reached the summit of human glory, since they boasted Aeneas as their ancestor, certain writers spared his memory. Among these is Sisenna, who is said to have represented Antenor and no one else as the betrayer of Troy. Then Livy, a most famous author, exonerates them, saying that they were protected by the Greeks in accordance with the law of hospitality, which the ancients held especially sacred and because they had always favored peace and the restoration of booty and of Helen. An honorable excuse indeed, but not needed by either Antenor or Aeneas, seeing that Capys, Helenus and many others who have never been considered traitors passed safely out of Troy with the consent of the victorious Greeks—unless, indeed, they were guilty upon some other count.

Between these [various opinions] you or anyone else may be the umpire. You may, if you please, with Dictys and Dares, regard these men as traitors. You may, if you prefer, on the authority of Sisenna, acquit Aeneas, or with Livy acquit them both and treat Dictys the Cretan and Dares the Phrygian as apocryphal writers. I do not believe that the precise truth can be discovered from the books that I have read, especially since we have the tradition of twenty-five centuries, and tradition does not ordinarily persist if its report is false.

Such, my dear Anthony, is my judgment upon these two problems. If I have been rather tardy in giving it, lay this to those occupations of mine to which you refer. If I have not given you satisfaction, ascribe this to my ignorance; for I am always more ready to learn than to teach.

Farewell! Live happily and strive, I beg you, to show yourself a true man, a credit to your family and beloved by all. Amen.

Here endeth the treatise *De Tyranno* published by Coluccio Pierio of the family of the Salutati.

Chapter 3

BARTOLUS OF SASSOFERRATO

On Tyranny

(C. 1355)

Bartolus of Sassoferrato (1313–57), the most learned jurist of his day, studied law at Perugia and Bologna and held teaching appointments at Pisa and Perugia, the latter of which he transformed into one of the premier institutions devoted to the civil law, until his premature death at age forty-three. His scholarship was honored by Holy Roman Emperor Charles IV and was recognized as authoritative in Spain, Portugal, and England. *De tyrannia* served as the *locus classicus* for all examinations of the legitimacy of monarchy in the fourteenth and fifteenth centuries.

The text is a reprint of Bartolus of Sassoferrato, *De tyrannia*, in Ephraim Emerton, trans. and ed., *Humanism and Tyranny* (Cambridge, Mass.: Harvard University Press, 1925), 126–54.

———— ✳ ————

The Treatise of Bartolus upon Tyranny

Chapter I

§1. My first inquiry is as to the derivation of the word "tyrant." It is derived from the Greek word τύρος, in the Latin *fortis* or *angustia*, wherefore powerful kings were called tyrants. Later it came about that the word was applied to the worst of kings who exercised a cruel and wicked rule over their peoples, that is oppression (*angustia*), because they oppress (*angustiant*) their subjects. This is the opinion of Hugo. That τύρος is to be understood as I have said appears from the interpretations in Scripture, where it is rendered by *angustia*, or *tribulatio* or *salvatio* or *fortitudo*. This will be of use to us when we come to consider the nature of the tyrant and how he is to be recognized as such.

Chapter II

§2. I inquire next as to the definition of a tyrant. Gregory,[1] in the second book of his *Moralia*, gives this definition: "A tyrant properly so called is one who governs a commonwealth arbitrarily (*non jure*). But it must be remembered that everyone of a proud spirit (*superbus*) practises tyranny after his own fashion—one in a state through an office which has been conferred upon him; another in a province, another in a city (*civitas*), another in his own house, while another may practise tyranny through his own inner malice, regarding not God in his inmost thoughts, and though he lack the power, doing what evil he can. He is a tyrant at heart, being governed within by iniquity. For, if one is a tyrant who outwardly oppresses his neighbors, it is enough if one inwardly desires power in order that he may oppress them."

§3. Such are the words of Gregory, and they are to be kept as a rule of action. Let us briefly consider them.

"*Proprie tyrannus, etc.*" As a king or a Roman emperor is a lawful and true and universal ruler, so if anyone gains this office unlawfully he is a tyrant in the strict sense [*proprie*].

"*Non jure principatur, etc.*" This is true because he lacks a sound title, being chosen unlawfully, and he is [to be] condemned, or else he is crowned without being elected and afterward condemned by a judgment, as in the case of King Saul in I Kings [Samuel], c. 13, where the prophet spake: "Thou hast done foolishly, thou hast not kept the commandment of the Lord thy God which he commanded thee; for now would the Lord have established thy kingdom upon Israel forever. But now thy kingdom shall not continue, etc." It is evident, therefore, that a king forfeits his kingdom through sin, and therefore he is a tyrant because he does not rule according to law. Above, however, I was speaking of a universal tyrant, but here of a special one, who is not a tyrant in quite so strict a sense.

§4. "*Omnis superbus, etc.*" Pride [*superbia*] is the root of all evil, and this is especially true of a tyrant. There (§5) follows in that passage the analysis of five kinds of tyrants. One is a general tyrant over the whole Empire of Rome, another of a province in which he rules not according to law, another of a city, another of a house and another of himself. Whether there can be a tyrant of a neighborhood we shall have to inquire, and on this point I will speak later.

"*His per acceptam dignitatis potentiam.*" This must be determined by what precedes or what follows.

"*Alius in provincia.*" In a province no one can lawfully have supreme power such as I mentioned above in speaking of the state as a whole. The procedure is different if one is made *praeses* of a province for a given term or during the pleasure [of the appointing power], and at the expiration of his term refuses to make way for his successor. Such an one is a tyrant and falls under the *lex julia majestatis.*

"*Alius in civitate.*" Our discussion will be chiefly occupied with the tyrant in a *civitas.*

"*Alius in domo.*" How this is to be understood, I will discuss later.

"*Alius latentem nequitiam exercet apud se.*" The tyranny of this one remains concealed, being solely in his own thoughts, and this is not a matter for a jurist to consider, since no man can be punished for his thoughts.

§6. Still, we must remember that if one plans an attempt or causes an attempt to be made, even without success, he is to be punished as if he had succeeded. In the passage [of Gregory] which follows, reference is made to punishment after examination by the Eternal Judge, and therefore I do not inquire into this point, but leave it to the theologians. I emphasize, however, the phrase "*habere potestatem appetit ut affligat*" because it may be useful to you.

§7. It should be specially noted that an act of tyranny consists specifically in the oppression of one's subjects. He is called a tyrant who impoverishes and brings suffering upon his own people, as has been said. The acts of a tyrant are of many kinds, as has been said. This is enough by way of comment on the passage [of Gregory].

Chapter III

[The closeness of Bartolus's reasoning is well shown here. In the previous chapter he has dealt with the various forms of usurped power in those units of population which have a regular, established government. But he was evidently familiar with cases of usurpation over groups which had no such recognized governmental mechanism (*jurisdictio*). His *vicinia* may be compared to one of our city "wards," i.e. a district within a larger political unit, set off for convenience of administration but having no independent governing system of its own. Here, says Bartolus, there cannot, properly speaking, be a tyrant—unless, indeed, the "ward boss" becomes so powerful that the lawful government cannot control him, "as the nobles are now doing at Rome." In that case he properly comes under the definition of a tyrant so far as that section of the civitas is concerned.

The same principle applies to outlying dependencies of a city. If in such a region a usurper becomes strong enough to resist the regular administration of the city officials, then he becomes a tyrant. In other words, tyranny is a de facto condition and must be dealt with as such.]

§8. I now inquire whether there can be a tyranny in a neighborhood (*vicinia*)?

My answer is: No, as is evident from Gregory's words, for he makes no mention of this kind of tyranny. It may also be shown by reason. The rule of a tyrant is the very worst kind of rule, as has been said, for it is directly opposed to the type of rule which is the best. A tyrant is a governor, though not according to the law, and it is, therefore, evident that where there is no government the word "tyrant" does not apply. But now in a neighborhood there has never been a king or any kind of government with jurisdiction, and hence there can be no tyrant. A neighborhood is not ruled by a distinct government but by the ruler who governs the whole community (*civitas*). Even if there be in a neighborhood certain specially powerful persons who oppress the rest, yet they are not (§9) tyrants, but simply stronger persons; unless, indeed, we suppose that in a neighborhood or in a certain district someone may gain such power that the general government can do nothing there without his consent—as the nobles are now doing at Rome—then he is rightly called a tyrant in that part of the city.

On the other hand it may be said that a city is generally divided into quarters or parishes, in each of which there are persons called *capitanei* or syndics who preside over the affairs of that section of the city. Now certainly it would seem as if where there is a government there might be a tyrant, but I reply that such persons have no right of jurisdiction even though they receive a certain power of restraint for the purpose of exacting fines, as in the case of crimes which they report. They are rather to be called the servants of rulers than actual rulers themselves. Therefore they cannot be considered tyrants but only as persons with a higher degree of power in virtue of their offices. They may inspire fear, and if they do this they fall under the above-mentioned clause: *si per impressionem*.

Furthermore, the evil doings of the powerful in a neighborhood can promptly be checked by the government of the city, and on this account they are not to be called (§10) tyrants. This explains why the blessed Gregory made no mention of tyranny in a neighborhood. By the same token I say that in manors, villages or encampments, outlying dependencies (*comitates*) of a city, where there is no jurisdiction either in law or in fact, there can be no tyrant, even though there be one person stronger than the rest. But if one should be strong enough to rebel and to hold his own against the city, so that crimes could not be checked there by the city officials without great difficulty, then he might become a tyrant.

Chapter IV

§11. I inquire next whether there can be a tyrant in a family (*domus*). It would seem as if this could not be, because, as has been said, no jurisdiction is exercised there. But Gregory says the contrary. In my opinion the paterfamilias may be said to have a certain degree of jurisdiction in the house, since he declares the law there in regard to his children and his slaves. So also the elder of the family has a certain kind of jurisdiction over his wife, his children and his slaves, and even the eldest brother or the uncle over those in the house who are under twenty-five years of age. If, then, one governs there contrary to law he may properly be called a tyrant. So that, if any one of the family should make a contract or any other engagement through fear of that person it would be null and void as if it were made through fear of a tyrant. If, however, an elder person has within the house a younger brother or brother's son over twenty-five years of age, the elder does not have that kind of power over him, since he is able to govern himself. In that case fear alone is not sufficient, but there must be proof of fraud or a general state of fear (*metus communis*), and the acts of such a junior cannot be annulled. We may also call the abbot of a monastery a tyrant if, being a usurper (*intrusus*) he rule there contrary to law; or if, though his title be a valid one, he rule tyrannically.

Chapter V

§12. I inquire now how many kinds of tyrants there may be in a commonwealth. I reply that from what has been said it is evident that a tyrant is one who rules not according to law (*non jure*), and since there are various ways of ruling contrary to law there are various types of tyrants. Some are open (*manifesti*) tyrants, others disguised (*velati*), others concealed (*taciti*). One may be openly a tyrant by reason of his conduct, another by defect of title. So in the same way a disguised tyrant may be such in practice or by defect of title. As to this let us inquire further.

Chapter VI

§13. I ask: What is a manifest tyrant by defect of title in a commonwealth? My answer is: One who rules there openly without a lawful title, as is evident from our previous definition. This may happen in divers ways. First, if the city or fortified place (*castrum*) in which he lives has not the right to choose its own ruler, and one acts there as ruler, he is a tyrant because he is ruling contrary to law, and he is subject to the *lex julia majestatis*. The same is true if an official, after his term of office has expired, continue in it against the will of him who has the right of decision (*ad quem spectat*) [probably the overlord].

§14. But if we suppose that the town or fortified place has the right to elect its own ruler and that the community has given to him some degree of jurisdiction, even though there is no doubt that this was done under compulsion; since what is done through fear is valid, even though it be [later] annulled by an action "*quod metus causa*" therefore he is meanwhile lawful ruler (*rector*), and it cannot be said that he is a tyrant by defect of title.

§15. Now we must consider in what ways the violence or cause of fear is applied against the people. I answer: When an army is led against the city without the consent of the overlord; or if the city is taken by assault with the help of foreign troops. If, however, one procures his election as ruler through a tumult or revolt by the help of citizens of the place itself, then the case is more doubtful, because it looks as if he were chosen by the dominant classes, as shown by the very fact that he has prevailed. In this case it must be said that he is not a manifest tyrant by defect of title but [a ruler] created by violence and fear.

But now supposing that one seizes upon the fortifications of a city with a moderate force and that through this occupation a reasonable fear falls upon the people? Certainly he is made ruler through fear. Or supposing he prevails, not by the help of the ruling class but through those of low estate, as commonly happens. Certainly in this case he cannot be said to be made ruler by the more important elements of the people, since men of that sort cannot be called to be *decuriones* or councillors.

So also, if he has done this with the help of people from the suburbs, or if with a moderate force of citizens he has stirred up a tumult while the rest were scattered in their own houses,—for a united few are more than equal to a divided multitude,—certainly this would justify a state of fear among the people. Or, supposing that at the outset with his moderate force he has driven out or killed one or more of the leaders of the city, on which account the people were justly alarmed; since it is written: "I will smite the shepherd, and the sheep shall be scattered." That such fear among the people is a reasonable fear is proved by many examples from history, especially in the book of Judges, and I say that, in the same way, if a ruler is chosen by means of a tumult or unlawful uprising he is a manifest tyrant by defect of title. And even if thereafter he rules well, still he is a tyrant—that is unless he be later legitimated [by an overlord].

That the above statement is true appears from this: that if he brings charges irregularly (*indebite*) against certain citizens and they are driven into exile at the time of his election, they may be considered as held in contempt because they ought to have been duly summoned (*pocari*). So that an election held while they were in contempt is invalid, and thus he is a manifest tyrant by defect of title.

From what has been said, therefore, the method of determining who is a tyrant becomes evident.

Chapter VII

[We come here to Bartolus's main interest: to establish, as far as may be, the continuity of legal obligations under changes of administration. The acts of a manifest tyrant *ex defectu tituli* are *ipso jure* invalid, and so are the acts of officials appointed by him. Those of officials chosen by the community itself *patiente tyranno* are also, in Bartolus's opinion, invalid on the general principle that even such officials could not be freely chosen while the tyranny lasted. On the other hand even a ruler who has won his office by compulsion is better than no ruler at all.

§17 presents some rather puzzling questions. The text appears to be corrupt, and I have done what I could to bring it into harmony with the general tenor of the author's opinions. Mr. Woolf has, perhaps, done wisely not to attempt a complete translation. The point seems to be that no tyranny however manifest can be pleaded to impair the obligation of all contracts. The test of an obligation is whether it was incurred through the regular operation of courts or under some form of compulsion by the tyrant. In the former case the obligation is valid, in the latter, *metus causa* may be pleaded as ground for release of the obligation. Here as elsewhere the practical Bartolus seems to base his opinion somewhat upon the duration of the tyranny. The longer it lasts the stronger grows the presumption of validity for its acts; otherwise the stability of the commonwealth would be proportionately endangered.]

I inquire whether acts done by such a manifest tyrant by defect of title or during his administration are valid.

§16. This question has several branches. I ask first as to the validity of those acts which are done by way of jurisdiction. It is certain that the acts of the tyrant himself, as of one having the right of jurisdiction, are *ipso jure* null and void. The same is true of the acts of officials appointed by him, and for the same reason. §17. But there is doubt as to things done in a city where a tyrant has been elected by other officials who were chosen by the community itself without opposition on the part of the tyrant. My opinion is that these acts are not valid, in accordance with the above-mentioned statute which says that whatever is done in the time of a tyrant is *ipso jure* null, and this is also in accordance with reason. For no official can be freely elected in a city where there is a tyrant, but the choice seems to be made by the tyrant himself.

Authority for this might be found in the decretal *de praescriptione* where it is said that in time of schism no [lawful] acts can be performed and no prescription runs. Now the period of a tyranny might perhaps be called a time of schism; for the tyrant breaks in sunder the unity of the whole state and thus evidently falls under the *lex julia majestatis*, as has been said. On the other hand in the decretal above cited it is not said that all acts are null except legacies made in favor of churches, and therefore all other acts appear to be valid. Besides injustice would [otherwise] be done; for if a tyranny should be greatly prolonged, shall we say that all suits and legal transactions in their courts shall be of no effect? It would seem to be a hardship in the case of suits brought against rebels or enemies of the tyrant, if such suits were to be *ipso jure* null. For no man is bound to appear before a judge notoriously hostile or in a place notoriously unfavorable to him.

§18. But some ordinances, judgments and legal actions have to do with persons living within the city, and here there is rather more uncertainty. We may compare the case with that of a free man held by another *sub patria potestate vel dominica* and, while under such control, performing some conscious act. Thus in the present case a people held under the power of a tyrant does certain things which officials chosen by the people would have done in any event, even if they had been free to act for themselves—as for example the decision of contentious cases which the tyrant allows to go through the regular judicial process. Such acts are valid, because they are done voluntarily.

There are certain other acts which would not have been done unless there had been a tyrant, and these are not valid because they are done, not voluntarily but through fear of the tyrant. For this I refer again to the decretal *decernimus*. For it is certain that, if there were no tyrant, action against churches could be taken only by regular officials and therefore such acts are declared [in the decretal above cited] to be absolutely without foundation on account of the character of the actors. These matters were treated as if we were speaking of a minor who has done something which a prudent person of mature years (§19) would not have done. I am supposing also that if in trials injury is done by judges to persons whom the tyrant has under suspicion, restitution will be made to them on general principles. I am supposing further that the time for demanding restitution runs from the end of the tyranny, as in other cases it runs from the end of an absence or with the coming of age.

§20. Our second inquiry has to do with the effect of contracts, and these may be of many kinds. If the city makes a grant or a concession to the tyrant, such a contract is *ipso jure* null. For, if a promise made by a captive to the person who has thrust him into prison is not valid, so also a promise or other contract made by a city with the tyrant who holds it captive and, as it were, in prison is not valid, since a tyrant is said to hold the people in servitude. We can also say that such contracts are null in accordance with a provision of the civil law. For if contracts of this sort are annulled when made with a just ruler, how much more in the case of a tyrant ruling unjustly. Sometimes contracts are made between a tyrant and an individual under his power, and these are also null or may be annulled as being caused by coercion. Especially if the tyrant causes property to be sold to him by coercion; for in that case he falls under the imperial law which compels him to restore the property. Coercion is proved if the tyrant would not allow the property to be got together or threatened the possessor if he refused to sell, or sought other pretexts or made repeated demands upon one who did not wish to sell; for the request of a superior is a command.

§21. A contract made by a tyrant of this sort with foreigners, which subjects or obligates the city to another person, is invalid *ipso jure*. If he subjects the city to another person, even though he makes an agreement favorable to the city, he is held to be acting tyrannically, and the contract is invalid, as in the case of a fraudulent possessor of an inheritance. A contrary opinion is held by Hostiensis,[2] who maintains that such contracts are valid in so far as they are favorable to the city, as we say in the case of a ward. If, he says, a contract is partly favorable to the city and partly unfavorable, then, if there are separate clauses it is valid in so far as it is to the advantage of the city. But if there are many clauses connected together, then, if the city rejects it in so far as it is unfavorable, it cannot accept it in so far as it is favorable. I think this opinion is true enough and is good law in the case of a contracting party who knew that the man was a tyrant; (§22) for he has no remedy. But, if we suppose that the contracting party was ignorant of the tyranny, then he has a remedy by restitution.

§23. But if the tyrant does not make a contract, but sells property in separate parcels (*distrahit*) either himself or through his officials, receiving payments due to the state, are those who pay released from their debts? On this point it must be said that if they are debtors to the state in virtue of an agreement made with the tyrant himself it would seem as if they ought to be quit in accordance with a provision of the civil law. But that passage refers to the case of a contract made with a robber in his own name, while here it is a question of a contract made with a tyrant in the name of the state. Nevertheless it seems that the debtor may be released from his obligation as if it had been made with a son [under *patria potestas*] or with a slave.

Sometimes a debt is paid for which the debtor was obligated to the city in some other way than by an act of the tyrant, and in that case it would appear that the debtor is not released. This is well supported by Innocent *de electione, c. nihil* where the statement seems to be that one who makes a payment to a usurping official without lawful title is not quit.

My opinion is that the above rules are sound when the debt is paid to a robber or to a usurping official or to a tyrant who is not in a position to inspire fear in the debtor or to threaten him with harm—as, for example, if the debtor were of another city. If, however, the tyrant be able to inspire fear or to apply force or threats in virtue of the jurisdiction he is exercising—though this be only a de facto jurisdiction—since the debtor is subject to him, he is released if he pays the debt to the tyrant or to his agent. This is also in accordance with reason; for through violence applied to a debtor an injury is done to the city in whose debt he stands, and [thus] the tyrant is oppressing the city and the fault may be said to be his. If the substance of a debt due in kind is destroyed through the fault of the creditor, the debtor may be released by way of exception; but if it be due in money, then there is little doubt as to his right of release *ipso jure*.

§24. But perhaps it may be said that if a tyrant of this sort be in such a position that the sum paid to him may readily be recovered, then no ground for exception should be allowed to the debtor. But, as I think, this distinction applies to the case where violence is used against a person to the injury of that person, but not where the injury is done to his creditor [that is to the city], for the reasons (§25) stated. I assume also in what I have said above that one must allege fear of the tyrant, and for this it suffices that the tyrant have made a law or given public notice ordering the payment to be made. For, if one has made a payment in view of such notice [this is evidence that] he had reason to fear violence, and that is sufficient. From what has been said it is evident that if collectors or other officials appointed by the tyrant collect money and afterward hand it over to the tyrant himself or dispose of it according to his orders, they are not to be held liable.

§26. Sometimes a tyrant of this class neither makes contracts nor sells property in parcels, but suffers property of the community to waste or its rights to be lost by prescription. In that case I think that no right of prescription runs against the community. I say also that if the tyrant exercises any jurisdiction which properly belongs to the city itself, claiming that his right derives, not from the city but from some other source, then, as far as he himself is concerned, he would seem to be making use of another's name, but, as far as the city is concerned, to be using his own name, if by that use the city retains its right.

Chapter VIII

§27. In this eighth chapter I take up the question of the tyrant *ex parte exercitii*, that is, as shown by his conduct. Even though his title be sound he is none the less a tyrant. I say that he is a tyrant because he rules "tyrannically," that is, his actions are not directed toward the common good but to his own advantage, and that means to rule unjustly—as is the case de facto in Italy. But now, that the method of proof may be made more clear, let us come down to specific acts, which for the most part (§28) consist in the oppression of subjects.

These acts are clearly enumerated by the famous Plutarch in his *de regimine principum*[3] under ten headings. First, it is the practice of tyrants to cause the ruin of powerful and distinguished men of the community, so that they cannot rebel against them; for we see that they murder even their brothers and blood relations, and that is an indication of the very worst kind of tyranny. Second, they banish their wise men, lest they discover and attack their iniquities and stir up the people against them. Third, they not only cause the ruin of study and education, but they prevent the training of capable men because they are always in fear of detection by wisdom. Fourth, they forbid private associations [*specialitates*] and public meetings, even lawful ones, through fear of uprisings. Fifth, they keep a multitude of informers about the place; for the man who is conscious of wrongdoing always believes that people are speaking ill of him and plotting against him, and for this reason he gladly listens to such informers. Sixth, the tyrant keeps the community in a state of division, so that each part may be in fear of the rest and so may not rebel against him. Seventh, the tyrant takes pains to keep his subjects poor, so that they may be fully occupied with getting their living and have no time for plotting against him. Eighth, he provokes wars and sends his fighting men abroad to prevent them from hatching plots and because through wars men are kept poor and withdrawn from study, which is what a tyrant desires. Also in this way he keeps soldiers in training for his own use in time of need. Ninth, he makes up his bodyguard, not from citizens but from foreigners, for he stands in fear of his own countrymen. Tenth, when there are factions in the city he always attaches himself to one of them in order to break up the other.

§29. Such are the opinions of Plutarch, and now let us examine them.[4] First: To cause the ruin of specially capable persons, even of a brother, is a tyrannical act. This is true unless it be for a just cause, as, for example, in the case of Romulus and Remus. For who can doubt that if any powerful person in a city creates disturbance or sedition he ought to be banished by any just judge? If then the cause be a just one the act is not that of a tyrant. Second, the same rule applies to the ruining of wise men, if the cause be just. Third, the destruction of study and education: I understand this to apply to such pursuits as are suited to the [given] community. If, however, a ruler breaks up such pursuits as are not adapted to the community, this is not the act of a tyrant. Fourth, that assemblies, even lawful ones, are not permitted: If an offence is once committed by them it is certainly right to dissolve them; for I have known persons to come together under a pretense of religion and straightway to throw the town into confusion. We must, therefore, judge by the kind of persons assembled whether it is the act of a tyrant to break up a lawful assembly. Fifth, the keeping of informers in a city: This may be the act of a just ruler if it be done for a lawful purpose. A good ruler may employ informers to punish crimes and other offences in the community; but a tyrant uses them against those who may injure his own position and therefore his act concerns only his own advantage. Sixth, that the tyrant strives to foment divisions in the city: This is a tyrannical act, seeing that it is a primary duty of a just ruler to keep the peace among the citizens. Seventh, deliberately keeping the people in poverty is plainly an act of tyranny; for the good ruler cannot properly take anything for himself nor afflict his subjects with burdens upon either their persons or their property. Eighth, that incitement to civil war is in itself (*simplicite*) a tyrannical act: Sometimes a civil war may be a just war, but an unjust war is an act of tyranny pure and simple. Ninth, maintaining a bodyguard of non-citizens may be a just measure; for a people may be so uncontrollable and so obstinate that the ruler, just though he be, cannot rely upon them. This is especially apt to occur in a newly recovered territory, even under a just master. For this reason emperors sometimes drove out the inhabitants of a city and settled them elsewhere. So also we sometimes see good rulers building fortifications or collecting munitions in a city where their rule is a lawful one. But such things, in the case of a just ruler are due to some exceptional cause, whereas with a tyrant they are of ordinary occurrence. Tenth, adhering to one faction and oppressing another is an act of tyranny pure and simple, since the final purpose of a commonwealth is the peace and good order of the citizens—as has been said.

§30. All the above, then, are indications whereby a tyranny can be proved, and especially these two: the promoting of divisions in the community and the impoverishment of citizens and abusing them in their persons or in their property. All this has been abundantly shown in the preceding chapters. From what has there been said it is evident what a tyranny is.

Chapter IX

[Now, supposing the fact of tyranny to be established, what are the legal means for getting rid of it? The most obvious answer is, of course, through some action of the overlord to whom the tyrant is technically responsible, and Bartolus's function is to describe the legal basis for such action. This he does in §§31–33 by references to formulas of the Roman public law.

As a matter of fact, however, such a rigid application of Roman discipline was impossible in the existing conditions of Italian politics, and Bartolus gives us here the clearest illustration of the closeness of his touch with the political actualities of his day. The tyranny of Taddeo Pepoli at Bologna was one of the most marked cases of *defectus tituli*. He acquired and held his power by violence, but his rule of ten years (1337–1347), was, on the whole, a benefit to the community. After three years the papal government in its capacity of overlord found it advisable to accept the situation and "legitimated" the tyrant by creating him "Vicar of the Holy See." The defect of title was thus removed, and the responsibility for a proper *exercitium* was technically assumed by the Papacy. The motive of the emperor Charles IV in distributing titles among the tyrants of Lombardy is obvious. He thereby recouped himself for the heavy costs of his senseless Italian expedition (1355) and fancied he was buying support for his fantastic schemes of imperial grandeur. The Legate in the Mark of Ancona is undoubtedly Cardinal Egidio Albornoz, who developed the policy of adopting local tyrants as papal vicars into a regular system. His motive is clearly outlined by Bartolus, who had every opportunity to study this interesting experiment in practical politics at close range. He "threw over his less valuable cargo in order to save the more precious." Yet the jurist holds in reserve the fundamental principle of right: If the legitimated tyrant continues to do the works of a tyrant, he is a tyrant still, and is to be dealt with accordingly.]

§31. *Qu.* In the case of a count, duke, marquis or baron whose title is regular but who is proved to be a tyrant by his conduct (*exercitio*) what action ought his overlord to take?

Resp. He ought to depose him; for he who acts in this manner holds his people in servitude, and it is the duty of an overlord to deliver the people from servitude. §32. But under what law do those fall who rule without a clear title? It is certain that they are subject to the *lex* (§33) *julia majestatis*. As to the ruler who has a clear title but is shown to be a tyrant by his conduct, I say that, because he oppresses his subjects in their persons he falls under the *lex julia de vi publica*. Also, because he encourages factions in the community and thus prevents the courts from acting regularly, he falls under the same law *de vi publica*. Further, by imposing new burdens and new taxes he incurs the penalty of the same law, which is deportation. Thus he forfeits all rights under the civil law and, as an infamous person, loses his dignities and his offices. He also falls under the *lex julia de ambitu*. Perhaps also he is liable to the penalty of death. I say, further, that a person exercising such a tyranny, if he conspires against the prince or his officers openly or secretly, is *ipso jure* a traitor to the Empire and forfeits his office, according to a novel of the emperor Theodosius.

Chapter X

§34. *Qu.* What shall we say of a policy which we have seen followed by the Supreme Pontiff, by the Emperor and by legates [of the Papacy]? Certain persons whom they well knew to be tyrants and whom they had [tried] to repress by forcible means, they have created bishops of the Holy See or vicars of the Empire, as, for example, Clement VI did at Bologna with Taddeo dei Pepoli and his sons. The same thing was done by the emperor Charles [IV] with the tyrants of Lombardy, and the same again by a legate in the March of Ancona with many tyrants.

Resp. It is to be presumed that such great lords would not do these things without urgent cause, and such cause may be of two kinds:—First, some great and pressing necessity which they have to meet. For, as a careful sailor throws over his less valuable cargo in order to save the more precious, and as the prudent house-father makes a choice of his more valuable goods for rescue [in case of danger], so a just overlord comes to terms with a tyrant and makes him his vicar in order to accomplish great and pressing reforms. The second reason may be consideration for the subjects of the tyrant. For, as physicians who follow Nature, when a disease cannot be cured without great danger to the patient, strive to support Nature and prevent the disease from going any further and thus Nature comes to her own assistance—such is sometimes the policy of a just prince, when, seeing that a tyrant cannot be deposed without great injury to his subjects, he makes the tyrant his vicar for their sakes, so that being less in fear he will be less oppressive to the people. Meanwhile some accident may occur by which the tyrant may be deposed in accordance with justice and without injury to the people. Yet, in spite of the validity of their titles, these tyrants are none the less tyrants if they continue to do the tyrannical acts above mentioned, for such acts do not enter into the commission with which they are entrusted.

Chapter XI

§35. *Qu.* Whether prosecutions brought by a tyrant who has a good title are valid? I say, that he either prosecutes exiles who have rebelled against himself, in which case the process is not valid, since no one is bound to appear before a notoriously hostile judge, as was said above; or else he proceeds against his fellow citizens, and then the process is valid until the tyrant is removed together with his office.

§36. But what if a process has already been begun in consequence of which a verdict is to be pronounced [by his superior] against the tyrant, do his acts performed while the case is pending and before judgment is pronounced hold good? I reply:—If the accusation be of some crime for which he would *ipso jure* be deprived of his office or would be declared a slave or an infamous person, then his acts after the trial has begun are not valid. But if the case is such that he would be deprived of his office only in consequence of the judgment to be delivered, then his acts meanwhile are valid, because meanwhile he retains his office. In the same way, if a contract be made or terminated with the tyrant, the transaction is valid,—it being understood that the agreement does not bring the city into subjection,—as I will explain later. I say also that if one is under the power of a noble person and has a lawful title, then, even though he be a tyrant in his conduct, he is, nevertheless, to be regarded as a privileged person so long as he is allowed to hold his office;—not so, however, if his title be defective.

I say further that if one having a good title becomes a tyrant through his conduct and causes an increase [or extension] of his power to be granted him by the people, such power would not be valid, on the assumption that the people would have acted from fear—as was said above. Also, any contract which he may have made involving the subjection of the city or laying any burden upon it would not be valid; for he is not acting as lord of the city if he deprives it of its liberty.

Chapter XII

[Up to this point Bartolus has been speaking of open, manifest tyranny. Now he takes up the more subtle problems of a tyranny which is either veiled (*velata*) or implied (*tacita*). Tyranny may be concealed either by extending the tenure of a properly conferred office beyond the term for which it was granted or by converting a subordinate office into one of a higher grade. The type of tyrant here presented is, perhaps, the most frequent and the most puzzling as a legal problem. How can a tyrant be convicted if he "keeps himself in retirement, does not act in person, and seldom appears at the City Hall, while the public officials obey his agents and his written orders"? Here is the perfect picture of the "party boss," as Bartolus knew him in the Italian city-states and as we know him in every corner of our "free republic." It is the "invisible government" of which we hear so much in our public prints, always silent but always alert to take advantage of every shift in the political breeze. But how is it possible to "get" such a concealed tyrant? Bartolus perceives the extreme difficulty of obtaining conviction by evidence on oath and therefore declares his opinion that proof may properly be drawn from the facts of the case. His illustrations are illuminating. If land is claimed as a deposit from a river, although no person has seen the process of this deposit going on, still the fact that it is there is sufficient evidence that the river has brought it. And, though no one can perceive the generation of a child, the fact of its birth under given circumstances is good evidence of its parentage. So the fact of party violence and oppression in a city where one person is notoriously stronger than the rest is proof enough that such acts proceed from him and that he is therefore a tyrant.]

§38. I now proceed to inquire in regard to the disguised or concealed tyrant, that is one who under some cover rules over a community contrary to law. This cover may be of two kinds according to the title which he causes to be granted to him. We have to remember that a tyrant is properly to be compared to a king, as we have said above. But it is an essential part of a royal power that it be perpetual, also that it have complete jurisdiction, as appears in our previous chapters. Now from these two qualities have come two ways of concealing a tyranny. First, that a person causes a certain jurisdiction to be granted him and then, after a time, to be granted to him anew. Such a jurisdiction seems to (§39) be rather that of a judge than of a tyrant. On this point I say that although he have jurisdiction and cause it to be conferred upon him in his own city, yet he has no title to it; for no person can have a jurisdiction of this sort. He has not an *imperium merum et mistum*, but only a simple (*nudam*) jurisdiction. And so what we said above about the tyrant *ex defectu tituli* holds good of such an one, since he receives no title.

§40. But if we suppose a community in which the people, either by privilege or by custom, have an unquestioned right to confer power, and therefore a title granted in the first instance would be valid, then we have to consider whether the man becomes a tyrant from the mere fact of renewal or extension. This would seem to be the case by common law, for such a renewal is not lawful—nay, he falls under the *lex julia de ambitu*. If, however, we suppose that the power of the people is so great that it can dispense from that law, then we should have to inquire whether during the first period of his rule he had made himself so strong that the people were forced to elect him for a second term. In that case, since he would be elected through fear, he would indeed be a tyrant ex defectu tituli. But, if he be freely elected and afterward become a tyrant through conduct, then I give the same opinion as above.

§41. The second cover is that a tyrant may cause some title to be conferred upon him which conveys little or no right of jurisdiction:—for example, that of Gonfaloniere; or he may have the policing of the city entrusted to him, or may have himself made a captain of mercenaries or of the militia. In such cases he is not [properly] called a tyrant; for a tyrant must have complete jurisdiction like a king. He cannot be called a prince (*principalis*) who has no jurisdiction or only a moderate degree thereof. Certainly he is not a tyrant by reason of his title. But if through this function he attains such power that he manages the affairs of the city as he pleases and the [city] officials obey him as their master, then I say, if he acts tyrannically or causes others so to act, he is a true tyrant. For his orders are obeyed in the city like those of a prince, and yet he is not ruling according to law, since he is acting tyrannically, and he is therefore a tyrant.

But how can this be proved when a tyrant of this sort keeps himself in retirement, does not act in person, and seldom appears at the City Hall, while the public officials obey his agents and written orders? I answer that the proof is a difficult one since when things of this sort are done no witnesses can be called. In view of this a certain decretal ordered in a specific case that the proof should be by the oath of some person; but I do not think that this is a sound general principle; for in the decretal the juror is not affected by any preceding circumstances. Therefore I think the proof here must be secured in some other way.

We must consider that although some actions cannot be directly proved of themselves, yet they are capable of proof. I have shown this in my treatise on Alluvial Deposits. Though these deposits cannot be perceived while they are forming, nevertheless, from the fact that they have been formed it follows of necessity that the river has brought them. So also, though the generation of a child is not perceptible it is considered sufficient proof if it can be shown that it was born in a certain house of a woman cohabiting [there] with a [certain] man. For, while a proof would be convincing to the judge, these facts incline him at once toward a conviction. So is it in the present case. If it can be shown that there is discord in the city, one party being driven out, and that crimes and misdemeanors occur without punishment and that the citizens are oppressed and other things of the sort happen, these all come under the head of those tyrannical acts of which we have spoken above.

Further, if the person having the title is the most powerful man in the city and if it is a matter of common report that he causes the above mentioned things to be done, then, I say, a tyranny is sufficiently proved; for these acts could not proceed from anyone except from that most powerful person. Taken in connection with common report they are sufficient to lead the judge to a conviction, and this agrees with what we have said in the case of one ruling according to law—namely, that it is enough if it be so held and reputed.

§42. But now, are acts passed during the time of a tyrant of this class valid?[5] In reply I give the same opinion as in the case of a manifest tyrant who causes things to be done through officials elected by the community, [namely that they are not valid. See §17]. This is true when the greater part of the citizens are oppressed or burdened with taxes or kept in a state of discontent. If, however, some are held in exile or some within the city are badly treated by exclusion from the offices, while in other respects the city is well governed and the common good well cared for, then the person having a title of this sort or some similar distinction would not be a tyrant in the plain meaning of the word, since the common welfare is well looked after—which is the very opposite of a tyranny. But in respect to external relations or dealings with the [personal] enemies of the man thus superior to others, even though he govern the state well, I think we should say the same as if he were a true tyrant. There is no reason why one should not be called a tyrant as to outside territories and a just ruler within the community.

§43. For this reason we must take into account that, just as an individual is seldom found who is free from all bodily defect, so it is a rare thing to find a government which is wholly devoted to the common good without any admixture of tyranny.[6] It would be a divine rather than a human condition of things if rulers had no regard for their own interest and cared solely for the common (§44) welfare. We call that a good government and not a tyranny in which the common good prevails over the private interest of the rulers. This is laid down by Aegidius Romanus in his *de regimine principum*, 1. iii, c. 11, 2[7] and it ought specially to be borne in mind when we are considering how to prove whether a certain person is a tyrant.

§45. A third form of concealment is when one allows no title to be given him in the city but so manages all its affairs that everything goes according to his will. That such a man is a tyrant can be proved in the way described immediately above, namely that he is the most powerful person through having the greatest following. Also because it is a fact made notorious by common report and because he causes the aforementioned things to be done. It is of great importance [for the proof] that during the time of the tyranny things should occur by which the evil character of the tyrant may be made plain and the method of proof be made more clear. As to acts done in the time of a tyrant of this type I say what I have said just above. Whether there can be a tyrant in a neighborhood or in a certain quarter of a city I have already given my opinion.

PART II

On Civic Republicanism

Chapter 4

LEONARDO BRUNI

Panegyric to the City of Florence

(C. 1402)

Oration for the Funeral of Nanni Strozzi

(1428)

On the Florentine Constitution

(1439)

The greatest of Florence's "humanist chancellors," Leonardo Bruni (1370–1444) may be credited with conceptualizing "republicanism" as an "ism," as opposed to the traditional practice of studying republics, monarchies, and mixed regimes in the broader context of good government. Born in Arezzo, Bruni succeeded Salutati as Florentine chancellor and, like his mentor, provided powerful ideological defenses of the city's cause in numerous wars. His magnum opus is the twelve-volume *History of the Florentine People*, but he perhaps achieved his greatest influence by translating Aristotle's *Politics* and *Nicomachean Ethics* into Latin. The readings presented here highlight the main elements of aristocratic republicanism in Florence: the themes of unity, consensus, self-sacrifice for the common good, resistance to tyranny, and mixed government.

The translations were originally published in the following volumes: Leonardo Bruni, *Panegyric to the City of Florence*, in B. G. Kohl and R. G. Witt, eds., *The Earthly Republic: Italian Humanists on Government and Society* (Philadelphia: University of Pennsylvania Press, 1978), 135–78 (complete translation of Leonardo Bruni, *Laudatio Florentinae Urbis*, edited by Hans Baron in his *From Petrarch to Leonardo Bruni* [Chicago: University of Chicago Press, 1968], 232–63, translated by Benjamin G. Kohl); Leonardo Bruni, *Oration for the Funeral of Nanni Strozzi*, in G. Griffiths, J. Hankins, and D. Thompson, eds., *The Humanism of Leonardo Bruni: Selected Texts* (Binghamton: Center for Medieval and Early Renaissance Studies, 1987), 121–27; and Leonardo Bruni, *On the Florentine Constitution*, in G. Griffiths, J. Hankins, and D. Thompson, eds., *The Humanism of Leonardo Bruni*, 171–74.

---- ✳ ----

Panegyric to the City of Florence

Would that God immortal give me eloquence worthy of the city of Florence, about which I am to speak, or at least equal to my zeal and desire on her behalf; for either one degree or the other would, I think, abundantly demonstrate the city's magnificence and splendor. Florence is of such a nature that a more distinguished or more splendid city cannot be found on the entire earth, and I can easily tell about myself, I was never more desirous of doing anything in my life. So I have no doubt at all that if either of these wishes were granted, I should be able to describe with elegance and dignity this very beautiful and excellent city. But because everything we want and the ability granted us to attain what we wish are two different things, we will carry out our intention as well as we can, so that we appear to be lacking in talent rather than in will.

Indeed, this city is of such admirable excellence that no one can match his eloquence with it. But we have seen several good and important men who have spoken concerning God himself, whose glory and magnificence the speech of the most eloquent man cannot capture even in the smallest degree. Nor does this vast superiority keep them from trying to speak insofar as they are able about such an immense magnitude. Therefore, I too shall seem to have done enough if, marshalling all competence, expertise, and skill that I have eventually acquired after so much study, I devote my all to praising this city, even though I clearly understand that my ability is such that it can in no way be compared with the enormous splendor of Florence. Therefore many orators say that the themselves do not know where to begin. This now happens to me not only as far as words are concerned but also concerning the subject itself. For not only are there various things connected one with another, here and there, but also any one of them is so outstanding and in some way so distinguished that they seem to vie for excellence among themselves. Therefore, it is not an easy thing to say which subject is to be treated first. If you consider the beauty or splendor of the city, nothing seems more appropriate to start with than these things. Or if you reflect upon its power and wealth, then you will think these are to be treated first. And if you contemplate its history, either in our own day or in earlier times, nothing would seem so important to begin with as these things. When indeed you consider Florentine customs and institutions, you judge nothing more important than these. These matters cause me concern, and often when I am ready to speak on one point, I recall another and am attracted to it. Hence, they furnish me no opportunity to decide which topic to put first. But I shall seize upon the most apt and logical place to begin the speech, even though I do indeed believe that other topics would not have provided an improper point of departure.

I

As we may see several sons with so great a resemblance to their fathers that they show it obviously in their faces, so the Florentines are in such harmony with this very noble and outstanding city that it seems they could never have lived anywhere else. Nor could the city, so skillfully created, have had any other kind of inhabitants. Just as these citizens surpass all other men by a great deal in their natural genius, prudence, elegance, and magnificence, so the city of Florence has surpassed all other cities in its prudent site and in its splendor, architecture, and cleanliness.

So we see that in the beginning Florence observed a principle of great wisdom: Do nothing for ostentation nor allow hazardous or useless display, but instead use great moderation and follow solid proportion. This city was set neither in the high mountains, so that it would present itself impressively, nor in a broad plain of fields, so it would be open on every side. Rather, this city has both advantages according to the most prudent and best opinion, for one cannot live in high mountains without intemperate climate, without harsh winds, without storms, without great discomfort and hazard to the inhabitants; nor are immense and vast plains without the drenching rays of the sun, without impurity of air, without a hazy humidity. Therefore, having avoided these potential discomforts, Florence very prudently was situated where it is midway between the dangerous extremes (a proven principle for all things), both remote from the evils of the mountains and distant from the dangers of the plains. Hence, though Florence knows both kinds of environments, it possesses a mild and pleasing climate. The mountains of Fiesole face north like a kind of bulwark for the city and repel the immense force of the cold and the headlong rush of the strong northern wind. To the east, where the force of the wind is less, the hills are smaller. And in the other directions, the fields lay open to the sun and to the southern breezes. Therefore, in the area of the city there is a great tranquility and a fine climate, so whenever you leave Florence, in whatever direction you set out, you meet either a greater cold or a hotter sun.

This city, covering an area of both mountains and plains, is surrounded by an extensive crown of wall, not, however, of such a mass that the city would seem timid or fearful of its power, nor, on the other hand so neglected that it can be called imprudent or indiscreet. And what shall I say of the throngs of people, of the splendor of the buildings, of the decorations of the churches, and of the unbelievable and admirable magnificence of the entire city? By Jove, everything here is striking and decorated with outstanding beauty. But it is better to know things in comparison with other things than from themselves alone. Therefore, only those who have been away for some time and return to Florence fully understand how much this flourishing city excels beyond all the others. For there is no other city in the whole world that does not lack perfection in some important way: one lacks in its population, another in the decoration of its buildings, still another suffers the least of these in that it does not have a healthful site. Moreover, every other city is so dirty that the filth created during the night is seen in the early morning by the population and trampled underfoot in the streets. Really can one think of anything worse than this? Even if there were a thousand palaces in such a city and inexhaustible wealth, even if it possessed an infinite population, still I would always condemn that city as a stinking place and not think highly of it. In similar fashion, someone who is deformed in body will always be unhappy even though he might possess a great many outstanding qualities. Hence, filthy cities that may in other respects be very good can never be considered to be beautiful. Further, who cannot see that a city that is not beautiful lacks its highest and noblest adornment?

Indeed it seems to me that Florence is so clean and neat that no other city could be cleaner. Surely this city is unique and singular in all the world because you will find here nothing that is disgusting to the eye, offensive to the nose, or filthy under foot. The great diligence of its inhabitants ensures and provides that all filth is removed from the streets, so you see only what brings pleasure and joy to the senses. Therefore, in its splendor Florence probably surpasses all the cities of the world, and, moreover, in its elegance it is without doubt far ahead of all the cities that exist now and all that ever will. Indeed, such unparalleled cleanliness must be incredible to those who have never seen Florence, for we who live here are amazed daily and will never take for granted this fine quality of Florence. Now what is more marvelous in a populous city than never to have to worry about filth in the streets? Moreover, however big a rainstorm, it cannot prevent your walking through the city with dry feet since almost before it falls the rainwater is taken away by appropriately placed gutters. Hence, the cleanliness and dryness that you find only in the rooms of private palaces in other cities, you find in the squares and streets of Florence.

Perhaps another city is clean, but it lacks beautiful buildings. Another will have beautiful buildings, but it lacks a good climate. Another has a good climate, but it lacks a large population. Only Florence can claim to have all these qualities that are necessary for a prosperous city. And if you are interested in things from antiquity, you will find a great many remains from ancient times in both the public buildings and private homes. Or if you are looking for contemporary architecture, there is surely nothing more splendid and magnificent than Florence's new buildings. Indeed, it would be difficult to say whether the river that flows through the city gives more utility or more pleasure. The two banks of the river are joined by four bridges magnificently constructed of squared blocks, and these are placed at such convenient intervals that the river never seems to interrupt the several main streets that cross Florence. Hence you can walk through Florence as easily as though it were not even divided by a river. Wherever you go you can see handsome squares and the decorated porticos of the homes of the noble families, and the streets are always thronged with crowds of men. Of the houses built near the river, some are actually on the river's edge so that they are bathed by the water, while others are set back from the river so that there is a street between these houses and the river bank. Here large crowds of people gather to do their business and enjoy themselves. Indeed, nothing is more pleasant than this area, for walking especially at midday in winter and at dusk in summer.

But why do I concern myself with just one part of the city? Must I (like some fisherman) just move up and down along the river? As if this were the splendid part of Florence, and the other quarters not are equally beautiful, or even more so. What in the whole world is so splendid and magnificent as the architecture of Florence? Indeed, I feel sorry for other cities when a comparison is made with Florence. In other places perhaps one or at the most two streets in the entire city are filled with important buildings, while the rest of the town is so devoid of architectural distinction that the townsmen are ashamed to have visitors see these parts. But in our city there is really no street, no quarter that does not possess spacious and ornate buildings. Almighty God, what wealth of buildings, what distinguished architecture there is in Florence! Indeed, how the great genius of the builders is reflected in these buildings, and what a pleasure there is for those who live in them. Among these many buildings in Florence nothing is more impressive in size and distinction of style than the churches and shrines, which are numerous and are (as is proper for places of worship) spread throughout the city. These have been marvelously revered by those who worship in their various parishes, and are treated with exceeding piety. Indeed, in all of Florence nothing is more richly appointed, more ornate in style, more magnificent than these churches. As much attention has been given to decorating sacred buildings as to secular ones, so that not only the habitations of the living would be outstanding but the tombs of the dead as well.

But I return to the homes of the private citizens, which were designed, built, and decorated for luxury, size, respectability, and especially for magnificence. Indeed, what could be more pleasant and more beautiful to the sight than the entrance courts, halls, pavements, banquet halls, and other interior rooms of these homes? And how beautiful it is to see the well-ordered spaciousness of many of the homes and to view the curtains, arches, the paneled ceilings and richly decorated hung ceilings, and (as in many homes) the summer rooms separated from the winter ones. In these living quarters you find beautiful chambers decorated with fine furniture, gold, silver, and brocaded hangings and precious carpets. But am I not silly to go on enumerating these things? Even if I had a hundred tongues, a hundred mouths, and a voice of iron, I could not possibly describe all the magnificence, wealth, decoration, delights, and elegance of these homes. If there is someone who would like to experience them, let them come here and walk through the city. But don't let him pass through like a temporary guest or a hurrying tourist. Rather, he should pause, poke around, and try to understand what he is seeing. Now, it is very important that in other cities a tourist should not stay too long. In those cities, what they have to show is all publicly displayed and is placed (as it were) on the outward bark. Whoever comes into these cities is seen as a stranger; but if these tourists leave the well-frequented places and try to examine the interiors as well as the exteriors of the buildings, there will be nothing to confirm their first impressions. Indeed, instead of houses they will find only small huts, and behind the exterior decorations only filth. But the beauty of Florence cannot be appreciated unless seen from the inside. Therefore, the sort of careful scrutiny that brings shame to other cities only serves to raise the esteem held for Florence, for behind the walls of the buildings of Florence there are no fewer ornaments and no less magnificence than there is outside; nor is any one street better decorated or more handsome than another, but every quarter shares in the beauty of the city. Hence, just as blood is spread throughout the entire body, so fine architecture and decoration are diffused throughout the whole city.

To be sure, in the center of the city there is a tall and handsome palace of great beauty and remarkable workmanship. This fine building bespeaks by its very appearance the purposes for which it was constructed. Just as in a large fleet it is an easy matter to pick out the flagship that carries the admiral who is the leader and head over the other captains and their ships, so in Florence everyone immediately recognizes that this palace is so immense that it must house the men who are appointed to govern the state. Indeed, it was so magnificently conceived and looms so toweringly that it dominates all the buildings nearby and its top stands out above those of the private houses.

Indeed, I do not think that I ought to call this building simply a "fortress" but, rather, "fortress of the fortress." The minute you step away from the city walls you are surrounded on all sides by many buildings, so that the latter ought to be called the "city" while this thing surrounded by walls would more correctly be called the "fortress." And as Homer writes of the snow that it falls thickly on the mountains and hills and covers the ridges of the mountains and finally the fertile fields,[1] in like fashion handsome buildings cover the entire region outside the city and all the mountains, the hills and the plains, so that they seem more to have fallen from heaven than to have been constructed by the hands of men. How magnificent, how well designed, how well decorated are these buildings! Indeed, these country houses are even more spacious than those in Florence, for they were designed and constructed on very spacious sites and greater care was taken to make them comfortable and pleasant. As a result, no one who lives in them lacks room, or colonnades, or gardens, or stands of trees. What can I possibly say of the rooms and banquet halls, which are more magnificent and ornate than anything imaginable? And near these homes you find wooded groves, flowery meadows, pleasant river banks, sparkling fountains, and—best of all—the nature of the place itself fit for delight. Indeed, the very hills seem to laugh and to exude a certain joyfulness, of which visitors never seem to tire and which never grows stale. Thus, this whole region is rightly considered and called a paradise—unequaled in grace or beauty by any other area in the whole world. Surely anyone who comes to Florence is amazed when at a distance he sees from the top of a mountain the massive city, beautiful and splendid, surrounded by many country houses.

Nor does Florence's beauty at a distance become sordid when you come close, which happens when something is not really beautiful. But all things are so arranged and gleam with such true beauty that the closer you come to this city, the greater grows your appreciation of its magnificence. Thus the villas are more beautiful than the distant panorama, the suburbs more handsome than the villas, and the city itself more beautiful than its suburbs. Hence, when newcomers enter the city they forget the beauties and architecture of the outlying area because they are so stunned in their admiration for the splendor of the city itself.

Now I want to discuss another topic that I usually consider one of the chief arguments for demonstrating the greatness of this city. Florence has fought a great many wars and has been victorious over some very powerful enemies. It has fought several growing and formidable powers, and by its sound strategy, by its wealth and sheer willpower, Florence has even overcome those enemies to which it was judged to be very inferior and even incapable of resisting under any circumstances. Very recently Florence fought for many years against a very powerful and resourceful enemy with such great force that it filled everyone with admiration. For this Duke,[2] who had by his resources and power been a source of fear to the nations north of the Alps as well as to the rest of Italy, and who was elated in his hopes, prideful in victory, and destroyed, like a storm, everything in his path with an incredible success, found himself confronted by this single city that not only repulsed the invader and delayed the impetus of his conquests but even overthrew him after a long war. To these things done by Florence we shall devote time and space a little further on. For the moment, however, let us return to our subject.

I say, therefore, that everyone was so amazed by the dimensions of this conflict and by the duration of the struggle that they were wondering how a single city could muster the great number of troops and immense resources, not to mention the vast amount of money needed for the war. But this wonder, the great amazement of everyone, lasts only as long as men have not seen this beautiful city nor observed its magnificence. When men actually have seen Florence their amazement at its achievements ceases. Indeed, we see that this happens to everyone; no one ever comes to Florence who does not admit to this experience. As soon as they have seen the city and have inspected with their own eyes its great mass of architecture and the grandeur of its buildings, its splendor and magnificence, the lofty towers, the marble churches, the domes of the basilicas, the splendid palaces, the turreted walls, and the numerous villas, its charm, beauty, and decor, instantly everyone's mind and thought change so that they are no longer amazed by the greatest and most important exploits accomplished by Florence. Rather, everyone immediately comes to believe that Florence is indeed worthy of attaining dominion and rule over the entire world. For this reason one can understand how extraordinarily wondrous this city is whose beauty and magnificence cannot be adequately comprehended or related in words. For just as actual sight has more effect than a report, so opinion is inferior to a report.

Now I do not know what others might say, but, for my part, I think my argument is so persuasive that it alone is able to confirm conclusively the incredible excellence of Florence. Once someone has seen the city, it is no easy matter to cancel and erase the general impression of the city's greatness. The only way that this could happen would be if even stronger evidence of nobility and beauty in this very city not just weakened but even cancelled the impression of wonderment caused by the magnitude of its deeds. This would be analogous to the case of someone telling me of the incredible and unparalleled accomplishments of strength by a boxer in a series of contests; for example, I might hear that this one boxer wore out others with his fists and laid out others with his glove. If I heard that this one had knocked down and beaten a great many other boxers, or that he had stopped a speeding heavy chariot with his bare hands or carried a live bull for a hundred yards (a feat that is claimed for Milo of Croton);[3] or if I heard that when this boxer stood upon an oiled bronze shield no one was able to take him by force (a feat that we read was performed by Polydamas);[4] and if someone would tell me, already dumbfounded by these deeds, that these reported feats were really seen, and, more than this, add that, if someone actually saw and inspected this boxer's powerful body, no one would be greatly amazed about these stories, and even more fantastic ones would be believed. Now, I say, if someone were to relate and swear these things to me, immediately this image of a very strong man would necessarily come to mind, showing his powerful body and graceful movements and the strength of his members. In like fashion, once this magnificent and splendid city is seen, it dispels all doubts about its greatness and converts former disbelievers to the truth. To do so the city must have a peerless magnificence and grandeur in its construction. How would such a complete change of mind, judgement, and opinion happen if it were not for the fact that Florence is, in truth, more majestic and magnificent than the tongues of narrators can describe or the minds of the listeners comprehend? Indeed, let everyone praise this city, let them always praise it. There has never been anyone who actually saw Florence who did not find it much more impressive than he had imagined when he had merely had it described to him. For this reason I do not fear that many will condemn me for being rash and reckless in attempting to describe the greatness of Florence. Seeing such a city, I have never been able to control my total admiration for Florence, and admiring it thus, not to sing its praises. Therefore, if I cannot accomplish this goal adequately, which no one ever has been able to do, my failings should be excused rather than censured. But let us return to our subject.

Beyond the country houses there are the walled towns. And what should I say of these walled towns? Indeed, there is no part of the region lying beyond the country houses that is not filled with these impressive and splendid walled towns. The city itself stands in the center, like a guardian and lord, while the towns surround Florence on the periphery, each in its own place. A poet might well compare it to the moon surrounded by the stars, and the whole vista is very beautiful to the eyes. Just as on a round buckler, where one ring is laid around the other, the innermost ring loses itself in the central knob that is the middle of the entire buckler. So here we see the regions lying like rings surrounding and enclosing one another. Within them Florence is first, similar to the central knob, the center of the whole orbit. The city itself is ringed by walls and suburbs. Around the suburbs, in turn, lies a ring of country houses, and around them the circle of towns. The whole outermost region is enclosed in a still larger orbit and circle. Between the towns there are castles—these safest of refuges for the peasants—with their towers reaching into the sky.

Now the number of farmers is so great that all the available land is under cultivation. What shall I say of the abundance and quality of the crops? What of the large harvests of the fields? Indeed, these things are known to everyone and obvious to the beholder, so that they do not require proof. But I shall say this much: It is not easy to find a region that grows such a great multitude of inhabitants! Now there are many cities that do not have as many inhabitants as the Florentine countryside; still, it gives this population together with the populous city not only the necessity of life but even makes them independent of outside help either for necessities or even for luxuries. For this reason Florence, both inside and outside the city walls, should be judged as the most fortunate city in the entire world.

Now if there is anyone who would say that Florence is deficient because it is not a seaport, he errs, in my opinion, and considers a vice what is really a virtue. Proximity to the sea is perhaps useful for buying and selling products, but otherwise it is too salty and offensive. Indeed, there are a great many inconveniences that beset seaports and, worse still, dangers that they must of necessity undergo. When

Plato of Athens, without question the greatest of all philosophers, established in his book how a city might live well and happily and investigated diligently what must be present and what must be avoided, he believed it was very important for a city to be rather distant from the sea.[5] Nor did that very wise man consider that a city could ever be fortunate if it were placed either on the seashore or anywhere near the lapping of the waves. He discussed at length the harm and discomforts to a happy way of life that proximity to the sea entails or necessitates. Indeed, if we should wish to discover how serious it is for a city to be situated in such a position, we need only consider the danger felt by seaports from Tana and Trebizond all the way to Cadiz. Not only do these cities have to worry about what their neighbors are doing, what policies neighboring peoples debate, what they are planning and what their attitude is toward us and be aware of their internal conspiracies as well as frontal attacks; but, in addition, these seaports have to reckon with possible dangers at the hands of the Egyptians, the Syrians, the Colchians of Greece, the Scythians, the Moors, the men of Cadiz, and many other strange and barbarian peoples besides. Indeed, it is sometimes difficult to know the policies of neighboring states; how much more difficult it is to know what distant peoples are planning. Land armies, which are usually very slow, sometimes arrive before anything is suspected. Therefore, what is to be expected from the speed of fleets? And even if seaborne attacks do not presently happen, we are not entitled to believe that they will never occur in the future since we know for certain that they occurred in the past. Moreover, it would be very foolish when you might live securely and quietly to throw yourself into the path of danger.

But if you who love the sea and its shore so much are not moved by this line of reasoning, perhaps you will be convinced by examples from antiquity. Read the Roman and Greek historians, and consider in those works how much ill fortune, how frequent the destruction of maritime cities, how many cities, even while they flourished with wealth, men, and money, have been captured by an enemy fleet before they could undertake their own defense. If the skeptics will reflect upon these examples, they will begin to understand that this city that is not a seaport lacks nothing but, rather, possesses (as it does in other matters) a gift of Divine Providence. Troy, "the most noble capital of all Asia" and (as the tragedian says) "an outstanding creation of the gods,"[6] was twice captured and destroyed by a fleet: the first time by the sudden arrival of Hercules and Thelamones, the second by the trickery of Agamemnon and Ulysses. That flourishing city could not have been captured in any way except for the opportunities afforded by the nearness of the sea. A decade had been consumed in useless land-based assault when finally the attackers left in a fleet upon the waves—a very useful element for disguising plots. Then the Trojans believed that they were at last free of the lengthy siege, and, since no hostile force appeared before them, they suspected nothing, "but the Argive host with marshaled ships was moved from Tenedos, amid the friendly silence of the peaceful moon."[7] And a little later: "Others sack and ravage burning Pergamum, are you only now coming from the tall ships?"[8] These are the rewards of the sea! For such reasons is proximity to the sea deemed praiseworthy.

But why do I discuss such a distant example? We read that the very fine Italian city of Genoa was captured and leveled to the ground during the Second Punic War by a single sudden assault by Mago, the son of Hamilcar.[9] Do I need to remind you of the destruction of the Phocaeans and the Syracusans, of Alexandria and Athens? Who does not know that at the time when the Roman people ruled over the entire earth the sea was infested for many years, by predatory fleets, so that a number of cities belonging to the Romans suffered complete destruction? And this people who had conquered the entire world could not preserve its seaports from the incursions of hostile fleets. Add to this the polluted air, the changeable weather, the debilitating diseases that derive from the unhealthfulness of coastal regions, and the harshness of the entire area of the seashore. In view of these and so many other adverse conditions, is it not surprising that a prudent city avoids a harbor so that it would be as secure as a ship in port? It prefers to do without the waves of the sea in order to avoid undergoing waves of invasions?

What indeed would a city without a harbor lack? Although I fear how my views will be received, still I shall say what I feel. As in all other respects, in this matter Florence has benefited from sage advice and Divine Providence. Florence is distant enough from the coast to be entirely free from all the difficulties that proximity to the sea carries with it, yet near enough to seaports so that it is not at all deprived of the use of the sea. It is only in nearness to the sea that Florence is vanquished by seaports, and in this matter the vanquished city is in reality the victor. To be sure, seaports derive some advantages from their harbors and beaches, but these advantages are always accompanied by dangers and alloyed with vexations. Indeed, Florence profits from its nearness to the sea but derives only pure advantage from its situation; it is never disturbed by misfortunes or threatened by dangers. The comfort of Florence is never vexed or threatened by pestilential climate, by fetid and impure air, by the humidity of the water, or by autumnal fevers. Rather, its utility is as pure as can be, not dangerous and total. Indeed, it seems to me that Florence is distant enough from the western Mediterranean to enjoy at the same time the benefits of proximity to the Adriatic. This happy situation cannot be praised enough. If Florence were situated on either coast in addition to being plagued with innumerable different vexations because of its nearness to the sea, it would be inconvenienced because it was too distant from the other. Hence, it would suffer from being at two extremes at the same time: both too near to and too far from the coast. But since Florence is equidistant from either coast, it seems not content with one of them but has sought to utilize both coasts at the same time; almost as the queen of Italy, Florence sits equidistant between the Tyrrhenian and Adriatic seas. It is set in a very healthy climate and is not far from either plains or mountains. Here lie very fertile fields, there arise smiling hills. Florence is further supplied by a river flowing through its midst, which is both of great beauty and of even greater utility. And in the city there are admirable splendors, incomparable beauty, stupendous architecture, and enormous magnificence. Moreover, the surrounding villas provide great and unheard of delicacies, amenities not of this world, and indeed complete joyfulness, pleasantness, elegance. Indeed, Florence is so filled with greatness and splendor that it excels by a long way not just the cities of Italy but even those of all the provinces of ancient Rome.

This abundance of beautiful things, which affords such rich material for easily describing the city, has seized me so completely and forcefully that I have not had any opportunity to rest. Perhaps I have constructed my speech so disjointedly that in attempting to describe all the fine ornaments of Florence I have passed over the first and best ornament of all. Occupied with describing the other beauty and magnificence of this great city, I had almost forgotten that I should really be talking about the people, the size of the population, and the virtue, industry, and kindness of the citizen-body, which is Florence's greatest treasure and among the first things that ought to come to mind. Therefore, it is time for me to return to my point of departure and to render those who inhabit Florence their due. So we ought to acknowledge that we have wandered a bit, and we ought to return to the subject of our speech. At this time we ought to collect our thoughts, leave behind those topics that we have already treated, and turn toward the subjects that we ought now to discuss, so that we don't persist in this error any longer.

II

Therefore, now that we have described what Florence is, we should next consider what manner of citizens there are here. As one usually does in discussing an individual, so we want to investigate the origins of the Florentine people and to consider from what ancestor the Florentines derived and what they have accomplished at home and abroad in every age. As Cicero says: "Let's do it this way, let's begin at the beginning."[10]

What, therefore, was the stock of these Florentines? Who were their progenitors? By what mortals was this outstanding city founded? Recognize, men of Florence, recognize your race and your forebears. Consider that you are, of all races, the most renowned. For other peoples have as forebears refugees or those banished from their fathers' homes, peasants, obscure wanderers, or unknown founders. But your founder is the Roman people—the lord and conqueror of the entire world. Immortal God, you have conferred so many good things on this one city so that everything—no matter where it happens or for what purpose it was ordained—seems to redound to Florence's benefit.

For the fact that the Florentine race arose from the Roman people is of the utmost importance. What nation in the entire world was ever more distinguished, more powerful, more outstanding in every sort of excellence than the Roman people? Their deeds are so illustrious that the greatest feats done by other men seems like child's play when compared to the deeds of the Romans. Their dominion was equal to the entire world, and they governed with the greatest competence for many centuries, so that from a single city comes more examples of virtue than all other nations have been able to produce until now. In Rome there have been innumerable men so outstanding in every kind of virtue that no other nation on earth has ever been equal to it. Even omitting the names of many fine and outstanding leaders and heads of the Senate, where do you find, except in Rome, the families of the Publicoli, Fabricii, Corruncani, Dentati, Fabii, Decii, Camilli, Pauli, Marcelli, Scipiones, Catones, Gracchi, Torquati, and Cicerones? Indeed, if you are seeking nobility in a founder you will never find any people nobler in the entire world than the Roman people; if you are seeking wealth, none more opulent; if you want grandeur and magnificence, none more outstanding and glorious; if you seek extent of dominion, there was no people on this side of the ocean that had not been subdued and brought under Rome's power by force of arms. Therefore, to you, also, men of Florence, belongs by hereditary right dominion over the entire world and possession of your parental legacy. From this it follows that all wars that are waged by the Florentine people are most just, and this people can never lack justice in its wars since it necessarily wages war for the defense or recovery of its own territory. Indeed, these are the sorts of just wars that are permitted by all laws and legal systems. Now, if the glory, nobility, virtue, grandeur, and magnificence of the parents can also make the sons outstanding, no people in the entire world can be as worthy of dignity as are the Florentines, for they are born from such parents who surpass by a long way all mortals in every sort of glory. Who is there among men who would not readily acknowledge themselves subjected to the Roman people? Indeed, what slave or freedman strives to have the same dignity as the children of his lord or master, or hopes to be chosen instead of them? It is evident that it is no trifling ornament to the city of Florence to have had such an outstanding creator and founder for itself and its people.

But at what point in history did the nation of the Florentines arise from the Romans? Now I believe that in the case of royal successions there is a custom observed by most peoples, namely, that the person who is finally declared to be heir to the king must be born at the time his father possessed the royal dignity. Those offspring who are born either before or after are not considered to be the sons of a king, nor are they permitted to have the right of succession to their father's kingdom. Surely whoever rules when in his best and most flourishing condition also accomplish his most illustrious and glorious deeds. Indeed, it is evident that, for whatever reasons, prosperous times stimulate men's minds and call forth great spirits, so that at such moments in history great men are able to do only what is important and glorious, and what is accomplished then is always especially outstanding.

Accordingly, this very noble Roman colony was established at the very moment when the dominion of the Roman people flourished greatly and when very powerful kings and warlike nations were being conquered by the skill of Roman arms and by virtue. Carthage, Spain, and Corinth were levelled to the ground; all lands and seas acknowledged the rule of these Romans, and these same Romans suffered no harm from any foreign state. Moreover, the Caesars, the Antonines, the Tiberiuses, the Neros—those plagues and destroyers of the Roman Republic—had not yet deprived the people of their liberty. Rather, still growing there was that sacred and untrampled freedom that, soon after the founding of the colony of Florence, was to be stolen by those vilest of thieves. For this reason I think something has been true and is true in this city more than in any other; the men of Florence especially enjoy perfect freedom and are the greatest enemies of tyrants. So I believe that from its very founding Florence conceived such a hatred for the destroyers of the Roman state and underminers of the Roman Republic that it has never forgotten to this very day. If any trace of or even the names of those corrupters of Rome have survived to the present, they are hated and scorned in Florence.

Now this interest in republicanism is not new to the Florentine people, nor did it begin (as some people think) only a short time since. Rather, this struggle against tyranny was begun a long time ago when certain evil men undertook the worst crime of all—the destruction of the liberty, honor, and dignity of the Roman people. At that time, fired by a desire for freedom, the Florentines adopted their penchant for fighting and their zeal for the republican side, and this attitude has persisted down to the present day. If at other times these political factions were called by different names, still they were not really different. From the beginning Florence has always been united in one and the same cause against the invaders of the Roman state and it has constantly persevered in this policy to the present time. By Jove, this was caused by a just hatred of tyranny more than by the well-deserved respect due to the ancient fatherland. For who could bear that the Roman state, acquired with the kind of virtue that Camillus, Publicola, Fabricius, Curtius, Fabius, Regulus, Scipio, Marcellus, the Catos, and countless other very honorable and chaste men displayed, fell into the hands and under the domination of Caligula and other monsters and vile tyrants who were innocent of no vice and redeemed by no virtue?[11] To excel in this these monsters were in a competition of mighty proportions, striving with all their power.

As a result of these struggles, every means of cruelty was employed in the annihilation of the Roman citizens, as though the highest prize in the world would be given to them only if they left in Rome no nobility, no political vitality, and even no citizen-body. Therefore, when Caligula had committed as many crimes as he possibly could, and many citizens still survived in that great city, the emperor, weary of killing and massacring and unable in any way to have his cruel desires satisfied, finally uttered that evil saying that serves as a witness to his enormities: "Would that the Roman people had but one neck, so that I could chop it off with a single blow."[12] Clearly he did just that. Not yet satisfied with the blood of the citizen-body, he would have made the city empty had he lived a little longer. In addition, he drove a sword through the senatorial order, he cut down the most outstanding members of the consular ranks, he cut off families at their roots, and he daily slaughtered whatever plebs were still left in the city as if they were cattle in droves. To this monstrous cruelty he added even more monstrous outrages, which indeed are uncommon and unequalled through all the centuries and have never been recalled without a curse. Three of his own sisters were, in turn, ravaged by him, and then they were forced to live openly with their brother as his concubines. Are these the deeds of emperors? Are these our splendid Caesars whom many think are worthy of praise? What crimes and outrages are these, and what monsters are these men! For these reasons who will wonder that the city of Rome had such hatred against the imperial faction and that this hatred has even lasted down to the present?

Now has there ever been a more just cause for indignation? Has anything ever touched the people of Florence more deeply than the sorrow of seeing the Roman people, its progenitor and founder, which only a short time before had ruled over the entire world with great ability, suddenly lose its own freedom at the hands of the most criminal of men? These were men who, if the Republic had survived, surely would have been counted among the lowest dregs of society. And what should I say of Tiberius Caesar, although he ruled before Caligula? (There is no need to proceed in chronological order when discussing those matters where there is neither order or reason.) Indeed, what more loathsome, more shameful things have ever been heard or seen than the brutality used by Tiberius in his torturing and extermination of Roman citizens on Capri? What could be worse than that same emperor's lovers and gigolos, who were given to such evil and unspeakable types of sexual behavior that it is, I think, to Italy's shame that such degenerates once lived there? But if these emperors were base and evil, were those who followed better? And who were these? Were they not Nero and Vitellius and Domitian and Heliogabalus? Yes, of course they were. Now it's not an easy thing to point out what was the nature of Nero's virtue and humanity. To be sure, his mother Agrippina praised the piety of her son to the skies; nor could one who showed piety toward his mother be thought capable of being impious and inhuman toward other men. Indeed, this is the same emperor who, in his great mercy, set fire to the city of Rome so his subjects would not be troubled by the cold!

O Gaius Caesar, what manifest crimes have you visited upon the city of Rome! But I will remain silent on this topic, for there are some who are irate that Lucan, a very learned and wise man, wrote the truth concerning those crimes. Perhaps they do so not without good reason, for although you displayed many and great vices, these were sometimes overshadowed by many and great virtues. Hence, the safest course is not to discuss you at all. For the same reason I shall not treat your adopted son, even though I am not ignorant of the reasons that led you to adopt him. But I am passing over all this. I shall not call to mind either his fatuous cruelty or his prescription and slaughter of innocent citizens or his treachery to the Senate or his adultery and sexual perversions; for there were in him—as there were in his father—the vestiges of certain virtues that made his faults more tolerable. But those monsters to whom you handed over the empire were redeemed from their vices by no virtues, unless it is perhaps a virtue to destroy the state with all one's might or never to refrain from the vilest crimes. For this reason I shall not recall your other deeds, but I cannot forget, nor do I think that I should not be angry, that you paved the way for so many evils and outrages that your successors perpetrated with ever kind of iniquity and cruelty.

But to what end? someone will ask. Really there are two reasons: first, to show that Florence has not, without good cause, developed its political allegiances; and second, to make it understood that at the time when Florence was founded the city of Rome flourished greatly in power, liberty, genius, and especially with great citizens. Now, after the Republic had been subjected to the power of single head, "those outstanding minds vanished," as Tacitus says.[13] So it is of importance whether a colony was founded at a later date, since by then all the virtue and nobility of the Romans had been destroyed; nothing great or outstanding could be conveyed by those who left the city.

Since Florence had as its founders those who were obeyed everywhere by everyone and dominated by their skill and military prowess, and since it was founded when a free and unconquered Roman people flourished in power, nobility, virtues, and genius, it cannot be doubted at all that this one city not only stands out in its beauty, architecture, and appropriateness of site (as we have seen), but that Florence also greatly excels beyond all other cities in the dignity and nobility of its origin.

But now let us turn to another topic.

III

Since Florence derives from such noble forebears, it has never allowed itself to be contaminated by sloth and cowardice, nor has it been content to bask in the glory of its progenitors or rest on its laurels at ease and leisure. Since it was born to such an exalted station, Florence has tried to accomplish those things that everyone expected and desired it to do. Thus, Florence imitated its founders in every kind of virtue, so that in everyone's judgment the city seemed completely worthy of its fine reputation and traditions.

Moreover, Florence did not refrain from fighting to show that it stood out among the leaders of Italy. It gained for itself dominion and glory not by deceit or trickery, not by covering itself with crimes and fraud, but by wise policies, by a willingness to face dangers, by keeping faith, integrity, steadfastness, and, above all, by upholding the rights of weaker peoples. Nor did Florence strive to excel only in riches; it sought to promote its industry and magnificence even more. Nor did it consider it better to be superior in power than in justice and humanity. With these qualities in mind, Florence strove to be the greatest of states; with these it acquired its authority and its glory. If Florence had not followed this policy, it wisely and truly knew that it would be falling away from the virtues of its ancestors and that its noble forebears would be more of a burden than an honor.

But Florence chose the wisest and best course of action. The same dignity and grandeur of the parent also illuminates its sons, since the offspring strive for their own virtue. And you may be sure that if the descendants had been cowardly or dissolute or had in any way fallen away from virtue, the splendor of the ancestor would not so much have hidden their vices as it would have uncovered them. The light of parental glory leaves nothing hidden; indeed, the expectation that the virtues of the parent will be reduplicated in the son focuses all eyes on the offspring. Whoever fails in these expectations to live up to the brilliance of their ancestors seems to be not noble but rather notorious on account of their descent. However, just as the grandeur of the ancestors scarcely aids those who are degenerate, so this same grandeur magnifies many times those descendants who possess high and noble spirits. Indeed, as their dignity and influence grows, these men are carried up to heaven, and they are placed together with their forebears in one and the same place on account of their own virtue and because of the nobility of their ancestors. Indeed, we have seen it happen in Florence that many men stand out as examples of excellence because of their great deeds, so that it becomes very easy to recognize in them their Roman virtue and the greatness of spirit. On this account, while Florence has been honored by the accomplishments and the splendor of its descent, it is even more honored by its own excellence and achievements.

But I think that I have already said enough concerning the brilliance of the city's origins—indeed, this is clearly manifest of itself. Concerning the excellence of the state, that is, how Florence has prospered at home and abroad, we should now speak. But I shall be very brief, and this speech does not allow a complete history of Florence; rather, I shall limit myself to the highlights. Before I come to this topic, however, I think that it would be appropriate and advisable for me to explain something and alert the reader, lest anyone, having gotten a false impression, might condemn me for being rash or ignorant. The former derives from levity, the latter from stupidity, and both are to be avoided. Now I do not doubt that a good many foolish men will suspect me and think that I wish with this my panegyric to win the good graces of popular acclaim, that I want to curry the favor of the mob, and that I am trying to capture men's minds as much as possible. Thinking this way, they believe that I have overstepped the bounds of truth and that in embellishing my speech I have mixed the false with the true. I want to advise such men, or rather disabuse them, so they will no longer think this way and will banish all their suspicions of my motives. Although I certainly wish to be loved and accepted by everyone (and I openly confess that I wish and desire this), still I have never been so driven by this desire that I would pursue it by means of flattery and adulation. For my part, I have always thought that one ought to make himself esteemed by others through the practice of virtue; not of vice. And I have certainly never expected or asked for any favors as a result of this panegyric. Indeed, I would be very stupid if I thought that I would be able to purchase the favors of a large citizen-body with this literary trifle. But once I had seen this beautiful city, once I had come to admire its fine site, architecture, nobility, comforts, and great glory, I wanted more than I can tell to try and describe its great beauty and magnificence. This is why I am writing this panegyric—not to curry favor or win popular acclaim. Indeed, it is so far from being the case that I undertook this labor in order to gain favor so that I would consider myself to be very lucky if I didn't generate more ill-will than good feeling against myself as a result of this speech. Rather, the great danger, as I see it, is that all those who have hated to see Florence flourishing will become my mortal enemies as a result of this panegyric. In fact, even now I continue to fear this. Thus my panegyric will make me an enemy of all those who are envious of or hostile to Florence and of all those men who have ever been troubled, beaten, or conquered by the Florentines or whose forebears were so affected—all these men will hate me. Accordingly, I am very much afraid that this work of mine will cause only hostility toward me. But I shall strike a bargain that no reasonable person can refuse. If I say in this speech anything that is false, self-seeking, or impudent, I shall gladly suffer the hostility and enmity of my listeners. But if what I say is true and if I express it with a becoming moderation, my listeners have no grounds to be angry with me. What bargain could be fairer than this? Who could be so perverse and evil that he could be angry with me if all I were trying to do was to provide the city of Florence with an appropriate and true panegyric?

Now, from all that I have just been saying, it ought to be clear that I have not undertaken the composition of this speech to win favor, nor can anyone justify becoming angry with me. But such are the various and natures of men that I do not doubt that there will be many who will hold that the line of reasoning I have just given is of little value. And, indeed, there will be others for whom truth itself is hateful and vexatious. There will be still others who, either because of the baseness of their natures or their ignorance of the subject matter, will hold nothing to be true except what accords with their self-interest. These men will accuse me of vanity and will bring charges that I have written nothing that is genuine. To these I say that they should not try to treat me cunningly nor hasten to accuse me rashly; rather, they should always realize that their views are reprehensible and should especially remember that I am not talking about the virtue or excellence of individual citizens but about the entire community. Indeed, if one or another citizen in Florence has lapsed into some small sin, this is no good reason to reprove and calumniate the entire city, especially since in Florence the deeds of evil citizens are not imitated but are criticized and corrected.

Indeed, no city has ever been so well governed and established that it was completely without evil men. But just as the good qualities of a few men cannot really free the foolish and perverse mob from its infamy, so the perversity and evil of a few ought not to deprive an entire nation of being praised for its virtuous deeds. Now there are both public and private crimes, and there is a great difference between the two. A private crime derives from the intentions of the individual wrong-doer; public ones are the result of the will of the entire city. In the latter case it's not so much a question of following the opinion of one person or another as it is of following what has been hallowed by law and tradition. Usually the entire city follows what the majority of the citizen-body would like. While in other cities the majority often overturns the better part, in Florence it has always happened that the majority view has been identical with the best citizens. For this reason these accuse me falsely and do not let them point out to me the evil deeds of a few individuals. This would be just as fallacious as reproving the law-abiding quality of the Romans because of the corruption of Verres or the bravery of the Athenians on account of the cowardice of Thersites.[14]

Now if my auditors want to comprehend how outstanding a city Florence is (and I have justifiably praised it at length), let them travel through the entire world and select any city they wish and compare it with Florence—not just in splendor and architecture (although in these things Florence is unrivaled in the whole world), nor just in nobility of its citizens (though all other cities cede to Florence first place in this category), but in virtues and accomplishments as well. If they will do these things they will begin to understand what a difference there is between Florence and other cities, for they will find no other city that can compare in any of these praiseworthy categories to our Florence.

I have said "any," and so I shall prove it forthwith. If they find some city that is judged in the common opinion of men to stand out in some kind of virtue, let them give proof of that same quality in which the city is said to excel. I do not think they will find any city that, even in its own specialty, is not inferior to Florence. In short, a city cannot be found that equals Florence in any given category—not in devoutness of belief, nor in economic might, nor in concern for fellow citizens, nor in the achievements of its people. Let them enter in this competition whatever city they like; Florence will take on all challengers. Let them search throughout the entire world for a city that is thought to possess great glory in one special kind of activity, and let there be a comparison of the most outstanding accomplishments in the field in which their city appears to excel; they will be unable to find anything—unless they simply want to deceive themselves—in which Florence is not far superior. Indeed, the excellence of this city is a real marvel, and as a city worthy of praise in every kind of activity, it is really without equal.

Now I'm not going to discuss practical wisdom, a quality that everyone has always conceded to Florence in any case and that we have always seen practiced here with great capacity. Was there ever such beneficence as this city has displayed and displays now? For this quality seems intended to help as many as possible and all have heard of the city's liberality, especially those who have needed it most. Because of Florence's reputation for generosity all those who were exiled from their homeland and uprooted by seditious plots, or dispossessed on account of the envy of their fellow citizen, have always come to Florence as to a safe haven and unique sort of refuge. Hence there is no one in the whole of Italy who does not consider himself to possess dual citizenship, the one of the city to which he naturally belongs, the other of the city of Florence. As a result Florence has indeed become the common homeland and quite secure asylum for all of Italy. Here everyone, when he has need, comes and is received by the Florentines with complete goodwill and supreme generosity. Indeed, the zeal for generosity and concern for others are so great in this state that these qualities seem to cry out in a loud voice and are openly acknowledged by everyone. Hence, no one will ever think that he really lacks a homeland so long as the city of Florence continues to exist. The acts of generosity performed actually are even greater than this policy might seem to require, for exiles are not only received with a welcome hand if they are not completely unworthy but also are often helped with gifts in kind and in money. Maintained by such gifts, the exiles can remain in Florence with complete dignity or, if they prefer, they can return to their own homeland and try to recover their property there. Are these not the facts? Have even the malcontents of Italy ever tried to deny it? No, this policy has been witnessed by an almost infinite number of people who, when they had been struck with poverty at home or had been exiled from their own cities, were helped from the public treasury and were restored to their homeland by the goodwill of the city of Florence.

There is, further, the example of many cities that, when they were oppressed by the conspiracies of neighboring states or the violence of domestic tyrants, were sustained by Florentine advice, aid, and money and thus brought through a difficult crisis. I shall omit the embassies sent wherever trouble has broken out to reconcile opposing viewpoints, for indeed this city has always been very prompt to use its authority in reconciliation. Can a city that has undertaken so much for the benefit of neighboring states not be called beneficent? Can it really be praised enough for its great virtue and many achievements? Florence has never tolerated injuries to other cities, nor has it ever allowed itself to be an idle onlooker while other states were in trouble. First Florence always tries with all its might and moral authority to settle disputes through negotiations and, if it can, to reconcile differences to persuade the parties to make peace. But if this cannot be accomplished, Florence always aids the weaker party, which has been threatened or harmed by the more powerful. Thus, from the very beginning Florence has always extended its protection to the weaker states, as though it considered its duty to ensure that no people in Italy would ever suffer destruction. Therefore, Florence has never in its history been led by a desire for leisure or has it, because of fear, allowed any other state to suffer great harm. Nor did it think that it had the right to remain at ease and at peace while any other city or ally or friendly state or neutral nation was in danger. Rather, Florence has always immediately stirred itself, taken up the cause of other cities, and shielded them from attack. Thus it has protected those states that seemed to be lost and aided them with troops, money, and equipment.

Who, therefore, could ever praise Florence enough for its beneficence and liberality? What city in the entire world can surpass Florence in this sort of achievement? Has not Florence expended vast sums and undertaken incredible risks for the defense of other states? Has it not protected many states when they were in danger? Since Florence has defended those states in time of peril, they have naturally begun to acknowledge it as their patron. And since Florence has become such a patron, who will deny that it surpasses other cities in dignity, might, economic power, and authority?

To this beneficence and liberality there has been added an admirable faithfulness to allies that this city has always preserved inviolate with complete constancy. It was with a commitment to this principle in mind that Florence always carefully considered whether it could really provide complete protection before it entered into any league. As a result, when Florence agreed to something it never went back on its promise. Therefore, when Florence has thought something out from the beginning and come to believe that its cause is just, no manner of expediency has ever been able to influence Florence to break any pact, treaty, league, oath, or promise that it has made. For nothing can be judged more proper to the dignity of a state than a reputation for observing all its commitments. Conversely, nothing is worse than betraying promises. The latter is the action of evil criminals who are the greatest enemies of the states. They are the sort who (according to Cicero) say: "I have sworn with my tongue, but in my mind I have sworn no oath."[15] That is a deceit that a just city can never tolerate. Therefore, a good city ought always to make its commitments after due consideration. And once it has committed itself to something, it should never consider permitting anything to be changed except for those things that are not in its power.

Moreover, since faithfulness and integrity have been so highly valued in this city, it has scrupulously observed agreements even with its enemies, and, as a result, Florence has never been accused of defaulting on its promises. On account of this it has happened that not even the enemies of Florence have doubted that the city would live up to its agreements, and among them the name of Florence has always carried great authority. This is the obvious reason for the fact that several men, though they had previously been Florence's worst enemies, gladly committed their sons and wealth to the guardianship of this people. They believed in this city's good faith and humanity; they saw that the second quality prompted the Florentines to pardon former injuries and furnish all due services, while the first ensured that the city would scrupulously observe what it had promised. Nor were they disappointed in their expectation. Indeed, it happened that the Florentines administered the property with great diligence and restored it to those to whom it belonged, justifying those who had believed in the good faith of this people. Indeed, their example of committing property to Florence's care was soon followed by others, for this city has always taken pains to give each one his due and in all things to put honor before expediency in all its dealings. Indeed, it has been the case that Florence considers nothing useful that is not at the same time honorable.

But of these many fine qualities with which I find this city has been endowed, I consider none greater or more outstanding or more consistent with Roman virtue and character than a certain loftiness of spirit and contempt for danger. Whose virtue could this be except the Romans? The Romans waged wars at every period in their history, and they engaged in enormous struggles and great military campaigns and—what is very rare and more incredible still—they never, even in times of greatest danger and difficulty, wavered from their purpose or permitted the debasement of their lofty principles. The emperor[16] was angry at the gates, threatening the ruin and destruction of Florence, and there followed him a group of Florence's enemies, resolute and ready to kill. This enemy was encamped within a mile of Florence, and the city resounded throughout with the sound of steel and the shouts of enemy troops. Nor even Hannibal approached the Porta Collina in Rome with more hostile intentions than did this monster plan his assault before the walls of Florence. What was worse, that part of the city most exposed to the enemy was not, at that time, well-fortified. Consequently, it was believed that no Florentine there dared to use his arms or offer resistance. Indeed, this valorous city only showed contempt for the emperor's threats and menaces. While the enemy revealed for several days outside the walls, those inside Florence felt no fear; rather, everyone went about his business as though no danger threatened or no enemy army was nearby. Every workshop, store, and warehouse was open; there was no slackening of industry, certainly none of government. When the emperor discovered this he marveled at the high moral and greatness of the city, and he gave up the siege.

This city has been powerful not only in resisting attacks; it has been even more formidable in applying force in response to previous attacks. Now although Florence has never tried to harm anyone except when it was attacked first, yet when it has been subjected to an attack the city has shown itself to be a most valorous fighter in maintaining its dignity. Every time Florence has taken the offensive, the city has been transformed by its amazing desire for praise and glory. Therefore, Florence has always willingly undertaken great and difficult causes. It has never shunned any cause because of the greatness of the danger or the difficulty of the task. I can call to mind some very well-fortified towns that Florence has captured and innumerable trophies of neighboring cities that the Florentines have seized. There also have been some outstanding feats of military skill performed by the Florentine people fighting outside their country. But this is not the place to describe many different wars, nor would it be possible to relate so many great feats. That would require a book of its own, and indeed a big one, which I hope I shall undertake sometime in the future[17] and commit to paper, and therefore to memory, how single feats were accomplished by the Florentine people. At present I shall content myself with one or two examples on the basis of which one can readily understand how great has been the virtue of Florence in other events.

Volterra is an ancient and noble town in Tuscany, but because it is situated on a high mountain top, even men who carry no burdens scarcely ever go there. The Florentines undertook a military campaign against this town,[18] for virtue accustomed to overcoming the greatest difficulties did not fear the harshness of the terrain nor the disadvantages of the combat. Therefore, when the Florentine forces sent there began to ascend the mountain, they were met by the defenders rushing down from their higher position, and the two armies were soon locked in mortal combat. The number of troops was about equal, but the Florentines possessed an advantage in fighting ability, while the nature of the terrain greatly favored the Volterrans. They used their superior position not simply to stop the Florentine advance with spears and swords; they also rolled large stones down the slopes. The Florentines, with a great effort of their own, struggled up the slope, and neither the weapons nor the stones nor the enemy troops nor the difficulty of the terrain could stop their assault. So, having fought their way step-by-step to the top of the mountain in the face of the enemy, the Florentines drove the Volterrans behind their walls. With the first assault the Florentines entered the town, although it did all this without any outside help; fighting only with its own troops, Florence courageously covered itself with glory and honor.

This accomplishment ought to seem remarkable to others and especially those who have actually seen Volterra are especially amazed by it, for it is obvious that no town in all of Italy is better fortified. Moreover, the town was being defended by brave men who were fighting valiantly for hearth and home. Yet they were overcome by an even greater valor. Who, therefore, cannot but admire those who captured this well-fortified city in a single day? Who would not praise to the heavens the valor of those who captured Volterra? Such are the deeds accomplished by this city! Such are its virtues and its bravery! With the same high morale, Florence has often been conquered the Sienese, laid low the Pisans, and vanquished powerful enemies and tyrants.

Still, what is really remarkable is that Florence has undertaken military campaigns and endured great hardship more often for the benefit of others than for its own profit. It especially ought to redound to its credit and honor that Florence has suffered many dangers for the freedom and security of other states and that it has safeguarded the welfare of many others out of its own resources. The Pisans, a nation rarely at peace with Florence, began a war against the people of Lucca who were friends and allies of the Florentines.[19] Finally, it happened that the long-awaited battle was joined between the two peoples, and in this conflict the troops of Lucca were defeated and many of them captured. The Florentines were at that moment making camp in the countryside near Pistoia, and when they heard what had happened to their friends they did not lose courage, nor did they fear the Pisans, who were fired up by their recent victory. Rather, the Florentines immediately broke camp and hurried to catch the victors, so they were able to intercept the Pisan forces before they had reached safety inside the walls of their city. The Florentines immediately joined battle with the Pisans and changed the fortunes of war so that the Lucchese, who had formerly been prisoners, now captured a great number of the Pisans who survived the slaughter and led them in chains back to the city of Lucca. In this way the military prowess of the Florentines saved the Lucchese, overturned the victory of the Pisans, and won for themselves laud and honor.

But what ought to be praised most in this outstanding Florentine triumph? Their military skill, which enabled them to win; or their high morale, which prompted them to pursue the victorious Pisans; or their generous spirit, which led them to undertake so great a battle on behalf of their friends? I think that the three ought to be viewed as one and the same deed that is to be praised. But I cannot laud every great deed with appropriate praise. Not only do I fear that there is not enough time, but larger topics demand my attention.

It has been not simply to this or that city that Florence has shown its beneficence but to the whole of Italy. Indeed, it would be judged properly an act of small import if Florence has undertaken these endeavors only for its own safety, but it is a glorious matter if a great many states have known and enjoyed the benefits of the Florentines' efforts. Indeed, it is a fact that Florence has always been motivated by a desire to protect the safety of neighboring cities that found themselves at war. Whenever such a state was threatened by some neighboring tyrant or the greedy desires of a nearby republic. Florence always opposed the aggressor, so it has always been clear to everyone that Florence treated these as its own homeland and fought for the liberty of all Italy. Nor indeed would Florence, so motivated, have accomplished its goal except that many times the pious and just will of God favored the course of action taken by this city. I do not want to go back to old examples but, rather, shall relate what our own age has just seen. I think that it is obvious in any case that the whole of Italy has been liberated from the yoke of servitude by Florence on more than one occasion. But let us omit these other instances and consider only what was done very recently.

Can anyone so feeble of intellect or so devoid of truth be found who would deny that all Italy would have fallen under the power of the Duke of Lombardy had not this one city resisted his power with its troops and sound strategy?[20] Who in all Italy then had either power or resources comparable to that enemy? Who would have endured to the end the attacks of an enemy whose very name brought terror to every mortal? Indeed, his reputation struck terror not only in the Italians but in peoples north of the Alps as well! He was well provided with resources, money, and men, but, most of all, he possessed cunning and political wisdom. And he had great and formidable power. All of Lombardy, and nearly all of the cities on the peninsula between the Alps and Tuscany and the Romagna, were under his rule and obeyed his orders. In Tuscany, he held Pisa, Siena, Perugia, and Assisi in his grip, and eventually he even occupied Bologna.[21] Besides many cities and many powerful noble houses followed his name and fortune, either out of fear or motivated by hope for booty or perhaps led on by his trickery. His followers did not lack in financial rewards, gifts, and counsel. Indeed, the Duke could have been a happy—a very happy—man if he had but put his resources, his energy, and his genius to good purposes. No man ever possessed a shrewder or cleverer mind. He was present everywhere, he left nothing unnoticed, nothing untried. And he acquired friends: some with money, others with expensive gifts, and still others with the promise or semblance of his friendship. Sowing seeds of discord, he set the nations of Italy at one another's throat, and when they had worn themselves down, he stepped in and occupied them with his overwhelming power. So eventually his cunning ways prospered everywhere. Hence many governments, seeing these great powers, became very frightened and began to temporize. But the stout Florentine heart could never know fear, nor could it ever consider surrendering any part of its honor. Florence knew that it was a Roman tradition to defend the liberty of Italy against its enemies, precisely as its ancestors had dared to fight against the Cimbri, the Teutons, and the Gauls. These ancestors had not feared the ferocity of Pyrrhus or the deceits of Hannibal, nor had they ever avoided any undertaking that would preserve their dignity or their grandeur. Rather, they underwent great hardship in order to gain great glory. So the Florentines were ready to do anything if they felt it would vouchsafe for them the good reputation that had been handed down to them by their ancestors. It was with these things in mind that the Florentine people set out for war in great and high spirits. So this people thought that it would live with great glory or perish fighting valiantly for its principles. Moreover, the Florentines believed that the position inherited from their ancestors had to be protected, so that they could never place concern for their wealth before their own self-esteem. Indeed, they were prepared to lose money and life itself to maintain their freedom, considering their situation both realistically and courageously. Now wealth and money and such things are the rewards of the victors. But those who think that in war they should conserve their wealth, since they think they make themselves more secure with this wealth, are in fact serving the interests of the enemy more than their own. With such a high morale was this city endowed, with such a measure of military skill did it meet its powerful and resourceful enemy in combat, that Florence compelled him who shortly before had menaced all Italy and believed that no state could resist him to wish for peace and to quake behind the walls of Pavia. In the end he not only abandoned the cities of Tuscany and the Romagna, but he even lost a large portion of northern Italy.

O incredible magnificence and excellence of Florence! O Roman people and race of Romulus! Who would not now esteem the name of Florence with great honor on account of the excellence of its spirit and the vast dimensions of its deeds? What greater thing, what more outstanding feat could this city accomplish, or in what way could it better prove that the virtue of its forebears was still alive than by liberating the whole of Italy, by its own efforts and resources, from the threat of servitude? As a result of this feat, Florence daily receives congratulations, praises, and thanks from all nations. But all these accomplishments have been credited by Florence to the will of Almighty God. Always possessing a certain modesty, Florence has preferred to credit its deeds to divine intervention rather than claim them on account of its own virtue. Consequently, Florence has never become inflated in its successes, nor have its victories been accompanied by retribution against those states that Florence could, by right, have hated. Rather, it has always maintained complete humanity toward those whom it has conquered, so that those who knew Florence's courage in time of war experienced its mercy in time of victory. Of the many great virtues of this city this one stands out: to maintain its dignity at all times. Florence has shown no greater concern than making sure that it maintained its dignity in the process of accomplishing great feats. Therefore, Florence did not exult immoderately at its successes, nor did it collapse in times of adversity. It showed modesty in success, constancy in adversity, and justice and prudence in all of its actions. Hence, its great name had acquired even greater glory among men.

IV

As Florence is admirable in foreign affairs, so it has outstanding civil institutions and laws. Nowhere else do you find internal order, such neatness, and such harmonious cooperation. There is proportion in strings of a harp so that when they are tightened, a harmony results from the different tones; nothing could be sweeter or more pleasing to the ear than this. In the same way, this very prudent city is harmonized in all its parts, so there results a single great, harmonious constitution whose harmony pleases the eyes and minds of men. There is nothing here that is ill proportioned, nothing improper, nothing incongruous, nothing vague; everything occupies its proper place, which is not only clearly defined but also in right relation to all the other elements. Here are outstanding officials, outstanding magistrates, an outstanding judiciary, and outstanding social classes. These parts are so distinguished so as to serve the supreme power of Florence, just as the Roman tribunes used to serve the emperor.

Now, first of all, great care is taken so that justice is held most sacred in the city, for without justice there can be no city, nor would Florence even be worthy to be called a city. Next there is provision for freedom, without which this great people would not even consider that life was worth living. These two principles are joined (almost as a stamp or goal) to all the institutions and statutes that the Florentine government has created.

Indeed, the magistracies were created to carry out justice; they have been empowered to punish criminals and especially to ensure that there is no one in Florence who stands above the law. Thus, all conditions of men must submit to the decisions of these magistracies, and they must pay due respect to the symbols of these offices. In many ways care has been taken that these upholders of the law to whom great power has been entrusted do not come to imagine that, instead of the custodianship of the citizens, a tyrannical post has been given to them. Many provisions are made so that these magistrates do not lord it over others or undermine the great freedom of the Florentines. First of all, the chief magistracy that is commonly viewed as possessing the sovereignty of the state is controlled by a system of checks and balances. Hence there are nine magistrates instead of one, and their term is for two months, not for one year. This method of governing has been devised so that the Florentine state may be well governed, since a majority will correct any errors in judgment, and the short terms of office will curb any possible insolence. Moreover, the city is divided into four quarters so that each section can never lack its own representative, and from each quarter two men are elected. And these men are not chosen by chance, but they have the approval of the citizens for a long time and are judged worthy of such a great honor. Now, in addition to these eight citizens, the task of governing the state is entrusted to one man, outstanding in virtue and authority and chosen in rotation from these same quarters. He is the chief of the priorate and bears the standard that is the symbol of the rule of justice over unruly men. The nine men, to whom the government of Florence is entrusted, can live nowhere except in the Palazzo Vecchio, so that they may be in a better position to govern the city. They are not to appear in public without their sergeants, for their dignity demands that they be treated with respect. Indeed, because it sometimes happens that there is a need for a larger council, the Twelve Good Men are added to discuss public matters together with the nine priors. Besides, to these are joined the standard-bearers of the Companies whom the whole population supports and follows since it is necessary to protect liberty with arms. These standard-bearers are also part of the council, and, like the higher magistrates, they are elected by quarter. They hold office for a term of four months.

These three colleges do not have power over all matters to be decided. A great many decisions, once they have been approved by these magistracies, are referred to the Council of the People and Council of the Commune for final action. Florence thinks that what concerns many ought to be decided by the action of the whole citizen-body acting according to the law and legal procedure. In this way liberty flourishes and justice is preserved in this most holy city. In this system nothing can be resolved by the caprice of any single man acting in opposition to the judgment of so many men.

These men oversee the government, uphold justice, repeal laws, and ensure equity. The power to dispense justice according to the legal procedure, and especially the power of life and limb, is given to minor magistrates who are not citizens but foreigners brought to Florence from distant cities and states. This custom is followed not because Florentines don't know how to act as judges (indeed they are employed daily in this capacity in many foreign cities) but, rather, to ensure that, from the judicial system, enmity and feuding will not arise among the citizens. For it often happens that, led on by their desire to be lenient, judges mete out some punishment other than what the statutes allow. Such judges, although they may, strictly speaking, have been judging correctly, cause a great deal of hostility toward their office. More than this, it seems objectionable for one citizen to stand in judgment over the life of another in a free city such as Florence, for whatever a native judge does, even if he is very just, will be viewed by the other citizens as abominable and horrible. Because of this our judges are imported from distant cities, and for them the procedures are carefully prescribed so that they cannot deviate from them in any way. They enter their office with an oath that, like stewards, they will render account of their administration of justice to the people when they have finished their term of office. Thus in every particular, the people enjoy freedom and are in control.

Moreover, in order to make it very easy for each person in this vast city to receive his due, that is, so that while the magistracies are busy with some individuals will not lack justice and law, the authority to judge and hand down sentences concerning disputes among their own members has been given to certain groups. In this fashion, the heads of the guilds of merchants and bankers and other guilds have the right to hand down sentences on their members. There are still other magistracies that have been established to ensure the public good and the piety of the people: among these are numbered the officials of the gabelles, the heads of the Monte and the guardians of wards' property. These are among the more useful offices because they attend to promoting public and private welfare and health and piety in this great city.

But of all the magistracies, and there are many in this city, none is more illustrious, nor founded on loftier principles than that called the heads of the Parte Guelfa. Perhaps it would not be pointless to say something about the origins of this organization. Hence, a short digression will not be completely useless, I hope, and perhaps worthwhile.

After the defeat of the Florentines in pitched battle at Montaperti, it seemed certain that the city could not be defended on account of this great blow to the state.[22] Therefore, all citizens of high and noble spirits, so they would not be ruled over in the city by those who had obviously been traitors to Florence left their homes and hearths, and went to Lucca with their wives and children. In doing this they followed the outstanding and laudable example of the Athenians, who abandoned their own city during the Second Persian War in order to be able to live there someday in peace and freedom.[23] Therefore, with this in mind, these outstanding citizens, who survived that great battle, left Florence, thinking that by doing this they would have a better chance for revenge than if they remained starving and waiting their fate shut up behind the city walls. So they went to Lucca, and there they joined up with other Florentines who had been scattered in the course of the battle. Very soon they brought together arms, horses, and military equipment, so that everyone marveled at their energy and resolve. They performed many feats of bravery throughout Italy. The exiles often fought to aid friends and to defeat men of opposing political allegiance by their courage and military skill. Moreover, from every endeavor they always emerged victorious, so that it finally seemed that the time was ripe for what they wanted most: to remove utterly the stain and blot on their homeland. Hence they set out against King Manfred of Sicily, who was leader over different factions in Italy and who had contributed knights to the enemy army at the battle of Montaperti. The Florentine exiles were under the leadership of a great and skillful general whom the Pope had brought from France to curb the insolence of this same Manfred.[24] After a while the army came to Apulia—and I would really like to describe in detail the great courage that the Florentines displayed on that occasion, but this is not the place for a lengthy narrative. To put it very briefly, the Florentines fought so well that even their most bitter enemy felt compelled to praise their skill and bravery. Thus, after they won at Tagliacozzo in Apulia and destroyed their enemy, honored and laden down with spoils and booty, the Florentine army returned to Tuscany. Immediately they expelled from Florence those who a little while before had governed the city so evilly, and they wreaked a splendid vengeance on their enemies in nearby cities. At this point the Florentines established a college composed of the chief men who had been the leaders of the Parte Guelfa and had taken a leading role in this noble and just campaign.

From its very foundation, this magistracy has always had great authority in Florence. For almost everything has been placed under its care and vigilance so that Florence would never be turned away from the sound policies established by its forebears, nor would it ever come under the control of men of different political sentiments. What the censors were to Rome, the areopagites to Athens, the ephors to Sparta, these heads of the Parte Guelfa are to the city of Florence. This is to say that these are the chief men who oversee the constitution and who are elected from among those citizens who love the Florentine state.

Therefore, under these magistracies this city has been governed with such diligence and competence that one could not find better discipline even in a household ruled by a solicitous father. As a result, no one here has ever suffered any harm, and no one has ever had to alienate any property except when he wanted to. The judges, the magistrates are always on duty; the courts, even the highest tribunal is open. All classes of men can be brought to trial; laws are made prudently for the common good, and they are fashioned to help the citizens. There is no place on earth where there is greater justice open equally to everyone. Nowhere else does freedom grow so vigorously, and nowhere else are rich and poor alike treated with such equality. In this one also can discern Florence's great wisdom, perhaps greater than that of other cities. Now when very powerful men, relying on their wealth and position, appear to be offending or harming the weak, the government steps in and exacts heavy fines and penalties from the rich. It is consonant with reason that as the status of men is different, so their penalties ought to be different. The city has judged it consistent with its ideals of justice and prudence that those who have the most need should also be helped the most. Therefore, the different classes are treated according to a certain sense of equity; the upper class is protected by its wealth, the lower class by the state, and fear of punishment defends both. From this arises the saying that has been directed very often against the more powerful citizens when they have threatened the lower classes; in such a case the members of the lower class say: "I also am a Florentine citizen." With this saying the poor mean to point out and to warn clearly that no one should malign them simply because they are weak, nor should anyone threaten them with harm simply because someone is powerful. Rather, everyone is of equal rank since the Florentine state itself has promised to protect the less powerful.

Florence not only protects its own citizens in this way, but it extends the same protection to foreigners. No one here, citizen or foreigner, is allowed to suffer harm, and Florence strives to ensure that each is given his due. Moreover, the justice and spirit of equity in Florence promote toleration and humanity among the citizens since no one can be prideful or disparage others while all men experience the same benign rule. But who can be skillful enough to describe fully, in the short time remaining, the honorableness of life and high moral standards in this city? Certainly there are many great men of genius in this city, and whenever they agree to do something they easily achieve more than other men. Whether they follow the profession of arms or devote themselves to the task of governing the state, to study and scientific knowledge, or to business—in every profession and in every endeavor they undertake they excel far beyond other mortals. No other people surpass them in any respect. Here they remain patient in their labor, ready in time of danger, eager for glory, brilliant in giving advice, industrious, generous, magnificent, pleasant, affable, and, above all, civil.

Now what shall I say of the persuasiveness of their speech and the elegance of their discourse? Indeed, in this category the Florentines are the unquestioned leaders. All of Italy believes that this city alone possesses the clearest and purist speech. All who wish to speak well and correctly follow the example of the Florentine manner of speech, for this city possesses many men who are so expert in their use of the common vernacular language that all others seem like children compared to them. The study of literature—and I don't mean simply mercantile and vile writings but that which is especially worthy of free men—which always flourishes among every great people, grows in this city in full vigor.

Therefore, what ornament does this city lack? What category of endeavor is not fully worthy of praises and grandeur? What about the quality of the forebears? Why are they not the descendants of the Roman people? What about glory? Florence has done and daily continues to do great deeds of honor and virtue both at home and abroad. What about the splendor of the architecture, the buildings, the cleanliness, the wealth, the great population, the healthfulness and pleasantness of the site? What more can a city desire? Nothing at all. What, therefore, should we say now? What remains to be done? Nothing other than to venerate God on account of His great beneficence and to offer our prayers to God. Therefore, our Almighty and Everlasting God, in whose churches and at whose altars your Florentines worship most devoutly; and you, Most Holy Mother, to whom this city has erected a great temple of fine and glimmering marble, where you are at once mother and purist virgin tending your most sweet son; and you, John the Baptist, whom this city adopted as its patron saint—all of you, defend this most beautiful and distinguished city from every adversity and every evil.

———— ✳ ————

Oration for the Funeral of Nanni Strozzi[25]

———————

There was an ancient law of Solon (in my opinion, a very wise man) which was also confirmed and warranted by the custom of his very wise city: it provided that citizens who had died fighting for their country should be accorded, after the private ceremonies, a public funeral with a splendid display of words as well as outward things. The latter were devoted to the funeral procession, the former to the praise of those who had perished.

The same law provided for their children, so that the city took care of them as if they were public offspring, bestowing upon them public education and care and every consideration. Certainly a foresighted and excellent law, and worthy of the reputation of Solon, one of the Seven Wise Men! What more useful or more honorable law can be imagined than this, which beckons men by the prospect of honor to defend their country, and at the same time alleviates the parents' misfortune by undertaking to care for orphans? For generally, be they ever so brave, men retreat from danger not out of fear for themselves, but out of concern for their children, especially their little ones; to be willing to leave them abandoned and orphaned seems to be in some fashion contrary to nature's law which enjoins upon us the duty of nourishing and caring for the children whom we ourselves have produced. But surely there could be no greater justice or gratitude than for those who have been orphaned for the country's cause to be supported by the country as if they were its children. Thus the glorious death of the parents would not mean loss for the children, but an actual increase in their resources.

What moved me to recall this celebrated and praiseworthy law was the glorious death of a distinguished man, the Florentine knight, Nanni Strozzi, who died fighting in this war which our city and the Venetians are now waging against the duke of Milan. He has left young children behind, orphans destitute of parental care, for he set love of country before love of children. Since all the circumstances foreseen in Solon's law are present, we believe that he and his children have a deserved and just claim to all of its benefits. For what death could possibly come closer to the situation envisaged by the law? Those who can and ought to will make provision, I trust, for the honor of a public funeral and for the education and care of his children. Meanwhile we shall attempt to supply, in accordance with the law, a eulogy in keeping with his merit; it will be written as if it were to be spoken at the very end of the funeral.

To the honor of the funeral of this great man, we are now appointed to add the praise of appropriate words, so that honored by a magnificent display of outward things, and commended in distinguished fashion, he may go his fatal way in the happy knowledge that his country has rendered him his full due. The legislator's circumspect mind and foresight are praiseworthy in many respects; for when verbal embellishment has been added to the physical display, the gratitude of the living becomes visible and the virtues and deeds of the deceased are disclosed as if illumined in a kind of splendor, and the grief of his kinsmen is delineated in proportion to the glory of his accomplishments.

This important responsibility for pronouncing the eulogy which has been entrusted to me would not seem to me a burden at all if only I had the talent and the ability to satisfy what is expected in such a glorious type of address. But I know that it is very difficult to do this worthily, and that without great talent and great eloquence one should not attempt it, especially since in a public funeral eulogy it is appropriate to include a eulogy to the city, too. A city, however, demands a particularly sublime tone, if I may put it so, and a grand, distinguished style of address. It is not within the capacity of every man to exhibit such distinction; it requires a man with wide public experience, who excels in this very kind of speaking and in eloquence.

For any eulogy that suffers from some weakness will often detract from those you wish to eulogize, and their reputation will decline with the skill of the eulogizer, so that it is sometimes better to keep silent altogether than to embark upon a eulogy unskillfully. The desires of the listeners are totally discordant. To the kindly disposed, nothing seems enough, while the envious and malevolent listener rejects it all as excessive exaggeration; so that it is almost impossible, given such variations among men, to temper the ears of the multitude. Nevertheless, though not at all unaware of these difficulties, I have been persuaded by my feeling for the deceased and by my country's command to surmount them as well as I could. I beg, however, and entreat everyone who hears me to consider my effort rather than my achievement. And so, after these preliminary remarks, I turn now to the real subject of my address.

This funeral oration is one which calls for neither weeping nor lamentation. Grief should be reserved for those who, when they die, leave nothing that could console their survivors. This man's life was the best that could be wished for, and his death wholly glorious, so that it could seem a thankless task, given such an abundance of successes, to bewail either his manner of living or his manner of dying. If we were to try to explain these successes, we should have to say that a great many of them, and among these the greatest, fell to his lot by some sort of divine favor. Foremost honor is deservedly given to his native land, for that is the first and prerequisite basis of human happiness, to be put as object of veneration ahead even of parents. If we begin therefore with a eulogy of his country, it will be recognized that we have chosen the right beginning for our address.

For the city in which he was born is one of the greatest and most illustrious; it is possessed of a wide dominion, and universal respect. It was without question the chief city of the Etruscans, and is second to none of the Italian cities in birth, wealth or size. To the origin of the city the two noblest and most distinguished peoples of all Italy contributed: the Etruscans, who were the ancient lords of Italy, and the Romans, whose virtue and arms enabled them to establish an empire over the world. For our city was a colony of the Romans, who were assimilated with the older Etruscan inhabitants. The Etruscans, however, were always the first people of Italy, supreme in authority and wealth. Their power, before the empire of the Romans, was such that this one people gave its name to both of the seas that encircle Italy. From the Alps to the Sicilian Straits, the whole length of Italy was for many centuries ruled by this one people. This one people was responsible for bringing the worship of the immortal gods, and learning and letters, into Italy. This one people taught the other peoples of Italy all the arts of peace and war. As for the Romans, it is better to say nothing of their power, excellence, virtue, glory, magnanimity, wisdom, or of the greatness of their empire than to dispose of these in a few words. What city, therefore, can be of better or nobler birth, or be better endowed with the glory of ancient forefathers? Or indeed which of the most power-ful cities is to be compared with ours in this kind of distinction? Deserving also of commendation are our ancestors who, when they fell heirs to this city, established institutions and governed in such a manner that they seem to have departed as little as possible from the virtue of those from whom they were descended. They were guided by such wisdom in the enactment of sacred laws for the stability of the republic that these have become a model of good government for other peoples. Others, however, have never served as a model for the Florentines, who have managed by continuous attention to preserve or to increase their influence and power. Accordingly, there has never been a time within the memory of man when this city has not been the capital of Tuscany. Also deserving of praise are the citizens of this present age, who have extended the city's power even beyond what they inherited from their fathers, adding through the exercise of virtue and arms Pisa and other large cities to their dominion. But there is not time now to record all these wars and battles and great deeds. They would call for extended treatment, the labor of many years rather than a day. But leaving behind now, or deferring, foreign affairs, let us, if I may put it this way, look into and examine the body of the city itself.

The constitution we use for the government of the republic is designed for the liberty and equality of indeed all the citizens. Since it is egalitarian in all respects, it is called a "popular" constitution. We do not tremble beneath the rule of one man who would lord it over us, nor are we slaves to the rule of a few. Our liberty is equal for all, is limited only by the laws, and is free from the fear of men. The hope of attaining office and of raising oneself up is the same for all, provided only one put in effort and have talent and a sound and serious way of life. Virtue and probity are required of the citizens by our city. Anyone who has these two qualities is thought to be sufficiently well-born to govern the republic. The pride and haughtiness of the powerful are so vehemently hated that more severe laws have been enacted to penalize this kind of man than there are for any other purpose. The proud were finally conquered and compelled by the law's quite adamantine chains to bend their necks and to humble themselves to a level beneath that of the middle class, so that it is regarded as a great privilege to be allowed to transfer from the category of the *grandi* into that of the *popolo*. This is true liberty, this is fairness in a city: not to have to fear violence or injury from any man, and for the citizens to be able to enjoy equality of the law and a government that is equally accessible to all. But these conditions cannot be maintained under the rule of one man or of a few. For those who prefer royal government appear to ascribe a virtue to the king that they grant was never present in any man. What king has there ever been who would carry out all the acts involved in government for the sake of his people, and desire nothing for his own sake beyond the mere glory of the name? This is why praise of monarchy has something fictitious and shadowy about it, and lacks precision and solidity. Kings, the historian says, are more suspicious of the good than of the evil man, and are always fearful of another's virtue.[26] Nor is it very different under the rule of the few. Thus the only legitimate constitution left is the popular one, in which liberty is real, in which legal equity is the same for all citizens, in which pursuit of the virtues may flourish without suspicion. And when a free people are offered this possibility of attaining offices, it is wonderful how effectively it stimulates the talents of the citizens. When shown a hope of gaining office, men rouse themselves and seek to rise; when it is precluded they sink into idleness. In our city, therefore, since this hope and prospect is held out, it is not at all surprising that talent and industriousness should be conspicuous.

Our city has so large a population of citizens that, beyond the countless numbers living on their native soil, there are countless more spread out through the whole world. Without mentioning Italian cities, which are never lacking in Florentine citizens, and passing over those who live in Rome, Naples, Venice, Bologna, Ferrara, Rimini, Mantua and other Italian towns, there is not a place in the world so distant and so remote that it does not have a Florentine citizen living there. If you inquire about Britain, which is almost the farthest island in the world and situated in the ocean, you will find a great multitude of our citizens there; if you search Gaul or Germany, there will be a great number of our citizens where you least expected them. Why should I mention Paris, Barcelona, or Avignon? In these towns whole colonies of our citizens have been accustomed to live. What should I say about Pannonia, or about Sicily, once the most celebrated of islands? In sum, not to tarry further over particular towns, there is not a single place from Tanais and Maeotis to the columns of Hercules and the ocean sea in which a Florentine citizen will not be found. Accordingly, if the whole total of our absent citizens, scattered over the entire world, should be added to the multitude of those present, the result would be such an enormous population that no city of Italy could quite be compared with it in this respect.

In talent and intelligence our citizens are so capable that they have few equals, and no superiors. They possess shrewdness, and industry, and an ability to do things with speed and agility, and sufficient breadth of conception for the proper conduct of affairs.

Our strength lies not only in our government of the republic, in our domestic organization, and in our pursuit of business abroad; we also have a reputation for military glory. For our ancestors fought in the dust and battle-array of many a glorious war, with their warlike virtue conquered all their neighbors, broke a thousand enemy wedge-formations, and erected countless monuments of victory. Our city has moreover supplied the most powerful kings with their military chiefs; it has produced the leaders best versed in military science.

What should I say about letters and studies, in which our city enjoys by universal consent a great and brilliant preeminence? I am thinking and speaking not of vulgar and commercial subjects, although our people excel in these, too, but of the more cultivated and godlike branches of learning which are regarded as having a superior excellence and an eternal, immortal glory. Who can name any poet, of this or an earlier age, who was not a Florentine? Who but our citizens brought back to light and into practice this art of public speaking which had been completely lost? Who, if not our city, recognized the value of Latin letters, which had been lying abject, prostrate, and almost dead, and saw to it that they were resurrected and restored? Wherefore if Camillus (although he was not the original founder) is rightfully called the founder of Rome on the ground that he restored it after it had been lost and occupied, why should this city of ours not, by the same logic, be called the parent of the Latin language for restoring it to its splendor and dignity from its recent state of ruin and corruption? And just as we thank Triptolemus for giving us all the grain that has since been produced, so any literary or cultivated branch of learning, wherever it has developed, must be credited to our city. Now, even the knowledge of Greek letters, which had become obsolete in Italy for more than seven hundred years, has been brought back by our city so that we may contemplate the great philosophers and admirable orators and the foremost men in other branches of knowledge, not through the enigmas of inept translations, but face to face. Finally, humanistic studies them- selves, which are the best and most distinguished branches of learning and the most appropriate to humankind, being essential to private as well as to public life, were embellished by our native literary erudition and came, with the support of our city, to spread throughout Italy.

As for resources and wealth, I am afraid that it might inspire envy if I were to report our apparently inexhaustible supply of money. Evidence of it is this long Milanese war which has been waged at incredible cost, in which we are spending over thirty-five hundred thousand [florins], and nevertheless men are prompter in paying their levy now when the war is drawing to a close than they were at its beginning, so that there seems to be a kind of monetary force in our economy which sends up new shoots every day as if by some divine power.

——— ✳ ———

On the Florentine Constitution

———

Since you wish to know about the constitution of our city, of what sort it is, and how it is constructed, I shall try to describe it as clearly as I can. The Florentine constitution is not completely aristocratic or democratic, but a kind of mixture of the two. This is quite clear from the fact that certain noble families are forbidden, because they have too great a power of numbers and of force at their command, to hold the chief offices in this city; and this rule is anti-aristocratic. On the other hand, mechanics and members of the lowest class do not participate in the political life of the community; and this seems to be antidemocratic. Thus, avoiding the extremes, the city looks to the mean, or rather to the best and the wealthy but not over-powerful.

An assembly of the people takes place very seldom in this city, because everything is previously taken care of, and because the magistrates and the councils have such authority to decide matters that there is no need for the assembly unless a great change is required, in which case the whole people is convoked. Then indeed the people is sovereign, and the assembly is dominant, but as we have said this happens very seldom.

The highest office in the city is that of the nine magistrates, whom we call Priors. Only two of these are plebeians of the guilds; all the rest belong to the aristocratic and wealthy class. First among them is the Standard-Bearer of Justice, which no one can ever be unless he be distinguished by birth and reputation.

Besides the nine magistrates there are twenty-eight men who serve as councilors and assistants; these do not reside in the palace, but are summoned by the Nine, when it is necessary to discuss a matter regarding the community. They call them colleagues, but we might refer to them as senators. The nine magistrates, acting together with these senators, have a great deal of power, especially from the fact that nothing can be brought before the great councils which has not first been agreed to by the Nine and the senators.

The great councils of this city are two in number: the Council of the People, numbering three hundred, and the one drawn from the nobility, numbering two hundred. A matter which a council is called upon to consider must first be closely examined by the Nine and the senators, and after being decided upon by them, is brought before the Council of the People. If it is passed by this council, it is then brought before the other council, of the nobles. If it is passed by this council, too, the matter is decided, and we say that something voted in this manner has the force of law. This is the way we deal with matters of war and peace, of the making and dissolving of alliances, of audits, immunities and public charges, and with all matters of concern to the city.

If the Council of the People does not agree with the proposition decided upon by the Nine and their colleagues, it is invalid and cannot be brought before the other council. If, on the other hand, it passes the Council of the People, but the other council fails to endorse it, it is invalid. Thus it has to be approved three times: first by the Nine and the senators, next by the Council of the People, and thirdly by the Council of the Nobles.

I think that you can now see the outline of this polity. For the great councils take the place of the people and its assembly; the nine magistrates and the senators the place of the council, as these terms are to be found in the text of decrees: "Decreed by the Florentine Council and People," and this is how we interpret them.

Since the magistrates are concerned with all these matters, it remains to observe how and from among whom they are chosen. Every five years there are magisterial elections, which take place in the following way: the Nine magistrates, together with the senators and certain other persons, being assembled in the palace, scrutinize the whole list of citizens, voting on them one by one. Whoever gets two-thirds of the votes becomes eligible. This does not mean that he takes office immediately, but that he is designated as qualified to take it when it may fall to his lot. When all the votes have thus been taken and the qualified persons have been designated, each name is separately written down and placed in certain purses, by section of the city.

The city is divided into four sections, which we call quarters, and there are as many purses bearing the names of the citizens who have been designated as qualified for election. When the time comes to choose new magistrates, names are drawn by lot from the purses, two for each section of the city.

The standard-bearers have separate purses in each section, for this honor belongs by lot to each section of the city, since it is a kind of leadership that the whole city must share.

The election of the senators takes place in the same manner as that of the nine magistrates. There are two kinds of senator: one is composed of the captains of the *gonfaloni*, and each is chosen from his *gonfalone*. There are sixteen *gonfaloni* in the city, and each has its own captain. The second group of senators is composed of twelve men, called "good men," and they are elected, not by tribe but by section of the city, that is, three from each quarter. That is how the twenty-eight senators or councilors of the Nine magistrates are created.

As for the great councils, we have said that there are two: the Council of the People and the Council of the Nobles. Their members are chosen by lot, after everyone has first been scrutinized and found worthy, and the names have been put into purses by *gonfalone*, except that the elections do not take place every five

years, but whenever necessary. It is the common procedure, however, for all qualified officers to be chosen by lot, after they have been voted upon and found to be
qualified.

But the choice by lot is not the end of the process, if some other obstacle or
impediment turns up. There are many such impediments: age, nepotism, time,
privilege. The age restriction excludes youth from office: nobody can become a
member of the Nine or of the colleges if he is under thirty, nor standard-bearer if
under forty-five, nor a member of one of the great councils if under twenty-five.

Family relationship strictly prevents taking office. For if my brother, or father,
or son or any other relative is in the magistracy, I cannot take office as a magistrate.
The laws forbid two members of the same family to serve at the same time in the
magistracy.

The time restriction blocks those who have just been magistrates. For it is not
permitted for them to become magistrates again until three years have passed, nor
for a relative to become magistrate until six months have passed. If anyone has not
paid the assessed tax, or has otherwise failed to acquit his obligations to the community, these are also impediments.

Thus chosen, then, are the magistrates who conduct the public business of
the city.

The laws and the magistrates concerned with private law are different, the latter
not being citizens, but foreigners. For this function, notable and well-born persons
from other cities are chosen. They receive their salary from the community, to
induce them to come to serve as judges in our city. They judge in accordance with
our laws, and punish the guilty and the wicked.

They are of two categories: one of them has authority over financial and commercial cases and the like. The other is responsible rather for the correction and
punishment of evil-doers. The term of these offices is six months; when the period
comes to an end, these judges are investigated before leaving, and are held to
account for their conduct in office.

The reason for calling upon outsiders to fill these offices is to avoid the development of enmities among the citizens. For the man who has been condemned generally hates and complains against his judge, whether justifiably or not. On the other
hand, the outsider may impose punishments upon the citizens more justly and
independently than a citizen might. And as the death and blood of the condemned
leaves its stain upon the judge, this too seems harder to bear in a free and equal
city if the citizen has imposed such a penalty on a fellow citizen. Finally the outsider
will be more afraid than the citizen of the investigation of his conduct if he violates
the law. For all these reasons, they thought it better to have punishments imposed
by outsiders.

It would be appropriate next to speak of the laws of the city, but this part
demands a long investigation. For the present we shall say merely this: that the

city uses the Roman law, and was indeed a Roman colony. For Sulla the dictator established this colony, with the best Roman stock, with the result that we have the same laws as the mother-city, except for such changes as have been brought about by time.

Since the constitution is a mixed one, as we have said, it is correct to describe it as having some tendencies toward democracy, and some toward aristocracy. One of the democratic tendencies is for the magisterial terms of office to be so short. The highest office—that of the Nine—is no more than two months; some of the senators serve three, others four months.

The designation of short terms of office for magistrates is a democratic feature, and tends toward equality. Democratic, too, is the fact that we so highly honor and protect our freedom in word and deed, as the very purpose and objective of the whole constitution. Electing our magistrates by lot and not according to any property assessment is another democratic characteristic.

On the other hand, there are many features which show an aristocratic tendency. The system of preliminary discussion, and the impossibility of bringing a matter before the people until it has first been formulated, and the requirement that the people may not change the text, but must accept or reject it as a whole, seems to me most aristocratic.

This city too has experienced, as I believe other cities have also, various transformations from time to time, sometimes in favor of the many, sometimes in favor of the aristocrats. When, formerly, the people used to march forth under arms and fight its own battles, and (because the city was overflowing with population) could overwhelm almost all the neighboring cities, power in the city was in the multitude, and accordingly the people had the advantage, so that it was able to disenfranchise almost all the well-born. With the passage of time, warfare came to be carried out instead by hired foreigners, and then it seemed that political power should no longer be in the multitude, but in the hands of the aristocrats and the wealthy, because they contributed so much to the community, and had counsel to offer in the place of arms. Thus, as the power of the people gradually dissolved, the constitution became established in the form which it now possesses.

Chapter 5

POGGIO BRACCIOLINI

In Praise of the Venetian Government

(1459)

Poggio Bracciolini (1380–1459) spent the first fifty years of his public life in service to the papacy, both in Rome and abroad, before becoming—at Cosimo de' Medici's encouragement—chancellor of Florence in 1453. A Tuscan native trained as a notary, Bracciolini made profound contributions to Italian letters: he recovered scores of Latin and Greek manuscripts (including Lucretius's *De rerum natura*) throughout Europe, engaged in numerous public exchanges with fellow scholars (the most heated with Lorenzo Valla over biblical philology), and wrote a history of Florence that picked up where Bruni's left off. *In Praise of the Venetian Government* represents one of the most meticulous and enthusiastic analyses of the laws and mores of the republic of St. Mark, and, just as important, one of the most severe indictments of ancient polities such as Rome and Athens.

The text is a reprint of Poggio Bracciolini, *In Praise of the Venetian Government*, in Jill Kraye, ed. and trans., *Cambridge Translations of Renaissance Philosophical Texts*, volume 2, *Political Philosophy* (Cambridge: Cambridge University Press, 1997), 135–44.

--- ✳ ---

In Praise of the Venetian Government

I have long desired to praise as best I could the singular excellence in every department of the Venetian Republic, but have hitherto been prevented by my many occupations of an official and domestic sort, as well as by a certain diffidence as to whether I could find eloquence equal to the task. Now that I enjoy greater leisure, however, and bearing in mind that fortune favours the brave, I have resolved to set out in writing what I had long had in mind, with the double aim of celebrating such a magnificent city as it deserves and of encouraging other cities to imitate the institutions of this well-ordered republic by a rehearsal of their merits. If ever there has been a republic that deserved praise and celebration, if ever any held in honour the prescriptions of justice, if any ever through its good customs has maintained dignity and respect in all its dealings both public and private, if there has ever been anywhere where the common good was put before private advantage, that republic is surely Venice, a city whose repute eclipses all others that have ever been, or are or may be in future.

As Aristotle says, there are various sorts of constitution, of which two in particular stand out from the rest, namely monarchy and aristocracy, or what we call government by the best.[1] Indeed, Cicero says in De legibus that the best sort of constitution is that in which the best men, as he chooses to call them, are in power:[2] men motivated by desire for praise and esteem, who keep their fatherland safe, true lovers of the republic. Such a constitution, I can say with confidence, has only ever been found in Venice. With the Venetians, only the best govern the state, under constraint of the laws, and intent, everyone of them, on the advantage of the commonwealth without consideration of personal gain.

Aristotle never saw such an aristocracy, nor indeed had he read about the existence of one. For if he had ever had occasion to study this polity, in which one noble is set above the others as head,[3] though himself obedient to the rule of law, while the other aristocrats like the limbs of a body attached to the head follow the dictates of justice as a sure guide to action, he would doubtless have given this form of government preference over all others. Here he would have seen a quasi-king, as it were, and after him the aristocrats acting together with a common mind and a common voice for a common goal: the combination of monarchy and aristocracy in a single constitution. We must necessarily think that this is the best form of government of all. In fact, Aristotle himself says that it is better to be ruled by many good men than by one only.[4] In that case a monarchy must be inferior to an aristocratically governed republic in proportion as the talents of many people are more extensive and abundant and in practice better than that of one man alone, just as the benefits they bring would diffuse more widely than those of a single person; and their wisdom and integrity would carry with them greater advantages than his virtues could by themselves. This was the view of Lampridius in the Life of Alexander Severus, where he says: "Your grace is well aware of the saying you will have read with regard to Marius Maximus, that a republic is better, and so to say in safer hands, when the prince alone is bad than when the prince's friends are bad, for one bad man may be set straight by many good ones, but no one man, no matter how good, can possibly prevail over many bad ones."[5] How then shall we judge a republic which joins to a good leader excellent advisers and bends to one united will the talents of many men? Obviously, it is to be thought a very happy state of affairs and such a republic will be supreme above all others, even if Aristotle never knew it.

I imagine that Plato too, had he been able to examine this remarkable manner of governing a city, would have taken it as the model of his *Republic*.[6] There he sought the best possible form a republic might take, having laid down that it must be based on justice. Justice was in turn secured by reward and punishment, so that the good were encouraged to seek praise by having their virtue rewarded, while the bad were to be deterred from wrongdoing by the prospect of having their misdeeds punished. And this must be the very state that the philosophers were looking for, since it is on their principles that the republic is founded: here justice has mastery over all, and through justice the good are honoured and the evil punished, as each deserves.

To bring out more clearly by comparison the special qualities of Venice in the operation of justice, let us look at some ancient constitutional arrangements and the practices of antiquity. The Spartans come in for great praise for having supposedly lived for almost seven hundred years with the same set of laws and absolutely invariable customs.[7] But their form of government was always changing, and their state never stayed the same for long—now subject to kings, now to tyrants, now torn apart by different factions, now shaken with internecine feuds. All this shows that Sparta was by no means a peaceful and contented state but deeply unhappy and turbulent, given over not so much to the public weal as to private hatreds; and so at length, after many disasters, it passed under Roman sway.

The nature of the constitution enjoyed by the state of Athens is explained by the Greek historians. Power of decision on all questions rested with the common people, and what was agreed by plebiscite was taken to be ratified and binding. When the mob had been roused by these decisions, the leading aristocrats were apt to be expelled from the city, excellent citizens would be condemned to death by sentence of the people, their chief commanders punished by exile or prison. Athens was in turn in thrall to kings or cruel tyrants, or prey to the fickleness of the common people—a perverse city indeed, that rewarded the good service of its military commanders with all sorts of trouble, a city constantly unsettled by discord within or wars abroad, where reprobates were preferred to honest men, and scoundrels were actually summoned to occupy the offices of state. It was accordingly no surprise that their liberty was soon lost.

Similar failings led to the collapse of the state of Thebes, as it fell under alternating sway of the more powerful citizens and of tyrants, or was troubled by faction within the state: you might say it was more a mass of competing interests than a republic.

It is said that Carthage was a great and powerful republic, which engaged in a struggle for supremacy with the Romans over almost four hundred years.[8] But we also read that it had a variety of administrations all characterized by cruelty and barbarous savagery. It is certainly true that it either killed or exiled its generals, despite all their great qualities. So it is to be viewed more as a haughty and violent tyranny than as a proper republic.

The Roman republic was the greatest that has ever been seen and is celebrated above all the rest. In literature and oratory it equalled or surpassed all others, and in the arts of war it was without rival. It had many men of great stature across the whole range of human endeavour. Yet everyone knows the number and nature of the revolutions that took place in the free republic from the very beginning—the sudden reversals of fortune, the quarrels and feuds, the uprisings of a fickle populace, the great and frequent struggles between the fatherland and the mob, the trials of strength between the senators and consuls on one side and the tribunes of the people on the other. Alienation and hatred, wars which went beyond mere civil war,[9] theft and plunder, proscription of citizens and fine men driven into exile—in short, there arose in the republic commotions without number, like a stormy sea whipped up by the constant battering of waves. I shall not rehearse the acts of theft and sacrilege, the rapes and killings, the wrecking of cities, committed by consuls, praetors and other magistrates, nor the lust and greed of the Roman soldiery. I pass over the dreadful despotism showed towards subjects and the terrible crimes perpetrated in the provinces due to the unspeakable passions of our ancestors. Cicero witnesses that more allied cities were destroyed by quartering Roman soldiers than enemy cities by the force of their arms.[10] I shall not mention the various coups launched against the republic and the vast lands that were given over to Roman avarice. Why bring up Verres and Clodius and Catiline and all those other conspirators who were born for the destruction of Rome and her provinces?[11] I think it would be accurate to say that for many centuries Rome was not a republic at all but a den of thieves and a despotism of the cruellest sort. Neither law nor morals nor traditional institutions nor the courts counted for anything. Egged on by the tribunes, the order of the day was might and cold steel, leading to slaughter in the forum and in the temples. Cicero himself complained that the republic no longer existed, nor the courts nor the Senate, but everything was done at Caesar's whim.[12] There was a time with the early Romans when the republic deserved the name; but even then one has to take into account the Secession of the Plebs,[13] the willfullness of the Decemvirs,[14] the exiles of Coriolanus[15] and Camillus.[16]

The Venetian Republic, on the other hand, is very different from those of bygone ages—it is quite without those faults and vices which have been the ruin of other cities and republics. There is no discord or dissent among the Venetians as to how to govern the republic, no feuding between citizens, no factions or quarrelling, no open enmities. All of them take the same view, all of them with one mind rush to the aid of the republic, to which they direct their constant thoughts and on whose welfare they spend all their effort. Their whole aim and object is that their state should be as happy as possible. This may seem a thing very difficult to achieve in such a great city, but it will not surprise anyone who considers the manner of their government. There are a great many very ancient noble families with whom the governance of the republic lies. No commoner is granted the opportunity of civic service, public office being reserved for the nobility, and of the nobility only the foremost men. One and all accordingly behave like the limbs of a single body and act together with one mind for the city's safety and well-being, regarding it as if it were their own mother who was to be cherished and cared for.

The virtues of this city, then, are rightly thought to surpass by far all the others. The most conclusive proof is that fact that for seven hundred years and more, down to our own day, the Venetians have persisted with the same customs and institutions based on the laws, the doge and magistrates—something which has never occurred in any other republic.

Of all the many qualities to be praised in this marvellous state, the first is perhaps its location, which in my view adds greatly to the credit of the city. It is so situated that although it has no encircling walls nor ramparts to defend it, the Venetians could be safer or less fearful of siege engines or machines of war. No sudden charge or unexpected enemy attack holds terrors for them. Surrounded on all sides by sea, Venice is free from external threat, being five miles from the mainland and reachable only by sailed through banked channels, so that there is nothing to fear from that quarter. It is also equipped with only one port, which bigger ships cannot enter when they are laden; and the Venetian galleys and other boats can easily block off the approach of any enemy fleet. In all other parts the water is stagnant and marshy and cannot be used by large vessels. There is therefore nothing to fear either from cavalry attack or enemy ships. There is besides a broad wall of heaped-up boulders some twenty miles long, which is kept stable by great wooden piles:[17] this serves to protect the city from the full force of the waves and keeps the marshy lagoon undisturbed.

What is truly remarkable—the great and glory and ornament of Venice—is the vast Arsenal with its magnificent shipyards, which far surpass any others in the world and for whose maintenance special levies are raised. Here are berthed more than 100 galleys, all fitted out with weapons (to say nothing of those used for trade), and a great many cargo ships: they could if need be set to sea with a fully fitted-out fleet of 150 large ships inside a month. As for smaller vessels, they have an almost infinite number, the greatest part of them adapted to the transport of vital supplies. As one would expect, everything that is needed to support such a large city is imported in great abundance, so that the Venetians need fear no scarcity. The great number of ships makes a fine sight as they come and go, now to nearby places, now as far away as Pontus and the Black Sea and other ports of the infidels, besides trading voyages to Spain and France, Flanders and Britain. It is a great spectacle of the city to see them returning laden down with their various cargoes and then transferring their goods for transport to other parts of the Mediterranean or Italy.

I need not describe the splendours of their homes and palaces, the sumptuously built churches, the squares and public places—a whole city packed with craftsmen. Nor need I dwell on the modesty of the young or the dignity of the old, the natural authority of the men or the majesty of the Senate, of which one could truly say what Cineas said of the Roman Senate, that it seems to be made up of kings.[18] Indeed, all the citizens have an air of grandeur about them, with their fine clothes and elegant possessions, on which they lavish a good deal of care. In addition, the whole city is criss-crossed by canals as well as paved streets, and this brings them considerable advantages, since everything that they need for daily life can be brought to their homes in boats. The chief glory of Venice, however, is the size and splendour of the churches, which the Venetians adorn with various objects for religious veneration. But this they have in common with many other places. Where they really stand out from the rest is in the treasure of the church of San Marco, whose opulence and ornament make a marvellous sight. There is a great mass of silver and gold, and of pearls too and the so-called precious stones, which are both rare and highly prized.

I shall turn now to my second theme, the rational and orderly system under which everything is administered and carried out at Venice, and say something of the group of magistrates to whom the government of the republic has been entrusted from the very foundation of the city. From the beginning, the citizens elected a doge to act as their head, a man who was to be set above the rest and who would act in the republic's interests. Yet he is still subject to the rule of law, and though of a higher status he is on a level with all the rest when it comes to observing the laws. If he commits a crime, for example, he is duly punished by a magistrate according to legal prescription. On his own he is without power: he may not act in the name of the republic without being obliged to consult a committee of six men,[19] whose advice is binding; he cannot write state letters, open those brought before him or give any audience or official response. The council of six has the real power in the state, always subject to the laws. It is elected by vote of the Senate and may be removed by its decision, if the need arises, but nearly all members die in office. It may still be brought to trial, all the same, if it should act in any way that deserves censure. But the fact that, as they say, no doge has ever aspired to tyranny, save for one who paid with his life,[20] shows how deeply rooted in the Venetian mentality is the respect for decency and justice, and how modestly the doges have lived over these many centuries. And that unique case is all the more remarkable since ambition and the love of power are such widespread failings among mankind. But with the Venetians patriotism extinguishes all other passions and casts out whatever mad longings men have.

They realize that they are the guardians, and not the masters, of the laws. They realize that they share with others the responsibility for governing the city and are not entrusted with absolute power. The special merit of their laws is that they are completely solid and stable, and they remain in force as long as they continue to serve the republic. They are not repealed at the whim of individuals nor amended from day to day, but are kept safe by perpetual sanctions. Besides those I have mentioned, there are also ten men selected annually from the leading citizens, to whom is given the power of judgment over wrongdoers of all sorts in proportion to their crimes.[21] There is no appeal from their sentence, and their decisions may not be reopened. There is a special magistracy concerned with administration of the law, before whom cases of citizens and foreigners are tried.[22] The proceedings are not conducted on the basis of allegations written down by notaries or the trickery of professional advocates, but by equity, moderation and reason; this leads to a great saving of both time and expense. Nor do they place any reliance on outsiders to administer or deliver justice. Members of the magistracies themselves deliver the law, and their decisions are so temperate that there is seldom any dissent from them.

To these must be added the so-called Procurators of San Marco, men of probity and authority elected from the entire body of citizens, whose function is to supervise the finances of the church. They disburse for pious purposes any surplus remaining after the religious services and upkeep of the fabric have been seen to. There are also what are called officers of the night,[23] whose task is to mete out appropriate punishment for minor crimes, especially those committed at night.

In addition, there is a smaller assembly of two hundred men, called the Rogati, in whose meetings all those magistrates I have mentioned take part. In these sessions the doge presides on a raised dais, the rest being seated after him according to their status. Here decisions are reached after discussion on all matters concerning the state of the republic, and in particular on matters of war and peace. When the need arises, they convene an additional, larger Council [Maggio Consiglio], of which all nobles over the age of twenty are members. By their votes are elected all the governors and other officials who are entrusted with administering the provinces and towns outside the city, as well as those chosen for some special mission. It is open to all who may chance to be at this meeting to nominate and elect anyone they wish. The nominees who are elected by vote of the Council are obliged by law to give those who nominated them a certain cash sum. In this way two virtuous acts are rewarded: that of the man who nominates someone worthy office, and that of the nominee if he achieves office. Rivalry and contention among the citizens are thus centred on virtue and not on hatred or violence. All of them strive to become men of such high moral character in the eyes of their fellows that they will get more votes than the other candidates.[24] And votes are not won by campaigning or solicitation; so the path to high office lies open to the very best. Each of them thinks that they too share in the success if they nominate someone who is thought deserving of office by the Senate's vote. I remember that certain persons were once subject to a heavy fine for having solicited votes for a friend. In public affairs, they want men's judgment to be completely free, not bought with cash or entreaties. It therefore seldom happens that anyone is selected to govern others unless his own integrity has been tried and tested. If any governor shows himself greedy and cruel in relation to his subjects beyond what the law allows, severe punishment follows. The victims are allowed to make complaints and seek protection from injustice. The Venetian governors therefore keep their hands free of any stain of wrongful conduct, always acting in accordance with the laws, which are entirely devised with a view to the promotion of justice.

This manner of life, these habits and arrangements have never changed since they came into being. The city is governed with such reverence and equity, political power is so evenly distributed to all in office, honours are so equitably granted to the citizens, that the state appears to be preserved in this marvellous concord not by men's devices but by divine assent, not by an earthly monarchy but by some heavenly kingdom. Their whole concern and object, each and everyone one of them, is what they think will benefit the republic. If ever there is a diversity of opinion, as sometimes happens when matters of peace and war are being debated, the view of the majority is approved and followed, and even those who dissent will change their vote to conform with the larger party. No one perseveres in obstinate opposition, no hatreds or feuding unsettles the republic. Everyone permits his view to succumb to that of the majority. And so it happens that differing opinions are reduced to unanimity and are not the occasion of faction or conspiracy amongst the citizens. You would think that they were all of one will, one heart and one mind, one united view. No household with any decent man at its head, no brothers or relations ever seek their own private benefit with such concord and fellow feeling as the Venetians show in maintaining standing and prestige of their city. No one consults his own interests in their deliberations but all keep the common good in view.

A special merit of the Venetians is that when someone is condemned for a crime, sentence is carried out as soon as he is caught. Justice takes its course without special pleading or mitigation, without evasion or intercession on anyone's part. Exiles are rarely allowed to return to the city without paying the penalty. And though the Venetians are harsh in the administration of justice, they are nevertheless at the same time very reasonable. If a man is deprived of his offices for his sins, or exiled from the city or even put to death, he alone is punished for the crime. They allow the rest of his family or household, whether his sons or his relations, to be elected to magistracies, to take part in committee meetings, to attend the Council and undertake public duties, since they have done no wrong. It often happens that a father is driven into exile, while his son keeps the position and status that he had before, in accordance with the biblical prophecy that "the soul that sinneth, it shall die."[25] Only the guilty are punished in Venice the others keep their standing untouched. Nor may anyone rail at another's faults or subject him to verbal attack, in case it leads to vituperation or feuding between citizens. Once they have given their word, they stand by it with the utmost fidelity. Nothing is thought more shameful than to renege on a promise.

One great virtue which sets them apart from the rest is the secrecy with which they treat matters raised in the Council. Discussions of questions of state are regarded as highly confidential. Their decisions are shrouded in such secrecy that they only become known when they are put into effect. They discussed the execution of the general Carmagnola for almost eight months, and yet their deliberations were quite unknown until he was captured and paid the price of his folly.[26]

And what of their wonderful generosity towards those who have served Venice well? Everyone who has benefited the republic receives ample benefits in return. A great many men have been admitted to the ranks of gentry, and even to the nobility, for their good services towards the city. This alone puts it above all other cities past or present as a model of virtue, an exemplar of gratitude, a spur to good deeds.[27]

What shall I say of their upright characters, which they have kept intact and uncorrupted down the ages? They speak with the greatest candour, without sarcastic abuse, snide criticisms or bad language. Their conversations are marred by no odious quarrels or slander of one another, for they hold verbal and physical decency in the greatest respect, cultivating the virtue of decorum so highly praised by Cicero.[28] They pay the utmost honour to old age and adopt the good old Spartan custom of allowing older citizens to take precedence and have greater prestige the older they get.[29] The young people are given an admirable education: from their earliest years they are so brought up that you would think them born for a life of modesty and decency. They are given no schooling except what will fit them for literature and business. They also spend considerable effort on the pleading of cases, in which they are occupied for a good deal of their time. The older ones among them are particularly respected as they yield to their own elders in a graceful display of their dignified manner of life. This arrangement of their early lives leads to a well-spent youth and the emergence of better men, and ultimately fine and modest senior citizens. A man who has been schooled in decency from his first youth will find no difficulty or labour in following virtuous ways in later life. As Aristotle says, the upbringing and moral education one has received at the outset may well determine the course of the rest of one's life.[30] It rarely happens that an early life which has been coloured by bad morals and nourished on evil ways can turn out a good man and an upright citizen.

How flourishing our Christian religion is among the Venetians, and how highly valued, is demonstrated by the splendidly decorated churches and basilicas. There are a great many religious houses which the citizens go to for prayer and the frequent distribution of alms to the needy. They are very pious, especially in the matter of caring for citizens who have fallen on hard times and lost their livelihood. These they do not oppress or throw into prison, as often happens elsewhere; instead, they life them up and sustain them with hope of a better future. They reckon that the city's vitality is itself diminished if they abandon citizens who have suffered some disastrous stroke of fortune.

It is marvellous to see the care and effort they put into attracting people to live in the city. They offer a wide variety of employments and ensure a regular food supply, so that life for the common folk may be as convenient as possible. People of modest means are not burdened with taxes, nor are they exposed to injury or disaster, and the city is consequently always well populated. What really preserves the city and binds it together in concord is the scrupulous fairness of the tax system. It is not based on the arbitrary whim of the powerful: all the leading citizens pay tax according to their means as determined by the census. They alone take responsibility for the city's public expenditure; and the more people that pay, the less onerous the taxes appear to individuals, since a burden that falls on everyone equally is borne more easily. And so it happens that when they have to go to war on land or sea, money is always available, nor is an opportunity ever missed to carry out a job properly for want of funds.

In this matter of the control of public expenditure, they are in advance not just of Italian cities but of any country in the world. The census of the citizens and their resources has always been carried out in the old Roman fashion, and that has proved the salvation of the city. In time of war it is not a case of one man being ruined while another is enriched, as we see happening elsewhere, but losses hit everyone equally hard, as if from a single inheritance. For that reason they are very careful about declaring war and prefer to deliberate rather than to decide on a course of action. They are even cautious in their deliberations, bearing in mind the possible expense and danger and giving lengthy consideration to the likely outcome of events.

It is greatly to the Venetians' credit that they keep the northern Mediterranean free of pirates. If any of their citizens do fall prey to robbers on the sea, they make sure the crime does not go unpunished. They will pursue them wherever they go with a fleet of armed ships until they are taken and punished, or the stolen goods returned. But they are as concerned with restraining their citizens while they are in office and punishing those guilty of wrongdoing as they are with pursuing thieves and pirates. A father may castigate a son who occupies a magistracy, or a son a father, according to the nature of the misdeed. There is no place here for mitigation by intercession or pleading or the claims of friendship. The laws are supreme, and no one transgresses them, no one repeals them or bends them to his own interpretation. If someone pillages the treasury or squanders the resources they hold in common or secretly filches from public property or fraudulently tries to divert it to his own private advantage, he is at once convicted and given a stiff sentence. It is considered a great disgrace, and a matter of perpetual ignominy, when the names of such people are annually read out in public in the Council, in order that the stain of this infamy may deter others from such crimes.

Under the doge and these magistracies and by virtue of these laws, institutions, customs and constitution, the Venetian people have for more than seven hundred years not just kept their republic intact but daily extended their empire by land and sea, so that their glory now resounds throughout the whole world. In the time of Charlemagne, the Venetian doge was Maurizio, whose son was captured by the Lombard king Desiderius, and then freed and restored to his father by Charlemagne.[31] I should not deny—in fact, I freely admit—that there were a good many doges before Maurizio. But it is cause enough for praise and honour that an identical form of constitution has endured for so many years, something that has happened in no other city. When I come to consider the causes of the republic's durability, one reason in particular stands out: the justice which Aristotle said was the surest basis of any state has flourished here as nowhere else;[32] here laws, not men, are in charge. That virtue has by itself ensured the stability and durability of the Venetian republic to this day. No other city, no other kingdom, no other republic has existed so long, with such austerity and such integrity. Nowhere else has justice been held in such honour. Nowhere else has the law of the people been so deferred to. We must hope that, if anything in human affairs can last, this republic with its constitution and customs (provided always that faction is absent) may rival eternity.

Chapter 6

ALAMANNO RINUCCINI

Liberty

(1479)

Scion of a prominent Florentine merchant family, Alamanno Rinuccini (1426–99) studied philosophy with the Byzantine scholar Johannes Argyropoulos and translated the works of Plutarch and Isocrates, among others, into Latin. Rinuccini held high domestic and diplomatic positions in the Florentine government and was a trustee of the University of Florence. Originally a Medici partisan, he became disenchanted with the family's reign after Lorenzo de' Medici's consolidation of rule following the failed Pazzi conspiracy in 1478. Written from self-imposed exile in the countryside, the dialogue *Liberty* discusses Florence's past greatness and fiercely denounces the "tyranny" of Lorenzo.

The text is a reprint of Alamanno Rinuccini, *Liberty*, in R. N. Watkins, ed., *Humanism and Liberty: Writings on Freedom from Fifteenth-Century Florence* (Columbia: University of South Carolina Press, 1978), 193–224.

———— ✳ ————

Liberty

Preface to his brother, Alessandro:[1]

When I took up a way of life, my beloved brother, not much different from the one you yourself profess, I was encouraged by your advice and that of certain friends, but I know full well that my decision met with disapproval from some who envied me and some, perhaps, who did not understand. They did not like to see me give no further consideration to practically any of the affairs of the city and devote myself, almost like an exile, solely to the cultivation of this little house and farm. They did not approve of my leaving all public concerns and all unnecessary personal ones. We can silence their criticism, of course, by calling on the testimony of various famous men, but you alone seem enough of an example. You lived in the great English city of London, representing the richest and most eminent company of all that were there and enjoying the favor and good will of your superiors. The way you did business made it clear that only lack of desire prevented you from amassing an enormous fortune. All these things you put aside, however, and what is more, relinquished your considerable personal inheritance, in order to live a kind of life you thought would give you leisure with dignity and undisturbed tranquility. I could not do the same, for I was already committed to the care of wife and family, but I chose the nearest approximation, a life far from the crowded city and innumerable anxieties associated with the greed and ambition which it fosters.

I have been unable to avoid some well-meant reproaches from friends, however, and I have made, as you will see, a rather long answer to their objections. Rather than let them change my determination in the least, I won them over to my own opinion. After the grievous loss of my only son, I was living sorrowfully in the villa he himself had frequented and was avoiding the company of men. Two persons of our academy came to see me at that time on a visit of condolence. I shall not put their names in writing lest, if some of the talk that took place among us seems to attack a certain person, these men might have reason to complain that I published the freely spoken words of a friendly conversation. So I have invented names appropriate to their characters and sentiments, which I think suggest them both well enough. If you recognize them, I look forward to your comment on that. But if you cannot give me your opinion on the choice of names, I would still appreciate it on the substance of the discussion at least, and I look forward to hearing whether you agree.

This is how it all happened: they were returning from the Casentine and went out of their way to visit me. By chance they found me at home, reading something or other, and after the sort of things customarily said when friends first meet again, they spoke at length on the themes of comfort and consolation. Finally Alitheus, hoping to distract me from the oppressive grief that weighed on me, suggested to Microtoxus that he say in my presence what they had been saying about me on their trip.

So he began as follows.

Dialogue on Liberty Begins

Speakers: *Alitheus* (the Truthful), *Eleutherius* (the Lover of Liberty), and *Microtoxus* (the Short-Range Shooter)

Microtoxus: This little house and the land around it remind me of the Curii or Cincinnatus. The farm is beautifully cultivated though it looks to me basically quite small. Clearly all this delights you no end, Eleutherius, yet it provokes me to laughter or amazement. For up to now, when you stayed out of town so much, I always thought you were busy either in agricultural pursuits or in the enjoyment of a more beautiful house. I could easily understand your desire for open air and for escape from the prison-like confinement of the city house. After all, your very name, Eleutherius, indicates a love and zeal for liberty. But now I see your fields are well kept up and that your country house is much smaller than your city residence; I really don't see what has kept you away so long. I can't believe that you hate the city, like some people, who are lazy and want to enjoy a passive leisure. You abound in skills that not only keep you active in the city but bring you honor. And I think Alitheus agrees.

Alitheus: Frankly, Microtoxus, I am not as surprised as you at Eleutherius' decision to live in the country. And what is more, I admire his frugality and modesty, for he has set the limits of both farm and house to make them economical and to provide for all necessities, not to fulfill luxurious designs. When I consider his former life and character and especially, as you say, his name, I feel he has not set himself these limits just by chance but rather that he has chosen a life style. I think he has made a wise decision. If he wanted freedom to lead a good life, I think it is indeed more possible here in isolation than in the city.

Microtoxus: You have strange ideas, Alitheus. Why should he alone, among so many thousands, be unable to find freedom in the city? And particularly in the one city which professes to uphold liberty most among the states of Italy! She has spared neither treasure nor risk to defend not only her own freedom and the freedom of her citizens but also the freedom of many other Italian cities. All that I could easily prove on historical evidence, but to set it forth to you seems superfluous. You have given your attention to the talk of our elders and also to books, so you know these things very well.

Alitheus: Very true, Microtoxus. In all Italy, I think, there is no city that has so energetically and enduringly championed the cause of liberty. Nor is there any place where it has flourished in so pure and ample a form. For if you go from the beginnings to the present, you will find that this country's liberty has never been crushed by a foreign people or a tyrant. There is only the isolated case of Walter [of Brienne], duke of Athens, who was called in by a popular revolt and reigned as a tyrant through deceit and the support of a faction of the nobility, but he did not rule long, nor could he long suppress the fruitful tree of liberty, if I may so express myself. I am not sure, in fact, whether this whole episode is not perhaps greater proof of the native Florentine love of liberty than a totally uninterrupted history of freedom would be.

Consider what you said and what I said too: doesn't it make your crime and the crime of men like you even more serious and less pardonable? You received a treasure of such magnitude and magnificence from ancestors who, at the greatest cost of labor and money, preserved it and passed it on to you—and you, lazy, apathetic, and enfeebled by your blinded intelligence, let it slip through your fingers. I don't know, in view of all this, whether to blame your slowness of mind and coarse sensibility, if it happened without your even knowing it, or, if you did bear and suffer such losses consciously, to condemn your degenerate and effeminate softness. These are things to be avoided even at the sacrifice of one's life; for to me it is clear that an honorable death is preferable to a life of disgusting shame.

This truth did not escape the truly magnanimous mind and noble character of Jacopo and Francesco dei Pazzi and of the various heads of that family. Though they were flourishing, possessed ample wealth, had intimate connections with the most eminent citizens, and enjoyed popularity and the good will of the people as a whole, they scorned all these advantages "in the absence of liberty. Thus did they undertake a glorious deed, an action worthy of the highest praise. They tried to restore their own liberty and that of the country. You know that Fortune foiled their plans, as is often her way. Their resolution, however, and the action on which they embarked, deserve praise forever. Men of sound judgment will always rank them with Dion of Syracuse, Aristogiton and Harmodius of Athens, Brutus and Cassius of Rome, and in our own day, Giovanni and Geronimo Andrea of Milan.[2] But I don't know why this discussion has wandered so far from its starting point. The greatness of these men and of what they attempted certainly demand, not a little digression from us, but the full attention of an eloquent historian.

Microtoxus: Are you quite in the possession of your senses, Alitheus, saying such things to us and completely forgetting what I just said?

Alitheus: And what was that?

Microtoxus: I said that the state of Florence was always zealous in the pursuit of liberty, always remarkable among other states in this respect. That is why the word liberty is actually written in gold on one of her banners.

Alitheus: Let's think about that, Microtoxus. It seems to me the fine words and the golden letters clash with the facts. This sort of argument only adds to my sorrow, indeed, for I see so many of my fellow citizens are fooled and are wholly detached from reality. What could be stupider than to think you are what you are not? Or to imagine you possess what is completely out of your reach?

Microtoxus: I would like to hear something clearer and, if I may say so, more explicit, if you are going to talk about these things. I admit my comprehension is rather slow. Really all generalizations, or, to use the philosophical term, "universals," do completely and wholly contain the particular truth spoken of, but just the same such conceptions are not easy for everybody to grasp. These general statements are not fitted for practical application, since action must deal with particular things in particular situations. From you, therefore, I long to hear what liberty is and how we have moved away from it in the way we live, as well as how the way our friend, Eleutherius, lives is particularly free.

Alitheus: You must realize that you have just thrown the whole burden of this discussion on me. If some of what has to be said is unpleasant, it will be up to me to say it. Well, whatever comes of it, I am not going to be afraid to say what I really think among good friends. I shall answer as well as I can both the first parts of your question. Of the way of life Eleutherius has chosen, however, I think it is only fair that he himself should speak. No one can set forth better than he his reasons for living in isolation and what he hopes to gain thereby. It would be better actually if he handled all this talk of liberty, since, as you said in your first speech, liberty herself gave Eleutherius his name.

Eleutherius: This is not right. Since you two started the argument, I think you should finish it. I shall, like an honorable judge, keep watching to see which of you comes closer to the truth, and I may on occasion give my own opinion.

Microtoxus: Well said, Eleutherius. But we don't want you to get away without even getting your feet wet, you know, especially when the whole discussion began on account of you. So let's take the divisions just made by Alitheus, and leave to you the explanation of your total retirement to the country and of the philosophy behind your life style. You have been listening to us in cunning silence, while we seemed to be guessing, as it were, at your secrets, but now we won't do that anymore. I suppose you were laughing to yourself while we tried to understand someone else's mind by our own interpretation rather than by asking him questions directly.

Eleutherius: Your talk concerned things that are most worthwhile, and was very interesting—so I was happy to have served as the object of some speculation. Now I am really eager to hear Alitheus' ideas, which he promised us. For I think he will take his speech from the heart of philosophy. I know how hard he has been studying, especially these last years as a good student of Johannes Argyropoulos.[3] Like a good many of our friends, moreover, he has even kept a written journal on the lectures. I won't, as Microtoxus puts it, escape without getting my feet wet. If any need is felt for a word from me, I shall tell you whatever you want to know. Now let's listen to Alitheus. I noticed already how well he defined the parts of our topic.

Alitheus: I don't see how I can put off any longer fulfilling my promise to you. I do suggest, though, that we go sit in that grove over there, for this is a lovely time of day, especially in spring, and the walk through flowering vines and trees, and over blossoming flowers and grasses, seems to call to us. I know that it's just the work of nature, but this landscape—in its dimensions, its relation to the sun, and its shape—looks like the work of an artist. The grove is just far enough from the house so that if you go back and forth while you're reading or meditating, you get some exercise. The gentle slope offers a lovely view, and makes your walk not overstrenuous and fairly quick.

Microtoxus: What good ideas you have. The mild weather urges us to stay outside, not under a roof, and the very topic of our discussion suits the open air and not a walled-in place. Not to cross the space from the house to the woods in idleness, however, let Eleutherius recite for us, on the way, one of the poems of Theocritus' *Bucolics*.

Eleutherius: I shall, and it's a pleasure to do for you what I so often do even by myself. For I almost never wander through these places without a book of poetry. I shall begin, then, and when I fall into barbarisms, as they used to say in Attica, please correct my mistakes. You know how hard it is for a man used to Latin to speak Greek correctly. But be that as it may, I shall begin.

Microtoxus: A lovely poem and most suited to our bucolic surroundings. You spoke so well that you seemed a very Greek. Now, as you see, here we are at the wood. Let's sit or lie, whichever we prefer, beneath this spreading oak, and listen to Alitheus.

Alitheus: As you please. But hearing this poem delighted me so that I could have walked unawares all the way to Florence. I was enthralled by its sweetness and occupied also by thoughts of what I should say. To begin with that now, I shall use the method developed by Plato and define the subject of our discussion so that it is clear to all the participants. I think you will indulge me if I take rather many words to state with some precision what that subject is. There is no such thing in actuality, as an absolute and perfect definition composed according to the method of the philosophers, by stating first the category to which the thing belongs and then the essential differences that mark it off from other members of that category. They themselves admit that, because of the paucity and inaccuracy of words, there are many more things than there are words for things, hence always ambiguities. I think I may say roughly, though, that liberty is a kind of potential for enjoying freedom within the limits set by law and custom.[4]

Microtoxus: Right, but it hasn't taken you many words, Alitheus, to state the extent of this potential. Still, since we aren't trying to match the sharp wits of the dialecticians and their verbal parsimony, but really want the amplitude of the orator, I hope you'll explain each of these points more extensively and completely.

Alitheus: I'll be glad to, if Eleutherius doesn't mind.

Eleutherius: On the contrary, nothing could be more to my taste. I long to hear some words on this subject, which often concerns and troubles my mind. For I see a lot of people who neglect and utterly scorn this precious gift of Goel. Yet the love of liberty and longing for freedom are natural not only to man but even to the animals. The very brutes prefer poverty and hardship, accompanied by freedom, to a life of comfortable servitude. But too much of this, I see Alitheus is ready to speak.

Alitheus: You've heard my definition of liberty, as brief as I could make it. It seems reasonable to call liberty a kind of potential or capacity, for the man who is called free is able, at will, to use or not to use this capacity. If he is indeed free, nothing prevents him from leading the life of a slave, which he can do through ignorance or by a conscious, if perverse, choice. Such is the case, for instance, of men addicted to lust or avarice or some such vice; they voluntarily give up the use of their liberty. For who would call a man free if he's subject to avarice, anxious night and day, bending every effort to the pursuit of money by fair means or foul? Neither his body nor his mind is ever free from labor. Shall I continue and also consider the people who get entangled in shameful love affairs? At the nod of a lover, they vacillate a thousand times an hour—now filled with foolish delight, now tormented by horrible anguish. Shall I talk about ambition too? Tossed about by vicissitudes, ambitious men constantly attempt to command undistinguished little wretches. And, for the appearance of being in command, they actually subject themselves to men even worse than they are. Let's not list all the kinds of vice that enslave men and oppress them. I shall just cite the Stoic paradox, which is as true as it is elegant: "Only the wise are free."[5]

Only the wise, as the Stoics say, have extinguished the passions; or, in the language of the Peripatetics,[6] moderated them. Empty of conflict and distraction, they live in peace and tranquility and are directed by their own free will. Their senses, their reason, and all the powers of their soul agree in directing them to certain ends, and these they steadily pursue. This is not just the source of liberty, but of happiness, the goal praised and desired by philosophers. Perhaps its nature was best expressed by the writer who called it εὐθυμία,[7] a state of spiritual well-being, a state I would suppose, of peace and tranquility. The man whose mind is in this state truly is free and can live exactly as he wishes. It seems that liberty does not differ much from happiness. From these remarks it is clear, I think, why I defined liberty as a kind of potential. Now let us—if you do not object—look at the other parts of this definition.

Microtoxus: You have made amply clear that liberty is some kind of potential. Now it would be nice to know whether you think this potential is innate or acquired by training and practice, like running and jumping and wrestling.

Alitheus: A good question, Microtoxus. I too think this potential is much like any human faculty. Its basis, like that of any tendency or inclination, is a natural gift found in any well-endowed human being, and it may be perfected by the liberal arts and good education. Its origins, since it is actually also a certain appetite, I think are quite like the origins of the affections. It is like love, hate, anger and other such things, to which some men naturally incline and which others naturally shun. For I won't deny that some people are, by nature, more inclined than others to cherish liberty. Such is the character of all affections.

Eleutherius: My own observations confirm the truth and wisdom of what you say. I have seen plenty of men, not in the least attracted by any definite advantage, subordinate themselves to the vilest persons. Yet others could not be induced by bribes or terrible threats to make themselves the inferiors of their peers. In this sense liberty might reasonably be classed as a kind of fortitude. Even Cicero seems to think so in his book *De Officiis*, where he says of fortitude: "It makes anyone of a naturally strong mind unwilling to obey another unless his commands are just and legitimate and serve a useful purpose."[8]

I could give you many examples, both Florentine and other. But not to go far from home, Alitheus is such a man and, I admit, so am I. We have often talked about it in the past. I don't see why I should subordinate myself to men who are inferior to me in family and character, men who owe their higher status only to the depraved judgment of knaves and to the bold whim of fortune. But I don't know if we should even call it high status to hold offices that are awarded, in many cases, not for merit or education or good character, but by arbitrary choice, or for a price, or for reasons of shameful corruption. I am holding up Alitheus' discourse unduly, however. I am eager to hear his explanation of the rest of his definition.

Alitheus: I was very glad of your critique of these times. I found in it a kind of reply to certain thoughts that often torment me. But of that I shall find occasion to speak later. Now let us move on. We have defined liberty as a kind of potential for living, meaning by "live" to act and do things. I don't use the term here as Aristotle does where he says that to live is simply to be among the living. Such life is fully present not only in animals but in plants and in grass and in anything that has a vegetative soul. Here, however, I am calling life something that consists of action and is granted to animals, especially to men. For human life, as the philosopher says himself, consists of a kind of action. What I said of the potential for living, therefore, is the same as if I had said the capacity to act and do things. I think we do well to call this a free capacity, moreover, if it is not limited by force or by consideration of externals, but acts in accordance with the dictates of right reason. In the senate, or in court, or in any place of judgment, a man may be inhibited by fear or desire or something else from saying openly what he thinks. But would he then be free? He must dare to speak and to act. Hence, as I said before, liberty has quite reasonably been seen as part of fortitude. Both the free and the strong man reveals himself most clearly in action. We praise a man's strength, however, when he with reason exposes himself to bodily danger, while we admire his freedom when he is speaking and giving counsel. Frank and noble spirits must possess both virtues, it seems, for they neither yield to present dangers nor are terrified by threats. In states where liberty exists, these qualities are most useful, for there the citizens speak without subterfuge and give advice to the Republic based on their real convictions. I think it was right, therefore, to call this power to live liberty. Or do you perhaps disagree?

Microtoxus: I don't feel that anything has been introduced here altogether superfluously. Furthermore I won't take offense at anything you say or that I hear said about myself, as long as you'll please go on with the discourse you started. Even if I seem to know already what is coming, I still want to hear you explain what is meant by "within the limits of law and custom."

Alitheus: I noticed long ago, Microtoxus, that nothing worries you more than to seem to be hearing something for the first time. Let me tell you what I think though.

I would not call anyone unfree merely because he had to obey the law of his country. Obedience to the law is, as Cicero says, the truest liberty. So, we obey the law in order to be free.[9] Many actions can, in fact, be prohibited without diminishing personal liberty. I would not call it lack of freedom not to be allowed to strike one's fellow citizen with impunity, or to take his wealth by force, or to rape his wife. Then there is a myriad of things not prohibited by law but forbidden by the customs and conventions of the city. Anyone who does those things risks suspicion of madness. This, in my view, is not a threat to liberty either. I don't consider a man unfree because, if he wants to keep his reputation for sanity, he can't unlace his boots or eat his dinner in the piazza—that is, if he's a citizen of Florence, for these same things are tolerated in travelers. Custom likewise does not let a respectable man cavort or sing in the market place, though there is no law against it. I would not describe a man as less than free because, for fear of disgrace, he abstained from such activities. Would you?

Microtoxus: Not at all. What you say seems absolutely true, and nothing could be truer. I see how wrong I was not to understand the need for these last points in your definition. They are really no less important than the rest. Since you have done justice to the first part of our problem, now, and explicated your definition part by part, I am only waiting to hear you on the other half of the question. Please go on and explain in what ways we at present live without liberty, for this point I scarcely believe you can prove.

Alitheus: You are asking me to contemplate again a very sad situation. These things are painful to remember, let alone discuss. Dear friends, I cannot think about this subject without tears. It makes me ashamed, for I too was born in this city, and I too belong to our time. And I see the people who once commanded most of Tuscany and even some of the neighboring peoples, bullied today by the whims of one young man. Many noble minds and men of eminent seniority and wisdom wear today the yoke of servitude and hardly recognize their own condition. Nor, when they do see it, do they dare avenge themselves. They become, and this is worst of all, the unwilling adversaries of those who try to liberate them.

We have degenerated so much in our time from the virtues of our ancestors; I am convinced that if they came back to life, they would deny we ever sprang from them. They founded, cherished and increased this Republic. They gave it excellent customs, sacred laws, and institutions that further an upright way of life. Our constitution, as anyone could see, equaled or surpassed in its protection of the people's liberty the ancient constitutions of Lycurgus, Solon, Pompey, and the rest. The results proved it. As long as our state lived in accordance with its own law, it enjoyed preeminence among the other Tuscan cities in wealth, in dignity, and in power. All that time this city was a model, not of power alone, but of moral principles. Now I see the same laws despised by everyone till nothing stands lower. The desires of a few irresponsible citizens, instead, have gained the force of law.

Consider the facts, really. Isn't it well known that the basic principle of all liberty is citizen equality? This is a fundamental to keep the rich from oppressing the poor or the poor, for their part, from violently robbing the rich. On this basis everyone keeps what is his and is secure from attack. Judge for yourselves how secure things are in our country. Shall I describe the sale of justice? Most carefully, as long as our state was free, was justice kept clear of corruption. Now it is managed in a way that is sickening even to talk about. I cannot recall without great sorrow how no one dared, by word or vote, contradict the charges which, backed by plenty of false denunciations from certain individuals, were thought to be in line with the wishes of one powerful man. It came to the point where I considered it one of Fortune's gifts, and not one of the lesser ones, if a man could find some honorable reason not to participate in judgment. And yet at one time our state was well known for justice, and men from distant countries brought cases to be tried in Florence. Now when cases arise in the city, they are never judged but after long delay and great expense. The play of ambition and bribery or the wishes of the powerful are always involved. As a result the sentence often favors, not the man with right on his side, but the one with influence. There are many to tell how they have been forced out of their houses and lost their inheritance. They have been despoiled by force and fraud of their homes, their money, and all that they possess.

Why compare the freedom of speech that used to prevail in the senate and in all public meetings with the present silence? There once did shine the wisdom, the eloquence, and the fervent patriotism which graced some of our best citizens. Serious and responsible men used to consider all sides of any proposal freely, and soon got at the truth of things that way. There were not many errors made in council then. Once a decree was passed, it was not repented of the next day and changed to its opposite. Now, on the other hand, as there are just a few Catos sitting in consultation on the weightiest questions, we often see resolutions passed one day and reversed the next by the same body, perhaps because they received a word of warning from someone. Our state has been robbed of the advantage or convenience which Aristotle noticed in free republics—that they are one body served by many heads and hands and feet.[10] For it is practically the same as not to possess something, if, having it, you do not wish to use it.

Thanks to the arrogance of a few overbearing individuals and the apathy of the rest of the citizens, these few today usurp the power of all. Their impulses and ambitions decide everything, while almost no authority is left to the councils or the people. Silent is the voice of the herald so eloquently praised by Demosthenes, that used to be empowered by our government to call all citizens to a council. If, for custom's sake, it does occasionally still ring out, everyone knows it is meaningless. For men are too intimidated to give free and open counsel. Consider, too, the undeniably important power of the state to punish malefactors. Irresponsible criminals, whom no shame, no sense of right and wrong, no love of honor can deter from crime, can be coerced by fear of the judge and of punishment. Unless their boldness is curbed by that fear, no crime is horrible and cruel enough to make them hesitate. The absence of threats is for them an invitation to crime. And what do such scoundrels have to fear today? What holds them back, when the bribes and the influence of wicked leaders whom they delight to serve assure them of immunity and rewards? Men actually condemned to exile or prison openly walk the streets in front of everybody, released, not on the order of an official, but by the words of one citizen. Men condemned by the Committee of Eight to perpetual imprisonment are removed from jail on the whim of a private person, or rather of a tyrant.

And what about the way public officials are chosen these days? You know as well as I that, in free states, offices are filled by chance selection from certain lists. It is considered best for liberty and justice if all those who aid the Republic privately by payment of taxes are also given a chance to participate in its rewards and advantages. But now all the positions that bestow some dignity on a man and yield some profit are filled, not by lot, but by appointment. The result is that no good men, no men noted for prudence and nobility are chosen, but satellites of the powerful or servants of their desires and pleasures who will unquestioningly obey them and act as humble as ever they can. This, of course, lessens the authority of the legitimate government, or rather destroys it. Good men, furthermore, and men fitted for public affairs, react with the natural indignation of free persons and refuse to hold any office. This gives still more license, however, to the small group of criminals who harass and ruin the Republic. I could go on much longer, protesting against these disgraceful abuses, but my own grief, by God, and the repulsive character of the crimes involved, makes me want to stop. I cannot simply ignore, however, the most terrible abuse of all. This is an evil all our citizens should be trying to stop like a plague. While Italy in general has enjoyed great peace in recent years, what could be more shameful than to find that all our citizens, but for a few, have been drained by heavy taxes? These resources, moreover, collected on the excuse of purchasing agricultural surpluses or on some other stupid pretext, have all been diverted to serve one man's pleasures. No need to wonder, now, how they get all the money for urban and rural building at once, or where the money comes from to feed such crowds of horses, dogs, birds, actors, sycophants, and parasites. So much spent in so few months does in itself invalidate the impression of private wealth he supposedly wants to give. And he openly admits that he does not have to pay his debts. He has always extorted money on any pretext from all sides, from friend as well as stranger. He has always assumed that Fortune will always favor him, so that he can freely use the wealth of others, public or private, as his own.

These facts and others like them, Microtoxus, in my judgment simply undermine liberty. Liberty has been uprooted and thrown away. To hate such an undignified and corrupt condition like the plague is only natural. But I find the situation even more unbearably bitter when I reflect on what I have learned from the talk of older men and from books about our ancestors' long struggle to preserve liberty and citizen equality. They used to have periodic inquiries to expose wild behavior or, in legal terms, to uncover public scandal. Those who were convicted they exiled. This custom of ostracism goes back to the Athenians and has always been characteristic of free republics, for people knew that citizen equality is basic to the preservation of liberty. I am sure the fact has not escaped you, for instance, that Giorgio Scali received the death penalty. He was a noble knight and a very distinguished man who held high public office, but he had removed his follower, Scatiza Assecla, from the prefect's prison. The knight, Verius Circulus, was exiled for claiming a position above his fellow citizens. Curtius Donatus was expelled from the city because he took to wife the daughter of Uguccione Fagiolano. The people attacked him, and later he was defeated and killed in battle. Once he formed a connection with a tyrant, the people suspected he might have some sort of tyrannical designs. In those days there was real concern for liberty among the people. They wanted, that is, to keep things under their own control and to govern the Republic themselves. Now, on the other hand, the people seem to despair of themselves. They submit to an alien will and let the wishes of certain people subvert their lives.

This is not the result of natural and honest ignorance, but of coercion by force and threat. They dare not vindicate their rights. Yet this same people once fought powerful republics and great tyrants. They defended their liberty with success, first by sacrifice of blood and second by expenditure of vast wealth. We know how boldly, with what might and military cunning they made war against their neighbors when they saw themselves invaded or when, goaded by injuries and excessive provocations, they crossed the borders of others. They fought Volterra, Pisa, Arezzo, and Pistoia until all these cities came under their rule and dominion. They made Siena, Perugia, and Bologna suffer so much in war that by finally demanding peace, they were granting a boon. To speak of Lucca, it is true, is somewhat embarrassing.

We repeatedly conquered that city but we never could hold it, and though it has often come under Florentine government, for some reason it has always slipped through our fingers again. It really has seemed like a dragon that annually devoured Florentine money and blood.

It would take too long to list all the tyrants and princes the Florentine people have fought. They carried on long and bitter wars rather than suffer the loss, if only in name, of their liberty. They fought Manfed at Arbium and again at Benevento, where he died defeated.[11] Love of liberty made our ancestors, much as they always cherished the Christian religion and the cult of the church, unhesitatingly take up arms against a wicked pope. Such was Gregory X, who for three years denied our city the sacraments.[12] Later they made war against the Emperor Henry, who pitched his tents as near as the monastery of San Salvi.[13] For similar reasons, they fought Uguccione Fagiolano and Castruccio of Lucca.[14] These tyrants could do great damage to our city but they could not destroy our liberty. The same thing with Guido Tarlato,[15] who was leader and tyrant of Arezzo. Even Louis of Bavaria, coming to be crowned emperor of the Romans, tried in vain to subjugate Florence.[16] Mastino [della Scala, of Verona], that perfidious tyrant, took over Lucca and made her drop her obligations as a Florentine ally. He not only held that city against all law and custom, but also waged war against Florence. Against his stratagems and onslaughts, Florence made a marvelous defense.[17] Following Mastino's example the Milanese leader, Biscio of the Visconti, tried to drag the Florentines into his empire. He used no less fraud than force but in the end he grew weary of the struggle and was glad to sue for peace.[18] Then there was the greatest and most expensive war, the one against the terrible governors of the Papal States. They disregarded divine and human law. First by starvation, and when that didn't work, by war, they tried to rob us of our liberty. At that time Gregory XI ruled from Avignon, and the Florentines, led by the Eight appointed to wage the war, were able to make many papal cities revolt against the rule of the church.[19]

Not much later there was a full-scale war against Gian Galeazzo Visconti, the tyrant of Milan. That was a war that put us in great peril. It staggers the imagination to consider how much money it cost. For many years the Florentines waged that war without obtaining a true peace settlement, made in good faith. In the midst of peace the duke was setting traps for the Florentines and preparing further war. So they summoned Duke Robert of Bavaria into Italy on the promise of 40,000 gold pieces, and in a single night, they collected all that and more as the citizens carried their contributions to the magistrates. Such was their hatred of tyranny, such their love of liberty and country.

Great and mighty war was waged against Ladislas of Naples, that perfidious king, with the Florentines pouring out money: some spent on armaments and some intercepted by the treachery of the king. Yet they did purchase Cortona from that same king, and increase their dominion.[20] Later there were wars, not one but several, with Filippo Visconti, the duke of Milan.[21] That wicked tyrant and sewer of all crime used force and all sorts of cunning tricks to destroy our liberty. But our forefathers stopped him, and gave him occasion to do some worrying about keeping his own domains. Should I remind you of the wars with Alfonso, King of Sicily? Under the influence of Pope Eugene and the Sienese, he attacked the innocent Florentines, who were most loathe to fight, and waged a cruel war. Finally, he conspired with the Venetians so that he and they both expelled our ambassadors. Then he sent his son Ferdinand at the head of a huge army and himself invaded our borders. What happened? On both fronts the armies came back to their kingdom without loot, wholly disgraced, and ravaged by hunger and exhaustion.[22]

But the war we are now waging against Pope Sixtus and King Ferdinand[23] leaves me at a loss as to what to say. Both of them clearly declare in speech and writing that they do not seek to take away but to restore the liberty of the Florentine people, and that they war, not against the Florentines, but only against Lorenzo de' Medici. Everywhere they speak of him as a tyrant, not a citizen, and they have hurled at him alone the full range of ecclesiastical censures. I don't really know whether the struggle of those who oppose these attacks ought to be viewed as a defense of liberty or of servitude.

I wanted to review all this briefly, however, and to demonstrate by a quick summary of past events how great was our ancestors' concern always to preserve and guard liberty. They gave their blood, insofar as it was their business to fight, and later, when they waged their wars with foreign armies, they spent enormous sums. Nor were they satisfied with Italian forces; they brought to their side various transalpine princes. They called kings and emperors into Italy, such as Charles, king of Bohemia and emperor of the Romans, against the power of the bishop of Milan. Similarly against Ladislas of Sicily, they called in Louis of Anjou from France, and together with Pope Alexander V, arranged a friendly alliance with him. On the same principle, they paid heavily to get the count of Armenia to cross over into Italy and oppose what Gian Galeazzo was trying to do. They labored with special zeal, though not with success, to incite Robert, duke of Bavaria, elected Roman emperor, to come and fight that same Gian Galeazzo. And not to harp on ancient history, in our own day we have seen Rene, the alternate king of Sicily, called down from Provence to carry on against the Venetians the campaign of Francesco Sforza, duke of Milan, with whom we had become allied and associated. King Rene, to keep a presence in Italy as long as there was work to be done, left behind his son, John, styled the duke of Calabria. He lived a long time in Florence and avenged the city against the unprovoked onslaught of Alfonso and Ferdinand [king of Sicily and duke of Calabria of the actually reigning Aragonese house] when they tried to destroy her liberty.[24]

These things I had to say, excellent friends, concerning liberty. I am afraid I may have seemed to run on and on. But, by God, the subject drew out my talk beyond what I intended almost without my noticing it. If it bored you, I beg your pardon, but if it gave you some joy and pleasure, thank liberty herself, whose very name is a delight to the ear. Now, not to let ourselves be cheated of what was promised us, I think we may fairly expect to listen to Eleutherius while he gives us his reasons for living as he does.

Eleutherius: Your demand is just, Alitheus, and I can't in honesty evade it, much as I was hoping to. I had convinced myself that the seriousness and magnitude of the problems we have been discussing would make you forget my trivial and foolish concerns. But I do think it best to put all this further talk off till tomorrow. The sun, now inclining to the west, and the breath of a gentle breeze so pleasantly cooling the air remind us to think of our health. You know how good it is to take some moderate, not overstrenuous exercise before supper. That's what the doctors say. So, with your approval, let's go look at the various trees in that grove. It's just far enough from here to let us walk there and return home in time for supper.

Microtoxus: A wholly delightful and happy thought, Eleutherius. Nothing you could have suggested would do us more good. We wander through tall grass in the shade of the trees' green roof, we are surrounded by the varied songs of birds, and we approach a pleasant destination. These very delights, this abundance of honest pleasures, might even alter my opinion if I did not know you for a man destined to do greater things. Well, we shall argue about that later. Let's go now, and continue our little journey until we arrive at home. Then we shall see to our bodily refreshment, and surrender to rest and sleep.

Book II

Eleutherius: The next day, as dawn was breaking, I went to see my friends. They were already up and taking a stroll in the garden, where it was cool. When we had exchanged the usual words of greeting, I turned to Microtoxus and said, "Well, Microtoxus, did this night change your mind? Would you agree now that one is happier living in the fresh air, among wide fields, amidst the gratuitous bounties of nature? Or would you still prefer to be walled in on all sides by the city, to live as if in prison, and hardly to breathe freely?"

Microtoxus: We shall talk about these things later. Let us go slowly down the road which encircles the farm and sit in the meadow shaded by great oaks. You may follow me there now, and I shall be your leader.

Alitheus: Microtoxus, you made a fine choice of place. The heavy growth of oaks on the east provides shade and the field, surrounded by grapevines, is better furnished for our comfort with its soft grass and flowers than any room full of drapes and rugs.

Don't hold back any longer, Eleutherius, fulfill your promise to speak. Redeem your pledge now and tell us your reasons for your way of life. Though I agree with you and approve of your life, I still want you to say something convincing to Microtoxus here.

Microtoxus: I myself, before Eleutherius begins, would like to state my objections to his retirement. I don't want you to think I am afraid to state my views. Also, I don't see the need for a lot of repetition in case Eleutherius wants to rebut my arguments.

Alitheus: Wise words. I admit it is folly to try to judge a cause unheard. So state your position. We are ready to listen.

Microtoxus: I've always believed that a man of natural talents, especially if he has further profited by education, ought as far as possible to be useful to society. He ought to communicate to others what he has developed in his own life. Architas[25] is right, you know, when he tells us that we are born, not for our own sakes, but for our family, country, and friends, and that we are only in some small part our own. But a man who lives only for himself, who withdraws into solitude and occupies his mind with private affairs, neglects his duty. I might concede the privilege to persons defective in mind or body, and therefore unable to do their duty as regards society. But I think withdrawal is least permissible to a man whose limbs are unhurt and who possesses an aptitude for speech and for observation, especially a man whom long study of literature has made still more intelligent. Such a person would be useful to his fellow men in the city.

Nor can you reasonably be deterred by shame or modesty, Eleutherius, as if you were some outsider newly invited to take part in government. Long ago your ancestors were already contenders for the honors of the city. In time of grave danger they aided the state with large financial contributions, being second to no other family or to few. I find in the public records that when the office of prior was only eighteen years old in our city, one Senro Rinuccini was awarded this highest dignity. Do not imagine, for the records show clearly that it was not so, that men of humble station or condition or men without proven ability and character were elected to the highest office in the Republic in those days. Until 1347, as it happens, I find no others of the clan raised to this dignity; perhaps those who lived then overlooked them, or perhaps it was the paucity of men, always a problem in your family. In the year I mentioned, however, Eleutherius, an ancestor of yours named Francisco was made prior, and he held that office five times before 1365. Between the last and second to last time, he was also made a knight by Niccolo d'Este, then prince of Ferrara. He and Maffeo Pillio were sent to that prince as orators from the Republic, and he elevated them both to knightly rank. After these events, Francisco was created one of the Eight with undefined powers. It was a dangerous time for the Republic, for Bernabo, the tyrant of Milan, had occupied the fort of Miniato with connivance of a noble faction. The Eight appointed to direct that war by their full efforts and with the support and cooperation of the people of Miniato took it back from the tyrant. Thus it returned to Florentine jurisdiction and control. After that, however, your family, along with the nobles in general, was excluded from the government of Florence by a rabble of scoundrels who cruelly vexed all the good men except those who paid them off.[26] Not much later, nonetheless, Giovanni, his son, was made a knight by the people and became a prior as well. Your house did not again enjoy that dignity for sometime, until Francisco, son of Cino and nephew of your father, the knight Francisco, was elected to that office in the year 1437.

I remind you of these things, Eleutherius, which you know better than anyone, of course, only to make you see that, if you sleep or live in leisure and rest on your wealth, you disgrace your family. You accepted your dignity from your ancestors, I remind you, and it is up to you not so much to guard the ample fortune which they bequeathed to you as to carry on their official role and likewise gain public honors, which are just as desirable a heritage.

Eleutherius: You, Microtoxus, have certainly given us a lot of information about my ancestors and about our whole family. I am filled with admiration for your diligence. You have managed to put together facts I thought were known to few persons beside myself. For while these things are all true, still, being old truths, they have been generally forgotten. I know them partly because my father, Fillipo, told me, and partly from certain old documents. I carefully keep those documents, which I sorted out after much labor from numerous bundles of papers, for such things are often lost through the negligence of the very people they concern. This makes it easy for me to accept your rather freely spoken criticism. I shall answer your points one by one, as briefly as I can. I don't want to go into too much detailed exposition and bore you. When it comes to the actual reasons for my own decisions, however, I shall state my arguments at more length.

I won't deny, good friends, that I have spent my whole life in the study of books and have, as I believe, made the best of my education. For I did not limit myself, as many people do, to what is done by the faculties of grammar and rhetoric at universities; I did not devote all my time to the poets and orators and historians, though I read enough in them. But equipped with this kind of knowledge, I turned to philosophy, a study which merits the name of guide to life. I applied my mind and worked hard to get from my studies not just an ornamental polish or some honest intellectual pleasure but also guidance to right living.

There is much acute controversy among the best philosophers, as to the nature of the ultimate good. Plausible reasons are poured out on every side of the issue, but all do seem to agree on one point, that happiness, or synonymously, the highest good, is found in whatever makes men, as far as humanly possible, similar to God. According to all the best thinkers, moreover, whether our own theologians or pagan philosophers, in God there is no passion or motion. Whatever, therefore, makes the mind tranquil and free of passion, that, they admit must bestow happiness. If we agree with Aristotle's conviction that happiness lies, not in passivity but in action,[27] we shall conclude that tranquility is the essential foundation and basis of happiness because it allows us to devote ourselves properly to either action or contemplation.

I do not think it foolish to point this out because I have so often seen people mistakenly suppose that anything productive of tranquility itself is the dreamed-of goal, happiness. Thus there are people who say that wealth or status or some combination of external advantages is happiness, thinking that one of these can guarantee peace and tranquility. This, I think, is far from true. For desires and possessions, as is well known, plunge the soul into perpetual agitation and anxiety. The opinion of the Stoics may not be unfounded when they say that only virtue, a right spiritual disposition or condition, is happiness.[28] This is a hard doctrine, for the soul so disposed is, by habit or by the condition of virtue, emptied of all passion. What are generally esteemed excellent things such men have learned simply to scorn. They live as though they had no sensual capacities, or as though, having them, they had no use for them at all. That is what the Stoics ask. If anyone actually should reach this state of mind, I would consider him, not a man but a mortal god.

Aristotle, however, speaks more plausibly and more in line with every day experience.[29] He grants that men may have passions within moderation, with the proviso that their feelings must obey rather than oppose reason. Thus we may in moderation seek honors, wealth, and some pleasures. Since he considers happiness an active pursuit, however, he seems thus to allow us very little of it. For, weighed down by the body and its needs, we are obviously prevented from cultivating happiness and can give only snatches of time to contemplation. In this regard the Stoics' ideas seem better to fit the case, for they declare that happiness consists simply in the quality or condition of being virtuous. These problems really require more extensive treatment and subtler argumentation, however, so let's leave them to people who inquire into the fine points of this kind of discussion more for the sake of argument than with a view to application.

We'll let it suffice to draw the following conclusion from their arguments: Man's first concern is to seek inner peace and liberty and tranquility, and furthermore, he may do so in either of two ways—avoiding anything he might desire to possess, or learning so to moderate his desires as to have them diverge only minimally from the dictates of virtue and right reason. Having thus gained the mastery of our passions, we may live happily and well. A moderate worldly fortune will easily suffice us. We differ widely, then, from the foolish opinion of the mass of men, who think that the highest good, the goal that all should seek, is great wealth or the vulgar fame awarded and sought by the general public. Happiness is truly what the Greeks called εὐθυμία, a word we might translate "spiritual well being," or simply tranquility.[30] How I have hoped to attain this condition myself you shall hear. But I don't want you to think that I am trying to give other people a set of rules by which to live. I am not telling you what others ought to do, but simply what I have done and for what reasons. That is what you asked me.

When I read in the best authors that to a wise man nothing is so important as his own moral guilt, I understand this to mean that one should bear with equanimity whatever happens to one through no fault of one's own. Fault or guilt is properly defined as of two kinds: faults of ignorance, that is, and faults of wickedness or vice. Since by our own efforts we are able to avoid both classes of guilt, I have always believed that we are also obligated to avoid them both. It seems to me Cicero expressed it well and truly: "I have always wished," he said, "first to deserve honors, second, to be thought to deserve them, and only third—what many people consider the first thing—actually to obtain them."[31] With this philosophy in mind, I have mainly tried not to be barbarous, stupid, and ignorant concerning the customary activities of men living the common and civic life. I have tried to make absolutely sure that no one could ever justly call me a thief, a robber, a liar, a scoundrel, a slanderer, or an unjust man. Secondly, I have tried to give some evidence of my character to my fellow citizens, most easily, I thought, by service in office. I took the trouble, therefore, to fill, first the highest office of prior, and, not much later, that of member of the Eight. I don't know what others thought of me, but this is what happened: without my asking or even suspecting it, I was appointed along with some most distinguished citizens, to the post of prefect of grammar schools, and I was soon sent as an envoy on an important mission to the pope. There, if I had preferred private advantage, or rather foul disgrace, to the public interest, I might have had what people call a very successful career. But I would rather lose every possession I own than enrich a certain private person at the expense of the Republic. Through all vicissitudes, I have maintained this principle always: nothing could make me an abject careerist, a servile creature, a man with no dignity. I would not buy anything with deals and favors. I saw it all done so often and so shamelessly that I was embarrassed for these ignorant souls who wanted to be preferred above others and therefore acted so obsequiously towards their natural peers as to fill them with vast and unjustified delusions of grandeur. Too late these people themselves saw the mistake they had made. Then it was useless, for the disease was too advanced for cure.

This is why up to a certain point I did try to participate in government, though I considered it a wise precept that says "do not get involved in politics." Such, we know, was Plato's view, the Prince of Philosophers, when, in his old age, he saw the Athenians apparently gone mad.[32] The same can justifiably be said today of the Florentines, whose prolonged and bitter servitude has made them lay aside a long time ago all sense of honor, all moral sensibility, all manly vigor and love of liberty. Instead scoundrels and criminals, men one wouldn't want to call citizens, have reached such a pitch of audacity that they unhesitatingly overturn and betray and undermine everything for their own purposes. With virulent hatred, moreover, do they persecute anyone they think knows of their crimes but refuses to be a tool or accomplice. The result is that good men who do obtain a position in the government along with them live in great danger and acute anxiety. For to serve their greed would be vile and criminal, but for one to resist the power of a whole group is impossible. And the greatest horror of all is seeing crimes committed in one's presence which one could not even hear described without distress.

Although I am far from that wisdom which reached its height in Plato, still the little knowledge of literature that I have has freed me from the disease of avarice and ambition and taught me that the happiness all men seek is not to be found by amassing wealth, nor by gaining what the crowd thinks are honors, but by living in tranquility and freedom of spirit. I speak now of the sort of happiness to which a person placed in civic life can aspire in this valley of tears. Not that I have ever wanted to live passively in a state of idleness. An inactive and slothful life weakens the nerves of body and brain. But I have aimed for the middle way which would make me every day a better man. I am always learning something and becoming potentially more useful, should the state ever require my services. Since, as I remarked before, it is less painful to hear than to see things you cannot approve of, I spend much of my time alone, in converse with my own mind or with the books you have seen here, and I enjoy the liberty I wholly believe in. I have apportioned my time so that not a particle of it is wasted. I am always attending to my bodily health by taking exercise, or concerning myself with domestic matters, or cultivating my mind by reading and meditation. For nothing worth writing has come to my mind, seeing how much there is already in the way of all sorts of books, and how well they have been written in both ancient and modern times. If Nestor or Titonus were to return to life and devote all his years to reading, I think he would hardly find time for my contribution—if I wrote. If something were occasionally to bring me friends like you, therefore, to visit me here, I would not exchange my life for the life of those the poets call blessed, who inhabit the Elysian fields. Whatever it may be, I think my life is more blessed than the life of a city person, burdened by constant anxiety, humiliated by being unable to move a finger of his own will. Good men and loyal friends, now you have heard my philosophy. Perhaps I went into more detail than you bargained for. Whatever others may say, these sentiments will remain mine if you approve them. I so much respect your judgment that, if you agree, I shall consider myself armed against all criticism. If something seems amiss to you, however, I shall not refuse to change the present direction of my life.

Alitheus: The model of your conduct already impressed me before, but now, after your discourse, I feel convinced that no other is so conducive to happiness. Although I do not at present live so very differently from you, I shall after this strive to go more often to the country and enjoy solitude.

Microtoxus: Right, Alitheus. For, the ideas of Eleutherius have changed my mind so that I can think of nothing truer. Yet really I still don't believe that a man should shrink from work and from feelings of indignation, and should live for himself only. You turn your back on others and abandon your country, which should be your dearest concern. Aside from what we owe to immortal God, we owe our best to our country.

Eleutherius: This new plea, Microtoxus, and your freer discourse earlier tend to the same end. So I shall reply to both at once. First, consider whether that accurate list of the highly honorable offices held by my ancestors is not really an incentive to choose as I have chosen rather than to take the path you urge upon me. Who could justly reproach me for having enough pride to refuse to become a suppliant, begging from those wicked usurpers for my rightful inheritance and that of other good citizens? I should not remain long without public honor if I could regain it by recourse to justice or to arms.

What you said about the duty of a citizen, Microtoxus, was well and truly said. I too have thought long and hard about this, and therefore did serve my country as long as I could. I chose to act so as to be of some use to the state, and to show myself ready and willing to obey its orders with alacrity. Not my country but the criminals whose force took over all her laws and authority ignored my willingness to render good service. They sensed, of course, that I was repelled by their ways, or rather by their vices. Since that was so, why waste my time and effort? To coerce them by force was impossible, but to gain their approval by conforming to their way of life and to their crookedness would have been beneath me, I know, and totally dishonest. Should I have pleaded with them and flattered them to get what they owed me by law? And should I thus have humbled myself before men who had perverted all law and every sacred thing, who, to the great sorrow and indignation of good citizens, had usurped all authority and honor in the Republic? It is true, as once was said, good deeds done in a wrong context should be accounted villainy.[33] Likewise, in my view, honors won by foul means are blots on honor and degrading.

I did not believe that, as long as my own conduct had not disqualified me by immorality or weakness or lack of judgment from even the highest offices, I ought to seek office in a manner unworthy of my ancestors. I have met the standards of the best citizens of our time and the most eminent. They have judged me worthy of the highest honor of standard bearer, a grade no one of our family attained before. This makes me feel that my ancestors and even I have won sufficient honor. Of the three levels of honor mentioned by Cicero, I have at least attained two. And if I am excluded from the third, it is not my own fault, but on account of the unjust hatred and envy of malevolent men.

What excuse can they give for excluding me from the government? I carried out my mission, though in vain. They cannot say there was some flaw in my conduct, some contravention of orders, something done that was not in accordance with their orders. I had been given, by order of the people, full power to make binding agreements. I never used that power, however, unless specifically directed to do so by the highest magistrate. I can prove all this easily from public documents. I knew very well the duty of a good envoy and a loyal citizen. That man, elevated by Fortune's bold hand and by the imprudence of the foolish citizens, complained that I wrote publicly to the magistrate on great affairs of state, rather than privately to him. This does not bother me one bit. I shall always remember and declare that I was sent forth, not by one private individual, but by the whole people, by the highest public office, by the Republic itself. What right did he have to complain when, for friendship's sake, I even gave him a private report on the main points at the same time I handed in my official one? But with his usual arrogance he scorned this report, and left me without even the honor of a written acknowledgment. I would be dishonest not to admit that these things were somewhat upsetting.

When the pope in the council of cardinals, therefore, formally pronounced sentence against our Republic, I made a private report to him as well as a public one to the highest magistrate. Then he wrote and censured me for having spoken as I had in a public document. It is true that, both before and after my return, I did not hide my indignation. When the pope had left Rome on account of the plague and was traveling around, to the great discomfort and danger of his court, since he was no longer deliberating on matters that concerned us, I asked permission to return home. First I asked the magistrate and then him privately, but he kept denying my request. Shortly after, when without his knowledge I got permission from the Eight, he used the excuse that I came from plague-ridden parts to make the same Eight bar me from the city. I omit many details, I don't want to seem overconcerned with trivia.

The fact is I would have taken these blows calmly and not let them disturb my mind, had not far greater crimes and more serious evils inflicted by him on the Republic aroused my deep disgust. He accepted tyranny as a legacy from his grandfather, but exercised it much more severely than his grandfather did. He was more insolent than his father. He did not get reasonable advice from the citizens, nor did he listen to his own reason. He did everything according to the impulses of his willful spirit, and he dragged down the poor country. Spoiled in part of her wealth and altogether of her dignity, she has become the mockery of all Italy for enduring such a destructive and cruel tyranny.

Even certain princes, remembering our former dignity and glory, have come to pity our distress. It has reached the point where they use their resources to war on Florence only partly to avenge their own injuries at his hands, but partly to restore to the Florentine people their former liberty. This Florentine Phalaris has now gone so far in insolence that he considers himself greater than the greatest princes of Italy. When he receives favors from them in his need, he esteems those something owed to him by right.

This gives you some idea of his cruel oppression of the citizens, his fantastic audacity and incredible arrogance. He taxed them enough in recent years, while there was peace from external enemies, to vex and wound them. Now he has involved them in a war that is grave indeed, dangerous and pernicious. This war—as not only rumor but public letters sent by the pope and king to all peoples make clear—was undertaken not against the Florentines but against Lorenzo de' Medici, the tyrant of Florence, for the liberty of the people. This man, whose insolence, temerity, and ingratitude had wounded the most powerful princes of Italy, implicated the state in a grave and calamitous war, conducted by them, as they declare, not against the Florentine people but for their liberation from Lorenzo's fierce tyranny. It is a shame and a misery, altogether, to see the many fields laid waste, the villages and farms devastated, the many men taken prisoner, the many victims reduced to indigence and beggary. One might well sing to us the song of Hesiod:

Often the whole city suffers through one bad man.[34]

If I am unwilling to adore, to flatter and to bow before this man, can you blame me?

These, good friends, are my answers to the arguments of Microtoxus. I don't scorn the honors won by my ancestors nor do I lack the desire to follow in some modest way along the same path, if I may do so in liberty. I do not shirk labor and trouble. I would take on work, and danger too, for my country. But the truth is that I cannot peacefully tolerate our ungrateful citizenry and the usurpers of our liberty. I live, therefore, as you see, content with this little house and farm. I am free from all anxiety. I don't inquire what goes on in the city, and I lead a quiet and free life. There's never a day when I fail to read or write, and, except when it rains, I always take some exercise outdoors. If only I could have your company here, therefore, I should consider myself in paradise.

Alitheus: I think you have done very well, Eleutherius, and I myself, persuaded by your thoughts, shall try to see you and talk with you often.

Microtoxus: On such journeys, I promise to be your constant companion. But since we have talked enough now, let us dedicate the rest of the day to our health. Walking and talking, let us get ourselves a good appetite for dinner.

Chapter 7

GIROLAMO SAVONAROLA

Treatise on the Constitution
and Government of the City of Florence

(1498)

A Dominican friar and fiery preacher from Ferrara, Girolamo Savonarola (1452–98) gained religious and then political prominence in Florence following the 1494 invasion by the French king Charles VIII and the subsequent expulsion of the Medici. Savonarola's homilies on scripture contained invectives against luxury, gambling, and sodomy, and his public processions stirred up a religious revival in the city, culminating in the famous bonfires of the vanities. The friar wielded considerable influence over the popular government that was established in 1494, embodied in the institution of the Great Council, an assembly of thirty-six hundred citizens. In 1498, Savonarola's denunciations of clerical corruption under the Borgia pope Alexander VI caught up with him, and his aristocratic enemies in Florence were able to engineer his arrest and execution. Savonarola's *Treatise on the Constitution and Government of the City of Florence*, written as the friar's fortunes were turning sour, expresses his views on the importance of spiritual renewal, civic virtue, and mixed government for Florence—and it implies the veiled threat that a Savonarola-less Florence would return to the condition of Medici tyranny that characterized the rule of Lorenzo the Magnificent.

The text is a reprint of Girolamo Savonarola, *Treatise on the Constitution and Government of the City of Florence*, in R. N. Watkins, ed., *Humanism and Liberty: Writings on Freedom from Fifteenth-Century Florence* (Columbia: University of South Carolina Press, 1978), 231–60.

※

Treatise on the Constitution
and Government of the City of Florence

FIRST TREATISE

Chapter I
Government Is Necessary in Human Affairs;
on Good and Bad Government

The all-powerful God who rules the whole universe infuses into his creatures the excellence of his rule. He does so in two ways. Creatures lacking intellect and free will, he permeates with certain strengths and virtues so that they will naturally incline to take the right means toward the proper ends, making no mistakes unless, as rarely happens, something blocks their path. These creatures, therefore, do not govern themselves but are governed by God and by the nature he has given them, so that they achieve their proper purposes. Creatures endowed with intellect, however, such as man, are governed by him in a way that also requires their governing themselves; for he gives them intellect by which they can judge what is useful to them and what is not useful, and free will freely to choose what they like. But the light of intellect is weak, especially in childhood, and therefore a man cannot rule himself perfectly without the help of others. The individual person is by no means self-sufficient and cannot provide for his own physical and spiritual needs. Nature, we see, provides food, clothing, and weapons for all animals, and when they are ill they instinctively find their own medicines. None of this is provided for man; but God, who governs all things, has given him reason and the use of his hands to let him provide for himself. Because of his bodily weakness, moreover, man needs almost infinitely many things for his nourishment, preservation, and growth, and many arts in order to provide these things. Thus it was made necessary for men to live together and to help each other, some practicing one skill and some another, so as to form a body perfectly equipped with arts and sciences.

It is well said, therefore, that the solitary man is either God or a wild beast: for he is either so perfect a man that he is like a God on earth, having like God no need of anything or of anyone's help—such were St. John the Baptist, and St. Paul the first hermit, and many others—or he is like a beast, totally deprived of reason and hence without concern for clothing, shelter, cooked and prepared food, and the conversation of his fellow men, following only animal instinct. Since very few people are so perfect or so bestial, the rest are obliged to live with others, in cities, in castles, in country homes, or elsewhere.

Since the generation of men is very inclined to do evil, especially when there is no law or fear, they have had to find laws to restrain the aggressiveness of bad men, so that those who want to live well may safely do so. No animal, indeed, is more dangerous than man without law. The gluttonous man eats more avidly and insatiably than any other animal, not satisfied with the foods and kinds of cooking he knows, seeking, not the satisfaction of nature, but the gratification of unbridled appetite. Similarly in sexual matters, he does not obey seasons and nature's commands, but does things it is abominable to think of, let alone to hear about, and which no animal even thinks of. He also outdoes beasts in cruelty, for they do not make cruel war on each other, especially not on those of their own species, while man even invents new instruments for hurting others and new devices of torture and death. Aside from all these things, men have within them pride, ambition, and envy, and from these spring quarrels and intolerable wars. And yet, because men have to live together and want to live in peace, they have had to find laws by which the bad will be punished and the good rewarded.

But because only a superior authority can be a source of laws and because people can only be made to observe the laws by someone who has power over others, it was necessary to constitute some in authority, to care for the common good and to exercise power over others. For while every individual person pursues his own good, if none were there to care for the common good, society would be destroyed and the whole world would fall into confusion. Some men gathered together, therefore, to choose one individual to take care of the common good and to rule all others. This kind of government was called kingship and the one who ruled was called king. Certain other people, whether because they could not agree on one ruler or because it seemed better thus, set up a group of the chief persons and best and wisest in the community, to have them govern and hold public office in rotation; this was called aristocracy. Still others wanted the power of government to stay in the hands of all the people, who would distribute and rotate offices as they thought best. This form of government was called civil government, because it belongs to all the citizens.

The government of the community was created, then, to take care of the common good and to let people live together in peace, so that they might devote themselves to what is good and more easily pursue eternal happiness. A government is good, therefore, which uses all its strength to maintain and increase the common good, and to induce the people to be virtuous and live righteously, with special concern for religion. And a government is bad if it neglects the common good and cares for the private good of its members, careless of the character of the people and the way they live, except where this impinges on the particular needs of the rulers. Such government is called tyranny. We have made clear, then, the need for government among men, and what kind of government, generally, is good and what kind is bad.

Chapter II
Although the Government of One Good Man Is Best by Nature, It Is Not Good for Every Community

While that government is good which concerns itself with the common good, spiritual as well as physical, it may be administered by one or by the principal citizens or by all the people, and we must realize that, in principle, the civil form of government is good, aristocracy is better, and kingship is best. Given that the aim of government is the union and peace of the people, this union and this peace are much more readily attained and preserved under the rule of one than under more than one, and under the rule of a few rather than a crowd. For when all the men in a community must respect and obey one man alone, they do not form factions, but are all bound together in love and fear of that one. When there are more than one, however, some people respect one and some another; some like one, and others another, and the people are not so well united as when one alone rules. They are less sure to remain united the more people govern them. Unified power, moreover, is more effective than dispersed power, as fire is hotter when all the fuel is burning in one place than when it is scattered and burns here and there.

It is clear then that the power of government will be able to act in a more unified way if it is concentrated in one man than if it is given to more than one; it follows that the rule of one, when he is a good ruler, is by nature better and more efficacious than any other. What is more, the rule of the whole world and of nature is the best government, and as art follows nature, the more a human government resembles that of the world and of nature, the more perfect it is. Obviously since the whole world is governed by one ruler, and since all natural beings that manifest some kind of government are also governed by one (for example, bees are governed by a king, and the various spiritual faculties by reason, and the limbs of the body by the heart, and so on), it follows that human government by one ruler is by nature the best. Hence our Savior, who wanted to give the church the best kind of government, made Peter head of the faithful, and he established in every diocese, as in every parish and monastery, the rule of one, placing all the lesser rulers under a single ruler's authority, that of his vicar.

Speaking absolutely, therefore, the government of one when the ruler is good is preferable to all other forms of good government. Every community should, if possible, be so governed, that is, that the whole people will peacefully make one man prince, who is good and just and wise, and whom everyone will have to obey. But we must note that this form of government is not good and not possible and ought not to be attempted in every community, because it often happens that the one who rules absolutely is not good, but rather, in a certain place or with a certain specific ruler, bad. The case is parallel with that of spiritual life, which is lived in the religious state, and this in principle is the best state, yet it is not a state to be imposed on all Christians, nor should that be attempted, nor would it be good, for many could not bear it and would make schisms in the church. As our Savior says in the Gospel: "One must not patch old cloth with new, for the old will tear and become more torn than before, and one should not put new wine in old wineskins, or the old will burst and the wine be lost." Sometimes we see a food which is good in itself and even the best of foods, harmful as poison to a particular person; and a climate which is considered perfect may be harmful to certain constitutions. The government of one likewise is best in principle but to certain peoples, who are inclined to quarrel, it will do harm and be the worst sort of government. Among them the prince will suffer opposition and even assassination, which will lead to infinite evils, for his death will be followed by the division of the people into factions, and then by civil war with a variety of chiefs, and if one of them does win, he will become a tyrant, so that finally, as we shall show, the common good of the city will be wholly ruined. If a prince wishes to attain security and stability while ruling such a people, he will necessarily have to become a tyrant, he will have to exile the powerful, to expropriate the rich, and to irritate the people with heavy-handed oppression; otherwise he will never be safe.

Certain peoples, then, who by nature are such that they cannot tolerate the rule of one unless it is accompanied by great and unbearable oppression are like certain men, who are really used to living in the open and who, if they decide to live in good, well-heated rooms and wear good clothes and eat delicate food will soon grow ill and die. Wise men, therefore, if they must institute a government, will think first about the nature of the people concerned, whether their temperament and habits are going to let them accept the rule of one. If so, that is the government to be established. But if not, wise law-givers will try to give them aristocracy. And if that too will not be tolerated, they will institute the civil form of government with such laws as suit that people's character. Now let us see which of these three good forms of government suits the Florentine people.

Chapter III
Civil Government Is Best for the City of Florence

There can be no doubt (if anyone gives serious consideration to what we have said) that if the Florentine people would tolerate the rule of one, it should receive a prince, not a tyrant, who will be prudent, just, and good. But if we examine the opinions and ideas of the learned, we shall quickly see that, considering the character of this people, such a form of government does not suit them. For it is said that this form of government suits a people who are servile by nature, a people lacking either in vitality or in intelligence, whichever it may be. Those who have plenty of vitality and are physically strong and daring in war, nonetheless, if they lack intelligence, are easily subjugated by a prince. It is easy to trap them through the weakness of their minds, and they will follow their prince as the bees follow their king, and as we see the people of Aquileia do. Those that have brains but lack vitality, being cowardly, easily accept a single prince and live quietly under him, as do the oriental peoples. When a people lacks both, of course, the rule of one is doubly easy. But a bold people who abound in intelligence and in vitality cannot easily be ruled by one man unless he is a tyrant, for they are always plotting against their prince, using their cunning, and since they are daring too, they readily put their plots into execution. Italy, we know from past and present experience, has never kept long under the rule of a single prince. Indeed we see this little province divided into as many principalities as there are cities, and those cities are almost never at peace.

The Florentine people, however, is the most intelligent of all the peoples of Italy and the most farsighted in its undertakings. It has, as its history has shown again and again, a vigorous and audacious spirit. For, though this people is devoted to commerce and appears a quiet people, nonetheless, when it enters into civil or external war, it is very terrible and full of spirit. This the chronicles show when they relate its wars against various great princes and tyrants, where Florence has absolutely refused to yield and finally, in self-defense, has carried away the victory. This people's character, then, will never tolerate the rule of a prince, even though he be good and perfect, for the bad citizens always outnumber the good, and here, through their cunning and courage, they would either overthrow or kill him (since they are most inclined to ambition). Alternatively, the prince would have to become a tyrant. If we consider the matter further we shall conclude that this people not only finds the rule of one uncongenial, but it also could not accept aristocracy. Habit, indeed, is second nature, and as the rock's nature is to fall and it cannot alter this and cannot be raised except by force, so habit too becomes nature, and it is very difficult if not impossible to change men, especially whole peoples, even if their habits are bad, for their habits spring out of their character.

Now the Florentine people, having established a civil form of government long ago, has made such a habit of this form that, besides suiting the nature and require-ments of the people better than any other, it has become habitual and fixed in their minds. It would be difficult, if not impossible to separate them from this form of government. And, indeed, while they may have been governed by tyrants for many years, nonetheless, the citizens who usurped the principate in this period did not tyrannize in such a way as freely to deny the sovereignty of the whole. With great cunning they governed this people without attacking their temperament and their habits. They left the form of government as it was and all the usual offices, but saw to it that only their friends held those offices. The form of civil government has long been unchanged, therefore, and the people finds it so natural that to try to change it and give Florence another form of government would be no less than to run against their nature and against their ancient habit. This would generate such unrest and anger in this community that it would soon risk losing all its liberty. History shows this clearly, and experience is the teacher of all arts. Every time Florence has been governed by a small group of leading citizens, there have been great divisions among the people and no peace until one party or the other was thrown out, and some one citizen became a tyrant. This citizen, then, usurped the liberty and common good of the people, and their hearts remained discontent and restless. If Florence was divided and discordant in the past, through the ambition and rivalries of the leading citizens, moreover, it is still more so at present. Were it not for the grace and mercy of God, there would recently have been much blood-shed, the destruction of many houses, and fights and civil wars within as well as outside the walls, for the citizens who were exiled at various times by those who governed from '34 on have returned, and they had mostly nurtured various hatreds in themselves during this period because of the harm done to their houses and families. What happened with the arrival of the king of France, as anyone who was here and capable of judgment knows, should have been the death blow for Florence; but the council and the civil government then founded in Florence were not created by men but by God, and helped by the prayers of good men and women within the city, this government became an instrument of divine virtue, and it preserved the city's liberty. No one not wholly deprived of his natural judgment by his sins could consider the dangers that have threatened the city for the last three years and deny that it has been governed and preserved by God.

We conclude, therefore, that in the city of Florence the civil form of government is best, although in itself this is not the best form, and we assert this both because divine authority created its present civil government, and because of the reasons given above. The rule of one, though in itself best, is not good, let alone best, for the Florentine people, any more than the state of perfection through life in holy orders, though best in itself, is best or even good for many of the Christian faithful, while some other state of life which is not in itself best is best for them. We have made our first point clear then; that is, we have shown what is the best form of government for the city of Florence. It is time now to make the second point, and to show what is the worst kind of government for the city.

SECOND TREATISE

Chapter I
The Rule of One, When He Is a Bad Ruler, Is the Worst
Form of Government, Especially If the Ruler Rose
to Become a Tyrant from the Status of a Mere Citizen

The rule of one, if he is a good ruler, is the best of all forms of government and the most stable. It is less likely to turn into a tyranny than the government of more than one for the more people are in power, the more easily divisions appear among them and generate wider divisions among the people. Nonetheless, as this form is perfect and stable when it is good, so when it is unjust and bad, it is by nature the worst of all the bad forms of government. First, because evil being the opposite of good, and the worst the opposite of the best, so the government of one, being best when good, logically must be worst when bad.

Secondly, as we have said, united power is more effective than power dispersed; so when a tyrant reigns, the power of an evil government is concentrated in a single person, and as there are always more bad men than good and everyone likes those who are similar to him, all the bad people will try to follow this ruler. Those who seek rewards and honors will follow him with special zeal, and many more will follow from fear, and those who are not altogether depraved but simply love earthly things will come along either from fear or from love of what they desire; those who are good but not altogether perfect, moreover, will follow from fear and lack of courage to resist while few are perfect, or rather perhaps none are. So all the power of government will be concentrated in one man. This one man, however, being a bad and unjust person, will carry every evil enterprise to perfection and easily pervert every good thing. When a government consists of several bad men, one will get in the other's way, and they will not be able to do as much harm as they would like, nor as much as a single tyrant can do.

Thirdly, a government is worse, the more it leaves aside the common good. The common good, indeed, is the purpose of good government, and the closer it approaches that purpose, the better it is, while the more it departs from that, the worse it is, for everything gains its perfection by approaching its end, and by separating from that end, becomes imperfect. But it is clear that bad government by many departs from the common good less than does bad government by one, for if those who rule usurp the common good and divide it among themselves, divide, that is, the city's opportunities and honors, nonetheless being given to more than one, the common good remains to some extent common. But when all the common good is channeled to serve only one man, it does not remain common at all, but is altogether private. The bad government of one, therefore, is of all governments the worst. It departs most from the common good and is most destructive of the common good.

Fourthly, duration contributes to these arguments. The government of one is by nature more stable than that of several men and cannot, though it is bad, be as easily hindered and stopped as that of many, for all the members take their orders from the head and they have much difficulty in rising against it. Under a tyrant it is very hard to find a leader who will rise against him, for he is ever on the watch to destroy such men, and he prevents his subjects from gathering and generally is vigilant to stop all opposition. When a group of people constitute a bad government, they are easier to overthrow, for it is easier to gather good men around the one in the group who does well. And it is easy to sow dissent among the bad, to prevent their unifying, because each of them is only seeking his own private good, which makes it natural for them to quarrel. The bad government of one, in this respect too, is the worst of all; it is a hard thing to oppose and end it.

But although by nature the bad government of one is the worst, yet sometimes the worst miseries attend the bad government of a group, especially towards the end of it; for when such a government is bad, it quickly divides into factions, the common good and the public peace are torn apart and finally, if no remedy is found, one faction will have to win and to oust the other. From this event innumerable evils, temporal and bodily and spiritual, will follow. The worst and most important result will be that the government of a group will become the rule of one. From having been a mere citizen, the one who has most popular favor will rise to become a tyrant. And the rule of one who is bad is the worst of all governments (as we have said) but there is still a big difference between the government of one natural and true lord who has become a tyrant and the government of a mere citizen who has become a tyrant. The latter will do more harm than the former, for if he wants to reign he must destroy by death or exile or other means not only those citizens who actively oppose him but all who are his equals in nobility, wealth, or fame. He must get rid of all those who could possibly harm him, and this means vast suffering. The natural lord does not have to do this, because there is no one who is equal to him and the citizens, accustomed to being his subjects, are not likely to be conspiring for his overthrow. He does not live in the state of universal suspicion that characterizes the tyrant who started as mere citizen.

Peoples who have aristocratic governments will discover that, through the quarrels men readily start and through the ubiquity of bad men and gossips and slanderers, division may easily come and precipitate them into tyranny. Such peoples, therefore, ought to take precautions and to make most vigorous and severe laws to prevent any individual from trying to make himself a tyrant. They should punish him with the extreme penalty, not only if he has spoken of doing it, but especially if he has been trying to do it. While they should show mercy to any other criminal, moreover, in this one case they should show no mercy, except that the soul of the criminal should always receive assistance. They should never diminish the penalty but rather increase it as an example to all, so that every person may learn, not only never to attempt it, but not even to think of it. Anyone who is merciful in this situation or negligent in punishing such a case sins gravely before God, for he fosters the tyrant's beginning, and from his rule come the innumerable evils we shall talk about later. When bad men see that the punishments are light they become bold, and little by little they move towards tyranny, as a drop of water little by little hollows the stone. He who has failed to punish this crime seriously is responsible for all the evils that follow through the tyranny of such citizens. A people that has civil government should be more willing to tolerate any other evil and inconvenience arising out of civil government with its imperfections than to let a tyrant arise. And to help everyone understand the evil that comes from tyranny, although we have preached of it at other times, still we will speak of it in the next chapter, to make the dangers better known. We will touch at least on the major points, but if we wanted to tell all the omissions and abuses and grave crimes and evils that follow from tyranny, it would be impossible, for these are infinite.

Chapter II
The Wickedness of Tyrants and the Evils of Tyranny

Tyrant is the name given to one of evil life, the worst kind of man in the world, who wishes to rule all others by force, especially if that man was once a mere citizen. First, it must be said that he is proud, since he desires a position above his equals, and even above those better than himself, whom he should more justly have to obey. He is envious, likewise, and suffers whenever other men gain any glory, especially when citizens of his own city achieve high renown. He cannot bear to hear others praised, though he often pretends pleasure and listens with pain. He delights in his neighbors' disgrace, and longs for every man to be slandered so that he alone may stand in high honor. He lives beset with fantasies of grandeur and with melancholy and with fears that always gnaw at his heart; therefore, he is always looking for pleasures as medicine for his condition. There is hardly a tyrant, perhaps there never has been one, who is not lustful and devoted to fleshly delights. Since he cannot maintain himself in that state or give himself all the pleasures he wants without plenty of money, however, he necessarily also yearns, with inordinate passion, for property. Every tyrant, therefore, is greedy and rapacious and a thief. He not only steals sovereign power, which belongs to the whole people, but also steals the property of the community, as well as whatever he desires to take from individual citizens. Sometimes he uses cunning and hidden means, and sometimes obvious ones. It follows that the tyrant commits virtually all the sins there are. He is steeped, first of all, in pride, sensuality and avarice, the roots of all evil.

Secondly, once he has taken power, which was the whole object of his desire, there is nothing he will not do to keep it. There is no crime which he is not ready to commit when it is a matter of keeping power. Experience confirms that the tyrant stops at nothing and spares no one when it is a matter of keeping his position. In mind, therefore, or in actual practice, he commits all the sins in the world. Thirdly, because from his perverted kind of government all the sins of the people follow, he is himself responsible for all, as though they were his sins. It follows that his soul is totally depraved. His memory always reminds him of injuries and desires revenge, while he instantly forgets the favors of friends. His intellect is always busy plotting fraud and treachery and other wickedness. His will is hate-filled and perverse in its desires. His imagination is crowded with false and wicked visions.

All his exterior senses are ill-used, whether to satisfy his concupiscence or to wound and deride his neighbor, in expression of his overflowing rage and scorn. All this comes to be because he has made it his purpose to hold such power as it is, in fact, difficult if not impossible to hold for long, for nothing violent can last. He is thus trying to maintain whole by force something which naturally breaks, and he must be ever vigilant. He is devoted to an evil end, and therefore must create an evil order.

Since the tyrant cannot ever think a good thought or remember or imagine or do things that are not evil, if he does do some good it will be not for his own citizens but for foreigners. He maintains friendships with lords and masters of foreign peoples, for he views his citizens as rivals and is always afraid of them. He tries to use foreigners to strengthen his position at home. He wants his rule to be secret, and to seem not to be governing at all. He says and he makes his henchmen say that he does not want to change the city's form of government but only to preserve it. He wants to be viewed as the preserver of the common good, and therefore he shows mercy in small things, gives audience occasionally to mere boys and girls or to poor people, and often defends such persons even from minor wrongs. He longs to appear as the author of all the honors and dignities that are given to citizens and wants everyone to feel that these come from him. As to the punishments of those who err, however, or of those who are found guilty by his henchmen in order to bring them down or make them less fortunate, these sufferings he blames only on his officials, and excuses himself for not being able to help. Thus he acquires a good reputation and the love of the people, by making the officials bear the hatred of those who do not see through his stratagems.

He also tries to seem religious and dedicated to the service of religion, but he only does certain exterior things, like going to church, giving to certain charities, building or decorating churches and chapels, and other such things, all for ostentation. He even likes to converse with religious persons, and he falsely confesses to those who are really religious, so as to seem to have been absolved. Yet he ruins religion by usurping the benefices and giving them to his satellites and henchmen, as well as wanting them for his sons. Thus he usurps both temporal and spiritual goods. He wants no citizen to do anything fine, to outshine him in building a palace, or giving feasts, or endowing churches, or backing works of government or wars, for he wants to appear unique. Secretly he often ruins great men, and having brought about their downfall, he will appear to exalt them more than ever, so that they themselves may think they are obliged to him, and so that the people generally will think him merciful and magnanimous and give him their support.

He does not leave justice to the courts for he wants to favor and to kill or ruin whomever he pleases. To get wealth he seizes the commune's money and invents new taxes and revenues. With this money he feeds his satellites and pays off princes and other captains, often without regard to any need of the community. He wants to keep the military well off, and to make them his friends, and he can burden the people with taxes more honorably if he says it is needed to pay the soldiers. For this reason he tends to make unnecessary war and to cause others to make war for no purpose. He does not seek or desire victory nor to diminish foreign powers, but he does it just to keep his people lean and to stabilize his position. He often uses the commune's money to build great palaces and churches, and he displays his arms everywhere and feeds men and women entertainers, for he wants to stand in solitary splendor. To men he has raised from a low condition he gives the daughters of noble citizens for wives, both to lower and destroy the name of the noble families and to exalt such low persons as will be loyal to him. These have no generosity of soul, but they need him, being commonly such vain persons as consider his friendship the ultimate beatitude.

He eagerly receives presents in order to collect property, but he seldom gives to other citizens, preferring to bestow his gifts on princes or other foreigners in order to win their friendship. When he sees something that he wants, belonging to a citizen, he praises it and looks at it and makes such gestures as show his desire, so that the person will, for shame or fear, give it to him. He has flatterers around him to urge the person to make the gift. Often he makes people lend him things that he likes, and then does not return them. He despoils widows and orphans, while pretending to be their defender, and he seizes the goods and the fields and the houses of the poor for parks or pastures or palaces or other purposes that will give him pleasure. He promises to pay the owners a just price, but he never pays half what he says he will. He does not pay those who serve in his house as they deserve. He wants people to serve him for nothing. His satellites he tries to pay only with the goods of others, giving them offices and benefices that they do not merit and taking the offices of the city from others for their sake. If any merchant has a great deal of credit, he strives to make him go bankrupt, for he wants no one to have as much credit as he.

He raises bad men to high places, men who would be punished by the law if he did not protect them. These will then defend him because they thus defend themselves. If he occasionally gives a wise and good man a high position, he does it to show the public that he is a lover of virtue. He always keeps a sharp eye on the wise and good, however, and does not trust them. He also makes sure by the way he maintains them that they cannot hurt him.

Those who fail to court him and do not present themselves at his house or come to his public appearances, he considers enemies. He has followers everywhere who try to draw the young to themselves and provoke them to evil, even to oppose their own fathers. These get the young men to come to him and try to implicate all the youth of the country in their evil counsels. They make the youth hostile to all whom he views as opponents, even to their own fathers. He also tries to induce them to consume their goods in feasts and other delights so that they will be poor and he alone will remain rich. He does not like any office to be filled without consultation with him; or rather, he wants to fill them all with his own choices. Down to the cooks of the palace and the servants of the public officials, he does not want any jobs given without his consent. Often he gives offices to a younger brother, or to the youngest of a family, or to one with less qualifications of skill and character, in order to make the older and better persons envious and angry, thus creating discord. No opinion can be given, nor any praise bestowed, nor any peace arranged without him, for he wants always to favor one party and degrade whichever does not suit him as well.

All the good laws he cunningly tries to corrupt because they are opposed to his unjust government, and he constantly makes new laws to suit himself. In all governmental and administrative positions, within as well as outside the city, he has busy spies to tell him whatever is being done and said, and these give their own laws to such persons as they appoint to lesser offices, so he makes himself the refuge of all criminals and the nemesis of the just. He is supremely vindictive, and tries to avenge even the slightest injuries with great cruelty, so as to make others afraid, for he is afraid of everyone.

If anyone speaks ill of him, that person had better hide, for he will persecute him even to the ends of the earth, seeking revenge by ambush or poison or other means. He is a great murderer, for he wants to remove each and every obstacle to his rule, though he always presents himself as just the opposite, and very grieved by the death of others. He often pretends that he wants to execute some murderer who has been working for him, but secretly arranges his flight and, after a certain amount of time, that person will pretend to seek forgiveness and will be taken back and maintained close to him.

The tyrant wants to be the best at everything, even at little things, such as games, and rhetoric, and jousting, and horse racing, and scholarship. In any field where there is competition, he will always try to be first, and if he cannot win on his own talents, he will cheat and use some stratagem.

To enhance his reputation he makes it hard to see him. He often busies himself about his private pleasures while the citizens stand outside and wait. Then he gives them a brief interview and ambiguous replies. He would like to be understood by mere signs, for it seems he is ashamed openly to desire and demand what is in itself evil or to refuse what is good, so he speaks in broken phrases that sound good but he also wants to be really understood. He often jeers at good men, with words and by the way he treats them. With his close followers, he laughs at them.

He has secret communications with other princes and then, not telling what information he has acquired, he calls a council to discuss what is to be done. Everyone there gives the best answers he can, but the tyrant alone appears prudent and wise in the end, and well-versed in the secrets of the great lords. And for this he alone wishes to judge all men, and a little scrap of paper from him or a word sent by one of his pages counts more with any judge or official than any law.

Under the tyrant, in short, nothing is sure. Everything depends on his will, which is directed not by reason but by passion. Any citizen subjected to him hangs in suspense because of the tyrant's pride, any man's wealth is unsafe because of his greed, any lady's chastity and modesty are endangered by his lust. Especially at great feasts, there are male and female debauchees to corrupt the women and girls for him. There are often secret passages where the women are led away unsuspecting and find themselves caught in a trap. To say nothing of sodomy, which he likes so much that no boy who is at all attractive is safe. It would take a long time to discuss all the sins and wicked actions of the tyrant, but these will do for this treatise, and now we shall consider the particular problems of the city of Florence.

Chapter III
The Well Being of Florence Is Undermined by Tyranny; for Florence of All Cities, Tyranny Is Especially Bad

If tyranny is the worst form of government in whatever city or province it occurs, this, if we look at it as Christians, seems to me true to the highest degree in Florence. For all governments of Christian men ought to have as their ultimate purpose the salvation promised us by Christ, and this salvation cannot be attained but by good Christian living which (as we have shown elsewhere) is the best of all ways of life. Christians, therefore, ought to make both their local and their universal governments primarily encourage goodness in daily life. Since good living is nourished and fostered by religious institutions, these ought to be cultivated and preserved and expanded. It is not so much a matter of having more ceremonies as of encouraging more truth, and fostering good, holy, and learned clergy, both secular and regular. Bad men should as far as possible be removed from among the city's priests and monks. As the saints teach us, indeed, there are no worse men than these nor men who do more harm to true religion and good Christian living and every kind of good government. It is better to have few and good priests than many bad ones, for the bad ones provoke the wrath of God against the city. The gravity and number of their sins, which lead the majority of the people to sin likewise, and their persecution of good and just men, cause God to withdraw his hand and not let the grace of good government flow, for all good government comes from him. Read and reread the old and new Testament; you will find that all the persecutions of just men have tended to come from evil clerics, and that their sins have brought scourges of God on the people, and that they have always ruined good government by corrupting the minds of kings and leaders and whatever men were in power.

It is of the utmost importance that the city foster good living and that it be filled with good men, especially priests. If religion and morality improve, government is bound to be perfected. This is true, first, because God and his angels give especial care to bring it about. You can read in the old Testament in many places how, when religion flourished and increased, the kingdom of Judea went from good to better. The same is clear in the new Testament concerning Constantine the Great and Theodosius and other religious princes. Second, the prayers offered by those who are religious, and by the good people in the city, and by the whole community gathered at public feasts are efficacious. We read in the old and new Testament that cities have been saved from mortal danger by prayer and endowed by God with abundant spiritual and temporal goods. Third, good counsel is sure to maintain and increase the kingdom, for when the citizens are good, they are given special enlightenment by God, as it is written: *Exortum est in tenebris lumen rectis corde*, that is, in the shadows of trouble of this world, the righteous in heart are illuminated by God. Fourth, there will be unity, for where people live the good Christian life there cannot be discord; since the roots of discord, pride and ambition, greed and sensuality, are not there. Where there is unity, there is bound to be strength, and indeed past experience has shown small kingdoms made great through internal unity, while great ones have been quickly torn apart by discord.

Fifth, there will be justice and good laws, which good Christians cherish. As Solomon said: *Justitia firmatur solium*, that is, by justice the land is strengthened. The land will also attain wealth through good living, for since the people do not spend their wealth on waste, vast sums will collect in the treasury, with which to pay soldiers and officials and to feed the poor. By these means they will make their enemies afraid. Moreover as merchants and other rich men hear about their good government, they will gladly come to the city, while neighboring peoples who have been ill-governed by others will wish to be ruled by them. Their unity and the friendship of their allies will mean that they need few soldiers, and all arts and sciences and achievements will come to the city and vast treasure be gathered there, and its rule will expand in many directions. This will be a good thing, not only for the city, but also for other peoples, because they will be well-governed and because religion and faith and good Christian living will expand. This will be great glory to God and to our Savior Jesus Christ, king of kings, and lord of lords.

This is what tyrannical government prevents; this is what it spoils, for there is nothing the tyrant hates more than the worship of Christ and good Christian living. It is directly opposed to him, and opposite seeks to oust opposite. The tyrant, therefore, tries as hard as he can to remove the true worship of Christ from the city, though it persists secretly. If an occasional good bishop or priest or monk turns up, especially if he makes free to speak the truth, the tyrant tries carefully to remove him from the city or to corrupt his mind with adulation and presents.

And he is sure to give benefices to bad priests and to his own churchmen and to his henchmen. He favors the bad clergy who flatter him.

And he seeks always to corrupt the youth and all the good life in the city as something utterly opposed to him. That is a great, even a supreme evil, in any city or kingdom, but it is especially terrible in a Christian city, and Florence seems to me still the greatest Christian city . . . first, because this people is truly religious by inclination, as those who know the city know. It would indeed be very easy to create in this city perfect religious institutions and the best Christian life, if there were good government here. For, as we know by everyday experience, if it were not for the bad priests and monks, Florence would go back to the life of the first Christians and would stand as a mirror of true religion for the world. Even at present, in the midst of such persecutions of those who seek to live rightly and of good men, and with so many internal and external obstacles, excommunications and evil ideas in the air, we see these people living in such a way in this city of the good that (may I say it without offense to any other?) no other city can be named or exists where there is a greater number of righteous people or a greater perfection of life. If amidst persecutions and obstacles, she grows and is fruitful by the Word of God, what would she be if there were a quiet order within, and no opposition from lukewarm and bad priests, monks, and citizens?

The truth of this is confirmed by the well-known subtlety of the Florentines' minds, for we know how terribly dangerous it is if such minds turn towards evil, especially if they grow used to evil from childhood. For then they are hard to heal and will probably propagate a multitude of sins on earth. But if such minds do turn towards the good, it will be hard to pervert their goodness and they will be able to propagate the good in many directions. Florence, therefore, requires great care. It needs good government, and no one must be allowed to become a tyrant here; for we know how much evil tyranny can accomplish here and in other cities. Florentine tyrants have often been able cunningly to deceive the princes of Italy and to keep not only neighboring cities but even remote states in a divided condition. This has been all the more possible because the city is so affluent and so industrious. Thus it has repeatedly caused trouble for all Italy.

The rightness of our plea is also confirmed by the fact that, as we have remarked, tyranny, being a violent thing, cannot naturally endure. To express it in Christian terms, tyranny is permitted by God to punish and purge the sins of the people, but once they are purged, such government must cease. Once the cause is gone, the effect must disappear. If such government cannot endure in other cities and kingdoms, it certainly cannot endure in Florence without a fight. So many good minds cannot rest, and we have seen in fact frequent uprisings in Florence against whatever government there was. Such commotions and civil wars have sometimes brought upheaval to all Italy, and caused many evils. For the reasons I have given, and for many others that I must omit for the sake of brevity, it is fully clear that, if tyranny should be removed from any city and if anywhere any other kind of government can be more readily tolerated in its imperfections than tyranny with its horrendous effects, all this is even more applicable to Florence. Anyone who has really tasted of these things will easily understand that no punishment and no scourge in this world weighs like the sin of the man who tries or even wishes to try to become or to raise another as tyrant in the city of Florence. Any punishment that can be imagined in this present life is light compared with such sin. But the omnipotent God who is a just judge will know how to punish it as it deserves in this life and the next.

THIRD TREATISE

Chapter I
How to Found a Civil Government and Make It Work

Having decided that in Florence the best government is civil government, and that in that city of all cities tyranny is the worst kind of government, we must now see how one can be sure that tyranny does not arise in Florence and how civil government can be introduced. Sometimes tyrants gain power by force of arms, and as reason cannot resist force, we cannot in this case give any further instructions. We do intend to show, however, how provision can be made so that one citizen does not, as in the past has happened, take over, coming into power little by little, by cunning and not by arms, with the help of his friends. It may be said that for this purpose we would have to prevent any citizen becoming excessively rich, since money attracts followers and the very rich citizen can easily make himself the ruler. If we wanted to make this provision, however, it would lead to trouble. It is too dangerous a thing to wish to take the property of the rich and too difficult to set a specific limit on the private wealth of citizens. We shall assert, rather, that wealth is not the basic cause of one citizen's becoming a tyrant. A rich citizen possessing wealth alone, in fact, cannot attract the multitude of other citizens needed to support his government. Others have little to hope for from such a rich man. A small amount of money alone would not buy their consent to his tyranny. Each one would want a lot of money, and no citizen, no matter how rich, could actually buy as many citizens as he would need in such a big city. Having been made rich, moreover, the majority would naturally refuse with indignation to become the slave of persons viewed as equals.

Citizens in fact seek more than money, status, and fame within the city. They know that reputation helps a man grow rich. We must make sure, therefore, that no citizen is able, by any means whatsoever, to distribute benefices, and offices, and positions of dignity in the city. The true root of tyranny in the city is the fact that citizens adore positions of honor and want to be highly esteemed. If they think they cannot get benefices and honors by any other means, they willingly subject themselves to the person they believe can give them these things. Little by little the number of citizens self-subjected to the man with more authority increases, and so he becomes a tyrant. When there is a small group which usurps such authority, the people inevitably divides into factions which finally fight each other, and the one with the greatest following or the one who wins becomes the tyrant. It is necessary, therefore, to institute a system which lets only the whole people distribute offices and honors. One citizen, then, will not need to look up to another. Every man can consider himself the equal of any other. No one can make himself boss.

Because it is too hard to assemble the whole people every day, a certain number of citizens must be chosen to hold this kind of authority from the whole people. Because a small number, however, could be corrupted through friendships and family ties and bribery, this group must be large. Perhaps everyone would want to be in this group, and that could generate confusion. Perhaps the plebeians would want to get into the government, which would quickly lead to disorder. The number of citizens must be limited in such a way, therefore, that those who threaten to bring disorder cannot enter. Yet no citizen should have any reason to complain. Once this large group of citizens is established, which calls itself the Great Council, and which distributes all offices of honor, this group undoubtedly is the lord and master of the city. Hence it is necessary, as soon as the council has been created, to do three things.

First, to stabilize it in the right way and protect it with strong legislation, so that it cannot be deprived of power. Citizens who do not love the city well enough, however, and who care more for their own special interests than for the common good, would not want to join the council (but if they neglected it, the council could lose its power and be destroyed). One must make sure, therefore, that members who fail to attend at the appointed time, with no legitimate excuse, pay a fine, and a larger fine on the second offense, and that on the third offense, they lose their place in the council. Those who are not motivated by love to be active, therefore, though they ought to be so motivated, will be coerced. Everyone should care for the common welfare more than for his private affairs, and everyone ought willingly to risk his property and his life for the community's sake. So many good things, they should realize, proceed from good government and so much evil results, as we have shown, from bad government. Further legislation and penalties should be set up, as men gradually learn how best to make the council secure and to stabilize its control of the city. If that falls, all is lost.

Second, one must also make sure that this lord and master cannot turn into a tyrant. For just as one man who is a natural lord can be corrupted by bad men and become a tyrant, so a good council can, through the malice of bad men, become bad and tyrannical. Since dissolute and frivolous men, when there are a lot of them, are the cause of many evils in government, they must, as far as possible, be systematically excluded from the government. Heavy penalties must be established to prevent people's conniving with others, or asking others for agreement or for votes. If anyone is caught doing this, he must without fail be punished. Without severe penalties, we cannot preserve our state. We must diligently make arrangements that prevent the roots of evil and of flaws that would undermine the honesty of the council. It must not, especially its majority must not, fall into the control of bad men. That would mean instant ruin and tyranny would ensue.

Third, we must make sure that this system is not abused by exaggeration. The citizens must not be asked to assemble for every little thing. The true lords should personally decide only important matters, while minor matters fall to subordinates. The council must, however, preserve always the right to distribute offices and benefices. Everyone must pass through the gates of judgment. This, as I have said, will eliminate the source of all tyranny. The citizens should meet at regular and fairly convenient times to discuss the many things which will have to be done in these days of meeting. They will have to make the elections as quick and as expeditious as possible. We cannot say much about this or go into great detail, but if the Florentine citizens will stick with our principles, and accept what is said in the next chapter, they will be able to manage. As to details of procedure, with the help of God and their own good will, they will learn day by day from experience. Nor do I myself want to overstep the bounds of my condition and to give our opponents grounds for complaint.

Chapter II
What the Citizens Must Do to Perfect
Their System of Civil Government

Every Florentine citizen who wants to be a good member of his city and to help her, as everyone should wish to do, must first of all believe that this council and this civil government were ordained by God. This is true, indeed, not only because all good government comes from God, but also and especially because of the providential care which God has recently manifested in preserving the city. No one who has lived here for the past three years and is not blind and devoid of judgment would deny that, but for the hand of God, this government would never have been created against so much and such powerful opposition, nor would it have maintained itself to this day among so many traitors and so few friends. God, however, demands of us that we ourselves use the intellect and the free will he has given us. He has made all that pertains to government imperfect at first, so that with his help we can improve it. This government is still imperfect and has many flaws. We have hardly more than the foundation. Every citizen, therefore, should strive to perfect it. It can be made perfect only if all or at least the majority are blessed with the following four virtues.

First, fear of God. It is known that every government comes from God, for everything does. He is the first cause of all things and he governs all things. The government of things in nature is visibly perfect and stable, because natural things are subject to him and do not disobey. As they submit to all his commandments, he will always guide them to the perfection of their order and show them whatever they must do.

Second, love of the common good. When they hold offices and other dignities, the citizens must put aside all private interests and all the special needs of their relatives and friends. They must think solely of the common good. This concern will illuminate the eye of the intellect.

With their own affections put aside, they will not see falsely. With a firm grasp of the true ends of government they will not tend to go wrong in their decisions. They will deserve God's help, indeed, in fostering the growth of the common good. This, it is said, is one of the reasons for the expansion of the Roman empire, that they loved the common good of the city very much, and therefore God, to reward this virtue (for he does not want any good to go unrewarded, and yet their virtue, lacking the sanctification of grace, did not merit eternal life) rewarded them with temporal goods corresponding to their virtue. He caused the common good of their city to grow and extended their empire over the whole earth.

Third, love of one another. The citizens must drop feuds and forget all past offenses. Hatred, bad feeling, and envy blind the eye of the intellect and do not let it see the truth. Sitting in councils and in public offices, anyone who is not well purged in this regard will make many mistakes. For this God will let them suffer, for their own sins and those of others. But when they are well purged of such feelings, He will enlighten them. Beyond this, if they are peaceful and love one another, God will reward their benevolence with perfect government and growing power. This again is one of the reasons God gave such an empire to the Romans, for they loved one another and in the beginning lived in concord. Theirs was not divine charity, but it was good and natural charity, and God therefore rewarded it with temporal goods. If the citizens of Florence love each other with charity natural and divine, God will multiply their temporal and their spiritual goods.

Fourth, justice. Justice purges the city of bad men, or makes them live in fear. The good and just endure in high authority because they are gladly elected to office by those who love justice. They are enlightened by God in legislation and in guiding the city to a happy state. Justice will make the city fill up with goodness because it always rewards goodness; and the good men, wanting to live where there is justice, will congregate there in great numbers. God, for justice also, will increase the city's empire, as he did that of the Romans. Because the Romans exercised strict and severe justice, He gave them imperial power over the whole world. He wanted justice to make his peoples righteous.

The Florentine citizens, if they deliberate and use rational judgment, will see that they require no other government than the one we have described. If they have faith, moreover, that it was given to them by God, and exercise the four virtues we have named, their government will doubtless be soon perfected. They will arrive at good counsels together, in which God will illuminate their minds concerning whatever they seek to do. God will give them special light, moreover, because they are his servants, and they will know many things that they could not have found out for themselves. They will create on earth a government like that of heaven. They will be blessed with many spiritual and temporal blessings. If they will not have faith, however, that this government is given to them by God, and that they must truly fear God and love the common good, and if they follow only their own wills, without love for one another but with factionalism as always before, and if they fail to do justice, the government ordained by God will still remain. Only they and their children will be wholly consumed rather than receive the grace of it.

God has shown signs of his anger already, but they do not want to open their ears. God will punish them in this world and in the next. In this one they will always be restless and full of passions and sadness; in the other they will burn in the eternal fire. For they refused to follow the natural light, and even the divine signs which have been vouchsafed them, and to realize that this truly is their government. Some who failed to act righteously under this regime and were always restless with it are already suffering the pains of hell. Florentines! You have seen that God wants this government and signs have been given you, you know that it has not faltered despite attacks from within and without, and you realize that those who attack it are threatened by God with many punishments. I beg you by the bowels of mercy of our lord Jesus Christ, that you be content now to accept it. If you are not, God will send a greater scourge to assail you than he has done before. You will lose then both this world and the other. But if you support it, you will gain the happiness that I shall attempt to describe in the next chapter.

Chapter III
Those Who Rule Well Are Happy, and Misery Afflicts
Both Tyrants and Their Followers

This government is made more by God than by men, and those citizens who, for the glory of God and for the common good, obey our instructions and strive to make it perfect, will enjoy earthly happiness, spiritual happiness, and eternal happiness.

First, they will be free from servitude to a tyrant. How great that servitude is we have declared above. They will live in true liberty, which is more precious than gold and silver. They will be safe in their city, caring with joy and peace of mind for their own households and for making an honest profit in business. When God increases their property or their status, they will not be afraid of someone taking these away. They will be free to go to the country or wherever they want without asking permission from the tyrant. They will marry their sons and daughters to whomever they choose. They will be free to have weddings and celebrations and friends and to pursue science or art, whichever they please, and in other ways too, to build for themselves a certain earthly happiness.

Second, spiritual happiness will follow. Everyone will be able to dedicate himself to the good Christian life, and no one will prevent him. No one when in office will be forced by threats not to give justice, because everyone will be free. Nor will a man be forced by poverty to make evil pacts. The government of the city being good, riches will abound and everyone will work. The poor will earn money. The boys and girls will receive a holy upbringing. Good laws will protect the honor of women and girls. Religion especially will flourish, for God, seeing the people's good will, will send them good clergy. As the Scripture says: "God gives priests to suit the peoples." And these priests will be able to govern their flocks without hindrance, and good church officials and good monks too will become numerous. The bad, indeed, will not be able to live here, since contrary expels contrary.

Thus in a short time the city will be filled with true religion. It will be like a paradise on earth. The people will live amidst rejoicing and singing of psalms. The boys and girls will be like angels growing up in both the Christian and the civic life combined. They, in time, will create a government in this city that is more heavenly than earthly. The happiness of the good will be so profound that they will enjoy in this world a certain spiritual beatitude.

Third, not only will this earn the people eternal happiness, but it will raise the level of that happiness by a great deal. Their merits and therefore their reward in heaven will be increased. For God gives to those that govern well the greatest reward, since beatitude is the prize of virtue, and the greater a man's virtue, the greater his actions, the greater the prize. It is certainly greater virtue to rule oneself and others, and especially a community and a kingdom, than merely to rule oneself. It follows that he who rules a community merits in eternal life the greatest prize. Greater reward as we see in all the arts is given to the master who governs the undertaking than to the servants who obey his directions. In the military art, more is given the captain of the army than the soldiers; in building, greater reward is given the master builder and the architect than the manual workers. And so on in all the arts. The better the actions of a man, moreover, the more he honors God and makes himself useful to his neighbors, the more deserving he is. Certainly to govern a community well, especially one like the Florentine, is an excellent action. It will, as we have shown, bring great glory to God and benefit the souls and bodies and temporal prosperity of men. There can be no doubt then, that it merits a high reward and great glory.

We know that one who gives to charity or feeds a few poor is greatly rewarded by God, for our Savior says that in the day of judgment he will turn to the just and say: "Come, blessed of the Father, receive the kingdom prepared for you from the beginning of the world, for when I was hungry and when I was thirsty and when I was naked and wandering, you fed me and dressed me and took me in. And you came to visit me when I was ill, for what you have done to my little ones, you have done to me also." If God, then, gives great rewards for each man's particular charity, what reward will he give to the man who governs a large city well? Good government feeds many poor, provides for many who are wretched, defends widows and orphans, and takes out of the hands of the powerful and wicked the persons who otherwise could not defend themselves from their power, liberates the country from thieves and assassins, protects the good, and maintains good living and religious practice. Beyond all this it does infinitely more good. Similar loves similar, moreover, and he will love most whoever most resembles him. All creatures are similar to God, and all are loved by him, but because some are more similar to him than others, he loves them more. He who governs is more similar to God than he who is governed, and therefore surely, if he governs justly, is more loved and rewarded by God for this than for private actions when he is not governing. Whoever governs also takes more risk and suffers more weariness of mind and body than he who does not govern, for which again he deserves greater reward.

But the would-be tyrant is unhappy. First, he has no earthly happiness, for though he has riches, he cannot enjoy them because of the affliction of his spirit, his fears and continual worries, and especially because of the vast sums he must spend to remain in power. And though he wants to make everyone else a mere subject, he is the merest subject of all, forced to wait upon everyone in order to win people over. He is deprived of friendship, which is the greatest and best thing a man can enjoy in this world, because he does not want anyone to be his equal, because he is afraid of everyone, and especially because a tyrant is almost always generally hated for the evils he perpetrates. If bad men love him, it is not because they really wish him well, but because they want to profit from him. No true friendship, therefore, can exist among them.

Because of the evils he does, he does not have fame and honor. Others always hate and envy him. He can never really be consoled and free of melancholy, because he must always be vigilant and suspicious that his enemies may try something. He is necessarily always afraid. He does not trust even his guards.

He is spiritually unhappy also, moreover, for he lacks the grace of God, and all knowledge of him. Surrounded by sinners and by the perverse characters who

make up his assiduous following, he is bound to fall into evil ways. He will, therefore, be eternally unhappy, for tyrants are almost always incorrigible. The multitude of his sins means that sin has become a habit with him, extremely hard to
abandon. To give back all the property he has stolen, also, and to offer reparations
for so many evil deeds would mean being left in his underwear, a thing one can
imagine would be difficult to one accustomed to a life of such pride and indulgence.
He is also prevented by his flatterers, who make light of his sins and convince him
that wicked things are good, even by the tepid monks who confess and absolve
him, showing him white when they should show him black. Thus he is wretched
in this world and goes to hell in the other, where he is more severely punished
than other men. There stands against him the multitude of his sins and of the sins
he has caused others to commit. He is also condemned for the office he has
usurped, for, as the good ruler earns God's greatest rewards, the bad one is most
severely punished.

The tyrant's followers all participate in his wretchedness in temporal, in spiritual, and in eternal things. They lose their liberty, which is the greatest of treasures,
as well as their property and honors and sons and wives. For all these come into
the tyrant's power. They are always imitating his sins, in order to please him and
to be as like him as they can. In hell, too, therefore, they will participate in his
terrible punishment.

The citizens who dislike civil government because it stops them from being
tyrants all participate in the same wretchedness even though they are not actually
tyrants. They lack riches, honors, reputation, and friendship. All the lean ones
congregate around them hoping to repair their fortunes, and all the bad men
surround them. They must be always spending money, and the good people avoid
them. They have not a single real friend, for their followers try to rob them. Their
bad companions lead them into a thousand sins which they would not otherwise
commit. They are restless in heart and at all times filled with hatred, envy, and
complaints. Thus they have hell both in this world and the next.

Since (as we have shown), therefore, those who rule well are happy and are
like God, and those who rule badly are unhappy and like the devil, every citizen
should abandon his sins and his private affections to strive to rule well. Everyone
should work to preserve and increase and perfect this civil government, for the
honor of God and for the salvation of souls. God gave this government especially
to Florence because of his love for this city. Through this government, it can be
happy in this world and the other, by the grace of our Savior Jesus Christ, king
of kings, lord of lords, who with the Father and the Holy Spirit lives and rules in
saecula saeculorum.

PART III

On Florence Between Republic and Principate

Chapter 8

PAOLO VETTORI

Memorandum to Cardinal de' Medici About the Affairs of Florence

(1512)

Paolo Vettori (1477–1526), the younger sibling of his better-known brother, Francesco (who had a noted correspondence with Machiavelli), is certainly the least erudite author to appear in this collection. A politically active and likely quite profligate member of a wealthy patrician family, Vettori played a prominent role in the Medici's return to Florence in 1512 and thereafter held significant civic and diplomatic posts owing to the family's patronage. *Memorandum to Cardinal de' Medici* presents the unvarnished vision of a principality supported and maintained through the efforts—public and covert, legal and criminal—of a coterie of loyal aristocrats.

The text is a reprint of Paolo Vettori, *Memorandum to Cardinal de' Medici About the Affairs of Florence*, in J. Kraye, ed. and trans., *Cambridge Translations of Renaissance Philosophical Texts*, volume 2, *Political Philosophy* (Cambridge: Cambridge University Press, 1997), 239–42.

———— ✳ ————

Memorandum to Cardinal de' Medici About the Affairs of Florence

Most Reverend Lord, since it is necessary for you to depart,[1] I wish respectfully to write down for you what occurs to me; if I have not written wisely, at least it is done in good faith, as I must, for the prosperity of this government [*questo stato*] and of those who are linked with it.

Your ancestors, from Cosimo to Piero,[2] maintained power [*questo stato*] more by skilful management [*industria*] than by force [*forza*]. But you need to use force more than skilful management, because you have more enemies here and not very much ability to satisfy them; therefore, since you cannot win them over again,[3] you will need to become so strong and secure that they will be afraid to attack you. The way to achieve this is to maintain the body of faithful armed men [*questa guardia*], and in order to be more in control of them, you must be able to pay them more easily. Therefore, I would recommend a decision in the *Balìa* that the office of the Ten[4] allocates all the funds needed for the upkeep of these forces and places these funds in the depository of the Signoria, so that they will be paid to the commissary who will have special responsibility for these forces. In this way, the payments would be made more easily and secretly. You should contrive to have spies within these forces and keep the soldiers well disposed towards you. But all these forces will not be sufficient, because this city is very large, and there are too many discontented citizens. Moreover, you cannot trust all the members of the *Balìa*, or all the information that they gather. Consequently, if all the previously mentioned forces are not supplemented by others, they will turn out to be very weak or useless.

You cannot have military forces that are more reliable, or more numerous, or that will cause more fear in the city or inspire greater trust in your family [*Casa*] than infantry troops, because you must realize that during the past ten years the city has been very prosperous, and therefore the memories of this period will give rise to much resentment or hostility.[5] On the other hand, your countryside and rural districts [*contado e distretto*] have been very far from prosperous, so that you should be able to win over their inhabitants, even if you cannot regain the allegiance of the citizens. And if you arm the inhabitants of the countryside, and win over those whom you arm by defending them from provincial administrators [*rettori di fuori*] and from public officers in Florence itself [*magistrati di dentro*] who oppress them, and if in fact you become their protector, within six months you will be more secure in Florence than if you were to have a Spanish army in Prato ready to help you. Here is the way to achieve this: before you leave, contrive to get the *Balìa* to decide to give as much authority to the Signoria for raising infantry and cavalry as the Nine[6] had, because the constables who will be chosen for that purpose will need no further approval and will be entitled to delegate that authority to the man they think most suitable; you will therefore be able to appoint a commissary favourable to you and who will obey you. The funds of the Signoria, given directly to their depositary, will be sufficient for paying these constables.

There is something else that you should decide before you leave: how Giuliano[7] should act and from whom he should seek advice, about both internal and foreign policy. And I must warn you frankly that if this matter is not dealt with properly, confusion and harm could well result; and including myself among all the others, you will find all these citizens to be ambitious and cautiously self-seeking [*rispettivi*]. Because of their ambition, it is hard to satisfy them, and because of their cautious self-seeking, they will give unsound advice. There will be very few who do not think first of saving themselves rather than you, and who are not concerned with being able to stay in Florence themselves, even if you should be driven out. Hence, the advice given by such men is not unbiased, and Giuliano will not realize this, because he is not yet well versed in the affairs of this city; if someone who perceives troubles that are merely brewing does not stay close to him and warn him about them in good time, your regime [*lo Stato Vostro*] could come to such a pass that, even if it survives, it will be exceedingly weak. And if the situation were to be put right, fresh injuries would need to be done to the people. If such things are not done at once, they cannot be done later. All this is concerned with cautious self-seeking [*a' respecti*].

With regard to ambition, I wish to tell Your Most Reverend Lordship that, when you leave, that which keeps the citizens united in obedience will be removed, namely, your own personal authority and the respect it engenders. The discords will at once cause many problems for Giuliano, which he will not be able to overcome by himself, because he does not yet understand our affairs, and very serious troubles could result from this. Therefore, I would say that, before you leave, you must choose for Giuliano ten or twelve citizens, being careful to exclude any who are fair-weather supporters of your family. Giuliano should seek their advice on every matter, both at home and in the Palace,[8] both in secret and in public. Since it is possible that disagreements will arise among them, you need to choose from this number one or two, at the most, whom Giuliano, after previous consultations, can gather round him in order to discuss the proposals and opinions of everyone before making his decisions. If Your Most Reverend Lordship choose the twelve men well, especially those two trusted advisers, and begins to control affairs in this way, all the ambitions, troubles and contentions, though they will not altogether cease, will at least remain hidden, so that men become accustomed to this way of doing things. For men complain and shout when they see that shouting gets them what they want; but when they realize that their shouting is ineffective and does not cause the decisions made to be changed, they quieten down and learn to accept what has been done.

Another matter is that Your Most Reverend Lordship must decide is where you want affairs of state [*le cose di Stato*] to be handled. Dealing with all of them privately [*a casa*][9] would be too troublesome; if they are dealt with in the Palace, the Ten must deal with them, because the Signoria has always been the instrument [*il bastone*] and not the decision-making body of government [*il cervello dello Stato*]. Therefore, before you depart, you must reorganize the Chancery.[10]

In order that you may understand everything, in Lorenzo's day,[11] as far as I have been able to find out, the Chancery was organized as follows: Scala[12] attended to the letters of other rulers [*Signori di fuora*], which messer Marcello[13] does now; messer Cristofano[14] attended to correspondence about internal affairs, which Machiavelli[15] does now; ser Giovanni[16] dealt with the Riformagioni,[17] which ser Francesco[18] does now, and ser Simone of Staggia[19] the Tratte,[20] which is now the responsibility of ser Antonio Vespucci.[21] All these men have had their assistants. At the head of the Chancery of the Eight of Pratica and the Ten were messer Francesco Gaddi,[22] ser Alessandro Bracci[23] and ser Francesco, son of ser Barone;[24] and they had as assistants such men as ser Antonio della Valle,[25] ser Antonio of Colle,[26] Bernardo de' Ricci, ser Lorenzo Ficini,[27] ser Jacopo di Ruffino and Marco of Romena, and others that I have not discovered. But I certainly know that they had pairs of men, so that they could send them abroad together with ambassadors; and with regard to the latter, they began to establish permanent embassies in important places, like those of Ser Antonio della Valle in Naples, ser Antonio of Colle in Rome and Bernardo de' Ricci in Milan. At present, the duties of the Chancery of the Ten and the Chancery of the Signoria are not entirely distinct, because messer Marcello deals with letters to and from the Ten, and Machiavelli dealt with letters about internal affairs, before he went to the Ordinanza.[28] Then, for the last four years, Biagio,[29] the assistant of messer Marcello, has served there; and there are three or four assistants who write letters.

Although the Chancery is organized in this way today, during the previous regime [*nello Stato passato*][30] it was organized differently. For in the Ten a post carrying a salary of 194 florins was left vacant; this money was put aside to pay a well-qualified man to help messer Marcello as an equal. Yet another post carrying the same salary was left vacant: this was used by the Ten for dealing with letters concerning internal affairs. These posts were not left unfilled in order to save the Comune money by economizing on their salaries, and in any case the Comune was sufficiently provided with staff. Your Most Reverend Lordship must think how the staff of these chanceries can be reduced at the present time. And if you want the affairs of state [*le faccende di Stato*] to be controlled by the Ten, Giuliano will need to meet with the Ten at least once a day and have with him some of those citizens chosen to advise him; and the replies to be given to ambassadors should be decided there, and everything else that he considers necessary. He should have a chancellor attached to the Ten who has much experience of internal and foreign affairs, and this man should also write on Giuliano's behalf to the ambassadors about those things that concern your own rule [*dello Stato vostro particulare*], not deviating in any way from what has been decided. Moreover, if you should remove an experienced or trusted man, that would be an excellent beginning for your rule [*per lo Stato vostro*], because it is essential that it should be seen as something ordered by you.

With regard to the funds required for everything, I shall not say anything; I shall leave Guidotto[31] to speak about it, or others who understand more about it than I do. I shall say only that it is essential to create a depository that has credit facilities, so that its credit can supplement money when necessary, and men can be reimbursed with promissory notes and not have to wait for money to come from the public treasurers every time.

Chapter 9

NICCOLÒ MACHIAVELLI

Memorandum to the Newly Restored Medici

(1512)

Discursus on Florentine Matters After the Death of Lorenzo de' Medici the Younger

(1520–21)

Minutes of a Provision for the Reform of the Florentine Government

(1522)

Memorandum to Cardinal Giulio on the Reform of the State of Florence

(1522)

Summary of the Affairs of the City of Lucca

(1520)

Niccolò Machiavelli (1469–1527) would have secured enduring fame for any one of the roles he assumed during his life in Renaissance Florence: diplomat, military strategist, civil servant, poet, playwright. It was in his capacity as political philosopher, however, that Machiavelli earned eternal renown by sparking some of the most intense scholarly controversies in Western intellectual history. On the basis of his chief political works—*The Prince*, the *Discourses on Livy's First Ten Books*, the *Florentine Histories*, and *The Art of War*—many commentators consider Machiavelli to be the father of modern political thought or modern political science; some even ordain him the founder of "modernity" itself. The essays collected here take a decidedly local focus: four of them are proposals addressed to the Medici family on the matter of converting Florence's government from a principality to a republic; the final one is an analysis of the politics and government of the Tuscan city of Lucca. The essays exhibit Machiavelli's commitment to granting the popular assembly, the Great Council, a central place in a reestablished Florentine republic, but they also convey Machiavelli's sensitivity to the Medici's concern that their interests and those of their partisans will remain secure during and beyond the proposed republican transition.

John P. McCormick translated Machiavelli's "Memorandum to the Newly Restored Medici" ("Ai Palleschi") and "Discursus on Florentine Matters After the Death of Lorenzo de' Medici the Younger" ("Discursus Florentinarum Rerum Post Mortem Iunioris Laurentii Medices") from texts in Corrado Vivanti, ed., *Opere I: I Primi Scritti Politici* (Turin: Einaudi-Gallimard, 1997), 87–89 and 733–45. Mark Jurdjevic translated Machiavelli's "Minutes of a Provision for the Reform of the Florentine Government," "Memorandum to Cardinal Giulio on the Reform of the State of Florence," and "Summary of the Affairs of the City of Lucca": respectively, "Minuta di Provisione per la Riforma dello Stato di Firenze l'Anno 1522," "Ricordo al Cardinale Giulio sulla Riforma dello Stato di Firenze," and "Sommario delle Cose della Città di Lucca," from texts in Jean-Jacques Marchand, Denis Fachard, and Giorgio Masi, eds., *Arte della Guerra e Scritti Politici Minori* (Rome: Salerno, 2001), 645–54, 642–44, and 612–20.

Memorandum to the Newly Restored Medici

I would like to advise you against following the opinion of those who say that it would be beneficial to accentuate the defects of Piero Soderini with the goal of diminishing his reputation among the people.[1] If you examine such persons and their motivations carefully, you will find that they are not moved to benefit the present state but rather only themselves. First, as far as the people are concerned, the Medici could be accused of the very same nefarious aspirations that they attribute to Piero Soderini.[2] Therefore, stressing Soderini's deficiencies will not enhance this state's reputation, but only the reputation of those citizens who wished him ill and who openly opposed him in the previous regime. As things stand, it is commonly believed that these citizens opposed Soderini only to discredit his state to the people, whereas if he were successfully denounced, the people would say: "Ah, we see! What they said was true! These were in fact good citizens who rightfully criticized Piero, but who intentionally caused neither his downfall nor the ensuing events."[3]

Hence, if the new state thoroughly denounced Soderini it would do so not in a way that transferred his good reputation to itself but rather to his adversaries, who had previously criticized him.[4] To them, not to the Medici, would accrue the gratitude of the people. This is not in the least bit beneficial to the present state, which must endeavor to make these citizens odious to and not favored by the people, such that the former cleave closely to the new state—partaking in responsibility for whatever befalls it, good or ill.

If you carefully consider who these citizens are you will know that what I say is true. They recognize that they have incurred the hatred of the universality[5] for opposing Piero, an enmity that they cannot escape unless their denunciations are borne out as valid. They wish to purge the universality of this enmity in order to pursue their own advantage and not that of the Medici. But the cause of the present mistrust between the universality and the Medici is neither Piero nor his ruin, but rather the change in the city's orders.[6]

Again, accentuating the defects of Piero does not improve the reputation of the Medici state but rather that of particular citizens; this state would severely undermine itself by denouncing one who has been expelled and who poses it no immediate threat, while at the same time strengthening those who are still at home, those who offend the state every day and who might enlist the universality in overthrowing it. To underscore my point, I repeat: the present state need not worry about the threat of Piero Soderini but rather the threat posed by the old order.[7] It would benefit this government to attack it, not Piero. Certain citizens who whore themselves between the people and the Medici despise Piero; they desperately seek an opportunity to undermine his reputation with the people and so free themselves of the taint of having been his enemies. This they do for their own sake and not for yours—nor for the benefit of those who wish to be faithful to you in circumstances both fair and foul.

For the sake of clarity, let me put matters another way. Certain citizens support the Medici for fear of two things: first, to avoid being offended by the Medici for not supporting them; and, second, to avoid expulsion if the previous order were restored with Piero Soderini at its head. To cast Piero Soderini in an evil light, and so make the universality hate him, gives such citizens less cause to fear him. They would prefer to take his place of prominence should the previous order return.[8] In that eventuality, it would be better that they not appear to be your adherents but rather remain cool to the Medici's state. This is plainly not beneficial to the Medici, for they would be unable to reside in Florence whether the previous order were restored with Piero or without him. On the contrary, those citizens who wish such a restitution could not abide in the city should Piero return, but they would stay and do very well indeed if he did not. This is why they wish to tear down Piero's reputation: for their own security and not that of the Medici. Rather than serving the Medici's interest, this situation would prove most harmful and perilous to their house and their state. They effectively would be ungagging those many mouths that would then bite them, freely and without respect.

——— ✳ ———

Discursus on Florentine Matters After the Death of Lorenzo de' Medici the Younger

———

Florence's governments have often changed their forms because the state has never been either a proper republic or principate.[9] One cannot call a principate stable when the will of a single individual is deliberated over and confirmed by the consent of so many. Neither can one consider a republic sustainable when those humors whose satisfaction is necessary to avoid its ruin remain unsatisfied. The truth of this is borne out by the kinds of states that the city has established since 1393. Commencing with those reforms enacted by Messer Maso degli Albizzi at that time, we see a republic governed by aristocrats that was so defective that it endured barely forty years. Indeed, it would have lasted even fewer years if not for the unity generated by the wars with the Visconti of Milan.

Among its defects was the fact that scrutinies for office were established too far in advance, which facilitated rampant fraud and produced poor appointments. Because men are variable and prone to corruption, individuals who initially may have been truly worthy when deemed eligible to hold office later may no longer be so when they are actually appointed to office. Additionally, great men never sufficiently feared punishment for engaging in the formation of sects, which is always the ruin of a state. Furthermore, the Signoria, which enjoyed too little reputation and too much authority, could execute and despoil citizens without appeal and could too readily call the people to a *parlamento*.[10] As a result, whenever a reputed citizen managed to control or circumvent it, the Signoria became less the state's defender and more the instrument of its usurpation. Alternatively, as already noted, it enjoyed a low reputation because it contained unworthy men, as well as many who were too young; also, its terms were excessively short, and it dealt with matters of little genuine gravity.

That state was disordered in yet another not insignificant way: it deferred excessively to the advice of private men over public matters, which diminished the authority and reputation of the magistrates in a manner that is contrary to all civil orders. In addition to these disorders, there was another one as important as all the rest combined: the people did not play their appropriate part in the state. All these factors contributed to infinite disorders such that, as noted, if external wars had not kept the state steady, it would have come to ruin much sooner than it actually did.

Then came Cosimo's state, which inclined more toward a principate than a republic. It endured longer than the previous state for two reasons: first, it was established with the favor of the people; and, second, it was governed by the prudence of two men, Cosimo and his grandson, Lorenzo. Still, a certain weakness inhered in the fact that large numbers had to deliberate over plans that Cosimo wished to enact, such that he often incurred the danger of losing the state. This resulted in frequent *parlamenti* and many exiles under this state, and, eventually, during the accident of King Charles's invasion, it collapsed.

Immediately thereafter, the city resolved to restore the form of a republic, but unfortunately not in a mode that would ensure durability: the orders that were instituted failed to satisfy the humors of all kinds of citizens; moreover, the state proved incapable of meting out appropriate punishments. Indeed, it was so flawed and so far removed from the model of a true republic that a life-tenured gonfalonier, had he been wise and wicked, could have readily become prince; had he been righteous and weak, he could be readily expelled, with the ruin of the entire state ensuing. It would take far too long to elaborate all the reasons for this, so I will mention only one: the gonfalonier was surrounded by no one who could, if the former were good, defend him, and if he were wicked, curb and correct him.

These governments were all deficient because every attempt to reform them was aimed not at the satisfaction of the common good, but rather to benefit and secure only a single party. Such security always proved elusive, however, because there ever remained another malcontented party, which invariably proved to be a formidable instrument for those who wished to innovate the state.

There is only left to consider the state from 1512 to the present time, its deficiencies and strengths—but because it is a recent and familiar matter, and thus well known by everyone, I will omit a discussion of it. In any case, the duke's recent death necessitates a full discussion of new modes of government. In order to demonstrate my loyalty to Your Holiness, I believe that I ought not err by failing to express my thoughts. First, I will convey the opinions that I have heard others express, and then I will present my own—if I err at all in this regard, I trust that Your Holiness will absolve me for being more loving than prudent.

Some insist that no more reliable form of government could be ordered than that which reigned in the times of Cosimo and Lorenzo; others prefer a more widely inclusive government. Those who prefer a government similar to Cosimo's say that all things return easily to their nature. They say that Florentine citizens naturally honor your house, they enjoy the graces that it has bestowed on them, they love the things that they have always loved, and they have become accustomed to maintaining a certain habit for sixty years. Thus, on this view, Florentines can do nothing else than follow the previous ways and return to their former spirits. Furthermore, they believe that it is only a few who adhere to an opposite way of thinking and who engage in contrary habits, and thus that the latter can be easily eliminated. Beyond these reasons, they invoke necessity, arguing that Florence cannot function without a head. Because it must have one, they conjecture, it might as well come from a house that tends to be adored; rather than, either absent a head, the city become confused, or, turning to an alternate head, the city settles for someone less reputed and less familiar to everyone.

One could respond to this opinion with the observation that such a state is dangerous because it is weak. If Cosimo's state suffered in those times from the many deficiencies outlined above, they would be doubled in the present. After all, now the city, the citizens, and the times are quite different from what they were then, such that presently it would be impossible to create a state similar to that previous one that could endure in Florence. First, that state had the universality[11] as a friend, while this one incurs its enmity. Those citizens had never in their lifetimes enjoyed in Florence a state more inclusive of the universality than that one. These citizens remember one that they consider more civil and with which they were more contented. In Italy back then there was neither an army nor a power that the Florentines with their arms could not repel, despite often standing alone. Now, with Spain and France here, we must be friends with one of them, whom, should they be vanquished, would leave Florence prey to the victor—a situation that never transpired in the past.

Previously, citizens as a matter of course paid heavy taxes; presently, through either incapacity or bad habits, they are no longer inclined to do so—and efforts to rehabituate them in this respect prove to be odious and dangerous affairs. The Medici who governed in those times were born and reared among fellow citizens such that they governed with familiarity and thus gained grace from the latter. Because they have now become so great as to transcend the bounds of civility, such familiarity, and thus such grace, is no longer possible. Consequently, given how much men and times have changed, nothing could be more delusional than the belief that now an old form could be imposed on entirely different matter. If back then, as I stated above, the Medici were in danger of losing the state every ten years, now they would certainly lose it. Furthermore, no one should believe it to be true that men readily return to an old and familiar way of life. They may do so when they consider the old ways more pleasant than the new, but when they like it less, they can return to it only under compulsion; and they will endure it only so long as that compulsion persists.

Additionally, it may be true that Florence cannot function without a head, and that among various private heads it would surely love one from the House of Medici more than any other. Yet, if it were to choose between a private and a public head, it would always find the public head, whatever house he came from, more preferable to the private one.

Some say that it is impossible to lose the state without an external assault, believing furthermore that in such circumstances there is always time to befriend the invading enemy. But this is grievous self-deception: usually friendship is not necessarily forged with the most powerful adversary but merely with the one that happens to be attacking you at that particular moment, or with the one that your spirit or imagination inclines you to love. It can easily happen then that your friend loses, leaving his fate to the discretion of the winner; at which time, the latter may decide against coming to an accord with you, either because you were tardy in seeking it to begin with, or because you have incurred his hatred as a result of your friendship with his enemy.

For instance, Duke Ludovico of Milan and King Frederick of Naples would have readily negotiated an accord with King Louis XII of France, if they could have (and he with one of them, if possible); and both lost their states as a result of their failures to do so—such are the countless factors that often impede efforts to secure treaties. All things considered then, one cannot call this kind of state either secure or stable because too many things may prove a source of precarity. Therefore, it should not be pleasing to Your Holiness or to your friends.

Regarding those who desire a more widely inclusive government than this one: I say that if it is not expanded in a way that results in a well-ordered republic then that widening will quickly ruin it. If such persons explained quite specifically what it is that they want, then I would respond to them with greater specificity; but if they continue to speak in generalities, I can address them only generally. I would like the following answer to suffice for now: apropos Cosimo's state, it must be said that no state is stable that is not a true principate or a true republic, because all the governments between these two are deficient. The reason could not be clearer: the principate's one path toward demise descends in the direction of a republic, while, likewise, a declining republic ascends in the direction of a princi-pate. Yet, those states in between incline toward not one but two possible paths to their demise, either toward a principality or a republic—in this resides their instability. Therefore, Your Holiness, if you wish to provide Florence with a stable state, one both worthy of your glory and compatible with your friends' well-being, you should order either a true principate or a true republic, with each of their respectively appropriate qualities. All other accomplishments will prove futile and excessively brief.

I will refrain from discussing a principate in any detail, owing to the difficulty in establishing one here, and the absence of any instrument to make it possible.

Furthermore, Your Holiness must understand that in all cities where there is widespread equality among citizens, only with maximum difficulty can a principate be established; and in those where there is widespread inequality, a republic cannot be ordered at all. For instance, in order to found a republic in Milan, where there is extensive inequality among citizens, it would be necessary to eliminate the entire nobility, and reduce everyone to equality. Because so many there live in an extraordinarily extravagant fashion, laws are insufficient to constrain them; rather they require a vigorous voice and overweening power to control them.

Alternatively, to establish a principate in Florence, where there is great equality, it would be necessary to institute significant inequality: one would have to elevate nobles with great castles and villas, who would defend the prince with arms and attendants by strangling the entire city and province. A prince acting alone without a supportive nobility could not maintain a principate; he would require there to be between himself and the universality an intermediary that acts as his auxiliary in ruling. As we see in France, the gentlemen control the people, the princes control the gentlemen, and the king controls the princes.

In short, to establish a principate in a city where a republic would be more appropriate requires efforts arduous, inhumane, and unworthy of anyone wishing to be deemed merciful and good. Therefore, I will forego any further discussion of a principate and speak only of a republic. Indeed, Florence is very eager to take on such a form, and Your Holiness is very much inclined to provide it— people believe that you delay in doing so only in the hopes of maintaining your greatness and your friends' security in Florence. I have devised a way to make both things possible. Thus, I want Your Holiness to understand my thinking, so that, if any good inheres within it, you can make use of it, and furthermore appreciate just how much I wish to serve you. For you will see that in this republic of mine your authority not only endures but increases, and that your friends remain honored and secure; alternatively, the universality will have manifest reasons to be content with it. I pray, with the greatest reverence, that Your Holiness neither blame nor praise my *discorso* without reading it in its entirety. Moreover, I pray that you not be alarmed by certain alterations in the magistracies, because where things are poorly ordered, the less of the old that is retained, the less of the bad likewise remains.

Those who order a republic must take account of the three different qualities of men who make up all cities, that is, the first, the middle, and the last. And although Florence is characterized by the equality noted before, still an elevated spirit motivates some citizens who think themselves entitled to maintain pre-eminence over others. When ordering a republic, it is necessary to satisfy these men—indeed, the previous state was ruined for no other reason than failing to provide them such satisfaction. This simply cannot be accomplished unless majesty is bestowed on the highest ranks of the republic, a majesty that is sustained by their persons.

It will be impossible to confer such majesty on the first ranks of the Florentine state without changing the present configurations of the Signoria and the colleges. Because of the manner in which such offices are created presently, men of gravity and reputation seldom sit in them, and the state's majesty is either diminished entirely, displaced elsewhere, or entrusted to private men—which contravenes all political order. This must be corrected in a way that satisfies the highest ambitions within the city. Here is such a way.

Annul the Signoria, the Eight of Pratica, and the Twelve Good Men, and, in order to enhance the government's majesty, replace them with sixty-five men of forty-plus years of age (fifty-three from the major guilds and twelve from the minor ones). They should remain within government for the duration of their lives in the following mode: Create from among them a gonfalonier of justice for a two- or three-year term (if a life-termed one is deemed undesirable); divide the remaining sixty-four citizens in half, with each set of thirty-two governing alongside the gonfalonier in alternating years as ordered below in perpetuity. These all together will be called the Signoria.

Each year's thirty-two should be divided into four parts of eight members, each of which should preside with the gonfalonier for three months in the palace, assuming the magistracy with the usual ceremonies, conducting all the affairs of the Signoria as it does today. Then, along with their companions among the alternate thirty-two, they will have all the authority of and the capacity to conduct policy presently associated with the combined Signoria, Eight of Practica, and the colleges, which were annulled above. This, as I have written, will be the first head and first organ of the state. This order, if considered well, manifestly bestows majesty and reputation unto the head of the state; for men of gravity and authority will always, quite obviously, fill the highest ranks of the city. There will henceforth be no further need of conferring on public matters with private men, which, as noted, is always pernicious for republics; from now on, the thirty-two who, in any particular year, do not sit in the magistracy, will provide requisite advice and counsel. And Your Holiness, as I will explain, may elect to this rank all your friends and confidants. But now let us consider the second rank of the state.

As I said before, I believe that there are three qualities of men, and, therefore, it is necessary to have three types of ranks in a republic, but no more. Hence, you would do well to clear up of the confusion of councils that have long confounded the city. These were instituted not because they served a civil way of life, but because they fed the appetite for office of ever more citizens, improving the city's health not a bit but providing instead opportunities for sects to corrupt it.

If, therefore, I am attempting to erect a republic comprising three groups then it seems to me that the Seventy, the One Hundred, the Council of the People, and the Council of the Commune should be annulled. These should be replaced with a Council of the Two Hundred, comprising forty-year-olds, forty of whom should come from the minor guilds, and 160 of whom should come from the major ones— none of these may also be eligible for the Signoria. These two hundred should serve for life and be called the Select Council.

This council, in tandem with the reconfigured Signoria, should have all the authority and responsibilities presently enjoyed by the councils we are explicitly annulling. Your Holiness may appoint this second rank of the state, just as you may appoint the first. To accomplish this, and to maintain, regulate, and supervise these new orders (and those still to be described), and for the security of your authority and of Your Holiness's friends, I recommend the following: Your Holiness and the Most Reverend Cardinal de' Medici must retain, through the Balìa, as much authority during the length of both your lives as does the whole Florentine people. To this end, the Eight of Guardia and the Balìa[12] ought to be established whenever you deem them to be needed. Moreover, for the state's security and that of Your Holiness's friends, the infantry should be ordered by dividing it into two bands, over which should be appointed, through Your Holiness's authority, two commissioners, respectively.

We see from the matters discussed above that we have satisfied two qualities of men and confirmed your own authority over the city and your friends' security within it; arms and criminal justice are placed in your hands, the laws abide in your breast, and all the heads of the state belong to you. It remains now to satisfy the third and last rank of men, which is the entire universality of the citizens; these will never be satisfied unless their authority is restored or if such a restoration is promised to them—anyone who believes otherwise is quite unwise. Because to do so all at once would serve neither your friends' security nor the maintenance of Your Holiness's authority, it will be necessary partly to restore it and partly to promise to restore it fully such that the universality enjoys complete confidence of actually gaining it back.

Therefore, I think that it is necessary to reopen the Great Council, with a quorum[13] of one thousand or at least six hundred citizens, to distribute all the offices and magistracies as it did before—except for the aforementioned Sixty-Five, the Two Hundred, and the Eight of Balìa, which, during the life of Your Holiness and of the cardinal, you would continue to select. And so that your friends would be certain, when the council is to make a selection, that their names have been placed in the bags, Your Holiness will appoint eight *accoppiatori*,[14] who may secretly select or reject anyone they like. In order for the universal to believe that those ultimately selected for office were actually drawn from the bags, the council must be allowed to choose and send two citizen scrutinizers to observe the placement of names in the bags.

No stable republic can ever be established without satisfying the universality. And if the Great Hall is not reopened, never will the universality of Florentine citizens be satisfied. Reopening this room and rendering to the universality this distribution is simply necessary to once again make Florence a republic. Be sure of this, Your Holiness: whoever thinks about seizing the state from you will above all other things plan on reopening it. Therefore, it is better to reopen it under terms and with modes that are safe, and thus remove from your enemies the opportunity of reopening it to your dismay and your friends' destruction and ruin.

By ordering the state in this manner, if Your Holiness and the Most Reverend Monsignor were immortal, it would be unnecessary to do anything else. However, you must at some point pass on, and yet you desire to leave behind a perfect republic fortified with all requisite parts, observed and recognized by all to be so. Thus, so that the universal may be content with it (through what is both restored to them and promised to them), the following additions must also be ordered.

The sixteen gonfaloniers of the Companies of the People should be created in the same mode and for the same duration as they presently are. They may be selected through your own authority or by the Great Council, whichever pleases you more. The *divieto*[15] should be increased only so that the magistracy will be spread more widely throughout the city, and, to the same end, none of the sixty-five citizens may be deemed eligible to hold it. Once the Sixteen have been created, four provosts should be selected by lottery from among them to serve for one month; thus, all the gonfaloniers will have served as provosts by the end of their tenure. From these four, one should be selected to reside for one week in the palace with the nine presiding signori, such that by the end of the month all four will have resided there. The sitting signori residing in the palace are permitted to do nothing in the absence of the provost. The latter need not necessarily speak but merely serve as a witness of the signori's actions. The provost may with good cause impede their proceedings and demand that these be discussed by the entire Thirty-Two as a whole.

Likewise, in such circumstances, the Thirty-Two will not be permitted to deliberate anything except in the presence of two provosts. The latter possess no authority other than the ability to put a stop to deliberations among the Thirty-Two and appeal them to the Select Council. In a similar manner, this council, that of the Two Hundred, is forbidden from doing anything without at least six of the Sixteen, among which there must be two provosts, being present. The Six are empowered to do no more than—when three of them concur—demand that a matter be transferred from the Select Council to the Great Council. The latter council may not gather together without twelve gonfaloniers present, among which there must be three provosts, all of whom may participate like any other citizen within the Great Council.

This ordering of these colleges is necessary beyond the lives of Your Holiness and the Most Reverend Monsignor for the following reasons. First, if the Signoria or the Select Council fail to deliberate properly on account of disunion, or if they act against the common good out of malice, someone will be available to suspend their authority and confer it on another council. After all, it is not a good thing for one magistracy or council to undermine the public good when another is available to advance it properly. It is also good that citizens who hold the state in their hands should have others who watch them, and who can either deter them from engaging in bad behavior, or deprive them of their authority when they are using it badly.

Second, in abolishing the present Signoria and depriving the universality of the people the possibility of becoming signori, it is necessary to compensate them with a rank commensurate with the one that has been taken away. In this manner, the magistracy of the provosts is greater, more honorable, and more useful to the republic. Moreover, for now it would be best to select the gonfaloniers ordinarily, so that the city conforms to its proper orders; however, they will not be allowed to exercise their office without Your Holiness's permission—in fact, you might put them to use in reporting on certain actions pertinent to your authority and your state.

Beyond this, in order to establish a perfect republic beyond the lifetimes of Your Holiness and the Most Reverend Monsignor, so that it is not lacking in any regard, it will be necessary to order appeals from decisions rendered by the Eight of Guardia and the Balìa. An appellate body, composed of thirty citizens selected from the bags of the Two Hundred and the Sixty-Five combined, would be empowered to call both complainants and the accused within a specified time frame. No one would be allowed, during your lifetimes, to avail themselves of this appellate body without your permission.

Such appeals are necessary in republics because bodies comprising few citizens seldom exhibit the fortitude to punish great men; therefore, to achieve such a result many citizens should participate in these judgments, and do so in secret, so that they cannot be blamed individually for outcomes. These appeals will also prove serviceable in your lifetime, as the Eight will be encouraged to judge cases expeditiously and justly; that is, they will judge rightly out of fear that you would subsequently allow an appeal to proceed. To avoid the prospect of too many appeals, these may be limited exclusively to instances of fraud in the amount of at least fifty ducats, and applied only to instances of violence entailing broken bones, spilled blood, or damages exceeding at least fifty ducats.

Let us consider all these orders to constitute a republic, which, absent your authority, lacks nothing necessary that has been disputed and discoursed at length above. However, during the lives of Your Holiness and the Most Reverend Monsignor it remains a monarchy, for you command the arms, you preside over criminal justice, and you hold the laws close to your breast. I know not what more one could desire for a city. You will see no reason why those among your friends, who are good and wish to live with what they have, should have cause to fear, as Your Holiness will retain so much authority and they will sit in the first ranks of government. Also it is inconceivable that the universality of citizens themselves would not be content as that part of the state that distributes magistracies has been restored to them and that little by little more of the state will fall into their hands. Sometimes Your Holiness might consider permitting the Great Council to fill open slots among the Sixty-Five and the Two Hundred, while you yourself would continue to do so when circumstances require it. Therefore, I am sure that in a short time, through the authority of Your Holiness, who would man the helm over everything, that this present state would be converted into the other kind, and likewise the other into this kind, such that they would each become the same, all within one body, with the city's peace and Your Holiness's perpetual fame resulting. Always your own authority would address whatever defects might become apparent over time.

I believe that the greatest honor earned by men is that which is voluntarily bestowed on them by their patria. I believe that the greatest good that men achieve, and that which is most favored by God, is that which they provide to their patria. Moreover, no man is exalted for his actions more than those who reform republics and principates through laws and institutions; after those who became gods, these were the most lauded. Because there have been few with the occasion to do so, and even fewer with the ability to do so, small indeed is the number who have done so. So highly esteemed is this glory by those who singularly pursue it that those who have been unable to found a republic in fact have done so in writing, such as Aristotle, Plato, and many others. They wished to show the world that if, like Solon and Lycurgus, they could not found a civil way of life, they were prevented from putting it into practice not through lack of knowledge but through lack of power to make it happen.

Heaven, therefore, gives to a man no greater gift, nor shows him no more glorious path than this. Hence, among the infinite felicities that God has bestowed on your house and on the person of Your Holiness, this is by far the greatest: to give you both the power and the matter to make yourself immortal, and, consequently, to far surpass the glory of your father and grandfather. Consider well, Your Holiness, that by maintaining the city of Florence on present terms the slightest accident may bring forth a thousand dangers; and even before they arrive, Your Holiness must confront a thousand inconveniences that would be excruciating for any man—just how excruciating, the Most Reverend Lord Cardinal, who has been in Florence these past months, can confirm. These inconveniences come in part from many citizens who are presumptuous and insufferable, and in part from many who, feeling as though they do not live securely at present, demand only that order be brought to government. Some say in this regard that the government should be rendered more widely inclusive, while others say it should be rendered more narrowly restrictive—with neither coming to particulars regarding the mode of achieving either because everyone is confused. While they feel that they enjoy little security under the present mode of living, they know not how to improve the situation; moreover, anyone who might actually know they refuse to trust. Such widespread confusion is enough to confound even the most well-regulated brain.

To escape these troubles, then, there are only two modes: either retire from giving audiences, and discourage men from requesting them, even in the customary way, or refrain from speaking when not asked to do so, as did the late illustrious duke; or, order the state in a mode through which it will administer itself, such that Your Holiness need only keep half of an eye on it. Of these two modes, the latter liberates you from many dangers and inconveniences; the former liberates you only from inconveniences. Regarding the dangers that you incur if matters stand as they do presently, I will offer a prediction. When accidents supervene while the city has failed to be reordered comprehensively, one or another thing, or both things simultaneously, will ensue: a head will be set up hastily and tumultuously, one who will defend the state exclusively with arms and violence; or, one party will rush to reopen the Great Hall and will pounce on the other as prey.

God forbid that either of these two things should happen; but please consider, Your Holiness, how many dead, how many exiles, how many extortions would result if they do. It would make even a very cruel man, let alone a highly merciful one like Your Holiness, die of sorrow. There is simply no other way to escape these evils than to provide the city with orders through which it can stand firm. This will always be so when everyone plays a part in such orders, when everyone knows what he must do and in whom he can trust; and when no citizen of whatever rank, either out of fear for themselves or out of naked ambition, desires to undertake an innovation.

---- ✳ ----

Minutes of a Provision for the Reform of the Florentine Government

---

Jesus Mary

Our most magnificent and esteemed lords[16]—considering that no law or order is more praiseworthy to men or acceptable to God than that by which one orders a true, united, and holy republic, in which one freely counsels, prudently deliberates, and faithfully carries out; in which men are compelled when deliberating affairs to abandon private interests and direct themselves only to the common good; in which the friendships of wretched men and the enmities of good men have no place; in which the appetites for false glory are extinguished and those for true and glorious honors are inflamed; in which hatreds, enmities, disagreements, factions, from which then are born deaths, exiles, the affliction of good citizens, and the exaltation of miserable citizens, do not have those who would feed them, but would be entirely pursued and extinguished by the laws; in which in public councils one can listen to what men wish and freely discuss and debate what is heard; and having considered, moreover, how many factions and divisions have in the past and at all times disturbed, divided, and destroyed the city of Florence; desirous to see if it is possible to find a way by which, with the satisfaction of the people and the security of every good and honest citizen, the republic of Florence should be governed and administered, and to that end, being in every instance exhorted and urged by the most reverend monsignor, Lord Giulio, the most illustrious Cardinal de' Medici, and advised and helped by his most prudent and pleasing advice; having invoked the name of omnipotent God and of his eternally virgin mother, and of Saint John the Baptist and any other advocate and protector of the city of Florence, so that what is begun for the good and peaceful life of the city of Florence will have a most happy progress and outcome—decree and order that:

By virtue of the present provision[17] all preeminence, order, and authority is meant to be and is in effect restored to the council, formerly called the Great Council, that it possessed to the fullest extent from the month of August 1512 and earlier. Immediately upon the final conclusion of this provision, the chancellors of the Tratte[18] should prepare the purses and anything else necessary to prepare so that said council can carry out those things over which it has authority, distributing honors and creating magistracies, offices, and councils in the same mode and manner that they used to create and distribute them in the specified prior period.[19] And in order that the said council can carry out the above responsibilities, it is decreed that, shortly after the council's powers are restored, the workers[20] of the palace are obliged to restore the room in which the council formerly assembled, so that it can now assemble in its previous and ancient orders: and the treasurer of the Monte is obliged to pay said workers the funds necessary to restore the room, after the funds are allocated by the officers of the Monte.[21] And because past experience has shown that it was difficult for one thousand citizens to gather, to facilitate assembly, where before there could not be fewer than one thousand citizens, it is established that hundred suffice; and moreover, thereafter, all those who assemble there must be eligible for the council according to the laws of city and not owing taxes;[22] and said council must assemble on the same days, times, and ringing of the bell according to which it traditionally assembled.

Considering also that it is through known experience that when the city was in its former laws and in those that suited more a free way of life, a standard bearer of justice for two months was useless and one for life was dangerous, to avoid these problems it is established that future standard bearers of justice will be elected and chosen for three years, the term of the first standard bearer beginning on the first day of next May and finishing every three years, as follows. The election of the first and subsequent standard bearer will be done in this way: that at least four days before the beginning of next May, our most excellent lords will name at least three citizens, forty-five years of age, eligible for the council and whose taxes are up to date, notwithstanding the following prohibitions: all those nominated must be elected from the council and then voted on in the council, one by one, according to age; and of them the one who has the most black beans, provided he has half the beans plus one, will be appointed standard bearer. If no one wins the election the first time, they are voted on again, and whoever has the most black beans, irrespective of their number, becomes the standard bearer; and in the case where there are two tied candidates, they will return to the vote as many times as necessary until one defeats the other.

This standard bearer, thusly elected, shall have the same salary, preeminence, and authority that the laws stipulated in 1512 when Giovanbattista Ridolfi was standard bearer. At the end of the three years, at least fifteen days before the end of term, the sitting priors should summon the council, having proclaimed the summons at least three days prior, in which all Florentine citizens eligible for the council can participate, irrespective of the state of their taxes. From the pouch of the council one hundred electoral officials should be drawn, each one a Florentine citizen by virtue of membership in a major guild, forty-five years of age, and irrespective of the state of their taxes. Then all candidates are voted on in the council, one by one; and all those who win the election by half the black beans plus one must be voted on a second time in the council, and whoever has the most black beans, irrespective of their number, will be elected standard bearer for said term of three years and under the above conditions; and these procedures will be observed in the future every three years. If in the final election there are tied candidates, they are voted on as many times as necessary until one defeats the other. If it happens that a standard bearer should die before the end of his term, a successor will be appointed for the remainder of the term according to the above method.

After the final conclusion of this provision, the currently functioning Councils of the People, the Commune, and the One Hundred shall be abolished;[23] and because the city should not lack a median council that will attend to matters that the Great Council cannot, it is established the current Council of Seventy will become a new Council of One Hundred, and it will have all the authority, together with the priors and colleges, that the Council of Eighty formerly had;[24] and further this council will deliberate about and ultimately obtain all the imposition of monies that will be conducted in the future. At least sixty of said councilors will suffice for assembly, in addition to its priors and colleges, and any motion put before them should obtain the approval of two-thirds of the councilors present. Nonetheless, this means that the appointment of men who will have to impose a tax, extraordinary tax, or loan, or grant any exemptions, whether serious or light, appertains and belongs to the Great Council, in the manner stipulated by the law that will be made about this. It will also be the responsibility of the One Hundred, assembling in the manner described above, to reform the Monte every year. If any of the members of the Council of One Hundred are missing, through death or other reasons, their replacements will be arranged as follows: the names of all the members of the Council of One Hundred will be put in a pouch, and for each replacement ten electioneers will be drawn who will nominate someone for voting in the Great Council. Whoever has the most black beans, having won the vote by half the black beans plus one, becomes a member of the council; and this procedure will be followed in the future.

If it happens that for whatever reason any council, office, or magistracy is not filled by the Great Council, it is established that, for those nominated to the unelected council, office, or magistracy, at the next meeting of the council there will be a vote, for some or all of the missing offices, to generate the number of magistracies that must be filled. For each person that must be elected, the names of two people with the most black beans, irrespective of the total number of black beans,[25] will be put in a purse, and the drawing will proceed, and it is understood that the person or people drawn is or are elected to this or that particular magistracy.

The priors, colleges, and ministers of the palace must be present for the baggings and scrutinies that the Great Council will make in the future, as the old rules of said council stipulated. After the final conclusion of this provision all the laws and orders prohibiting *parlamenti* that were established in the past will be renewed;[26] they are all to be strictly observed.

The magnificent lords desiring again that this peaceful and popular state being ordered might be of benefit to citizens, to the tranquility of the city and everyone's common health, and to inhibit those scandals that can grow in the beginning and create things that would be lacking for the perfection of a peaceful regime, which one cannot see or know without experience, but through the comfort and counsel of many wise, good, and loving citizens, it is established that shortly after the final conclusion of this provision our present magnificent lords must deputize twelve citizens, eligible for the council, up to date in their taxes, and forty-five years old of age—ten for the major guilds and two for the minor guilds. They will be called the Reformers; and of them, together with the Most Reverend and Holy Lord Giulio, Cardinal de' Medici, will have the same authority as the people of Florence have to reform and reorder anything that they judge necessary to reform and order for the benefit and tranquility of the city; and they are able to make laws, orders, and statutes that will possess the same power and worth as if they had been created and ordered by the entire people of Florence.

And so that everyone will see that this authority thus reserved is entirely for the benefit of the freedom and tranquility of the city and the true free way of life for a republic, it is first established that: Having created the twelve citizens above, it is established that the current *balìa* will be abolished and will no longer have any value or authority. In addition, the authority given to the Reformers outlined above and to the Most Reverend Monsignor de' Medici will last no longer than one year, to begin the first of May next year and to conclude as follows: after said year, the twelve citizens and said Most Reverend Monsignor will remain without any authority, neither will they able to extend their authority or give it to others, through any method, whether direct or indirect. These Reformers may not diminish the number of the Great Council, nor take from it any distribution or election of office, councils, or magistrates; all appointments to councils, offices, and magistrates belong to the Great Council, except for that described below.

Furthermore, the said Reformers may not give authority by name to any citizen nor appoint someone to a magistracy. All the appointment of citizens that must be made to office, councils, and magistracies that they have either created or reformed belongs to the appointments and elections process of the Great Council, in the manner established by them.

So that in the beginning of this government, as we said above, any scandalous person does not have the opportunity to create dissent because of his private passion, and so that those of malignant spirit, whether through desire for vendetta or some other scandalous reason, will have some brakes to hold them back, such that this new government will have authority and people in it will be secure, it is established that the Reformers, together with the cardinal, will have authority to elect all the *signorie* that will sit from the beginning of next May until the last day of October of the present year. There are three signorie in total, and after this time the appointment and elections of priors will return entirely and permanently to the Great Council.

It is established for the same reasons that the election of the Eight of Ward and Balìa of the People of Florence, who will sit in office until the end of next December of this year, will belong to the Reformers; after which time the election of the Eight will return entirely to the Great Council. It is also established for the same reasons that the next election of Standard Bearers of the Companies of the People and the next Twelve Good Men belongs to said Reformers; after the next election the election of their successors and all others who will be elected after that will return entirely to the Great Council. The Reformers and the cardinal may reform the chanceries of the Signoria and of the Eight of Practice, or rather the Ten of War, in any manner they deem appropriate and appoint people to their chanceries as they see fit; the chancellors of the Signoria must be confirmed each year by the Signoria, and those of the Ten, that is the Eight of Practice, must be confirmed by the aforementioned magistrate or magistrates.

———— ✳ ————

Memorandum to Cardinal Giulio
on the Reform of the State of Florence

———

I believe that all those who love a communal way of life will approve, of all the states that existed in Florence, a standard bearer of justice with a long term of office and the Great Council. Because of this, I would do both of these things without further reflection.[27] It is true that there are various ways of creating both, because the old number of one thousand would be pleasing to one person while another would prefer a smaller number. This would not bother me because no one would be excluded from coming there. And as for the standard bearer that would have to be created this first time, it could be done in the Council of the Commune in the following way: draw the names of twenty electioneers who would elect twenty citizens as candidates from the council and then vote on them. All those winning half the votes would be sent to the council for voting, and the person with the most beans would become the standard bearer. In undertaking this reform, Your Lordship could also elect this standard bearer by virtue of your authority. Once these two things are done, it would be necessary to think about other aspects of the republic, and here I think there would be some difficulty. For my part, among the orders that exist at present, some I would leave and expand, and others I would abolish. Those that I would abolish are the Councils of the People and the Commune, because the Great Council takes their place; those that I would . . . [the text is unfinished].

———— • ————

Summary of the Affairs of the City of Lucca

———

The city of Lucca is divided into three parts—one called San Martino, the other San Paolino, and the third San Salvatore.[28] Its first and most supreme office consists of nine citizens, three elected from each of the three parts, along with one other who is their head and who they call the standard bearer of justice. Together they are called the Signoria, or rather, wishing to refer to them by an ancient name, the Ancients. After this they have a council of thirty-six citizens, which is named after the number;[29] they also have a council of seventy-two citizens, which they call the General Council. On these three bodies rests the entire weight of their state, in addition to those particular matters that will be explained with respect to each of these bodies. The Signoria has exceptionally broad authority over the countryside, but none whatsoever over its citizens. But inside the city it alone assembles the councils, proposes the matters for deliberation, writes to the ambassadors and receives letters, assembles the *pratiche*[30] of their wisest citizens, which they call *colloquii*—and this prepares the way for the deliberations that will be carried out in the councils—monitors events, records them, and in fact is like a first motor of all the actions undertaken by the government of the city.

This Signoria sits for a term of two months, and those who sit are ineligible for the following two years. The Council of Thirty-Six together with the Signoria distribute all the honors and benefits of the state; and because they wish during the distribution always to have at least thirty-six sitting citizens, in addition to the Signoria, each member of the Signoria at each meeting can call two substitutes who sit with the same authority as the Thirty-Six. Their method of distribution is as follows: every two years they put into a pouch the names of all the members of the Signoria and the standard bearers who will sit for the next two years. To do this, the Signoria and the Council of Thirty-Six assemble in a room dedicated for this purpose, and they put the scrutineers, along with a friar, in an adjacent room, while another friar stands at the doorway between the two rooms. The rule is that each sitting member of the councils nominates whomever he likes. The standard bearer then gets up and speaks in the ear of the friar in the doorway leading to the scrutineers the name of the person that he nominated and for whom he wishes the others to vote. Then he goes in front of the scrutineers and puts a ballot in the urn.[31] When the standard bearer has returned to his seat, one of the older members of the Signoria takes his turn, and then the rest go one at a time. After the Signoria, the entire of Council of Thirty-Six takes its turn, and each member, when he gets to the friar and not before, asks who was nominated and who he should vote either for or against. Not knowing the answer until he hears it, he has only the amount of time it takes to go from the friar to the scrutineers to decide. Once everyone has voted the urn is emptied, and if the candidate has three-quarters of the votes he is written down as a member of the Signoria; if he does not get the votes, he joins the ranks of the defeated. Once the first candidate has been voted on, the eldest of the priors goes and nominates another person into the ear of the friar; then each one casts a vote: and in this way, one at a time, everyone nominates someone and usually they manage to elect the next Signoria after three rotations of the council. To have a complete roster, they must have 108 successful candidates and twelve standard bearers; once done, they elect sorters from among themselves, who determine by sortition who will sit during certain months and who will sit during others. Once the sortition is complete, they make the results public every two months.

In the distribution of other offices, they use a different method from this one. They conduct a scrutiny for them once per year such that, for an office with a six-month term, they elect two officials at every scrutiny. In the scrutiny process they follow this rule: first they post an announcement declaring that, given their election of officers for future years, whoever wants to hold office must go to register. Whoever wishes to be considered for office must be registered by the chancellor, who puts the names of all those who were registered into a purse. Then, the council that makes the appointments having assembled, the chancellor begins by drawing a name from the purse; if the person whose name drawn is present and says "I wish to be considered for this office," the vote is held. If he wins by three quarters of the vote and the office is filled, it is set aside, and for that office there are no further votes. If he does not win, his name is torn up, and he can no longer be considered as a candidate. Another name is drawn, and if the person drawn is present he announces which office he wishes to be considered for. If he is not present, he has charged someone who may speak for him, and they proceed thus until all the offices for future years are filled, based, as I said, on two people for each of the offices whose terms are six months.

It is worth noting the difference between these electoral techniques and those used by the Florentines and others because in Lucca the person voting for the Signoria must go to the urn, whereas elsewhere the custom is that the urn is brought to the voter. In the election process elsewhere, the office that needs to be filled is established first, and then they draw the names of the people who compete for it; they wish that many people compete and, given many eligible candidates, that the office will go to the person with the most favor. But the Lucchese do the opposite: they first draw the man and then declare the office to which he should go, and they wish that that declaration will go to the person drawn. The person drawn measures his strengths and accordingly chooses an office. And if he makes a bad choice,[32] he bears the consequences and for that year is no longer eligible for office. If he succeeds, the office is his. They do not wish the office to be put to another vote through which it might go to someone with more support because it seems injurious to them that someone could take what was already given to another person. Which, then, is the better of these two methods, the Lucchese or yours,[33] or that of the Venetians, I leave to others to decide.

The General Council, as I said, is made up of seventy-two citizens, who assemble with the Signoria, and further, each member of the Signoria can nominate three citizens who, sitting along with them, have the same authority as members of the Signoria. The General Council sits for a year, the council of Thirty-Six sits for six months, and they have only one prohibition: that those sitting members of a council may not be elected to the following one. The Council of Thirty-Six renews itself;

the General Council is appointed by the Signoria and by the twelve citizens elected by the Council of Thirty-Six. The General Council is lord of the city because it makes and unmakes laws; it makes truces, alliances, exiles, condemns citizens to death, and finally there is no appeal from its resolutions, nor any way to obstruct its decisions provided they have been approved by three quarters of the council.

In addition to the institutions above, they have three secretaries who serve for six months. They function, as we would say, as spies, or, by a more lofty name as state inquisitors. They can banish or kill a foreigner without any consultation; they monitor affairs in the city; if they learn about any plan against the state involving citizens, they refer it to the standard bearer, to the councils, and the colloquia, so that it can be investigated and dealt with. Beyond this, they have an additional three citizens who sit for six months, called *condottieri*, who have authority to recruit infantry and other soldiers. They have a Florentine[34] *podestà*, who has authority over each and every citizen in civil and criminal matters. They also have magistrates with authority over merchants, guilds, over the roads and public buildings, as all other cities do. With these modes they have lived to the present day and maintained themselves in the midst powerful enemies.

Judging from the result, one cannot but generally praise them; however, I also wish that we consider which elements in their government are good and which are bad. The Signoria not having authority over citizens is most wisely ordered, because all the good republics have done likewise. The Roman consuls and the doge and the Signoria[35] of Venice did not have and do not have any authority over their citizens, because the highest symbol of a republic is already so esteemed that if you were to add authority bad effects would result very swiftly. The head of a republic will not fare well without majesty, as we find in Lucca, because with two-month terms and long bans on reeligibility, by necessity many men of lesser standing sit there: that rule is not good, because the majesty and prudence that does not exist in the public one seeks in private. It follows from this that they need to call their colloquia of citizens, who belong neither to magistracies nor councils: a well-ordered republic would not use such a device. If one considers who sat on the Signoria of Venice or who was consul in Rome, one sees that the heads of those states, if they did not have authority, had majesty, because as it was good to lack the former, so it was bad to lack the latter.

Their method of distributing the Signoria and offices is good, civil, and well considered. It is true that it deviates from the methods of past republics, because in those republics the greater number distributed, the middle ranks advised, and the few executed. In Rome the people distributed, the Senate advised, and the consuls and the other minor magistrates executed; in Venice the Council distributes, the Pregàdi advise, and the Signoria executes.[36] In Lucca these orders are confused, because the few distribute, and the middle ranks and the many both advise and execute; and even though in the republic of Lucca this has not worked out badly, nevertheless someone establishing a republic should not imitate it. The reason why things have not worked out badly is that honor and profit in that city are pursued with little ambition, because on the one hand those who pursue them are weak, and on the other, the seeker, being rich, esteems his business affairs more than honors and profit and as a result attends to the politics less than the person who would rule over him. Then the authority that each member of the Signoria has to appoint two or three people during each meeting calms many of their friends. Again, the small number of citizens there, along with six-month terms rather than lifetime conciliar appointments, means that each person desires and seeks to be involved, because many people who doubt that they would be elected believe that they are friends with a member of the Signoria who will bring them into the deliberations, such that it matters less to them to be appointed to the Thirty-Six or Seventy-Two.

These councils also have another rule when they assemble that helps satisfy the people and speed matters along: if the council assembles and the term of service has expired among the councilors that must be present and they therefore lack people, the Signoria can send out its servants, and the first citizens they find, they bring into the council to make up for the deficiency in number. It is also well ordered that the General Council has authority over the citizens because it is a powerful brake to strike against those who would make themselves great. But it is not well ordered that there is not a magistracy of a few citizens, maybe four or six, that can punish, because disorders follow if either one of these two methods is lacking in a republic: the many serve to punish the great and the ambitions of wealthy citizens; a small number to instill fear in the ——[37] and to brake the insolence of the young, because every day in this city things occur that the majority cannot correct, from which follows that the young become audacious, and youth is corrupted and, once corrupted, can become an instrument of ambition. Lacking this method of restraining the young, Lucca thus witnessed this insolence grow and cause bad effects in the city. To restrain them they passed a law many years ago called the law of the unruly, by which they mean the insolent and badly behaved. The law stipulates that twice per year, in September and in March, everyone who has assembled in the General Council writes down the names of people that they think should be banished from their state. Reading then the list of names, whoever is nominated ten times or more is voted on, and if he receives three-quarters of the vote he is banished from their land for three years. This law was very well considered and did a great service to that republic because, on the one hand, it is a major restraint on men, and on the other, it does not create an excessive amount of exiles, because, in the first three years since it was proclaimed, as many people return as depart. But that is not enough, because the young who are noble, wealthy, and have powerful relatives, given the narrowness of the vote, do not fear it. We see in our times that a family, called the Poggio, has grown from which every day arise bad examples for a good republic, and for which until now they have found no remedy.

Some might consider it poorly ordered that all Lucchese votes must win by three quarters. To this one replies that, because all affairs in republics are debated in terms of a yes or a no, a yes is much more dangerous than a no; and they must guard more against those who wish something to be done than those who do not wish it to be done. For this reason it is judged less bad that a few people can prevent a good thing than they can easily accomplish something bad. If this difficulty[38] is good, nonetheless it is not good in general because there are many things that would be good to make easier, and punishing their citizens is one. If their punishment had to be decided by a two-thirds vote, relatives and friends would have a harder time obstructing it. This, then, is what one can say about the government in Lucca and what in it is good and bad.

Chapter 10

FRANCESCO GUICCIARDINI

On the Method of Electing Offices in the Great Council

(1512)

On the Mode of Reordering the Popular Government

(1512)

The Government of Florence After the Medici Restoration

(1513)

On the Mode of Securing the State of the House of Medici

(1516)

Often credited with establishing the methods of modern historiography in his epic *The History of Italy*, Francesco Guicciardini (1483–1540) is also an under-appreciated but decisive figure in the history of political thought, as manifested by his *Dialogue on the Government of Florence*. Guicciardini served over a long political career in prominent roles as diverse as the Florentine republic's ambassador to Spain, and as both military commissioner and provincial governor for Medici princes and popes. A major intellectual interlocutor of Machiavelli, the younger, wealthier, and more socially esteemed Guicciardini reflected on what he called "true and complete liberty" and "the civic way of life." Guicciardini was perhaps the first political thinker to endorse the institutional arrangements associated with modern representative government: members of the general citizenry, although perhaps discouraged from holding office themselves, elect public officials from a much smaller pool of worthy, wise, and notable candidates. Guicciardini's institutional model relieves common citizens of most of the political duties they exercised in ancient democracies and many medieval republics, such as holding lottery-distributed offices, debating policy in large public councils, and deciding political trials in similarly sized assemblies. Instead, he proposes that average citizens apply their general good judgment to the appointment of "virtuous and valiant" magistrates, and that they approve or reject—but never help formulate or amend—laws proposed by those magistrates. Guicciardini hoped that this novel political arrangement would defuse both the violent interelite conflicts and populist insurrections that threatened and often extinguished liberty in republics like Florence. As expressed in the constitutional reform proposals gathered here, Guicciardini thought that electoral politics constrained and enabled a republic's elite in a novel manner: the desire to hold office deterred magistrates from corruption or usurpation, while still leaving them sufficiently wide discretion to deliberate over and make laws conducive to the common good. By devising institutions for distributing offices that discourage violence among elites or between the latter and the people, Guicciardini hoped that liberty would flourish in republican regimes; by establishing the electoral interdependence of elites and people, Guicciardini expected more responsible behavior on the part of both segments of society. Guicciardini presciently anticipated that this model of republican government would allow the size of the citizenry to expand in unprecedented ways, securing "the fruits of liberty" for more and more individuals.

Natasha Piano translated the following: Francesco Guicciardini, "Del modo di eleggere gli uffici nel Consiglio Grande," "Del Modo Di Ordinare Il Governo Popolare," "Del Governo di Firenze dopo la restaurazione de Medici," and "Del Modo di assicurare lo stato alla Casa de' Medici," from texts in R. Palmarocchi, ed., *Dialogo e Discorsi del Reggimento di Firenze* (Bari: Laterza, 1931), 175–217, 218–59, 260–66, and 267–81.

---- ❋ ----

On the Method of Electing Offices in the Great Council

In Florence, it came to pass that the Great Council distributed the city's office and dignities based on who won the most votes in the election. The majority (*lo universale*) found this process too narrow, and therefore it was proposed that the officeholder would be selected by lottery among all those who won more than half the votes. Below I shall discuss the reasoning of those who favored the majority-vote system:

Excellent citizens, many hold the opinion that opposing this provision will displease your Excellencies because it will seem as though it works to rob you of your advantages. Nevertheless, I have so much confidence in your prudence and your love of *patria* that I am convinced that each one of you will eagerly hear anyone who volunteers what he thinks about this subject. If his reasons for supporting it seem sound to your Excellencies, they should convince you that this course of action will serve the public good more than personal self-interest. If the arguments do not seem convincing, you should not judge the speaker as evil. In fact, you should praise him as a good citizen because he was willing to honestly state his opinion without fear of retribution and without fear of displeasing your Excellencies.

Excellent counselors, those who order popular governments and republican liberty know that they must secure two primary ends: First, and most important, they must ensure that every single citizen is equal before the law. No distinction between rich and poor, nor between the powerful and the weak, can exist. Everyone must feel sure that his person, property, and condition cannot be affected beyond what the laws and orders of the city dictate, which is the reason liberty was instituted in the first place. The second end is that the benefits of the republic—that is, the honors and the public offices—are widely distributed so that as many citizens participate in government as possible. Because we are all children of the same mother, everyone must enjoy his advantages (*ai commodi suoi*). Besides, it is said that the good multiplies with the inclusion of more people. Yet these two ends are different insofar as the first must be instituted without any exception whatsoever. The more that everyone is held equal under the law, the better. One can never have too much equality in this regard, for it will never generate disorders in a well-regulated city.

But this is not the case with the second end. Wideness (*larghezza*) and broad participation is necessary only insofar as it does not result in disorder and damage the public good. Preserving the public good is more important and does not necessarily follow from such wideness. The city is a body, and as far as its internal and external affairs are concerned—such as the observation of justice and the laws, and the way to maintain and amplify the dominion—the souls of the magistrates reign and govern it. When the magistrates know how to bear the weight of government, the affairs of the city go well; when the opposite occurs—that is, when the magistrates are inadequate—the city is governed poorly, and everything becomes disordered and goes to ruin. The truth of this principle can be seen in your private business affairs. If a silk or wool dealer knows how to manage expenses and keeps a close eye on everything that needs to be done, profits abound, and capital multiplies. If, on the other hand, he is not adequate, the shop (*la bottega*) does not do well, and in due time *duccati* become *lire*, and sometimes compound into *grossi*. However, in republics, no magistracies are granted without scrutinizing the candidates [through election] (*sanza prima squittinargli*). Although forgoing scrutiny [election] allows more people to hold office, it is more important that the city is well governed, and therefore that electoral procedures remain intact. If more narrow procedures do not reflect a universal mandate but still help procure the effect [of good government], this is a minor inconvenience compared to what would transpire if offices were placed in hands that would mismanage the city.

Once your council was instituted, this method wisely secured both ends of government. When the Great Council became the distributor of all internal and external offices, it cut off everyone's arm so that no one could make himself great, thereby forcing everyone to be held equal under the law. This foundation removes the means through which an individual can become great by preventing anyone from accruing enough authority to hand out honors and offices to whomever he pleases, and consequently, it prevents him from fostering friends and a following. Distributing offices by election in the council created a well governed city because the magistrates were more discriminately chosen (*più scelti*). If one hundred men judge whether a citizen is well suited to an office, the judgment will undoubtedly be more secure if sixty men agree, as opposed to merely fifty. Furthermore, the person who obtains the most votes is obviously the person approved by the most people; it does not make sense to put someone in office who the city favors less than someone who earned more votes. Those who put majority-vote procedures in place wisely organized it in this manner for good reason: because the city is better governed this way. It should not be altered, even slightly, as those who want to make a new order suggest, without a very compelling justification.

I constantly hear that this method of election is too narrow and that it displeases the people. The people, it is said, would have never run the Medici out and created the Great Council for things [election procedures] *not* to be opened in a way that ensures everyone participates, as should be the case in a free government (*governo libero*). If elections were decided by others, your Excellencies would have reason to complain. But because the people distribute the offices to whomever they want, however they want, there is really no wideness or narrowness to be spoken of except that which they create themselves. I do not know why the people complain that offices are given to whomever one wishes,[1] and how [this process] can be lambasted, because today the people are the prince of everything, as of course they should be, since government should serve the most numerous citizens. If things were ordered so that the person preferred by the minority prevailed, or the people had to concede to others the right to decide the election, there would be legitimate grounds for complaint that the people do not hold enough authority. Only then could it justifiably be said that the people are the manservant (*famiglione*) but not the boss (*padrone*). But the distribution of offices has remained fully with you (*voi*): you are the ones who count the anonymous, unweighted votes; that is to say, you do not know nor take into consideration who cast which vote but are concerned only with their quantity. Therefore, it cannot be said that the people do not maintain complete authority. It is a real sign of true liberty that the person who wins the approval of the most number of men in this council is proclaimed the winner.

When multiple parties proliferate in every other magistracy in the city—for example, in the colleges and in the Eighty—they always follow he who has won the most votes. Why should we not should employ the same method in the Great Council, where the participation of a larger number renders the decision less likely to be corrupt than the decision of a smaller group? Many will say that the candidates who can win the most votes are always the same few and that many who merit office are excluded, which causes discontent because it seems strange to the citizens, who, after believing that they were finally going to participate, find themselves in the same position that they were in before—in an unbreakable cycle. There are numerous convincing responses to this concern: if one merits office, he does not need the approval of individuals but of the whole people; the people judge better than anyone because the people are the prince who make decisions dispassionately. In the past we praised elections decided by tyrants, so why are we now lambasting the elections decided by the people? You (*lui*) know better than any of us that, if nothing else, we distribute offices only to those who seem to deserve them most.

I do not deny that the people occasionally make errors when employing the majority vote system because one cannot always recognize and judge the true quality of his fellow citizens. But these mistakes are undoubtedly minor compared to those that would transpire if any other method were employed. Besides, each day these mistakes will diminish because the longer we employ this course of action, the individuals of the citizenry will become more studied and better known: one day actions of this one citizen will be witnessed and adjudicated, and tomorrow of this other fellow. The people, who will increasingly feel like owners of this council, will realize that the government really belongs to them. Consequently, they will put more thought into their judgments and better scrutinize the comportment and habits of their fellow citizens—something the people did not do beforehand. The populace will thus become an even better judge of which men merit office, and there will be no impediment to giving offices to these men.

The council's short history demonstrates this point. In the first few months, elections were far more disorganized than they were later because the people were not familiar with the citizens. In a government with newly established liberty, the citizens are not accustomed to this way of life, and they are filled with doubts that the regime was truly made to their advantage. This immediate state of affairs generates thousands of errors, suspicions, and confusions, which are often the cause of wild elections, but with time these outcomes dissipate. Every day things become more clear, and they continually improve. Those who deserve office and develop a following can hope that, in time, some opportunity will present itself so that each man can become better known and honored according his merit. This requires that these men must defer to what the people desire, and even endure (*tollerare*) for a short while the particular danger that comes with all this—that is, the desire to make a new order pernicious to the city.

Nor is it true that elections always produce the same candidates. If we were to examine previous instances, we would see that the candidates vary. If nominating in this setting [in the Great Council] were permitted, it would become even more clear. Previous examples demonstrate that those who held office are not all of the same quality, but rather of various sorts and ranks of the city. Indeed, they vary to such a degree that no one could say that the elections are managed by sects and bribes. If the offices are not held by as many people as they desire, this is not inconvenient because the people like it this way. The people do not deserve to be lacerated or criticized if they decide to place their affairs in the hands of those who are more often chosen, which actually can benefit everyone in the government of the city because it employs the most competent ministers possible. Each one of you strives to implement such employment practices in your own business affairs. In fact, even when you find yourselves with a good minister, you leave him behind for a better one. If it seems strange to see someone who has been given offices or dignities many times, it does not seem odd to the people, who ultimately look for their city and dominion to be well governed. When the people judge that this man has had enough turns, they hold the beans that have the power to replace him with another, casting the former candidate aside forever, or for however long they wish.

Every day calls for an election, but this defect can also be mended with time. You can trust that things will improve because the nature of the people is to desire wideness, and in the few months that this council has existed, the disorder that comes from such wideness has not been grave enough to cause concern. No wonder the people are lovers of the city and their own liberty: the times in which we live are strange and dangerous, and therefore they want their magistracies to be in the most capable hands. Among the expenses and dangers that we currently face, an ounce of the disorders that could result from incompetent magistrates would be the greatest of burdens, and these disorders are not worth all the pleasure that comes from wideness. When the city is on better terms, wideness can be permitted more safely. In this more dangerous environment, the good citizen, if he does not hold the offices he would like to obtain, should approve the good ends that move the people, and find more happiness in the public good than in his own personal command. He must remember that right now, every citizen enjoys the principal fruits of liberty: to not fear being oppressed beyond the dictates of the laws; to have no one above the magistracies; to not need to show deference or submission to anyone; to distribute the honors and offices of the city; to have as much authority before the law as the richest and most powerful man. If you had been promised half of these things two years ago, you would have been happy. Now that you have all these things they seem like small matters because you do not have everything that you desire. In the future, you may very well obtain all or part of what you now lack, and you should console yourselves with this: what you now lack is not taken away from your authority in principle, nor by tyranny; rather you have deprived yourselves of it by your own will for the public good, in which you still participate just like everyone else.

Do not think that I am ungrateful for the offices and benefits that you have bestowed on me, nor that I disapprove of wideness in areas where such policies can be instituted honestly and without damage to the public good, nor that I do not desire for you to obtain all the good that you can possibly acquire, because I have enjoyed great honor from your humanity. But I do not think that the proposed amendment will procure this good effect, and moreover, I believe that your interests could be achieved in a more prudent and temperate fashion. I have no doubt that if all those who won more than half the votes were reduced to election by lottery, these elections would not produce the sort of officials that will satisfy your interests. There are many in this council who are more interested in other affairs and do not invest as much time following matters of state as they should. These men would likely win because it is the nature of men to err more in giving than in taking. These men have many friends and relatives who make coalitions (*che ognuno va a partito*), and with their votes and their allies' votes they favor their own partisans; even though there are of course some men who, based on their diverse natures, are scrupulous enough to cast a white bean.[2] In effect, there are many reasons why men favor their own partisans: parentage, friendship, compassion, indolence, ignorance, and conscience. I say these things reluctantly, honorable advisers, because I hate casting aspersions on those who have benefited me, but necessity forces me to in this case. Here is the honest truth: many who are inadequate will be able to earn more than half the votes, and those who obtain this number will be placed on an equal plane with those men who are adequate to the tasks of the magistracy, and even those who are more than adequate. Out of these men, the one who can earn the most votes must be distinguished from the rest because, as a result of these benign inclinations, a couple hundred voters that judge more diligently and scrupulously than the others can tip the scale so that the elections usually fall to those who are more capable.

If the magistracies go to incapable men, your affairs will be governed poorly. The dangers that follow will be infinite and manifest because, if the magistrates that you appoint to the courts are incapable, they will disorder judicial matters.

Liberty was introduced primarily to guarantee justice. This guarantee cannot remain intact with incapable judges at the helm because they will permit many oppressions that must be avoided at all costs. If the rectors that you appoint to govern our dominions do not know how to govern well, thousands of disorders will transpire among the subjects. This will harm those involved, diminish your reputation, and fill your land with great discontent, which could eventually cause rebellion and intensely disrupt your affairs. If the *signori*, the Ten, the Eighty, those who command wars, and other lords of your state are inadequate, they will not manage affairs well, neither will they make good alliances nor take advantages of good opportunities. Not only will you be unable to recover Pisa and resolve the huge plague before you but your troubles and dangers will multiply every day and you will face thousands of discords and vigorous wars. You will be forced either to lose a large part of your dominion and maybe your liberty, or face enormous expenses that will come out of your own pockets. The hoarding of offices that was proposed for your own interest will cost you one hundred times more than the meager gain that one of you could have obtained from all the offices combined.

As you can see, times are treacherous and our state is in grave danger, like a ship amid a turbulent ocean, or a sick man whose life is in jeopardy. We advise that the state needs your diligence and good government now more than ever, and therefore, it is imperative that you authorize good doctors and dismiss the bad ones. You do not govern your private affairs as they suggest you ought to govern the public ones. In addition to resolving the present difficulties we face, the city needs direction in order to encourage virtuous men to reveal themselves. Lovers of our patria need to be more esteemed than others so that your children and descendants can direct souls toward virtue and public life, so that they conduct themselves with diligence and consequently become loved and highly esteemed by citizenry. Everything must be done thoroughly and conscientiously so that citizens love and think well of you. You run the risk of extinguishing industriousness and the love of virtue, and of removing any distinction between good and evil, not only further aggravating present problems, but disordering your government in perpetuity and ruining the good education of your children.

Honorable citizens, do you not think, that in Venice, whose example inspired this Great Council, their citizens have the same desire that you have for honors and offices? Do you not think that they also see many who are dissatisfied because they do not win elections as often as their peers, and consequently complain? Nevertheless, they continue to maintain this method of the most votes because they have seen from experience that it facilitates the best form of government, enabling them to prosper and expand their empire. The Romans employed this method and never elected magistrates otherwise. If you follow the road these republics have taken, you can hope for the same effects that they experienced; if you take another road, you should not be surprised that your ends are different. In Sparta, a city full of virtue and fame, there was one citizen who was not elected to the Council of Three Hundred. He returned home happily, rejoicing that in his republic there were three hundred citizens more useful than himself. Your citizens, finding themselves enjoying new liberty and not yet properly guided, do not have all that they think they deserve, and so they make a lot of noise, smearing the judgment of the people who currently enjoy security and liberty. They author useless and irrational laws; they look for every opportunity to cause confusion, nor can they handle being judged by anyone else but themselves. If your Excellencies give in to their impudence and ambition, they will come to you every day with new ideas and new disorders, wishing to alter the order of things, and to ruin all well-ordered matters. In fact, when they see that their evil ways enhance their reputation and strength, they will drive you straight off a cliff because they do not have the honor and strength of the republic in mind—only their own appetites and passions.

The ancients write, and it is very true, that free governments become disorderly only with license. This can mean only that when government is excessively wide too many important matters are put into too many hands. From this follows confusions within the city, a divided citizenry, and, ultimately, the loss of dominion, or tyranny. This danger is all the more threatening amid newly established liberty, where the orders of good government are still not yet well founded. In this respect, wideness is like all other things: things go well when it is moderated, but it becomes a vice and spoils when it tends toward extremes. I could recount thousands of examples, but here is the point: licentious liberty appeals to everyone for a short while, but in the end, this interest dissipates, and ruin ensues. The excessiveness that everyone thought made liberty more enjoyable is the very thing that destroys it, converting liberty into tyranny. However, excellent counselors, everything depends on you: from honors to debts, everything that pertains to this city and this dominion is commissioned to your direction and prudence and must be well governed. The magistrates must be people who know how to bear the weights that you bestow on them so that your children mature and aspire toward virtue, love of patria, and so that their good works entitle them to honors, nobility, and riches.

All these things become confused and disordered if you take away the provision that mandates majority vote. The election of good magistrates and the opportunity to cultivate your citizens, and especially the youth, toward virtue depends on preserving this procedure. If you do, you can hope to conserve liberty and your own security, and additionally enjoy the benefits of the republic in the times to come. But if you have so much ambition and desire for the present offices that you forget the good of your patria, you will disorder judicial procedures, the government of your subjects, and the preservation of your state. Instead of the honor of an office you hope for, you should defer to God and your own conscience. It could easily happen that you spend infinite sums, face infinite dangers, and in the end, lose your liberty.

On the Same Subject (In Contrario)

I am of a very different opinion, excellent citizens. You most certainly do not use your liberty too licentiously. In fact, I would accuse you of governing yourselves too respectfully and with too much modesty. You behave like a man who has been recently introduced to liberty after a long period of servitude, and who consequently cannot shake his servility. This submissive behavior manifests itself in timid and abject actions that retain the memory and vestiges of your ancient servitude. Because, thank God, you maintain not only your liberty but also an empire and dominion over others, you ought to become addicted to greatness and generosity. It is the duty of citizens that love liberty and honor not to deprive themselves and withdraw under false pretenses of respect and modesty back to their original habits of servitude. On the contrary, you must motivate yourselves; avail yourselves to the superior (*eccelso*) spirit and vigor that the boss (*padrone*) and prince of such dominion ought to have.

Excellent counselors, no one can deny that all citizens should participate in the honors and offices of this republic. It then follows either that those who are excluded are not citizens, or that they are treated like all other citizens. If the advantages (*commodi*) and honors are not open to everyone, part of the city remains in charge of power and the other in a permanent state of servitude. In this event, advantages and honors become private possessions. Not only are the excluded men deprived of something that reasonably belongs to them, but also the very securities and equalities, granted by the fact of all being equal before the law and the officers, and for the sake of which these liberties were invented, would thus be altered and weakened. If magistracies and government are always possessed by the same few, the others never participate, and who doubts that reputation and greatness would remain in those few office-holding hands? Precisely as a result of holding office, judges and magistrates generate such great respect that every subsequent election pits one category of reputable men against another sort that is perpetually at great disadvantage [because he has not been able to accrue the honor and prestige that comes with office holding, thereby creating inequality].

Anyone who contemplates these two ends of government [equality before the law and participation in office] knows that they cannot be separated, but rather that they are inextricably linked. Without one, you cannot have the other. Broad participation and communication (*communicazione*), so to speak, is reasonable and just in every free government, but even more so in our own, because, for seventy years, a large part of us were violently excluded from every dignity and emolument. Theoretically it would be just not only that we now enjoy our share in government, but also that we participate more than the others in order to make up for lost time. Nevertheless, to appease those who are not comforted by your Excellencies, and to avoid provoking discord in the city, I approve a more modest approach. I suggest that you rest content, leave the memory of the past behind you, and demand only your share in government participation, which is in itself laudable and modest. However, do not let yourselves be deceived and under pretenses of some species of good relinquish your share. This would constitute timidity and abjection and serve as a sign that you still do not entirely recognize that you have returned to a state of liberty.

I confess that it is useful for the city to fill the magistracies with adequate men. But I also must assert that, just as it is useful and reasonable that everyone bears taxes and inconveniences, so too must everyone enjoy emoluments and advantages, because this is one of the substantive ends of liberty. When we must choose between these two options—between the magistracies being left in the hands of those who do not govern well or creating a more narrow government—necessity would force me to confess that narrowness is preferable, *but* both are bad, and we must find a way to avoid making this choice. If I am not mistaken, such a course of action is easy to find—in fact, we have already found it: the magistracies need not become disordered with lottery. A temperate and convenient openness, not a slovenly one, can exist in our government. The one element [lottery] actually includes the other [scrutiny of merit through a preliminary election]. In our city harmony and concord of voice can occur. The ancients said that the city must imitate music in that all republics must be temperate, and so, as the proverb goes, it will be a salad not only composed of lettuce, but *de omni genere musicorum* [there will be every kind of music]. Those who for seventy years managed the horse tack (*basto*) will be permitted to ride on horseback upon their appropriate turn.

Those who oppose this provision say that when offices are elected by majority vote they are assigned to those who most deserve it because it is reasonable to think that those elected are most deserving if the majority corroborates this opinion of them. I would share this view, if those who were entitled to vote—that is, the men of this council—were of the same kind (*qualità*) and of the same station (*grado*). If there were no reason to think that these men varied by quality and rank (*grado*), one could rationally believe that the best were the ones who the majority agreed on. But a defect in this reasoning arises when you consider that all of us that make up this council are not of the same station (*grado*), nor do we have the same means. There is one sort of men, those who are from the fours and up—those who are wealthier and therefore considered more noble, or those who have enjoyed reputation from their fathers or ancestors—that think that the state belongs to them, and that we—those of the threes, twos, and aces—do not deserve dignities, but rather that we should be happy with a few petty offices, and have the rest of us carry all the burdens, like we have in the past.

These men have in their head the procedures (*modi*) and distinctions that were made between the fourteen and eleven offices,[3] and the *mazzocchio*.[4] They are used to those tyrannical procedures, so it strikes them as just that things are governed similarly in the future. It seems right to them that those who are not of their circle, unless they come from some extremely ancient noble house, are incapable of holding the dignities that matter. However, all these men who, in a word, do not remember that we are all citizens, pretend to be of a higher quality than others. They hand out favors to each other and form coalitions when they vote (*quando vanno a partito*), and give us—those of the threes, twos, and aces—nothing but white beans. Unless one of us is extremely virtuous and achieves the level of an Aristotle or a Solon, they presume that giving us an important office undermines the magistracy's reputation, and pollutes the office itself. On the other hand, we see each other as equals and do not form coalitions (*partiti*) within our own ranks. In fact, because we are not yet deceived by old opinions and habits, we often believe that they [the upper classes] deserve some office or other. This is the real reason why, even though we can easily find someone among ourselves capable of any task, he can never earn the majority of the votes: the person who wins the most votes must necessarily win among the fours and above, who are always supported by their peers along with some of us; but we can at most achieve support only among ourselves, and they will give us only white beans.

It is not virtue, prudence, or experience that earns them the most votes, but rather the nobility, property (*roba*), and reputation of their fathers and ancestors. It is neither to the benefit of the city, nor because the magistracies are in the hand of God knows who, but simply because they appropriated the state to themselves based on the presumption and false opinion of their own self-worth. There are just as many good, courageous citizens among the threes, twos, and aces as there are among the sixes, fives, and fours. There are just as many lovers of liberty among the lowers stations; in fact, there are probably more among them than among the higher stations because we do not long for anything except a free way of life, while they hope to have a narrow state headed by tyrants, like they have had in the past. If creating coalitions were based only on virtue and if other criteria were not considered, I would agree that the judgment of the majority is a sound course of action, and I would not doubt that every quality man would find a place for himself. But they drown us in their nobility and reputation, which brings with it a certain splendor that continues to dazzle us. It seems timely for me to say something about this, not in the way many other writers have spoken about the subject in the past, but in our own terms and according to our way of life in this city.

Today the nobility, or to use their own vocabulary, "the good men" (*uomini da bene*), is not a title used to designate an ancient bloodline of this city, which perhaps would be in some sense more reasonable. Instead, this term denotes several houses that for some time have maintained a certain status above others in the state. In fact, there are a few ancient houses whose men of prestige (*uomini da roba*) have diminished and have not maintained the splendor required of the station. They call these houses blemished (*intignata*), and they (*uomini da bene*) seek to elevate them close, but just below their own status, repairing them amid broken wheels, like they try to place us (*come ripongono noi altri*). Whoever considers the foundation of their nobility will not find any real reason that they have obtained so much glory. If they ever enjoyed success, it was because they prospered with fortune and the favor of the time, but even more often because of tyrants, or because some wealthy man among them found a way to ennoble himself with his money. Some of them curried favor with the heads of state in ways too shameful to mention. It was not virtue but extraordinary circumstances that hurled them to such honorable status, and we must keep these circumstances in mind. If your ancestors were modest citizens in their service, and did not seek to make themselves great through these means, this does not make you any lesser than them, nor does it mean that you should play a more minor role in the city. In fact, on the occasions when they have been given offices, your magistrates have done much good for the republic and not bad, like most of them [the upper classes], who have been ministers of narrow states and are enriched through these [sinister] arts.

They call themselves good men (*uomini da bene*), as if we are bad men; indeed, they have used this title to expropriate and oppress others. A few repute themselves to have inherited the mantel that their fathers and grandfathers, who were either very reputable men in the government of the state, or wise and respectable men, passed down to them, as if we do not know that often sons are the exact opposite of their fathers, and that virtue and brains are not hereditary, but rather come from nature or God's will. However, I no longer take them into consideration, nor do I regard those citizens as more useful to the city because most of them simply had more luck than my ancestors. Because magistracies were given, or taken, on this basis, I need not know if one's father was wise or virtuous; I need to assess what the man in question is or is not: if he is similar to his father or grandfather, I should respect him, and maybe give him the benefit of the doubt in honor of his ancestor's memory. But if he is of another type, I should not keep him in consideration, especially because it is more shameful that he did not know how to imitate the good examples that he grew up around. Nor need I demonstrate any honor in my behavior toward someone who desecrated a robe that was once beautiful.

There are others who enter this group through their wealth. Nothing can be more dishonest because wealth is completely dependent on fortune, and tomorrow a rich man can easily become impoverished. Many times, it is purchased through usury or other dishonest and viperous arts, and those who have unjustly gained titles of nobility (*la roba*) deserve to be punished. Everyone sees it as a bane that these men are honored, that those who are the worst are called good men (*uomini da bene)*. Notice that the reasons why everyone thinks those men deserve to be preferred over all others are not based on their virtue, merit, or prudence, but in their fortune, favors, and illicit business practices (*guadagni*). Nevertheless, we are so thick (*grossi*) that we hold them in higher regard than we hold ourselves. We do not realize that we are all born in the same city, that the patria exists for all of us, and that we are all capable of office. Wealth, favors, and good fortune should not distinguish us—only virtue, prudence, generosity, and love for this city and government. However, excellent counselors, it would be necessary for everyone who participates in this council to put these considerations aside and cast his vote for the person most capable of governing, or, alternatively, that those of us from the threes, twos, and aces act as they do and give our votes only to one of our own. Given that we are far more numerous, we can quickly make them realize what it means to only favor one's own and disfavor all the others.

The first option is impossible because they will never change their opinion of us. The second would be scandalous and divide the city. Anyone who wishes that we remain united and that everyone should play a role in government has proposed this provision [to introduce lottery]. If this provision were to succeed, it could afford some of you the occasional opportunity to become a candidate, and perhaps even to be selected for office. Introducing this procedure will not result in the magistracies falling into incapable hands because incapable men will not be able to earn enough votes to become candidates [for the lottery] in the first place, and with each passing day incapable men will be less likely to even be considered because their characters and insufficiencies will become better known. It will never or rarely be the case that half of the council is deceived and judge someone adequate who is actually not, nor will enough private matters converge behind one candidate that he can have so much favor. In fact, if a disadvantage exists, it will be at our expense, because many of us let ourselves become dazzled by their condition more than we judge their aptitude for office, something that does not exist in the reverse situation: if they are not taken by our virtue, then they will never add us to the coalition (*partito*).

Removing the majority vote system will not open the way to incapable men, but rather remove the impediment that we today face because we do not possess the property (*tanta roba*), reputation, or ancient parentage that they do. Although this method creates more openness in government, that does not mean that it will make more noise; nor should anyone fear that disorders will ensure. The communal magistracies do not go to one person, but to many, so that it may arise that no one constitutes enough of a majority to be the decided winner; but this is rather unlikely considering our peers generally make a profession of being governed and often voluntarily concede to one who supposedly knows more. It would be more honest to tolerate this small disorder that this procedure might engender, rather than exclude us and our peers forever, as if we were enemies of the city or from another city, or as if we were donkeys, whose task is always to carry wine and to drink nothing but water. We pay our taxes and carry the burdens much more than they do because we are poorer and every tax has a much higher significance for us than them; why, then, should we not be entitled to have access to advantages as well? If being a citizen entitles us to be members of this council just as they are, then having more clothes, more family, and better fortune does not make them more citizens than we are. If we take stock in he who has the greatest aptitude for government, then we demonstrate as much spirit, sentiment, and language as they do, and we exhibit less passion and desire, which ultimately corrupts their judgment.

They say that Rome and Venice always used the method of majority vote. As far as Venice is concerned, it is true, but there are many reasons for this. First, that city does not have a popular government but is founded on their *gentiluomini*, who are more capable of subjecting the people under their thumb; nor is there any fear of external threats (*tiranni*) because their geographic location prohibits cavalry from entering the city. In Rome, they do not honestly explain what happened: There was indeed a time when the *grandi* possessed the state, and consequently the people rebelled and raised themselves up against them. Their equivalents [to our nobility] knew that they could never win with a majority-vote system, and therefore they adopted a more robust method that is in no way comparable to our own. They divided the city into two parties; in our terms, between the sixes, the fives, and the fours on one side, and the threes, twos, and aces on the other. Thus, the Romans ordered by law that the offices were divvied—that is, each part of the city was entitled to half of the magistracies. If we were to propose this method, you all would forget the Romans, who you use as examples only when it is convenient, proclaiming that this policy is a mad and dishonest attempt to divide the city. You would never admit that the method of majority vote is far more dishonest because it removes any opportunity for those who merit office to obtain it, or that it divides the city far more, because one part, placed outside the circle, so to speak, needs to despair more than when they are subjected to tyranny. Under tyranny, they [the people] are oppressed by force, so they have reason to complain without shame. Now, each day they are placed beneath the authority (*sotto titolo*) of those who do not deserve it, breeding legitimate resentment and danger.

Continuing with the majority vote system will not nourish prudence (*le intelligenzie*). Fewer votes can constitute a checkmate: 150 or 200 men that put their votes together are capable of pushing someone through easily. Nor will the laws of the city be repaired because a number of this size cannot be combated easily; if the magistrates are beholden to a certain few, how will they punish the errors of those with exalted status? And even when justice could be pursued, is it not more laudable and holy to have a republic ordered so that these errors could not transpire in the first place, rather than one that encourages them? Pray tell, what prudence (*intelligenze*) will result from such a system? The kind of prudence exhibited by the quality of those men I spoke of above? The prudence of men who conspire to only vote for themselves and their peers, fostering that concord among them that is so natural but meanwhile suffocates us? We can address this only through violent and scandalous modes, which we could easily employ because we far outnumber them, or through the more temperate and pleasant mode proposed, which sweetly, and without public damage, allows everyone to enjoy real liberty.

I speak of real liberty because so far, they have only shown us what liberty means, without really granting it to us: on the one hand, they gave us the power to vote, and they convinced us that we could all equally take part in all honors and advantages; on the other, they managed to set things up in such a way that they can still enjoy all advantages with our own consent, with no violence and no explicit oppression, and we are, therefore, still their servants in many respects. We go to the council meetings with the same furor for liberty with which bears look for honey, yet we do not realize that it is a useless effort that entails continued servitude, and that, if we make an advancement at the end of each year, it always turns out that we have not gained anything relevant.

Therefore, excellent citizens, if these terrible conditions are not resolved, and if this honest, just, and easily introduced provision, which currently resides in your own hands, is rejected, you will encourage the spirit of all those who labor only to secure their own advantages. Moreover, you will have nothing to complain about except your own weak spirit and ineptitude. You are citizens of this city just like they are, yet you give yourselves very little reputation, and to them far more than they deserve. You allow yourselves to be persuaded by their false reasoning, that is, that you are not capable of serving in the government of the city, and when given the opportunity to equalize yourselves with them and reclaim your share of the honors and offices, you cowardly demure to the cast of men who regularly and willingly place their property and lives in danger to achieve such status. It will bring you not only danger, but also great shame. It will augment their arrogance that they maintain through their families, and they will treat you in a way that will force you to desire a remedy at some point, but then it will be too late.

Your fate remains in your own hands, and you can either bring yourselves in practice and in name to a true state of liberty and to enjoy its fruits, or confine yourselves to liberty only in name—a false liberty that is really servitude and deprives you of all offices and honors. I beseech you to make the same judgment and become men and citizens of this patria, and contradict those rumors of your insufficiency and ineptitude. If you were to do this, you would truly be free, and truly be citizens of this city, equal to those who currently repute themselves to be better than you, and you would leave to your descendants varying degrees of wealth, honors, and nobility. But if you refuse your rights (*il commodo vostro*), you will remain without these advantages forever—true servants, true naïfs. In the end, you will realize that everyone gave you the opportunity to insert yourselves into the history books of this shop, but that ultimately you are merely butcher boys (*garzoni*), and that procuring for yourselves your due is too arduous a task, and that they will always retain all the advantages of this republic.

On the Mode of Reordering the Popular Government

Two main reasons make me think that, unless of course God helps her, our city is bound to lose her liberty and her state (*stato*) within a few short years. The first is that after the many disasters (*nafraugi*) that have befallen Italy and the constant fighting among the several princes, it seems reasonable that one of these princes will emerge as a great power and defeat the minor ones, thereby potentially reducing Italy to a state of monarchy.[5] Considering how difficult it was for Italy to defend its common liberty (*libertà commune*) in a time when there were no foreign princes, it will be even more so now with such large birds preying on her entrails. In this event, we would find our city gravely endangered because we do not have sufficient forces to defend ourselves. We live unarmed and find the city, in comparison to former times, with little money because trade, which has kept us alive in the past, has declined.

The second reason is that our civic way of life (*vivere civile*) does not resemble the way of life in a good republic—with regard to both our form of government and our other customs and habits. Our government risks either becoming a tyranny, or declining into popular anarchy. License to do evil is universal, while the laws and the magistrates are neither respected nor feared. Virtuous and courageous men (*uomini virtuosi e valenti*) have no opportunity to demonstrate and exercise their proper *virtù*. We do not reward those whose works genuinely benefit the republic. Men are consumed by a universal ambition to aspire toward every honor, and a presumptuous desire to insert themselves in all public roles of whatever importance. Men's spirits are effeminate and indolent, accustomed to a delicate, and with respect to our means, extravagant way of life. There is very little love of true glory and real honor. Instead, men are very much motivated by riches and wealth. These reflections give me little hope, and yet I do not despair because I believe that we can heal a great part of these maladies, and that even though the cure is very difficult, it is, nonetheless, not impossible.

I do not imagine that one or two laws of limited application can yield sufficient change. We must make a great heap of all things and mix this mass into one matter, and then take it apart and reshape everything, just as the pasta maker makes something edible from pasta dough: if the first batch does not come out well, he piles everything together and shapes the dough into a new form. Or better yet, we can follow the example of a competent doctor, who, when finding a body full of so many diseases that he is unable to apply a specific treatment, seeks to address the causes of the illness and tries to affect a new state of health in the whole body. While this remedy is very difficult and requires a good doctor, it is not impossible. It is true that this remedy works better with a young patient than with an old one, a fact that discourages me all the more because our city has now already grown ancient. Nonetheless, I would not despair if some gifted mind would apply his talents to the task, and if wise men[6] were as motivated by this task as they usually are by making money or doing harm. Indeed, men should embrace this undertaking with more ardor because the difficulty of the task promises greater glory.

I confess that to heal the city entirely would require many things, all of which are practically impossible because the city exhibits bad habits and its men [are] poorly disciplined. One who would undertake the endeavor of reforming everything at once could easily fall short and accomplish nothing at all. But I would also commend one who would apply his spirit to things that are less difficult, and who would be content to address the few things that are now possible. It would be no small feat for one to lead the city from her present poor condition to, at least, a mediocre disposition. In fact, it would be enough to make a start because, by providing the city with the initial opportunity, we could hope for greater success in the course of time than would appear possible from our present lowly station.

Before all else, the city must maintain enough forces so that it can, at the very least, defend itself and not live in continual fear of external aggression (*insulti esterni*). Good internal order and the rule of law would be of little use if the city were subject to being overcome by outside force. Therefore, the city must be amply provided with defenders. Our old means of defense [mercenaries] are weaker than ever because the city's capacity to make money has been greatly impaired. Public revenues are insufficient and mostly absorbed by the public debt,[7] private citizens are not as rich as they once were, and trade in the city does not flourish because many other places and peoples have acquired and continue to learn the art of profit making. Moreover, those citizens who are rich are not used to being encouraged to help their *patria*, as was the case in ancient times. Rectifying these issues would prove extremely difficult given the present popular regime, and it would be more useful to apply that toil and effort to a reform project that would profit the city more substantially. In any case, clearly the city could not sustain a large expense of seventy or eighty thousand *ducati* a month, and is incapable of providing for such a large sum in short order.

Therefore, we cannot pretend that the city can sustain itself with a large army of mercenaries over a long period of time, as it has often done in the past. Because we can no longer rely on foreign forces, we must consider defending ourselves through the force of our own citizenry. Arming citizens is not alien to a republican and popular way of life. When a city gives itself a good justice system and good laws, these arms do not portend danger, but rather utility to the patria. This is borne out not only by reason, but also by the example of ancient republics—Rome, Athens, and Sparta—that defended their liberty and expanded their empire through their own arms. Nor is this a completely novel enterprise within our city. In the histories, we read that in the early enjoyment of their liberty (*libertà*) our very own people made up the battalions entirely on their own and with great success. This example should encourage our spirits, and not leave us feeling disheartened. Clearly, with the proper diligence, the city can be easily persuaded to endure the creation of a civic militia. Although the measure [establishing the present civic militia] was adopted against many opinions and with little favor or order, it has taken such strong hold that today everyone approves of the measure.

There are infinite reasons why making war with one's own arms is incomparably more useful than mercenary armies. First, a city that relies on foreign soldiers risks being deceived. This is especially the case for a republic because it is less unified than a principality and cannot maintain the bonds a prince develops with his soldiers. No obvious remedy exists for this lack of unity. Giving full power to one person endangers the existence of the republic, and dividing power equally results in chaos: no one really expects to be another's equal, and each man seeks to be singled out with rewards, consequently reducing military affairs to a marketplace in which men wheel and deal with each other for such rewards. When foreigners serve the republic in good faith, they do so not out of love. Serving can provide some glory, but not all men are motivated by such a goal. Because they are foreigners, their interest does not align with the republic's, and they necessarily split into factions. He who puts his trust in his own citizens and subjects incurs none of these risks because, as already stated, he does not have to worry about being deceived by them; moreover, he need not worry that they, like mercenaries, will deliberately proceed too slowly in order to drag out wars and extend their monetary compensation. Who doubts that citizen-soldiers exhibit intense (*sviscerato*) love and, not merely a desire, but an ardent desire to win? When the city is suddenly attacked or when it wishes to execute a military venture that requires speed, it could equip an army within a few days, but it takes far longer to gather mercenary forces from distant places or foreign provinces. In the event that the army suffers defeat in one battle, the whole state is not necessarily lost. A new citizen-based army could be raised at once—an impossibility in the case of foreign troops that could not be gathered together in sufficient time. It is easy to see the importance of this matter.

The Romans would never have been able to defend themselves in so many wars, especially against Hannibal, had they not been able to spring back and quickly generate new troops from among their population after defeats. Carthage fell to Scipio because the city was disarmed once its mercenary forces fell. During our own times, who doubts that if the Venetians could have reinforced their troops with their own people after the defeat at Vailà they would not have lost all their landed territory (*stato*) in eight short days?[8] Not being able to do so brought them to dire straits where, if the emperor were another man or if the alliance among their enemies had lasted, a single day or one inconstant mercenary leader would have cost the city not only its dominion, but also its liberty.

State (*lo stato*) and rule (*lo imperio*) constitute nothing but violence over subjects, occasionally palliated with some pretense of decency. Wishing to preserve the state without weapons and forces of your own, but rather with the help of others, is like wanting to practice a profession without the tools of the trade. In short, a city that lives unarmed can only poorly prevail over others and only poorly defend itself against its enemies. I would add that, when a city takes up this way of life [defending itself with its own arms] it costs much less to sustain its troops. During times of war they are paid like any other soldiers, and during peace time the costs of ordinary provisions and maintenance reverts back to the citizenry itself. In this manner, at least, the defense of our country would not be placed in jeopardy, considering that Tuscany and our territorial dominion is geographically well situated and sufficiently abundant to feed her inhabitants. It would be wise to introduce within the city itself the regulations of infantry that we have established on our territory's periphery and on the city's outskirts, and to add to this men of arms and light cavalry. Establishing these modes does not necessitate that we overexert ourselves right now—in fact, it would be relatively easy considering our amply populated city and state. Truly, so that the city and the countryside does not fill with factions and discord, a good judicial system should accompany the citizen army, which is easy to do in theory but harder in practice, as I will discuss at greater length below.

Once ordered with our own arms, which is the most important matter, the structure of our internal government deserves more than slight consideration. We must approach this question with great attention, and carefully consider the best way to order ourselves. There is no point in arguing over whether an administration composed of one, the few, or the many constitutes the best type of rule, for liberty is proper and natural to our city. Our past was lived in liberty, and we have been bred with it. Our ancestors gave us the tradition of liberty, and when necessary we defend it with all our means and with our very lives. Liberty is nothing but the supremacy of law and public decrees over men's individual appetites. However, laws do not have lives of their own (*legge non hanno vita*) and cannot be observed on their own; rather they require ministers—that is, magistrates—to enforce them. In order to live under the rule of law as opposed to the rule of men (*sotto particulari*), it is essential that the magistrates do not fear individual persons and should not owe their office to one man or to a few such that magistrates are not compelled to govern the city subject to the will of others. A popular way of life is therefore the foundation of liberty. It is grounded in and its spirit is embodied by the Great Council, which distributes the magistracies and dignities of the city.[9]

Keeping the Great Council intact renders it difficult for anyone to make himself overly powerful (*farsi grande*) in the city because no single man's authority can confer office and prestige on any person, and therefore no one in office needs to subject himself to one man out of fear or in hope of political gain. Without this check on individual power, the city is not free, nor can it be; it will otherwise inevitably fill itself with sects and factions, and in the course of a mere few years, it will wind up in the hands of one man. Not only am I in favor of the Great Council, but I also much prefer the way it is currently composed since it has gradually and judiciously (*discretamente*) excluded those who formerly who did not participate in government, so that now the council no longer consists of only plebs and peasants. It was necessary to open the way to enable everyone to sit in the council; indeed, if we were to restrict or even sift through the populace to make only certain citizens eligible for this office, it would no longer qualify as a *popular* council. True, this openness (*larghezza*) allows for a few crazy people and many ignorant and mal-intentioned ones to participate in the council; nonetheless, all things considered, it is clear that the elections and judgments that emerge from the council do not exceed the bounds of reason. And if by chance there are some judgments that are questionable, they should be endured because it is far more convenient to live with some small disorders than to see one man hold all the power of good and evil within his hands. Perfection cannot be found in any one thing, but in those things that are generally approved with the fewest defects.

The Great Council was thus properly made to include all those who participate in government (*stato*). I have often considered whether it would be wise, for the election of magistrates, to extend the electorate beyond those who are able to hold office to a larger number of those who cannot participate in government. We have seen from experience that the majority of the council's errors in electing officers comes from the appetite to distribute appointments so widely that every elector (*che ognuno di chi squittina*) desires to obtain office himself. This would cease to be the case if those who were not entitled to hold office were allowed to vote on the candidacies of those who were. These men would then not hold out hope that they would themselves be elected, and therefore they would not be influenced to vote for men other than those who they believe actually merit office. We have the examples of the ancient republics where an infinite number of men were involved in the designation of officials. We read among other things that the Romans granted citizenship to many *cum iure suffragii*, which in my view means nothing more than the power to elect officials while being denied the right to be elected. This, as we have said, explains why a voter will have no personal interest in one man being elected over another, but given man's natural inclination to seek the good when not constrained by private interests, will reasonably choose the one who appears to him most deserving. Nevertheless, being an innovative idea of considerable importance, I myself am not entirely committed to the position. If it [this idea] were to gain popularity, I would stress that its use must be limited; that is, that popular power would be limited to electing officials and not be extended to initiating legislation.

Having endorsed the Great Council and affirmed that it is the foundation of liberty—the very soul of our body politic—we must now turn to important matters of the state that concern war and peace. Initial discussion of laws that need to be adopted or renewed should not be conducted in the council because they are too important. Many object that the election of magistrates is of equal importance, but it is nonetheless made in the council. I respond that the two cases are not parallel. First, a large electorate is necessary for the preservation of liberty, which would not exist if offices were distributed at the discretion of one or of the few. This is not the case with other matters, whose resolution neither dries up the city's liberty nor risks particular men becoming powerful in a way that threatens common liberty. Moreover, legislation often requires the type of speed and secrecy that is impossible to achieve in large assemblies. Furthermore, while the election of magistrates is indeed important, it is not all that difficult to judge: the people rely on the reputation and estimation of men, which is based on a broader popular conception, composed of many opinions, as opposed to the judgment of one particular person. Popular judgment does not err all too often in elections, and when it does it is not usually of such grave consequence.

This [effective and salutary popular judgment] is not the case with legislation. Laws require the consideration of wise men (*uomini savi*), for when laws are driven by the appetite of the multitude, they are clearly always harmful or useless. Popular judgment is even less suited to daily votes and deliberations concerning the prosecution of war, the negotiation of peace, and the like, the truth of which one cannot truly grasp unless he is very wise, and where one error is capable of subverting the city's entire state and dominion (*stato e dominio*). Therefore of course great disorders occurred in the ancient republics, such as in Rome and especially in Athens, when they relied on the people's participation in these matters. We read that for this reason their states faced much ruin. Present times offer the example of Gonfalonier Piero Soderini, who asked the Great Council to decide whether to mount an attack against Pisa. The people's favor of the plan and their desire to proceed against the opinion of all the wise men of the city brought nothing but danger and disgrace.

Consequently, such deliberations must be conducted by wise and experienced men in smaller bodies of restricted membership. Now, one of the strongest foundations of liberty is the equality of citizens, meaning that no individual exceeds the others beyond a certain measure. This equality cannot exist where the same people hold the magistracies perpetually—that is, where the same people always remain in power. Change is necessary. Conversely, the business of politics also requires experienced men who attend to affairs of the state assiduously and who are capable of devoting specific attention to them. It is therefore appropriate that a single man occupies a distinct and exalted (*cua precipua*) office entrusted with the secrets of the state. One sees that the number one carries with it perfection [and unity], and while it need not be the case that this office is filled by one private man, it would be beneficial for our city to elect a gonfalonier for life, or at least for a number of years, because it would lead to many positive results. We see with the Venetian example that having a doge for life served as the great bedrock of their republic. Conversely, eight years after a popular way of life was established in our own city, we see the opposite effect: no one single person specifically tended to the maintenance of government, consequently convulsing the republic so often that its health came more from God or chance than from our men or our wisdom. It is evident that if it had not been destined otherwise, our city would have certainly gone to ruin.

It is therefore wise to make a single head of state in a similar fashion. However, it is not enough to simply have the Great Council with one gonfalonier. If other measures are not provided, a gonfalonier, with his great authority and reputation, would govern everything at his own discretion with a tyrannical flavor. Instead, it is necessary to give [the gonfalonier] half of a council of citizens, one similar to the Eighty,[10] composed of elected men and the elite of the city (*fiore della città*) with whom he would consult and deliberate the republic's important matters. In this way, he would not have to deliberate with the multitude on these issues and defer to a popular solution; at the same time it would inhibit him from arrogating too much of the city to himself. If this type of council did not exist, then it would be necessary for the gonfalonier to consult with both the Signoria[11] and a magistracy comprising a few citizens, which would always conform to his ways, because he holds office for life or for many years. Or, alternatively, it would be necessary to seek the counsel of many unskilled people (*imperiti*), who, as a result of their ignorance, would make many errors, or over whom the gonfalonier would exert excessive influence. For one sees from experience and reason that the multitude never supports itself on its own, but always attaches itself to and is dependent on a prop, hence breeding weakness in the latter. And it will be stickier with one who is very magisterial and reputable, thereby rendering his potential power too great.

One of the most crucial elements for maintaining true and complete liberty is surely this: There should be a method (*mezzo*) to regulate the ignorance of the multitude and control the ambition of a single gonfalonier. It is essential, then, that all men of intelligence and reputation participate [in government]. The method must involve the participation of men of quality so that they do not become resentful and alienated, and look to plot against the ungrateful (*causa di contentarsi poco e pensare a cose nuove*). The Eighty were established at the beginning of the popular government for this purpose, but the ignorance of the multitude enlarged it to include men who did not merit the office, and those who should have always been included were many times excluded. As a result, the poor quality and constant variation among the men that currently make up the council came into being, and it did not retain its proper authority. Consequently, the council did not bear the weight of the republic, and many errors ensued, which made the power of the gonfalonier dangerously great. Nonetheless, if the city is to conserve its liberty and become well ordered, it is necessary that this council be filled with more men of quality and authority. I will speak of the particular means by which this should be accomplished below.

Good and free republican government therefore rests on three foundations: The Great Council—an entity crucial to liberty, a gonfalonier for life or at least for a long time, and a group of a good number of citizens who determine and advise over important matters of state. These three elements, if ordered reasonably, would make this part of the government of the city well instituted and perfect. Thus far I have spoken of these orders abstractly and confusingly; it is now necessary to describe each institution more precisely, speaking of each one separately in the order mentioned above.

All the city's magistrates, officials, and offices, whether consultative or administrative, should be created by the Great Council. By upholding this principle, no one can claim that the state is controlled by one or by the few. It is true that putting the entire government in their hands means that it is essential that elections are conducted properly and that appropriate men are selected. We have witnessed the disorder that resulted from giving the dignities of the city to insufficient men, whether out of ignorance or malice, and the extreme consequences of this disorder. Beyond the damage done by having incompetent men govern, the indiscriminate handing out of honors irrespective of virtue or merit disillusions the goodwill of those who are capable, encouraging the audacity and inhibiting the shame of those who are evil (*cattivi*). If it were evident that the people refused to elect those who failed to comport themselves well or those who developed a bad reputation, this would motivate those with good souls and inhibit those with evil ones. Without upholding this distinction between good and evil, the reward that serves as one of the two bases of republican government [reward and punishment], according to the ancients, would be lost.

The origin of this disorder came from the ambition that gripped everyone to seek every honor and to abuse one's liberty insolently, which is natural among all peoples who are not well governed. This desire was fostered by the law that included among those eligible for office everyone who won more than half the votes, and that then selected the victor by lot among them. In an assembly where so many are ambitions, so many are evil, and so many are ignorant, it is no wonder that many are able to obtain such a [bare] majority. The method of selecting the men with the most votes should be adopted again, as it was employed in the first years of the council. Clearly, it was evident that, *ut plurimum*, elections were good then. Indeed, had this method been preserved, elections would have progressively improved as the state became more consolidated and as fewer suspect men would alter the judgment of the people.

This electoral procedure would be better and more reasonable because it is unjust that one man who is supported by eight hundred out of one thousand and another who is disliked by everyone outside of five hundred plus one are placed on equal standing. It is contrary to the nature of popular government, where the people, not lottery, should be prince, and where the prince, not fortune, should disperse honors. Two arguments can be advanced against this view: first, that it gives rise to enmity and bad blood between two candidates who consider themselves equals, such as when one sees the other preferred over himself without apparent reason, and sometimes indeed unfairly, because it cannot be denied that irregularities (*estravaganzie*) occur. The other argument is that in a popular government where everyone pays taxes, it is proper (*conveniente*) that everyone participates in a share of the offices, especially those posts that carry a salary (*utili*),[12] and yet, with highest majority vote electoral procedures, the offices are quite narrowly dispersed.

Nevertheless, I still would not veer from the method described above because it better conserves the intent of distributing the honors and offices well, which is the most important thing of all. If the state were in a more secure condition (*in modo fermo*) such that its citizens accepted it as a given and acknowledged that it could not be altered, I would not propose any distinction. But because the state is still young and continues to waver (*balenando*), for the sake of greater peace, it should be arranged that the more important magistracies, such as the Signoria, the Ten, and the Eight, are elected by the candidate who wins the most votes, or at least selected by lot among the top two nominees.[13] This should also apply to the more important external offices, such as the captains of Pisa, Arezzo, and Pistoia.[14] There is another type of office of a more administrative character, but not as important, such as, internally, the offices of tower, the country, and the like, and, externally, all the vicarates and large *podesterie*.[15] These offices could be decided with greater wideness (*paratiti piu' larghi*); that is to say, for each office four or five candidates could be nominated, and the winner decided by a mixture of sortition and election (*e nello andare a partito mescolare la sorte e la nominazione*). The third type of offices are those that handle few administrative matters but are founded on their honor or utility, such as the *camarlinghi* and the minor podesterie and many of the honors of the city. These could be left as they are currently dispersed. This method could still be criticized because it fails to correct all the defects stemming from this excessive inclusiveness (wideness) and also because it is against the practice of all republics, none of which, as far as I know, ever used this type of sortition to make appointments. They must be accepted, nonetheless, as the lesser evil, remembering that rarely is anything entirely perfect, but rather that wise men satisfy themselves with what exhibits fewer imperfections.

This brings us to the second consideration of the Great Council regarding the law: legislation should not be immediately introduced in the council because this would generate great confusion and it would be contrary to every order of a well-governed republic. Instead, legislation should first be discussed in bodies of more restricted membership, and only then submitted to the council to be approved or rejected. I readily agree that the law, being of universal importance, concerning every member of the city, should be decided in the council. However, I would prefer that there be no public discussion, unless on the order of the Signoria, and then only in favor of what is proposed, for a thousand disorders would ensure if everyone were permitted to argue on either side. Public discussion is beneficial when legislation is not examined in other chambers, but because they come down to the council already digested and discussed in more narrow bodies and already presumed useful, it is unnecessary that they are yet again debated. The council's approval does not require that the council reexamine every proposal from the beginning, but because the law binds everyone, it must not be said that it is made by the few and without universal consent. This requirement also serves as a check to narrow governing bodies, preventing them from transforming the regime or for some other pernicious purpose. In order to allow greater maturity of thought to the proceedings, it would, in fact, be desirable that the proposals are published some days in advance, so that they are made known to the people and allow for meetings and discussions before the council comes to vote on them.

Whether taxes and raising money should be voted on in the council, I think, is a more difficult matter. On the one hand, experience demonstrates that the people resist voting for taxes, to the point that many times once the funds have been approved they arrive too late to serve the intended purpose. It could also happen that funds are needed for a secret purpose of which the public should not be made aware. If the council's approval is needed, then that purpose needs to become manifest, because the people would never give their consent without being convinced of an urgent need. I would add that when the people deliberate these matters, they, *ut plurimum*, are inclined to adopt unjust and harmful methods that are both harsh and unprofitable. Because the council consists of more poor men than rich ones, they would not distribute the taxes proportionally. Instead, they want the rich to pay everything and not hear a word about it, which is unjust and dangerous. Although the rich should of course contribute to the city, it is foolish to ruin them because they provide honor and ornament to the city, and because they should remain capable of coming to its assistance on future occasions as well.

These arguments demonstrate that the council should not be trusted with these matters. Conversely, money is of great concern to everyone—being, as they say, second nature (*secondo sangue*). Trouble and discord can arise if everyone must make payment decided by the few. Furthermore, taxation would lead to disturbances if taxes were administered in a dishonest manner or if they burdened the poor more than the rich. Taking both sides of the argument into consideration, I conclude that because raising funds is such a serious component of the administration of the state—without it the state could neither defend nor offend—it is necessary that these matters are not deliberated in the council for the natural reasons mentioned above. Experience has frequently shown that the people's failure to approve payments in time has meant that not even one hundred thousand ducati were sufficient to put to right something that originally required ten thousand. It is true that a procedure in which only a small number determine the payment of taxes could cause upheaval (*alterazione*). I would favor, therefore, that the final decision lay with all the following: the intermediate council along with the signori, the Ten, the colleagues, and the Eight; as well as a few of the other leading officials such as the captain of the [Guelf] Party,[16] the conservators, the Six of Commerce,[17] and other such magistrates; so that there are two, or better yet, three hundred citizens who deliberate on these issues.[18] Such an ensemble would be better positioned to make good decisions, because it would include more prudent men who would let reason persuade them. In addition, the intervention of so many different men decreases the probability of dissatisfaction and the desire for a change [of government] (*fare alterazione*), for almost every family would be represented, and there would be very few who would not be represented.

The second foundation of good government is a gonfalonier. It is first necessary to determine how much authority he ought to have, and then to determine whether he should serve for life or for a limited term. This certainly deserves a great deal of thought because if the gonfalonier is too free and unconstrained, he could become so powerful as to cause great harm to the city and to pose a great danger to liberty. And yet, controlling him is also difficult, because you want him to serve to a certain standard without tying him down so tightly that he becomes useless. The gonfalonier must, first of all, serve as the head of the Signoria in the same manner and in the same form that he has to this date. Consequently, if the Signoria continues to maintain the supreme and unlimited power and reputation it now has, a gonfalonier capable of directing it would have in his hand all the force of the city. Experience shows that a gonfalonier who remains for a long while in his exalted office, with the prudence and reputation he will likely acquire, will practically always be able to prevail; and it stands to reason that this will be the case because the members of the Signoria are almost always weak. Such weakness is inevitable considering the complicated laws governing election to the Signoria. Both families and particular individuals are subject to prohibitions (*divieti*)[19] of long duration with regard to the composition of the Signoria itself and the associated colleges. This dignity is, and always has been, spread among a large number. Hence, many ignorant and worthless members are appointed who, lacking knowledge or distinction, have neither the ingenuity nor spirit to stand up to the gonfalonier, who can therefore sway and bend them to his will.

This would not be the case if the Signoria were made up of prudent and respected men, who would be able to disagree with [the gonfalonier], and therefore would be disciplined by reason and not overawed by authority. This is why the doge of Venice, despite holding a life appointment, has little power: because he is always flanked by the first men of the city. The weakness of our signori has given Piero Soderini immoderate authority, and because it affects everything, this must be repaired in one of two ways. Either the membership of that supreme magistracy, the Signoria, should be restricted to a small number of chosen men; or, it should remain large and continue to allow broader access, however with limits imposed on its authority in matters that otherwise make it too powerful. Restricting membership to a smaller number of select men would be beneficial if it could be done; because that magistracy is more important than all the others, it would be quite useful if it were filled with men capable of carrying a heavy burden.

However, one must also consider the city's tradition, according to which living with great splendor and honor in the government palace is seen as a universal right—indeed, so much so that one who has not been elected to the Signoria does not feel himself to be truly Florentine. This is such an ancient custom that it would be difficult, in my opinion unthinkable, to persuade the people to change it. Instead, we should proceed carefully to curb and limit some of its power and excessive authority.

The Signoria's present authority is great. With a power of six votes,[20] it can do practically anything with only a few exceptions, such as conducting peace treaties and alliances, raising mercenary armies, and electing officials. The Signoria has unlimited power to examine and deliberate civil matters as well as criminal ones, and it can freely execute citizens or send them into exile. Although these matters can be appealed to the [Great] Council, the procedure is poorly organized and not always observed. The Signoria can thus direct all these matters either directly or indirectly, because all [other] officials are subject to its orders.

I would add that with regard to affairs of the state, the Signoria can respond to letters from [foreign] lords and ambassadors and consult the Eighty only when and about such matters that they see fit. No taxes can be imposed, and no law or provision for raising money can be approved without the consent of two-thirds their members. In sum, the Signoria can do anything, and those things that it cannot do, no other body can do without its consent. And even though the magistrates are elected by the council, the Signoria nonetheless makes appointments on certain occasions and for certain offices and commissions, choosing some of the chancellors and notaries attached to certain magistracies—a matter of no small consequence. In this manner, on account of his high stature and authority, and the weakness of his fellows in office, the gonfalonier can be said to always be in command. It follows, then, that his power is too great for a free city and a free way of life, and therefore it is necessary to take the appropriate measures to prevent this.

Before anything else, the first and most pressing thing that must be done is to remove the power of the Signoria, acting with a majority of two-thirds, to pass sentences of death, exile, or loss of political rights, or to impose any penalty on any citizen for any sort of reason of the state—as well as its power of instructing other magistrates to do any of these things. This is the first and most essential protection that must exist in a republic: the right to live and act freely without fear of being molested by any individual. One might object that sentences pronounced by the Signoria in the name of the state can be appealed to the council based on the law of appeal passed in 1494. I answer that this [law of appeal] is not sufficient because it renders acquittals too difficult to obtain. The majority of two-thirds needed to win a case must essentially be obtained against the authority of the Signoria and before a naturally suspicious people, full of ignorance and enmity toward great and excellent men, and therefore not an adequate judge in cases of this kind. Such cases could be brought before a special tribunal like the Forty (*quarantìa*),[21] or be entrusted to some other magistracy, about which we will speak more below. For now, it suffices to say that it is not right that the Signoria condemns citizens for reasons of state; because [the Signoria] is always in the hands of the gonfalonier, such power makes him too fearsome.

Having removed this power from the gonfalonier to make men fear him, it is also necessary to remove his power to win them over with hope [of gain]. The Signoria must not have the authority to distribute to the citizens offices of any kind, nor should it maintain the ability to directly or indirectly name ambassadors or commissioners, unless it is a matter of sudden necessity for brief periods. It should not be permitted to entrust civil servants (*secretarie di Palazzo*) with missions of these kinds without permission from the Eighty or any council acting in its place, unless there exists a similar need for urgency. These prohibitions serve the purposes mentioned above and, in addition, eliminate the possibility of negotiations with foreign princes by such means. The signori's ability to remove any official with two-thirds majority, including chancellors and public secretaries, is harmful because it is subject to manipulation by the gonfalonier. As Piero Soderini's example demonstrates, this power makes the Signoria subservient to the gonfalonier, as they serve as his instrument to circumvent legislation and direct affairs of the state according to his will.

Legislative procedure also gives the gonfalonier excessive power. Because proposed legislation requires the consent of the Signoria, it is difficult for any law to be enacted against the gonfalonier's will. New laws can alleviate the defects and correct the errors that become apparent, and when the gonfalonier identifies a law that does not suit him, he can correct it by imposing the appropriate law on those who oppose his interest. It is necessary, therefore, that legislative procedures be sufficiently open so as to prevent the gonfalonier from imposing his will. We shall speak below about the means of getting around this, when we discuss how affairs of the state should be deliberated (*consulte*) so that multiple procedures and deliberative bodies hinder the gonfalonier from doing whatever he pleases.

It is now time to consider whether it is salutary for the gonfalonier to maintain the authority that was granted to him by the law of 1502; specifically, to have particular responsibility for justice and the right to preside over any magistracy dealing with criminal matters. The pertinence of this question depends on another: whether the gonfalonier should serve a limited tenure or a life appointment. If his term is limited, of course it matters little whether he maintains this authority, because no gonfalonier, unless compelled by the law, would use it arbitrarily of his own free will knowing he must return to life as a private citizen. Thus, this question becomes relevant only when the gonfalonier holds a lifetime appointment. In this case, I would grant him this power with the exception of affairs of the state. It would be a useful power, if he chose to use it. When, for instance, a noble or powerful man is guilty, the magistrates often lack the courage to punish him because they fear his power, and know that at some point in the future their interest or their family's interest may come into his hands or into the hands of brothers or relatives of the accused. Worse still, the magistrates even have reason to fear violence against their individual persons. A gonfalonier appointed for life would not have such fears. His use of such authority would be beneficial to the city. Nor would it give him excessive power that he would be feared, because it is usually lesser and younger men, rather than elected officials, who come before the court on such charges. In any case, this is not a very important issue, not only because few would make use of this power, but also because by reorganizing the city in the manner described below, it will no longer be necessary to prod (*sprone*) magistrates as much as the present moment requires.

The final concern regarding the office of the gonfalonier remains to be decided: whether he should be appointed for life or for a limited term. There are good arguments on either side (*hinc inde*), but ultimately, we must consider the two principal reasons that made us elect a gonfalonier for life. The first, the intense disorders that afflicted the state, and the other, the inability to properly address the serious problem of criminal activity. In response to the latter concern, the gonfalonier was given the right to preside over any magistracy. To enable him to use this power, it was necessary to make his appointment for life, for if he were temporary he would have the same reasons to incline toward the hesitancy (*fredezza*) that characterized the other magistrates. Today there is less cause for this concern, especially if the gonfalonier's authority is limited in the manner detailed above, and the administration of justice and the method of reaching verdicts are reorganized in the manner explained below. Leaving aside matters of justice, then, the whole question is whether, with regards to government (*rispetto del governo dello stato*), it is better to have a gonfalonier appointed for life or for a limited tenure.

There is no doubt that when the gonfalonier is good and prudent, it is more useful for the city that he serve for life. Because he is always in that office, he concentrates on the government of the state and has no other concerns or objectives beyond to administer well what the republic places in his charge. He acquires greater experience in all sectors, learns how to better manage events, acquires a growing understanding of the citizens he interacts with as well as the populace, and consequently becomes increasingly better equipped to address the exigencies of his office. He could act to the benefit the city and everyone in it with less apprehension than if his term were limited. The knowledge that he would end his life in this position steadies his spirit and removes any reason to seek the favor of one faction over another in order to be reconfirmed or reelected later, after the period of exclusion from office elapsed. These are persuasive reasons for the gonfalonier to be chosen for life.

On the other hand, the best guarantee that he will be a gonfalonier and not an absolute prince is, of course, a limited term of office. Knowing that he will have to surrender his office in the course of time will naturally remove any thoughts of usurping more power than the laws allow him. Should he entertain such thoughts, he would lack the means and followers [to usurp such authority] because he would lack the power and prestige that he would have were he appointed for life. Should he be inadequate, stupid, or evil—which is certainly quite possible—then it is best that the city should have the prospect of being free of him rather than endure him forever. One cannot rely on the possibility of him being deposed because it would never happen, partly because his friends and followers would prevent it, partly because not everyone would be discontent, and partly because not everyone would know his defects. It is also worth considering that a limited term would give greater satisfaction to more citizens. Leading citizens, on whom the concord of the city depend, will be more peaceable and attached to the public good if they can hope to achieve this rank themselves. These are the arguments in favor of the opposite point of view.

Taking both perspectives into consideration, I prefer that the gonfalonier be appointed for life because his permanence could bring greater benefit to the city. I believe, furthermore, that there should be a dignity and supreme rank in the city so that a deserving citizen can aspire to this exalted position through a frame of law and liberty: a dignity by which those who strive and spend their whole lives in the public's service could foresee a place of eminence to which their good conduct and patriotic activity could lead. They can hope to be rewarded for their good works without resorting to tyranny or encroaching on the rights of others. Although only a few will likely be motivated by this ambition, this enthusiasm would still not be futile. It has always been the case that the virtù of a few citizens have built and upheld every well-governed republic, and that glorious works and great deeds have always been initiated and accomplished by a few hands. Leading great things and becoming head of a free city require great skill and virtù that rarely coalesce in one individual. In order to act with great ardor, one must be motivated beyond their love of the city, but also by a spring of ambition, an appetite for grandeur, and the prospect of achieving a supreme rank (*e di condursi in qualche sommo grado*). Who can doubt that such ambition is laudable and most useful when it is served by earning the reputation of being a good and prudent citizen and by benefiting the country as opposed to flouting its laws and fostering factions? One who does not respond to this motivation must have a certain coldness to him, and one who fails to respond to the stimulant of glory will never accomplish noble and lofty things.

It is good, therefore, to demonstrate the prospect of achieving such an exalted rank in order to excite this type of honest ambition in the spirit of great men and create the opportunity for glorious accomplishments. Others, who are less high spirited and exhibit less talent and ability, will aspire to the other magistracies and dignities of the city, which will satisfy their ambition in measure with their degree. However, a small meal will not satisfy those with greater appetites. The limitations discussed above will eliminate any desire or thought of enlarging his authority or the threat of him becoming too powerful, because the citizens would not expect any gain or harm from him. In this case, I think it would be easy to make suitable laws, and discuss daily affairs of the state independent of him, and in this case I cannot see how he could become too powerful. I am hopeful that good election procedures will produce capable men of good quality. The institutions and checks to which the gonfalonier will now be subject will undoubtedly make it easier to bring redress to issues than has been the case up to now.

Having decided who the gonfalonier should be and what power he ought to have, we must now turn to who should elect him. We do not want to undermine the assumptions made above—that is, that the Great Council must be the distributor of offices—and therefore, it is necessary that the council elect the gonfalonier. However, the importance of this magistracy cannot be overemphasized, especially because every epoch produces only very few men capable of the task. The people may be able to identify men of courage and wisdom based on their fame and reputation—which is enough to assign the other offices—but they lack the subtle and detailed discretion required to examine and weigh the qualities of the man on whom so much will depend. To my mind, the best procedure would entail the following: Every time the office of the gonfalonier becomes vacant, the intermediate council composed of wise and prudent men (which will be discussed presently) ought to nominate three citizens for the said office by a two-thirds vote. The three nominees should be published to the Great Council, which should proceed to a vote two or three days later. The nominee who receives the most votes would be proclaimed the gonfalonier for life. By adopting this procedure, it is reasonable to expect that the three most capable men in the city will be nominated because they would be selected by the most prudent men. Although the people could err and not select the most capable of the three, this mistake would be of lesser consequence than if the people were given a broader choice. This procedure also ensures that the office would not be a gift of a few individuals or the work of factions or sects, but ultimately granted by the people. Furthermore, having the consent, so to speak, of both the Senate and the people eliminates the possibility of someone ingratiating himself to the people more than to the Senate, or vice versa. In fact, seeing that he must convince all groups, he will not use any other method beyond good works and deeds in order to be agreeable to everyone.

Now that we have discussed the extremes of the one and the many—that is, the gonfalonier and the Great Council—we must now turn to the middle: the council that will connect the extremes, and serve as the helm in charge of all important events. This council will have to sustain a significant burden, which requires that all wise men capable of governing participate in it so that these decisions are taken by those who know and understand such matters. We shall discuss which men and how many of them should participate; who and by what means they ought to be elected; their term lengths, authority, and rights; and how they should be consulted by other bodies.

This council ought to consist principally of the Signoria because it would not make sense for any council to meet without them. The colleagues were entrusted with the task of safeguarding liberty and therefore should be present when such matters are discussed. It is suitable that they be given this honor, and practice can compensate for any potential lack of ability or quality. To these must be added a group (*deputazione*) comprising the best men of the city. Although there are not many men sufficiently well versed in matters of state that deserve to be included, there must, nonetheless, be a broad enough membership to safeguard liberty, especially so that decision making will not be reduced to merely a few hands.

Besides, in a free government (*in uno vivere libero*), it is useful to broaden member-ship as much as possible so long as it does not incur great detriment. To my mind, [this council] should be composed of roughly two hundred members, including the Signoria and the colleagues. In ancient republics such as Rome, Carthage, Athens, and Sparta, they called this council a Senate, and they were composed of many members. In Venice, there are two hundred *pregati*, which are the same thing as senators. This number, as we said above, is necessary for the preservation of liberty because in a free government, the few could do much harm and get away with anything with the help of the many (*male portrebbono e' pochi giustifare el tutto co' molti*). Such a large number will inevitably include many inadequate and incapable people, but this should be tolerated, nonetheless, as the lesser evil. In fact, it would not cause as much damage as it may seem. Because the knowledgeable men of reputation will discuss events with solid arguments, the others will follow those who know more. When six or eight influential men are united, there is no chance that the others would not follow. When the most knowledgeable men disagree, as often occurs in the counsels (*consulte*),[22] listening and examining the formulation of arguments will open the minds of the mediocre men, who will either discover or at least follow the truth. Matters will not be presented in a raw manner without preparation, but rather at a more advanced stage of deliberation and maturity, requiring a final decision rather than a rehashing of all the facts and details from the beginning.

The whole point of this Senate (*consiglio*), if it is to be useful, is that all the men in the city who are reputed to be wise serve as part of it on a permanent basis. It is not enough that the majority [of the wise men] serve, because sometimes it happens that only one man sees more than all the others and he presents an opinion that, albeit developed on his own, is accepted by all once his arguments have been heard. At the end of the day, the entire weight of the government is effectively placed on the shoulders of very few. This is the way of all republics—ancient and modern. Therefore, the manner of appointing these council members must be such that this fundamental principle remains unshaken because it is essential and affects everything.

I am not convinced that these council members should be created once and serve perpetually, because I would like them to remain incentivized to conduct themselves well by having to present themselves frequently to the vote of the people. One could institute an election based on the greatest number of votes and a one-year term in office. It could be feared, however, that the people, as experience has shown, will tire of electing the same people every year, and, given everyone's ambition to be elected, the council will suffer such great turnover that it will be destroyed, as we witnessed in the case of the Eighty. It is therefore necessary that they are appointed for life, or, alternatively, that eighty of them are regularly elected in the council as the current practice dictates, and that these men should always meet together and consult with another eighty or hundred citizens who are appointed for life, and who are the first and best citizens of the city. In this manner, one could be certain that the [best] leaders are always present while still allowing for some change among the others who are less important, giving satisfaction to the whole without detriment to the republic.

It is difficult to entrust the election of life senators to the people because it risks endangering the regime or altering its structure. All those who have served at any time as gonfaloniers of justice, members of the Ten at least twice (because that magistracy has become very accessible in the course of time), or as ambassadors and commissioners-general elected by the Eighty would need to be perpetual members of this chamber. Because there might be some men who deserve the office but have never held one of these dignities, thirty further members should be elected by the Signoria and the colleagues and by the other permanent council members. It may turn out that this number is too large, but it should, nonetheless, be tolerated for the moment. It could be that when future members die they are not replaced until the number of members dwindles to one hundred. Once this target is achieved, members could be placed in the following fashion: the council, that is the Signoria and the Eighty together with the perpetual members choose by scrutiny[23] thirty citizens for each vacancy. The three receiving the most votes, but more than two-thirds of the votes, should be put to election before the Great Council, and the one receiving the most votes would be elected in the same way the gonfalonier would be elected.

This council should be entrusted with the following powers: approving mercenaries (condotte) proposed by the Ten and creating ambassadors and commissioners. The latter should not be elected by the people because these posts require special skills (esercizi apartati) and the people lack the subtle discretion needed to evaluate them. These officials should be appointed on the basis of greater or lesser social standing commensurate with the nature of their post, and this, again, the people cannot judge because they are usually ignorant of the purposes for which these posts are created or the secrets that surround them. The council should also be responsible for reconfirming palace chancellors, which is not the business of the people. All laws should be deliberated in this body before going to vote, and it should give final sanction for raising funds. As I will explain below, it should serve as a court of law in the city; it should create a gonfalonier and replace its own members through the method explicated above. The Ten of Balìa, though elected by the Great Council, ought to be chosen from among the intermediate council. This intermediate body should give counsel in all matters of state and be involved in policy making, in the way that we shall presently explicate.

In a republic, the method of creating laws and provisions governing daily affairs is quite difficult and restricted to a small number of people. They must be first proposed by the members of the Signoria, approved by the review committee (*fermatori*), passed again by the Signoria and the colleagues, accepted by the Eighty, and then finally, after all this back and forth, they are put before the Great Council. No doubt this procedural rigor (*stretezza*) was put in place for a reason. Creating legislation is a task of great importance that could alter the regime and the orders of the city at any time. The procedure was intended to prevent seditious men who like to see upheaval (*cose nuove*) from disturbing the well-being of other citizens. Reason attests to the necessity for such rigor, but so does the example of ancient republics, from which we learn that they experienced infinite riots (*moti*) only because it was every seditious citizen's right to propose new legislation to the people in a broad assembly. Conversely, such narrowness (*stretezza*) can also be noxious: if it is unreasonable to allow new laws to be easily proposed in such large assemblies, it is equally unjust and wrong to permit one man, or a few men, to hinder the presentation of legislation that may be judged salutary. Of course, if we keep to our present ways, a gonfalonier for life will most certainly be able to impede any provision, because it is quite difficult to get six signori to agree to oppose him. Even if such agreement were possible, the brief terms of the Signoria, the frequent changes of the Gonfalonieri di Compagnia and the Twelve Good Men, and the confusion that ensues ensure that the gonfalonier could easily impede legislations simply by creating well-devised delays. Even when the gonfalonier is opposed, such narrowness enables a very few citizens, if they are informed in time, to block such legislation. I do not believe that such narrow procedures are attributable to the initial liberty of the city, but [come] rather from the authority of the few, who, fearing that the council could dismiss them with a single decree, and not having enough authority to deprive the popular council of legislative power, wanted to ensure, through these strict procedures, that no law could be created against their will. This great disorder is inconsistent with a free way of life and must be corrected.

Another disorder arises when the Signoria, at the gonfalonier's suggestion, desires to make a law, however, because for some reason it worries that the law will not be approved, it draws it up and sends the law to the Eighty on the same day. When this occurs, the law will pass with little difficulty because the colleagues are always weak men. The law is spontaneously thrust on the Eighty, where, even if there is someone who might recognize its defects, there are not enough of them to vote it down. Nor can such a law's defects be detected through public engagement, because public discussion cannot take place without the Signoria's approval, and then only to speak in favor of the proposal. Once passed by the Eighty, the law finds little opposition among the people, who cannot think of any reason why it should not be approved (*che no sa piu' che bisogni*). In ancient times, they dealt with this anomaly by providing that every provision needed to be published for a certain period before being put before the college or the council. However, a proviso was later added that it was in the Signoria's power to block its publication. These are all tyrannical measures that serve to make a mockery of the city's liberty.

To remedy these drawbacks, I would allow two methods for creating new laws. The first would keep the current method and procedures intact but add two stipulations: the first, that once passed by the colleagues, they would have to be read at the meeting of the intermediate council, which I call the Senate, preceding the one where the vote will be taken, allowing for at least one day between. This vote should not be subject to change by the Signoria in any fashion. As a result of this advance notification, the Senate would not be caught off gaurd and would have time to fully examine the proposed legislation. The second is to provide that everyone, senators and committee members alike, be free to argue in favor or against the proposals in any way he sees fit. Such freedom of discussion would not be beneficial in the Great Council because it would generate too much confusion that could never be allayed; but in a Senate instituted primarily to examine the most important matters and guide the city, it is proper that these matters should be fully debated. Free discussion was prohibited so that reasonable or foolish provisions would be approved out of weariness, [the council] having heard only one side of the matter. A free city demands that such matters be brought forward easily and become the objects of deliberation without hindrance; however, the ensuing deliberations and investigations should thereafter be restricted so that decisions are reached only after mature consideration. This is what best befits the way of life in a good republic. The present procedures do the opposite—that is, proposing legislation is difficult, but the manner of consultation makes it easy to obtain decisions. These are the mechanisms introduced by tyrants, who take away liberty substantively while preserving its color and name in matters of small consequence—old mechanisms from which the city has not sufficiently distanced itself.

The second means of advancing legislative proposals (*provisioni*) would be for each member of the Signoria to be able to propose any piece of policy he pleases without needing the consent of his peers, provided that it be announced at a Senate session and that everyone be allowed to argue for or against the proposal. A favorable vote of three-fourths of the Senate ought to be sufficient to bring it before the Great Council. The member proposing the measure should assume the gonfalonier's present role of persuading the council to adopt it. In this manner, one person or a few people would not be able to prevent useful measures because it would only take one signore to present it to a large body. At the same time, this would not leave the way too open, because the Senate would have to approve it by three-fourths vote, as opposed to the other method that requires only two-thirds. Moreover, weak men would not be up to the task [of proposing legislation] because they would need the backbone to know how to justify and defend it before those who are against it. Laws regarding money should not, however, be adopted using this method, but only the first because creating openness in this discussion could generate turmoil and unjust practices. Such matters are of great importance and concern because they affect everyone, and, in these cases, men usually judge based on their own self-interest rather than based on what is the most reasonable or beneficial for the city.

Gonfalonier Piero Soderini demonstrated great skill in directing discussions of daily affairs according to his own will. This arose partially from the excessive authority he garnered as a result of the circumstances mentioned above and partially though his shrewdness in bringing matters to discussion under the most opportune conditions. In some instances he would have discussions brought to the Ten with restricted procedures, other times to the Eighty alone, and yet on other occasions to the Eighty together with larger councils, choosing which procedure he thought would best serve his proposes. When he saw that there was a wide range of opinion he selected the one that he liked the most. He submitted matters to vote sometimes by voice, sometimes by ballot—expediencies that make a difference—thereby making shrewd use of either the more open or restricted procedures with significant consequences.

Additionally, the current practice of voting by district (*quartiere*) is inefficient (*inetta*) and does not foster good discussion. I would like to see, then, first and foremost, that the office of the Ten be permanent, in war and in peace, while maintaining their present authority for dealing with affairs of the state. However, the Ten should not be able to decide independent of the Senate the matters that will now inevitably come before them. Moreover, the instructions that they give to ambassadors when they go abroad, which are now provided by the Signoria and the colleagues, will now be discussed and decided by the Senate. The Senate's power would require that every important matter, however few, would be brought before it, except those that demand the utmost secrecy. I would like to see the Signoria consult with the Senate about all events, and that the Ten have the ability to do the same, with or without the Signoria, who, in any case, should attend the meetings.

Discussions should be arranged in the following fashion: The magistracy that requests the advice (*consulte*) should present its case having prepared a reasoned argument, but also with the ability to advance more than one opinion. The magistracy need not all agree on their proposals; rather, each individual member should be able to say what he thinks, even if it is contrary to the opinion of the whole. This in place, every senator will be able to take the podium and argue for or against, and add or eliminate things to the proposal. All members should be able to do this. Then, either immediately thereafter or on another date, they should take a vote, and the position with the greatest number of votes must be adopted. Because it is unlikely that it will happen spontaneously in the beginning, the magistracy in question could compel the members to speak by nomination, and, with the process of time, it would become their habit. By following this procedure, the gonfalonier would not possess more power than the others because everyone would be brought into the discussion by arguing on one side or the other. In this manner, the affairs of the city would be discussed more openly and more thoroughly than they have in the past. This procedure engenders another good effect: where citizens do not have the opportunity to demonstrate their public worth, those who speak little are considered wise; by contrast, engaging openly in daily debates about policy and legislation offers the opportunity to those who want to prove their worth to make themselves known, and makes it possible to distinguish them from the others, like gold from lead. In this manner, men's abilities would be identified by evidence, not by hearsay, which is of great benefit to the city.

To stabilize this form of government requires upholding the rule of law and prohibiting the establishment of popular assemblies (*parlamento*),[24] which easily function to abolish popular government (*el vivere populare*). This expedient of holding *parlementi* was introduced because liberty is natural to our city as is the participation of the people, without whom nothing important could be accomplished. Those who desired to usurp power (*farsi grande*) in any period have always known that in order to establish a tyranny one could not extirpate liberty altogether, and that, instead, it can be established only by maintaining the shadow or semblance of liberty. Therefore, requiring the consent of the people and the councils to make new laws and appointments, but knowing that it could not be obtained through ordinary procedures, they invented this strategy of calling the armed people together in the piazza to approve what they proposed by voice. This amounts to forcing the people through military power to consent to everything proposed all the while pretending that it is done by the voice and will of all. Therefore, in order to secure liberty, it is necessary that the popular councils determine all matters, in good order and by ballot, and, consequently, to abolish the general assembly (*parlemento*), which is nothing but a means of forcing the people to approve what they do not actually want.

It would be nice not to have to continue further, and that it would suffice to discuss who should defend the city and how it should be governed internally—that is, to speak of the Great Council, the Senate, the Signoria, and the gonfalonier. But it is inevitable in any city that mistakes and crimes of every variety will be committed, which must be punished for the sake of the city's preservation. Ancient legislators proclaimed that republics rest on two pillars, reward and punishment, and so it is necessary to discuss who should conduct criminal trials and by what procedure.

The institutions (*ordini*) introduced and advanced above not only establish liberty and provide for good government but also amply provide for the remuneration of those citizens who act and conduct themselves well. I speak of the rewards that worthy citizens are entitled to expect in a republic—not those rewards that are sought from princes and tyrants. The opportunity to participate in the benefits (*utili*) of the city according to one's own merits (*grado*), and to be elected to offices and honors that befit one's virtue and conduct are the rewards that the patria regularly grants to her citizens. By contrast, opportunities to enrich oneself or usurp what belongs to others, exceptional authority and power to distribute offices however one pleases, or to protect criminals from justice, are all acts that bespeak tyranny. The spirits (*animi*) of good and generous citizens, however, must be nourished with distinctions and dignities that are compatible with liberty. They must enjoy the respect and reverence of others, and a measured but certain glory will be of sufficient satisfaction to them. The government described above would go a long way to bringing about these effects because the more restricted distribution of important offices through election, as compared with the present practice, would necessarily result in men of reputation receiving a greater share of the offices. Given the ability to publicly discuss policy and legislation—to argue for or against any proposal—would distinguish the courageous men from the others, rendering honor and prestige attainable for the virtuous—not, as is the case today, dependent on the nobility of one's house or the coattails of one's father or ancestors, but rather on one's own deeds and virtues. In this manner, an excellent man born of an obscure father would not be considered second-rate, and a truly second-rate man with a distinguished lineage would not be held in high repute. Good works and virtue would be compensated, then, in a suitably republican fashion, and, correspondingly, vice and stupidity would be met with obscurity and lack of honor. The opportunity for men to demonstrate their worth would produce the following positive effect: when all see that the good is esteemed, men develop an appetite to comport themselves well and are motivated to develop those qualities that elevate them to a higher rank and to supreme glory.

Certainly, in my estimation, I do not see how a greater reward can be offered to a man of a noble (*generoso*) spirit than being the head of a free city, having acquired that position neither by force, nor party affiliation, nor family connection, but rather by cultivating reverence, authority, and a good reputation (*una buona opinione*) for prudence and love of the city. I believe that this distinction, achieved by men in ancient republics, most notably in Athens by Pericles—that is, the knowledge that one is recognized and esteemed only for his virtues and talents—is worth more than all the power and authority of a tyrant. Happy are those souls who feel this flame, which burns only in noble hearts. Happy are those republics in which that ambition abounds, for it is here that the arts that lead to great achievements flourish. In these republics, virtue, good works, and the ardent desire to achieve great and generous deeds that benefit the republic are found in both the people who strive to achieve eminence (*autorità*) and those who already possess it. The greatness and fame of such men is neither contrary nor harmful to liberty, because it is not acquired through sects, factions, or cunning machinations, nor is it received from others but is beholden to the Great Council and therefore to the people (*el popolo*), who could remove him from power if he falters from the path of doing good. In fact, [this fame and reputation] is extremely useful and necessary, for only a few in any age can bear the burden, and hardly anyone will take it up if there is no reward or recognition to be gained from it. It is therefore necessary to have such pillars, without which republics could not last. May God grant that out own city will be full of this type of ambition and authority (*autorità*), and that all souls become motivated by such desires. In this way, there would be fewer misdeeds, which would make it less difficult to put the city's system of justice in good order, by matching crimes to punishments, which I shall deal with at once.

In our city there are many bodies that have jurisdiction over criminal matters, with some overlapping in a certain order of priority. Others are distinct, dealing with particular kinds of cases. The Eight and the conservators of the law are at the head of all these courts. I do not count the Signoria, because, although its power is supreme, it has other responsibilities as well, and it was created for other purposes, which is not the case for the others mentioned. In any case, the appropriate powers of the Signoria over criminal matters were detailed above. Therefore, we must now examine whether the power and jurisdiction (*balìa*) of these institutions should be restricted or expanded. Regarding all criminal offenses—excepting the crimes of the state—the power and discretion that the judicial institutions now possess must undoubtedly remain as they are presently. Punishment for these kinds of crimes should not be referred to the councils but instead should be undertaken by particular courts designated for specific purposes and who, accordingly, enjoy full powers (*balìa ampla*) in their proceedings. For if they must act within reason (*co'termini di ragione*), hardly anyone would ever be punished because it would be impossible to conclusively prove most charges without the means to do so. Moreover, many difficulties would arise if judicial verdicts always had to conform to the exact letter of the law. Legislators create uniform law and cannot take into account every particularity, and therefore, the statues dictate the same punishment for many cases that in fact deserve to be treated differently depending on the different circumstances.

Another difficulty remains: Should these special magistracies be authorized to judge political offenses (*li errori apartenenti allo stato*)? The problem arises because it involves a fundamental principle established above—namely, that the preservation of a free city requires that its citizens have no reason to fear the powers exercised by any particular individual in office. Granting these magistrates power over such decisions violates this principle. Six members of the Eight or seven of the conservators could do much harm with the power to behead or exile anyone they please. Nevertheless, I still think these magistracies ought to retain these powers, even with regard to political trials (*casi apartenenti allo stato*), to prevent straightforward cases from being sent to appeals courts and assemblies. And besides, in reality, the danger mentioned above does not exist, because four of their members change every six months [thus] there is no reason to fear that they will punish anyone in order to aggrandize themselves (*farsi grande*). Nor is there any danger that personal resentments harbored by any of their members will lead them to harm some citizens, because verdicts require the assent of two-thirds of the magistracy. Indeed, experience shows that these magistracies proceed with caution in proceeding against citizens. It is much easier to count thousands of citizens who have not been punished, or punished very lightly, than to find anyone punished excessively by these special magistracies.

A remedy against this danger, however superfluous it may be, would be to permit citizens to appeal verdicts brought against them in political trials. I would not like that these appeals be brought to the Great Council because these are matters that require great maturity and gravitas. Verdicts of death or treason should be subject to appeal to the Senate, without the colleges being present but only the Signoria. To deal with cases of lesser penalties, forty or fifty members of the Senate could be chosen by lot to serve as the appellate judges, so as not to burden all of them. A two-thirds majority would be required for acquittal; otherwise, the convictions would stand.

This suffices for the power of the special judicial magistracies. However, this alone does not constitute a solid basis for the administration of justice. Out of attachment to family and friends, out fear of offending others and making enemies, or out of weakness and ignorance and sometimes out of wickedness, magistrates frequently proceed so weakly and so slowly that our city's system of justice obviously lies in ruins (*guasta*), producing the most disgraceful and harmful state of affairs. License and a readiness to harm others has multiplied in everyone. In a few short years, we have witnessed how many unusually excessive and violent acts have been committed—unparalleled breaches of our city's customary behavior, which is naturally pacific, not aggressive. Our youths have become haughty and violent bullies (*spadaccini*) who use violence and insolence only against those who are too weak to defend themselves. We have heard how often our citizens have committed many transgressions against the powerful and the weak all over the open country and subject territory, and how often our magistrates commit acts of injustice, cruelty, and oppression (*tirannerie*) over our poor subjects because they only want to advance their own interest by means fair or foul without any respect for God or the city or of man. This greatly damages the reputation of our city and leaves our subjects discontent, even hostile, which will no doubt have grave consequences in the event of violent war. Furthermore, some citizens have audaciously plotted or conspired against the regime, and despite the evidence of probable cause of the clues pointing to their guilt, the judges, out of weakness, let them be.

After several years, the law of the Forty was adopted in response to such disorders. However, this law was poorly conceived and had so many defects that it has been criticized and attacked, in part by those who did not want to see crimes brought to justice and in part by those who feared that it would increase Piero Soderini's power, whose constitutional authority (*per lo ordinario*) already made him too powerful. Out of this concern, many raised great obstacles to passing the law regulating the administration of justice that he put forward. There are many problematic elements about the law itself, but most of all, people were displeased that he would seek to pass a law to punish the fault of others but from which he would be exempt and without a superior authority. He had already unconstitutionally usurped many powers (*arrogate molte autorità fuora delle legge*), contrary to the best interest of our city. The draft [of the law] was good, but it had some defects in its details, which, if corrected, could turn it into a useful and salutary statute.

Therefore, I would propose that when all crimes, whether political or other offenses, have been denounced, either openly or anonymously, to one of the competent judges, and when these case have not been decided within a certain time period (roughly one month), they should be brought before a special tribunal or the Forty. I think the tribunals ought to vary in character based on the type and gravity of the crime, as I shall explain below. These boards should be in charge of the prosecution and the proceedings of the entire case. The accused must have the right to appear in his defense, either in person or by proxy—whichever he finds best. The appeals board should have the right to question the accused all over again in any manner they see fit, and they must be required to hand down their verdict within two months. The verdict should be done in writing (*polizze*) in the same manner that the Forty employed, in which each individual openly expresses his opinion, whether in favor of or against the accused. If the accuser is known, he should now press the charge openly. For a sentence to be passed, it requires three-fifths majority support.

I would like that cases involving the state have recourse to the entire Senate with the participation of the Signoria but not the members of the colleges. To deal with accusations against those holding office, whether in or outside of Florence, I would draw thirty senators by lot and another thirty members of the Forty, which I will discuss in more detail later. To deal with all other crimes of any kind, there should be a tribunal of sixty citizens who are not senators but who are elected by the Senate and hold this office for a one-year term. They must not be barred from eligibility for other offices, and they ought to receive a yearly stipend of fifty ducati. They should, however, be excluded from reelection for a two-year period. Creating these different kinds of courts allows for the possibility of treating political trials, which are more important, with greater maturity of judgment, and to provide for other cases in a manner commensurate with their importance.

There are several possible objections to this view. The first is that the ease with which appeals can be made is subject to criticism. Only three of the Eight or four of the conservators are enough to unsettle a decision, even if they are against the majority of their fellows. Therefore, it becomes rather easy to harm or mistreat reputable men (*uomini da bene*) through the judges who may be provoked by some mad or wicked man who dreamt up a complaint against him. One could object to the written as opposed to oral procedure of passing judgment without discussing or examining the case. Finally, one could object to deciding important capital cases by only three-fifths vote when the laws of the city require two-thirds majority in cases of lesser importance. Nevertheless, these objections are not convincing enough to undermine my proposals. These features are essential; if otherwise the magistracy will be futile and fruitless. Above all else, it is clear that men of prominence will be able to avoid having to face an appeal if the magistrates are called up by the old law, for one who is unable to block a mere three votes is a very weak man indeed. This provision was introduced precisely because of the fear of those powerful men whom the lower judges do not dare, or cannot agree, to condemn. And if the procedures I suggest are not adopted, only precisely those cases just mentioned will be appealed—that is, those cases in which the magistrates through whom the appeal is made would already be inclined against the accused.

It is easy to believe that the court would resolve unambiguous cases and cases of obvious slander on its own; appeals would usually be resolved on the basis of reputation rather than on substantive charges. It is necessary to reach decisions by written ballots for the very same reason, for the fear that inhibits the first court from deciding the case by itself would prevent the court of appeal from expressing its opinion freely. The ample time of one month enables the accused to be heard and for the judges to discuss the matter, which means that they, who are more or less reputable men, would come to a verdict through healthy deliberation. This is especially true because our city is naturally predisposed to clemency and our men are more inclined to it than not. When there is no need for haste, which breeds suspicion and fury, things become less harsh and more humane. The reason for adopting a majority of three-fifths is because the majority of two-thirds is too difficult to attain. Exhaustion or tedium drive men toward the middle, which is unjust and results in either excessive or insufficient punishment. This is the reason for requiring a larger majority, but not so large that it engenders disorder. This works as much in favor of the accused as against him, because if a majority of three-fifths has the power to condemn him, a majority of three-fifths has the power to acquit him.

Now that we have demonstrated which judicial procedures should apply to private citizens and the other magistrates, we must now see which procedures the gonfalonier should be subject to during his term of office. He cannot be put on trial after he leaves office, because his term ends with his life. One the one hand, the dignity of his office and authority argues against having him be subject to daily annoyance and torment. On the other hand, it is against the city's interest that he be entirely immune to prosecution. To answer both demands, I would propose that although he may have no superior, each member of the Signoria ought to be entitled to accuse him before the Senate, but meeting without the colleagues, of any crime and ask for any punishment, forfeit of rights, fines, or even death or anything else. Condemnations would require a two-thirds majority. However, no one ought to be allowed to make such a proposition more than once during his tenure of office, to prevent the gonfalonier from being exposed to daily harassment (*cimento*).

I believe that the procedures and institutions (*modi e ordini*) outlined above correct many of the defects and drawbacks of our government. Following this pattern, the offices would be distributed appropriately, and the important affairs of the state would be discussed by the wise and leading men of the city. Virtuous citizens would be able to achieve a just degree of rank and power, but never so much that could undermine or endanger liberty. The capacity to punish crime would greatly deter evil, desirous men from usurping the public or private good. These measures would provide, if not perfect republican institutions, then at least better than mediocre ones. In order for it to be raised to an even higher level we would need to eradicate the roots of our overrefined sensibilities and weak spirits (*animi*) that make men effeminate and cause countless evils. It would be necessary to eliminate our regard and esteem for wealth because immoderate craving after riches eliminates the appetite for true glory, inhibits souls from cultivating virtues, introduces countless usurpations of the belongings of others, and encourages countless other dishonorable actions (*dishonestà*). Everyone is guilty of these universal evil desires and practices. Indeed, they run rampant not only in our city but throughout the world, where there exists only a great desire to enrich oneself and use wealth for self-indulgent purposes and evil ends. This corrupt way of life is nothing new; it has existed for many centuries, as is evidenced by the ancient writers who detested and denounced these vices in their own time.

Perhaps there are some remedies that could somewhat moderate these evils, but certainly not enough to have a notable effect on a malady that is so universal, so old, and so deeply rooted in the minds of men. To eliminate it altogether, one would need the knife of Lycurgus. In one day, he eradicated all wealth and sumptuousness from Sparta. He put together all the property of her inhabitants and then divided it equally among them and prohibited the use of money and all activities for which wealth is sought: sumptuous displays, banquets, many servants, luxurious clothes, and fine houses. It was certainly an admirable achievement, bringing about in one day in his city such moderation in living and such zeal for virtue and such low esteem for wealth, in addition to the many fine and glorious activities he made flourish in it. Anyone who has the good fortune (*grazia*) to order his republic in such a fashion is certainly very happy and glorious, and even happier to have reformed it in such a way that its institutions and laws should last for centuries; and so that while the republic lived under them, it was usually so strong and so powerful that it was the leading state of Greece. It was certainly preeminent in glory and famous for its virtues in the eyes of foreign nations. It was easier for Lycurgus to achieve this than for Plato, Cicero, and many other learned and prudent men to write about it. It is not surprising that in his own times it was believed that the Delphic Apollo's advice helped him, and rightly so, because reforming a corrupt city in such a laudable manner is a task for gods rather than human beings.

We can only marvel at and praise such a remarkable achievement, but we cannot permit ourselves to even hope for it, or even desire it for ourselves. Therefore, to speak now of things that are within our grasp, I would say that the malady is so deeply rooted that it is impossible to eradicate. It would be necessary, as Lycurgus did, to prohibit the activities and uses for which wealth sought, but given the weakness of men, this could be only an abstract aspiration. I certainly think that making our city well armed, and thus enabling Florence to achieve glorious victories, giving offices to men of good reputation and conduct, making it feasible to punish the crimes of those who err—that all these things together will make the people hold the rich in lower estimation than they do today. I would add another thing (which is often claimed but never well observed): to limit and moderate as much as possible luxurious clothes and jewelry, for they make the differences between rich and poor so obvious and spur men to seek wealth. Where regular avenues of profit prove insufficient, men are driven toward thousands of viperous and illicit means of gain. Such conduct is incompatible with the establishment of a republic whose aim is to remove the motive for attaining wealth. Luxurious habits are, furthermore, injurious to keeping the city rich for they impoverish it and cause endless amounts of money to be transferred to foreign nations. All these negative effects have no evident utility because they serve no reasonable purpose except to encourage a vain conceit and a womanly, rather than a manly, taste. Similarly, I would like to reduce dowries to moderate sums because excessive ones are harmful for the reasons mentioned above and because they do not conserve the equality of families and the nobility of blood, and last because it would be a great boon to worthy but poor men who have a harder time marrying off their daughters than do the wicked rich.

In conclusion, these are the things on which I think the city and its popular way of life should be established. There are many errors in detail, but I am of the opinion that the general contours and the final aims indicated make sense. May it please God, though our conduct does not deserve it, to see that this republic is transformed someday in this or some such manner with good institutions and good government. I would unreservedly give my life and possessions to see this realized in our times.

Completed the 27th day of August 1512 in Logrogno.

The Government of Florence After the Medici Restoration

Of all the cures and tools (*amministrazioni*) that men have at their disposal, nothing is more characteristic of a wise and circumspect man [than] that he, having diligently examined the weight of the responsibility before him, surrenders to its full examination and then decides [*capitolarla una volta e fermare el punto*] which mode and with which anchor he will steer his ship to port. We see that prudent and expert doctors use the most exacting diligence to understand the nature of a patient's sickness, and to diagnose which medicines and in what measure they are to be prescribed. Without establishing this diagnosis, doctors would tend toward prescribing treatment disproportionate to the illness and a diet contrary to the constitution and well-being of the patient, consequently resulting in the total ruin and death of the infirm.

This resolve proves necessary and laudable in all men, but most of all in the prince and head of state. Cities are made of infinite men characterized by infinitely diverse conditions and appetites, and they all demonstrate infinite degrees of ingenuity; therefore, so too are the accidents, humors, and difficulties in managing them infinite. It is necessary to understand these conditions and create the appropriate order with which they will be governed. The more difficult the case at hand, the more prudence and care is required, and the more important the effects that follow from this order. From good government follows the health and conservation of infinite men, and from the opposite, the city's ruin and extinction. In men's lives nothing is more precious and singular than this congregation and civil consortium. Just as one can judge a doctor by the health or death of his patient, one can judge the government of the state: if it is erected prudently and proportionally, you can believe in it and anticipate good effects; if it is otherwise constituted and governed poorly, who would expect anything but its ruin and destruction? This says it all, yet it is neither superfluous nor futile to investigate the matter more carefully—but at present I will discuss what occurs to me in the moment.

To speak more precisely, one must presuppose that the means of governing must be based on the diversity of governments and places that are to be governed: In some cases a king or a *signore naturale* governs; in others one maintains the state with violence and usurpation; in still others one governs a city that always served someone; or, then again, a city can be habituated to govern itself liberally and popularly, and to command others. Given so many types, speaking generally is insufficient; one should speak with the corresponding distinctions that apply to each case—but that would be too long of a discussion. Alternatively, one can restrict himself to a particular form, as I shall do here. My judgments and comments pertain to these specific Medici—that is, if they want to maintain the state and the government of the city of Florence. In order to better elucidate, I will first discuss [the Medici's] quality and being more generally.

For the longest time the city of Florence has been free: it has been popularly governed and maintained an empire and *signoria* in many parts of Tuscany. In Italian affairs it has always possessed more reputation and standing than other powers—reputation and standing that did not seem to accord with the dominion it possessed. This can be attributed to its location and the restless nature of the men who toil there: from the beginning, they knew how to be industrious, and they succeeded in becoming wealthy. These conditions made it so that in Florence all citizens savor the free and popular way of life; they would not want to accept as their rank the distinction that they actually deserve, and every citizen has an excessive desire for grandeur and power (*potenzia*). The Florentines are inclined to participate in politics and ponder matters of state and government. This applies to the present moment more than ever, considering that between 1494 and 1512 the citizens have been nourished by and habituated to a very popular and free (*liberalissimo*) regime. A government in which everyone presumes to be equal makes it difficult for anyone to willingly recognize superiors—let alone recognize a single authority who entirely and arbitrarily decides every matter. Even though in the past the house of the Medici was great, and especially Lorenzo (although the greatness of one epoch cannot be compared with another), now every matter small and large is commanded in plain view, whereas in the past matters were conducted through indirect channels but at least with more civil modes. Nor was absolute authority relied on in every case—and in those cases in which it was used, it was executed with finesse.

I add a crucial consideration: in the past, the Medici house did not happen on a purely popular government. Then the city was, and had been historically, divided by many factions, and at this juncture one of the factions and its head emerged as superior. At the point when the Medici prevailed, it did not seem as though the regime (*lo stato*) was completely replaced by an entirely unitary authority (*togliesse allo universale*); instead it seemed as though the bosses from one party were replaced with bosses from another. This replacement did not displease the middling and popular men because the mutation did not diminish their rank. In fact, since the *maggiori* were defeated, it ameliorated [the middling and popular men's] condition. In this manner the state of 1434 that came into Medici hands did not appear to be taken away from the people, but rather from Messer Rinaldo degli Albizzi, Palla Strozzi, and other like individuals. Furthermore, at that time, the Medici were not the absolute bosses of every matter but always acted through an alliance with some *compagni* [faction]. These *compagni* were always inferior to the Medici, but they still participated in some respect. The greatness of Lorenzo thus did not come in one stroke but developed slowly through the course of many years.

Today everything is different. In an instant, Medici power succeeded a popular and very wide (*larghissimo*) state. The state's authority and greatness were reduced absolutely to the authority of one. Consequently, there arose the notion that the state was taken away from the people and placed in the hands of a single man.[25] In the space of an hour, a regime that was accepted by the majority became a regime that the majority found detestable without any interval of time in between. This situation (*materia*) is rendered all the more difficult because the [Medici] regime possesses a great number of citizens as enemies. Now, citizens have no voice in the current regime whereas in the past they participated somewhat. These citizens are not the only enemies—there are many others who dislike this government. To better understand the nature and complexion of this group, we must break the enemies down into their component parts.

There are many men (either these men themselves or their fathers) who in 1494 unveiled themselves as enemies of the Medici. From that time until 1512 they continued in that course and way of life without reconciling themselves [to the Medici]: these men are implacable, and you should trust that on every occasion they will always obstinately do everything in their power against your state at full speed. Another category of enemies consists in the friends of this first group, both the natural friends or those that have become their friends through accidents. These men dislike that [the Medici] have taken the state and its greatness all for themselves. They do not believe that the honors and benefits of the city are distributed efficaciously, and they resent that deliberations and command [are] conducted singularly and absolutely, without consultation or participation of those who in a similar state would intervene. They dislike that in every magistracy, every matter, small or large, public or private, develops and proceeds independent of their involvement. This category further comprises of two types: one part, if they are not completely crazy, are forced to judge every case on the side of the Medici because, without them, they would be detested in any other regime, and they would belong neither to the useful nor the honorable citizens. They would struggle to live, because the majority of these men are not happy with their own means, but want to live extraordinarily and through pillage (*di ratto*).

The other subset of this group is used by the former. This secondary group— whether because of noble lineage, or because they are held to be good, or for being reputed to be prudent, maintained status in the popular state and would probably give their hearts to find prominence in every way of life within any kind of regime. Of these people, because in the estimation of others they have reasonable status in this state, you need not worry that this group will endanger itself by stirring dissension. But do not doubt that, should an opportunity against you arise, they would use it or at least allow the threat to develop. Nevertheless, if they are prudent or good, they should hope that this government lasts. Given the current state of the city, the discontent of the citizens, and the tricks that they [this secondary subset] pulled in the countryside and in the city itself, they can be certain that things cannot change without great damage and danger to the city. If this state is not maintained, they would run extreme danger because they would provoke the fury and anger of all those that presumed this group to be friends of the [Medici] state. If these individuals reasoned well, they not only would avoid confrontation with this regime but would with all their might help the forces that conserve it. This is what men of prudence would do. But because men are not all wise and, moreover, they deceive themselves in judgments of their own cases, I wouldn't place my confidence in the souls of a large part of this group.

The majority (*universale*) of the city remains to be discussed. In many respects, the majority is not happy with this government. It seemed to them that during the popular regime they participated in the state. They do not take well to being subordinated by one ruler or a few individuals. They dislike not being free to make family arrangements on their own accord. They, and especially the rich and the merchants, fear being hit with taxes and micromanaged in their business activity. All these things generate scorn and, from fear, discontent among the masses. Thus, gauging carefully (*faccendo bene il conto*), the Medici have few friends and can trust few people—in fact, they can trust only those who are dependent on them. In order to support and govern a city full of suspicious men and enemies, even more maturity and prudence is required than usual. A thorough examination and firm decision must be reached concerning the way in which to drive this ship. To me it seems like the principal and most important decision that needs to be made is which course of action to take. The first course of action aims to massage and win over the majority of the city, and to distribute the honors and offices (*utili*) with equality and efficiency. I am not saying that it must be a completely free and popular way of life, but one that supports or approximates a similar state, and one where individuals live justly and decently without committing injustice or allowing the great (*grandi*) to oppress the many (*piccoli*). The second course of action would grant the honors and offices to a restricted number of carefully selected partisans and would let them live extraordinarily and off of their countrymen. In effect, the regime would massage and caress this small group of partisans and wish that all the others support this group *pondus diei et estus* (in the weight and the heat of the day).

This is the most important decision. There exists a diversity of opinions because many, whether because their reason instructs them in such a manner or because their desire and appetite for distinction motivates them, would judge that by necessity the second course of action must be taken. They would allege that the primary motivation of he who governs must be the conservation of himself and his state. Given this intent, one must oppress and beat down those who are enemies and those who cannot be gained as friends. In this category, they would say, one must include not only those who are particularly inimical to the Medici, but also the majority of the city, who do not hate the Medici because of private fears and grievances, nor because they govern unjustly, but only because, having savored eighteen years of the sweetness of a popular way of life, they would want to return to it, and every other system would displease them. Only a good government favoring justice with largely distributed honors and offices would satisfy them. In fact, they would always desire a mutation to return to the Great Council and to participate in government and public administration.

If then the Medici have many enemies that are implacable and who would always rebel against them, they are forced to do two things: First, they must beat them down and diminish them so that these enemies can offend them less. Second, they must gain a good number of friends to make partisans and render them vigorous and powerful by enriching and fattening them. One can do no other but give them all the honors and offices to let them flourish and develop esteem for themselves. This would create so much good will because they would come to passionately love their greatness and, in order to conserve it, they would put themselves in the gravest danger. Knowing that their status resides with the Medici, and being enriched by them, more forces and authority would be needed to maintain them. Today no friendship is measured by any other metric besides utility, and where there is no dependence there can be no trust. One must incorporate those who the state elects and designates as friends in a way that they come to experience extreme wealth. Moreover, one must make them see that mutating the state would result in such great personal loss that they are forced to conserve it—not out of love but more out of utility, or rather, necessity. Doing this, they would become more robust but also necessarily more offensive to others. Consequently, provoked by regular reminders from the regime and motivated by their own cupidity they would fear the mutation of the state for fear of losing not only their honors, but also their professions and lives. They would resort to any means so as to maintain them. Any other mode that one takes is vain, because the enemies remain powerful, and friends few, cold, and weak. These reasons persuade one to take this course of action. And while these reasons seem very well explained, I nevertheless am of a different opinion.

———— ✳ ————

On the Mode of Securing the State of the House of Medici

The return of the Medici to Florence radically transformed the city. Either out of extreme necessity or because they could not see any other way of maintaining themselves, a few ruined and desperate exiled men sought the Medici's return. In exchange for satisfying the appetites of these few, not only the enemies of the Medici but the majority (*lo universale*) suffered because they were enjoying a popular way of life. Even the friends [of the Medici] who preferred the regime before 1494 did not celebrate, judging that their current poverty and circumstances would force them to suffer yet again and ultimately flee the city ruined while simultaneously causing the ruin of others.

The creation of Cardinal de' Medici into Leo X happened miraculously. Quite suddenly, after this moment, everyone's hopes and designs changed. Some thought that possessing the pontificate meant that they [the Medici] were absolved of past offenses and suspicions, which would consequently improve our own [Florentine] affairs. It was argued that their enemies would feel secure enough and live in a reasonable enough condition. Their friends, it was said, would throw themselves behind the state with warmth and vivacity. The people, in response to the sweetness of peace and the hope of no longer being burdened with taxes, would rest assured and develop a happy disposition. These factors would supposedly be further amplified by the greatness of a young, powerful pope so that conditions on all fronts should be ameliorated. Yet three years into this pontificate the purported effects of this theory have not materialized. The friends of the regime are unhappy—in fact, they are all cold and on edge. The people are more than unhappy, filled with jealousy and suspicion. The city's condition is quite miserable—a very damaging and dangerous condition for the state. It is difficult to govern when the people are enemies and you have not acquired partisans or powerful allies.

The greatness of the papacy may inhibit one from fully confronting this dangerous condition, yet it is extremely foolish to ignore it. Times change, and satisfaction always varies, which makes establishing a regime on a single man weak and shortsighted. When he dies, the effects of this disorder will emerge. In fact, these effects can emerge during his lifetime, as men constantly embroil themselves in trivial contests that can have devastating, unintended consequences. For example, as we saw last summer, the French invasion created a multiplicity of disorders, but instead of focusing on resistance for the public good, the Florentines thought only about their petty interests and conflicts.[26] Given this insecurity, the head of state should follow the example of the prudent sailor: during calm tides, he organizes his materials and instruments so that he can resist a future storm. Similarly, the man behind the wheel of the state should look ahead to organizing all members of the constituent body so that he can virtuously and vigorously defend himself against any accident that comes to pass. Anyone who considers the causes and origins of the evils before us knows that without much difficulty one could ameliorate the condition of this sick man, and if not improve him to optimal health, at least help him cultivate a better disposition.

The first component of the remedy consists in following: he who possesses the state must have the desire and motivation to maintain it. Assuming that he has this desire, he must render the state fruitful and useful for his own purposes. Who would invest time and energy into making something that did not satisfy him? It seems obvious that every man would seek to arrange the state to his own advantage, and yet there are some exceptions to this precept, especially in our case. Having produced such a young pope, these Medici have set their aspirations so high that the government of this city seems like a trifling matter. They clearly consider it among the most minor of their investments (*minori capitali*). Such disregard became evident when Giuliano, well before he developed the more grandiose ambitions that he holds today, explicitly renounced the city's government as a trivial, inconsequential preoccupation, and Lorenzo clearly shared this view. Nevertheless, their judgment cannot be more false. The way they maintain the government with their authority and power makes them the bosses (*padroni*) of the city and the entire dominion, which has profound consequences. Nor are they like typical absolute rulers (*signore a bacchetta*) who still govern through laws and commands (*legge e deliberazioni*). Instead, the Medici do what they want under the name of others and through means of the magistrates, who are appointed by the Medici and who obey them in every single regard.

Ordering Florence, one of Italy's principal regions, so that it retains great authority and reputation avails different productive possibilities for the Medici. While the pope is alive, they can utilize his power to acquire more states and expand their designs; once he dies, who does not see how important the support of this prudential ordering will be in maintaining what they have acquired? Their states will be quite difficult to conserve because they are new, and they will consequently face fierce opposition either from those inside who presume themselves to be leaders or hostile neighbors, or even the discontented population. In order to avoid this fate, one must organize the state well from the inside out. Doing so will make it easy for them to maintain themselves because their rule will not offend anyone, nor will it take away power from anyone except the citizens themselves, who, as I shall explain below, are easily satisfied.

This reasoning is so obvious that one needs no examples to defend it, and where an example is handy it requires very little elaboration to demonstrate the point. In Lombardy—the first acquisition they [the Medici papacy] have undertaken— they have already been forced to withdraw from Parma and Piacenzia. In Modena and Reggio they maintain an uncertain position with little if any strength (*utilità*) and many points of weakness, especially if they do not deal with Ferrara, which

they have already often debated returning to the duke of Ferrara. This is the necessary starting point and foundation of their endeavors. Without this step everything
they do will bring them ruin with time, that is to say, when the first adversity arises.
Maintaining this dominion will allow them to hold all the other pieces of their
state. If they do not maintain [these territories], they will never be called great.
Anyone who even remembers that they once possessed a dominion or produced
a pope will know that they were not the natural lords (*signori*) there. They will be
remembered as private citizens who, even if they were considered great at some
point, always remained so through private and civil channels.

I do not want to discuss whether their desire to make themselves great princes
through the papacy was well thought out or fallaciously reasoned. I will only say
this: Callixtus and Pio offer examples of ancestors who procured advantages from
the papacy that they themselves enjoyed and were able pass down to their descendants.[27] Yet we also have the example of Valentino, and the lesson to be learned
here is clear: privately acquiring great states is arduous but conserving them is far
more arduous. Infinite difficulties plague a new principate, and even more difficulties plague a new prince. Francesco Sforza offers us the only example, and while
he succeeded in conserving the new state he built in Milan, many circumstantial
reasons explain his success. Most important, he was a great man of virtue and an
excellent captain of that epoch. But he also stumbled on an opponent who constituted somewhat of an interruption in the Visconti's line of hereditary succession
as the natural princes of Milan. At the time, Madonna Bianca, the goddaughter of
Duke Fillipo, inherited power because she was the only successor in the line of
ducal descendance. This questionable legitimacy made it appear as though Sforza
did not oust a legitimate heir, but rather in some sense his conquest seemed to
exhibit a color of justice. Additionally, it must be remembered that Sforza found
a state that enjoyed some liberty, but nonetheless was solidly a principate. Liberty
there was disfigured just like servitude is disfigured among free peoples. These
conditions made conserving the new state very easy, but they are conditions that
those who conquer new dominions are rarely lucky enough to find. Most often,
conquered states are taken away from free peoples or natural princes. Conversely,
Sforza, one could say, occupied a vacant hereditary position, which did not rob
anything from anyone else. In fact, to the people it seemed quite beneficial that
Sforza conquered them, because they saw him as saving them from conquest by
the Venetians, who were of course their natural enemies.

But to return from this digression to our principal discussion: the second part
of the cure is that they [the Medici] are persuaded to make many good friends in
Florence—loyal and true friends who dedicate and apply themselves to important
matters. This will engender two salutary, and necessary, effects. First, it creates
men of reputation who possess credit and authority. These men of reputation will
benefit them [the Medici] because these men will become enthusiastic partisans

and important instruments for maintaining the state and its greatness. Every state and every emerging power need to foster dependents with varying degrees of rank and diverse offices, just like a head needs its limbs to support and serve him. Second, these Medici are quite young and were raised outside the city, detached from our affairs (*cose nostre*), and unable to dedicate themselves to the task of governing because of other concerns and obligations. Because they are no longer aware of our customs and the intricacies of governing this city, they often command in a destructive fashion, causing innumerable disorders—courses of action they would surely not pursue if they could discern what mattered most in our city. However, if there were a number of citizens who they could trust and who could speak the truth to them freely, these citizens could advise them on important matters so that they would not err, unless they were trying to do so intentionally.

Wise men with experience take advantage of the observations and the advice of others. Young and inexperienced men should especially do so because intelligence and natural judgment will serve them well. In order for this delegation of men to be fruitful for the Medici, they must be carefully examined; that is, this body of men must consist of carefully chosen citizens that maintain good standing in the city, and their friends must also be of sound mind and intention. To truly profit from this group, you must caress them by demonstrating trust in them. You must share with them facts and communicate with them what occurs in the city and the dominion, but always in a manner that reveals trust beyond superficial ceremony. If one feels trusted and loved, he will necessarily return this love and loyalty.

The person who has controlled this regime up to this point believes that its greatness has far surpassed all regimes that have come before it. He has wanted to handle all matters of the city and the dominion alone, and wanted all citizens and subjects to understand that there is no one else that can or should head the citizenry except himself. He has removed all reputation from the men of the state, and it has not done any good for anyone concerned. He wants it known that he makes every decision and that the citizens are nothing without him. Yet if one wants to maintain friends one must grant favor and reputation. Men cannot feel as though they are given hallowed titles of magistracy without any real administrative duties. Rather, the head of state must make these men believe that they actually command something. What good is it to for a citizen to be an *accoppiatore* if the entire magistracy has less power than one of the signori? Appeasing men of state and enlarging their favor creates partisan citizens who throw themselves behind other partisans and friends, which ultimately serves the state. By cultivating partisan friends in this manner, no one could make himself great in a dangerous or suspicious fashion.

Like all things, of course, this openness (*larghezza*) and trust would need to be moderated. I do not mean to say that one should entirely confide in this class of men or concede to them on every score; rather, the governor must always hold the bridle in hand. He ought to listen diligently and understand their opinions thoroughly, and decide to follow or ignore their advice only after listening carefully to all considerations in detail. Moreover, it is necessary to make sure these men are not left to their own devices so much so that they gather enough courage (*animo*) to surpass and oppress the weak and impotent—but this should not be very hard to do, either. In order to demonstrate how important it is that your friends and partisans feel useful, consider Lorenzo's example: although he was quite careful to make sure no other man surpassed him, he still gave out legitimate and significant offices during his rule. Giving men reputation enriched him in his own right, which proves that this policy is a reasonable and convenient one. These Medici could dole out offices better than Lorenzo ever did by feeding the unfruitful, unproductive men on the road to Rome with emoluments. And while they currently employ political patronage, they do so in a superficial and shortsighted way that does good neither to their friends nor to themselves. They should employ this strategy more pointedly. If they managed their patronage network well it could serve as a powerful foundation and defense of the state.

Of course, I am sure that on some level these Medici understand the strategic reasoning behind these principles [of political patronage] very well. While there are many reasons that have inhibited them from putting these precepts into practice, the most powerful inhibitor comes from their complete lack of trust in us. There are primarily two reasons for such distrust. First, they doubt the goodness of the citizenry. They believe that given the opportunity, citizens would look to govern only out of their own shortsighted self-interest and designs of usurpation, and to the detriment of the state. This concern is not all that reasonable because Florence, just like all places, is made up of good and bad men. There are of course energized bad ones with varying appetites for power. But there are even more men here who love this city and the public good (*il bene universale*). And the Medici could easily remedy the problems posed by the former, lesser sort of men. First, they can make sure to select confidants prudently, and second, as I said above, they must make sure that they do not concede complete trust to these men (*non si dare in loro preda*). In fact, it is important to buck and negate their actions once in a while, and to favor or disfavor them according to their behavior and merits.

The second reason the Medici doubt us is far more important. They may deny it, but it is clear from their quotidian management of the city that that they do not trust us personally. They do not believe that we love them enough to be used as a sturdy foundation for the benefit of their state. They remember being run out of the city in '94. During their long exile they made few friends. Their return was enabled by foreign forces without any of our support, except those very desperate few who resided outside the city, and who the Medici remember were also their enemies before the latter's exile. They know very well that those few were driven by desperation and extreme necessity to change sides, and that they cannot count on them for anything but inconsistency and disloyalty. The Medici have never experienced any loyal partisanship and true support, and therefore they judge all of us [ottimati] as mal-intentioned and cold.

They clearly hold such an opinion of us, and it will be our death. They do not confer with us, open themselves up to us, or even let us help disentangle matters of state. They are always reticent and reserved. But if I am not deceived, this is still a false and foolish course of action on their part. Citizens who are caressed and elevated in reputation, greatness, offices and honors will indubitably become their enthusiastic partisans, irrespective of this history. Patronage can stir something in a soul not entirely made of steel. And above all else, it moves self-interest, the teacher that disciplines all students. Self-interest makes men affectionate and partisan. I do not deny that certain natural inclinations, or love, or hate can move men, but when combined with self-interest, all human action becomes pointed and efficient. Without self-interest, human motive quickly disintegrates.

We no longer live in the time of the ancient Romans or the Greeks, when men had generous intellects and everyone aspired toward glory. No one in Florence loves liberty and popular government so much that, if given the opportunity to live better-off in another way of life, he would not jump at the chance. In fact, if he thought he could profit even slightly, he would take the bait and align himself so thoroughly with this new way of life that when the new regime mutated he not only would lose command, but would bring himself down with great ruin. But the truth is, in the popular republic of '94, even those short sighted, self-interested men never had the opportunity to satisfy their ambitions because the popular government of '94 came close to organizing itself into a beautiful republic with genuine liberty, especially in the beginning of Piero Soderini's magistracy. Only later, as the regime continued to enlarge (allargando) and thereby deform itself, did the hope that it could ever reform back into a proper republic continually diminish, until ultimately it devolved into a disordered, confusing mess. Nevertheless, this confusion would still be far preferable to what we would have if we were to witness yet another change (mutazione). That confusion and disorder would seem like finger food compared to what we could experience in today's politics, because, to my mind, the wideness that was then would be infinitesimal compared to that which would eventually be introduced; the difference would be more dramatic than the distinction between the narrowness of today and that of Lorenzo's time.

Such circumstances could provoke men's suspicions, rage, and ignorance sufficient to threaten the state. But no one that thinks that this current mutation was anything like what happened in '94, where the friends of the Medici, who were the flower of the city, were preserved and after a few short months were allowed to participate in government with the others. Today the situation is completely different, and it would be dangerous for anyone to even try such a thing. Those who see themselves as great and in good standing with the Medici know with certainty that attempting any mutation could run the risk of their exile, the loss of their wealth, and their ruin. You can bet that they would all affectionately run toward conserving and defending the Medici with every force they could muster because they know that their efforts would preserve and defend themselves. Nor is there any danger that anyone's greatness will surpass the Medici's because, considering that the entire state came to the Medici absolutely, there is no citizen established enough that the Medici could not easily quash at any sign of his advancement. Nor do the Medici need to worry about what happened in '66 from occurring again, where the Medici had to fight those who had in '34 been their friends. Nor is there a house in Florence capable of demonstrating excessive authority or greatness except the Medici themselves. Nor is there a citizen so rich that he worries about the winds drying up his wealth once in a while. And I would not worry that giving these men favor will bring danger, or that their coldness will hurt the state. We have plenty of examples from our own history, where for no other reason than for self-interest and to secure a comfortable position did men organize their wealth, arms, and friends to defend the state with more promptness and vivacity than anyone could ask for, such as in '58, '66, '78 and in many other cases. And the example of '94 does not negate my reasoning, because Piero's sinister modes and bad advice alienated friends and ruined everything. Therefore, returning to the conclusion of this section, I think that a delegation of a certain number of friends, chosen well, managed with discretion, treated lovingly under the above-mentioned circumstances, would not lack loyalty, love, or spirit in securing the [Medici] state, and would in fact be beneficial to it.

The third foundation is that the people and the majority (*lo universale*) is kept content, which will be difficult because the majority liked the popular government, and they dislike the greatness and absolute authority [of the Medici] that they now experience. This is all the more frustrating because, had it been possible to live and converse with them in a more civilized and equal manner, as it had been in the time of Lorenzo the Elder, no one doubts that this greatness would bother the people far less than it currently does. But now the thing is done, and their way of life cannot be moderated in this sense. Nonetheless one should satisfy the people in other ways as much as possible so that they are content. If it is not possible to remove all their displeasure, a great deal of it must be attenuated. If you cannot make them all love you, make a great part of them love you. Where there can be no love, be sure to eradicate hate, and where there is hate make sure it does not become desperation. This should not be difficult so long as you pander to their desires. The most important matters in which you must defer to them are: the finances of the commune, the justice of the civil courts, and the prevention of the powerful's oppression of the weak and less powerful.

Finances are crucial. Everyone knows that without a wealthy commune the citizens must supplement state expenses out of their own pockets—that is to say, through taxes and payments to the Monte. One must govern finances with complete transparency so that no one ever has reason to be suspicious. During the time of the Lorenzo, the financial administration and the office of the treasury was entrusted to a few hands with no outside visibility or mechanisms of accountability. Add to this that Lorenzo and his court spent almost unsustainable sums. Every time taxes were expected to be cut or the debt alleviated, a new arbitrary tax was imposed and assessed with partiality and malignity. The lack of transparency made everyone think that Lorenzo and his court were driving this superfluous spending and brutalization of the public finances, even when this was not in fact the case. Between this, the sinister tax ministers, and the fact that ordinary taxes were insufficient and new ones were levied every day—these factors made is seem that they were acting far more purposefully than they actually were, and consequently, it was believed that this was in fact their intended method to oppress the citizens. Countless suspicious and jealousies developed in the hearts of the entire citizenry, until suddenly, the city's military and commercial affairs came to a standstill: Military and commercial affairs were abandoned, the citizens became dumbfounded and anxious, not sure what to do, and the city lost all its momentum and motion. The only reason the city began to function again was because of fear of the French invasion and fear of a consequent alteration. This state of affairs had two deleterious effects: most obviously, universal hatred of the governors, or rather, universal desperation over them; the other effect is that the city, when its principal means of existence, industry, and military endeavors are frozen, becomes weak and poor. The weaker and more impoverished the city, the weaker and more impotent the boss (*padrone*). Similarly, the riches and reputation of the state generate riches and reputation for the governor. The more robust the tools that the state has at its disposal, the more vigorous and virile is the boss. Therefore if he wants to befriend the majority (*lo universale*) and to obtain greater reputation in all of Italy, he must closely follow public finances and expenses and must distribute these expenses fairly and efficiently. Following the finances diligently and openly will reassure men that they need not worry about financial administration, all jealousies and suspicions will dissipate, and men can return to their business activities without being burdened by taxes.

Now let us move to the second requirement: justice in civil matters. I am not talking about criminal trials, though of course it is necessary to ensure that justice is observed here too, and in these latter cases more openness is sometimes desirable. With the civil courts, it is necessary to make firm and strict rules that are observed and upheld, especially by the head of the state himself. Maintaining justice in the courts assures the boss's (*padrone*) security as well. Of all things, men cannot tolerate someone taking from them what is rightfully theirs, nor can they tolerate having restitution for some usurpation inhibited. It is necessary to deal with this in two ways: First, the rule of law must govern civil procedures. Cases cannot be diverted from ordinary modes to extraordinary ones as favors; for example, they cannot be extraordinarily summoned to the Signoria or similar places. Second, you must let cases of the *podestà* and of the *mercatantia* run their ordinary course.[28] These domains are the heart of this city; they are its helm and nerve. When justice reigns in these matters it protects the life and security of each individual. One must make sure not to intervene through either direct or indirect channels, nor with warm recommendations or general appeals. While you may think that general and nonpartisan recommendations (*raccomandazione*) cause no harm because [their] objectivity offends neither God nor men, it generates reasonable suspicion: those who see their ministers going about the civil buildings presume that these ministers are going around granting favors. Additionally it influences the judges, who, although they should always strictly follow the codes of justice, do not know if they are supposed to take these signs as commandments from the prince. In fact, it is necessary to entirely remove any preferential treatment (*raccomendazione*), whether substantive or ceremonious. These judges must be encouraged to be diligent and conduct themselves in good faith. They must believe the governor's soul to be impartial and on the side of justice, and the governor must demonstrate this commitment to justice with consistent affirmations of the judge's decisions.

To further secure these ends it is imperative to prevent a species of oppression that runs rampant throughout our dominion: We must reform our rectors and officials, who think of nothing other than enriching and fattening themselves with their complete disregard for justice and constant robbing on every front. They bring embarrassment to the state and even more harm considering the anger it generates among all subjects. For whatever reason God has not wanted to test us in this regard for some time, and if he did, we would quickly experience the disastrous consequences [if the countryside were to rebel]. Repairing these disorders would be marvelous. It is imperative that the government imposes strict rules that punish poor comportment and demonstrate a clear distinction between good and bad behavior. When evil men are not punished, like in present times, they will behave increasingly worse, and those extremely few men who aspire toward honor or who are honestly good are deterred from being so. We can no longer allow certain private citizens who prey on their weaker neighbors through the protection of the state and these corrupted magistrates. As it stands now, these private citizens buy off the magistrates and create estates for themselves with barely any money but merely through favors.[29]

And if someone were to retort: "If these private citizens are not permitted to take advantage of those around them, they will never be warm, enthusiastic partisans of the state," I would respond that this claim could not be any more dangerous. This flawed reasoning would make the governor infamous and create many enemies, not only out of those who are oppressed but also out of everyone who witnesses this oppression. And besides, appeasing these great citizens (*i cittadini grandi*) is not difficult; in fact, it is easier today than ever before. With the pontificate in hand, they [the Medici] have access to many spoils that can satisfy men. These spoils would not only render the heads of state (*capi dello stato*) enthusiastic partisans but would also invite many more good men of quality into the government. If the pope were to comport himself with the same measure and discretion that prudent men use in their own affairs, he would be well prepared for every accident that should come to pass and would create a strong foundation for the future of his house for years to come.

These are the principles *in quibus consistent leges et prophetae* (consistent with the laws and the prophets). In my judgment, these laws could be introduced and followed without much difficulty if the person who bears the burden of our affairs wants to dedicate the required time, diligence, and energy to secure these ends. Every time they would look to venerate the quality and foundation of the city and the government, which of course they should do, they would see a well-ordered and well-curated regime. Indeed, they would see that it bears optimal fruit and that this order constitutes the foundation of their security and establishment here. If they see no returns, as has been the case until now, and so it seems to them not worth undertaking the burden of organizing the state, I do not know what else to say to them except this: "you can continue to govern as you have in the past, and we shall see how it all ends: if it keeps working, I will be happy to be wrong; if things end poorly, I will be discontent, and so will everyone else considering that your ruin will bring down the entire city, or at least those who are considered your friends or favorites."

These foundations must be established and developed with agility. You must demonstrate yourself as grateful and human to the majority and live among them amicably; you must hold these ministers and *cancellieri* under your thumb, because their authority and greatness cannot be more disrespectful to this entire city and does not bear any benefit; in fact, their insolence, greed, and lack of expertise about our customs and way of life creates inordinate disorders and burdens. It is very important to leave men free to arrange their own marriages; using your authority to interfere or arrange them on their behalf is in effect useless and generates burden and hate. You could cultivate even more favor with the majority (*universale*) by occasionally demonstrating that you are concerned with the public welfare by helping with the Monte and the army, the two things that sustain life in the city. You must introduce good laws to reform the disorders that currently exist within the offices and among all its members. Finally, dress code must be reformed: the dress of men and women has deviated too far from its own customs, which cannot bring anything but bad effects to the private and public realms.

When it is seen that your spirit and interest is turned to these matters, everyone would come to your aid and guidance, bringing their affection. You would be considered the fathers of the city, whereas now you are seen as permitting every license. Currently, it seems as though you are disinterested in our affairs, which only contributes to the bad disposition and ill will that already exist ordinarily. If you were to do these things, I know that not only the city but even your own state [the Medici pontificate] would benefit. Without doing these things, I do not know what to say except that evil governors do not produce good effects.

I do not want to omit the following: There will always be those who hold the view that there would be more security [for you] to take control of the dominion and of the city absolutely, in fact and in title, instead of holding this government under the shadow of civility and liberty. Perhaps they have already tried to persuade you of this. I do not intend to dispute this here, but in my judgment, you could not take a more pernicious course of action for yourselves or for us. Moreover, this type of management would avail more difficulties, suspicions, and ultimately, more cruelty.

Notes

Introduction

1. On the experimental aspect of Renaissance political culture, see Mark Jurdjevic, "Political Cultures," in Michael Wyatt, ed., *The Cambridge Companion to the Italian Renaissance* (Cambridge: Cambridge University Press, 2014), 298–319; for a peninsular overview and recent methodological approaches, see Isabella Lazzarini and Andrea Gamberini, eds., *The Italian Renaissance State* (Cambridge: Cambridge University Press, 2012); Andrea Gamberini and Giuseppe Petralia, *Linguaggi politici nell'Italia del Rinascimento* (Rome: Viella, 2007).

2. On civic humanism's relationship to Florentine republicanism, see John Najemy, "Civic Humanism and Florentine Politics," and James Hankins, "Rhetoric, History, and Ideology: the Civic Panegyrics of Leonardo Bruni," both in James Hankins, ed., *Renaissance Civic Humanism: Reappraisals and Reflections* (Cambridge: Cambridge University Press, 2000), 75–104 and 143–78, respectively. On its ideological compatibility with Medici power, see Mark Jurdjevic, "Civic Humanism and the Rise of the Medici," *Renaissance Quarterly* 52.4 (1999): 994–1020.

3. A vision famously elaborated in Dante's *De monarchia*.

4. On medieval conceptions of sovereignty and legitimacy, see Walter Ullman, *A History of Political Thought: The Middle Ages* (Baltimore: Penguin, 1965); Walter Ullman, *Principles of Government and Politics in the Middle Ages* (New York: Barnes and Noble, 1961); Nicolai Rubinstein, "Le dottrine politiche nel Rinascimento," in M. Boas Hall, ed., *Il Rinascimento: Interpretazioni e problemi* (Rome: Laterza, 1979), 187–231.

5. Giovanni Tabacco, *The Struggle for Power in Medieval Italy: Structures of Political Rule*, trans. Rosalind Brown Jensen (Cambridge: Cambridge University Press, 1989).

6. Jane Black, *Absolutism in Renaissance Milan: Plenitude of Power Under the Visconti and the Sforza, 1329–1535* (Oxford: Oxford University Press, 2009); Gregory Lubkin, *A Renaissance Court: Milan Under Gian Galeazzo Sforza* (Berkeley: University of California Press, 1994); Danilo Marrara, *Riseduti e nobiltà: Profilo storico e istituzionali* (Pisa: Pacini, 1976).

7. John Najemy, "Political Ideas," in Guido Ruggiero, *A Companion to the Worlds of the Renaissance* (Oxford: Blackwell, 2002), 386–88.

8. For a study of these parallels, see Julia Emlen, Anthony Molho, and Kurt Raaflaub, eds., *City States in Classical Antiquity and Medieval Italy* (Ann Arbor: University of Michigan Press, 1991).

9. For numerous examples of these developments, see Lauro Martines, *Power and Imagination: City-States in Renaissance Italy* (New York: Knopf, 1979).

10. Felix Gilbert, "The Humanist Concept of the Prince and the Prince of Machiavelli," *Journal of Modern History* 11.4 (1939): 449–83.

11. Quoted in James Blythe, *Ideal Government and the Mixed Constitution in the Middle Ages* (Princeton, N.J.: Princeton University Press, 1992), 69.

12. For a survey of humanism's themes and intellectual context, see Jill Kraye, ed., *The Cambridge Companion to Renaissance Humanism* (Cambridge: Cambridge University Press, 1996).

13. Gary Ianziti, *Humanistic Historiography Under the Sforzas* (Oxford: Oxford University Press, 1998), 235–40; see also Andrea Gamberini, *Lo stato visconteo: Linguaggi politici et dinamiche costituzionali* (Milan: FrancoAngeli, 2005); Andrea Gamberini, *L'età dei Visconti e degli Sforza, 1277–1535* (Milan: Skira, 2001).

14. Jerry H. Bentley, *Politics and Culture in Renaissance Naples* (Princeton, N.J.: Princeton University Press, 1987), 198–201.

15. On Venetian republican culture, see Edward Muir, *Civic Ritual in Renaissance Venice* (Princeton, N.J.: Princeton University Press, 1981); William Bouswma, *Venice and the Defense of Republican Liberty: Renaissance Values in the Age of the Counter Reformation* (Berkeley: University of California Press, 1968).

16. In addition to defining the patriciate, the Great Council created laws and oversaw the electoral process; the Senate's responsibilities included diplomacy and governance of the city's mainland subject territories; the Council of Ten had jurisdiction over treason, sedition, and political crimes. On the evolution of Venice's institutions, see Frederic Lane, *Venice: A Maritime Republic* (Baltimore: Johns Hopkins University Press, 1973).

17. Robert Finlay, *Politics in Renaissance Venice* (New Brunswick, N.J.: Rutgers University Press, 1980), 113.

18. Francesco Vettori, *Scritti storici e politici*, ed. Enrico Niccolini (Bari: Laterza, 1972), 145–46.

19. Felix Gilbert, "The Venetian Constitution in Florentine Political Thought," in Nicolai Rubinstein, ed., *Florentine Studies: Politics and Society in Renaissance Florence* (Evanston, Ill.: Northwestern University Press, 1968), 463–500.

20. Machiavelli identified division and discord as the overwhelmingly central question of Florentine politics and made it the central focus of his history of Florence. Niccolò Machiavelli, *Florentine Histories*, ed. and trans. Harvey Mansfield and Laura Banfield (Princeton, N.J.: Princeton University Press, 1988).

21. On Florentine political institutions, see Gene Brucker, *Florentine Politics and Society, 1343–1378* (Princeton, N.J.: Princeton University Press, 1962), 57–83.

22. John Najemy, "Guild Republicanism in Trecento Florence: The Successes and Ultimate Failure of Corporate Politics," *American Historical Review* 84.1 (1979): 60.

23. On the Florentine guilds and their politics, see John Najemy, *Corporatism and Consensus in Florentine Electoral Politics, 1280–1400* (Chapel Hill: University of North Carolina Press, 1982); Najemy, "Guild Republicanism in Trecento Florence," 53–71.

24. I borrow the familial political metaphors from Edward Muir, "Governments and Bureaucracies," in Guido Ruggiero, ed., *A Companion to the Worlds of the Renaissance* (Oxford: Blackwell, 2002), 108–23.

25. Quoted in John Najemy, *A History of Florence, 1200–1575* (Oxford: Blackwell, 2006), 253.

26. On this style of patronage politics, see F. W. Kent, *Household and Lineage in Renaissance Florence: The Family Life of the Capponi, Ginori, and Rucellai* (Princeton, N.J.: Princeton University Press, 1977).

27. Quoted in Nicolai Rubinstein, "Machiavelli and Florentine Republican Experience," in Gisela Bock, Quentin Skinner, and Maurizio Viroli, eds., *Machiavelli and Republicanism* (Cambridge: Cambridge University Press, 1990), 4.

28. Quoted in Rubinstein, "Machiavelli and Florentine Republican Experience," 4; on Luca della Robbia and Florentine politics, see Mark Jurdjevic, *Guardians of Republicanism: The Valori Family in the Florentine Renaissance* (Oxford: Oxford University Press, 2008), 96–123.

29. Francesco Guicciardini, *History of Florence*, trans. Mario Domandi (New York: Harper Torchbooks, 1970), 3.

30. On the formation and management of the Medici party, see Dale Kent, *The Rise of the Medici: Faction in Florence, 1426–1434* (Oxford: Oxford University Press, 1978). On this style of politics more generally, see Paul Mclean, *The Art of the Network: Strategic Interaction and Patronage in Renaissance Florence* (Durham, N.C.: Duke University Press, 2007).

31. On Cosimo de' Medici's cultural patronage, see Dale Kent, *Cosimo de' Medici and the Florentine Renaissance: The Patron's Oeuvre* (New Haven, Conn.: Yale University Press, 2000); for a contemporary account, see the biography of Cosimo in Vespasiano da Bisticci, *The Vespasiano Memoirs: Lives of*

Illustrious Men of the XVth Century, trans. William George and Emily Waters (Toronto: University of Toronto Press, 1997).

32. Quoted in J. R. Hale, *Florence and the Medici: The Pattern of Control* (London: Thames and Hudson, 1977), 31.

33. Alison Brown, "The Humanist Portrait of Cosimo de' Medici, *Pater Patriae*," *Journal of the Warburg and Courtauld Institutes* 24 (1961): 186–221.

34. The definitive study is Nicolai Rubinstein, *The Government of Florence Under the Medici, 1434–1494* (Oxford: Clarendon, 1966).

35. Quoted in Kent, *Rise of the Medici*, 19.

36. This paragraph summarizes Ronald G. Witt, *"In the Footsteps of the Ancients:" The Origins of Humanism from Lovato to Bruni* (Leiden: Brill, 2000).

37. On this debate, see John Oppel, "Poggio, San Bernardino of Siena, and the Dialogue *On Avarice*," *Renaissance Quarterly* 30 (1977): 564–87.

38. Poggio Bracciolini, *De avaritia*, in *Earthly Republic*, 263.

39. On this and other major political themes of humanism, see Anthony Grafton, "Humanism and Political Theory," and Nicolai Rubinstein, "Italian Political Thought, 1450–1530," both in J. H. Burns and Mark Goldie, eds., *The Cambridge History of Political Thought, 1450–1700* (Cambridge: Cambridge University Press, 1991), 9–29 and 30–65, respectively.

40. Gene Brucker, *The Civic World of Early Renaissance Florence* (Princeton, N.J.: Princeton University Press, 1977), 300–301.

41. Quoted in Ronald G. Witt, *Coluccio Salutati and His Public Letters* (Geneva: Librairie Droz, 1976), 4; on Salutati, see Ronald G. Witt, *Hercules at the Crossroads: The Life, Works, and Thought of Coluccio Salutati* (Durham, N.C.: Duke University Press, 1983).

42. Hankins, "Rhetoric, History, and Ideology."

43. Jurdjevic, "Political Cultures," 307.

44. Jurdjevic, "Political Cultures," 304.

45. Hans Baron, *The Crisis of the Early Italian Renaissance: Civic Humanism and Republican Liberty in an Age of Classicism and Tyranny*, 2 vols. (Princeton, N.J.: Princeton University Press, 1955).

46. Riccardo Fubini, "Renaissance Historian: The Career of Hans Baron," *Journal of Modern History* 64 (1992): 541–74.

47. James Hankins, "The 'Baron Thesis' After Forty Years and Some Recent Studies of Leonardo Bruni," *Journal of the History of Ideas* 56 (1995): 309–38.

48. Quentin Skinner, *The Foundations of Modern Political Thought*, vol. 1, *The Renaissance* (Cambridge: Cambridge University Press, 1978), 41–48.

49. Mikael Hörnqvist, "The Two Myths of Civic Humanism," in Hankins, ed., *Renaissance Civic Humanism*, 105–42.

50. Jerrold Siegel, "Civic Humanism or Ciceronian Rhetoric? The Culture of Petrarch and Bruni," *Past and Present* 34 (1966): 3–48; and see Hans Baron's reply, "Leonardo Bruni: 'Professional Rhetorician' or 'Civic Humanist'?" *Past and Present* 36 (1967): 21–37.

51. Najemy, "Civic Humanism and Florentine Politics;" John Najemy, "The Dialogue of Power in Florentine Politics," in Emlen, Molho, and Raaflaub, eds., *City States in Classical Antiquity and Medieval Italy*, 269–88.

52. Quoted in Najemy, "Civic Humanism and Florentine Politics," 91.

53. Leonardo Bruni, *Panegyric to the City of Florence*, this volume.

54. This paragraph summarizes Nicolai Rubinstein, "Florentine Constitutionalism and Medici Ascendancy in the Fifteenth Century," in Rubinstein, ed., *Florentine Studies*, 442–62.

55. On the Great Council, see Najemy, *History of Florence*, 381–90; on Savonarola, see Donald Weinstein, *Savonarola: The Rise and Fall of a Renaissance Prophet* (New Haven, Conn.: Yale University Press, 2011).

56. Najemy, *History of Florence*, 390–400.

57. On the complex factional alignments of these years, see Nicolai Rubinstein, "Politics and Constitution in Florence at the End of the Fifteenth Century," in E. F. Jacob, ed., *Italian Renaissance Studies: A Tribute to the Late Cecilia M. Ady* (London: Faber and Faber, 1960), 148–83.

58. Roslyn Pesman Cooper, "Piero Soderini: Aspiring Prince or Civic Leader," *Studies in Medieval and Renaissance History*, n.s., 1 (1978): 69–126.

59. For more on these details, see Robert Black, *Machiavelli* (London: Routledge, 2013).

60. On Machiavelli's populism, see John P. McCormick, *Machiavellian Democracy* (Cambridge: Cambridge University Press, 2011); John P. McCormick, "Machiavellian Democracy: Controlling Elites with Ferocious Populism," *American Political Science Review* 95.2 (2001): 297–313; John P. McCormick, "On the Myth of the Conservative Turn in Machiavelli's *Florentine Histories*," in Nadia Urbinati, David Johnston, and Camila Vergara, eds., *Machiavelli on Liberty and Conflict: Commemorating the 500th Anniversary of the Composition of* The Prince (Chicago: University of Chicago Press, 2017), 330–351.

61. See Guicciardini's extensive quarrel with the premises of Machiavelli's *Discourses* in Francesco Guicciardini, *Selected Writings*, ed. and trans. Cecil Grayson and Margaret Grayson (Oxford: Oxford University Press, 1965), 62–124.

62. The explanatory footnotes to the texts by Machiavelli and Guicciardini were written by the respective editors of this volume. The reprinted texts include their original explanatory notes.

Chapter 1. Petrarch

HOW A RULER OUGHT TO GOVERN HIS STATE (1373)

1. An allusion to the pseudo-Cicero *Epistula ad Octavium*.

2. Julius Caesar *Bellum civile* 3.91.3.

3. An allusion to the assassination in December 1350 in Padua of Francesco's father, Giacomo II da Carrara, by a distant kinsman. As a result Francesco, then a young man in his twenties, succeeded his popular father to the lordship of Padua.

4. Francesco da Carrara contracted marriages for several of his daughters with the scions of noble houses in Italy and Germany, including the count of Oettingen, the count of Veglie, and the duke of Saxony.

5. An allusion to the border war fought with Venice in 1372–73, which Francesco da Carrara ended by agreeing to the payment of an indemnity to Venice while he maintained substantially his original frontiers. See Paolo Sambin, "La guerra del 1372–73 tra Venezia e Padova," *Archivio Veneto* 5th Ser., 58–41 (1946–47): 1–76.

6. An allusion to Cicero *Epistolae ad Brutum* 1.4a.

7. Cicero *Somnium Scipionis* 13 (=*De republica* 6.13), which was known in the fourteenth century only by its inclusion in Macrobius, *Commentarii in Somnium Scipionis*.

8. Romans 13:4.

9. See *Scriptores historiae Augustae* 19.8.8.

10. Cicero *De officiis* 2.7.23.

11. Cicero *De officiis* 217.23.

12. Cicero *Orationes Philippicae* 1.14.23.

13. Macrobius, *Saturnalia* 2.7.4. The same anecdote was told earlier by Petrarch in his *Rerum memorandarum libri* 3.34.3–4 (ed. Gius. Billanovich [Rome, 1943], p. 126).

14. Cicero *De officiis* 2.7.24.

15. Cicero *De officiis* 2.7.23.

16. Cicero *De officiis* 1.28.97; 3.21.82.

17. Suetonius *Caligula* 30.

18. Cicero *Pro Ligario* 12.35.

19. Suetonius *Divus Julius* 84, quoting Pacuvius.

20. See Suetonius *Divus Julius* 76.

21. Seneca *Epistulae* 9.6.

22. See Matt. 22:39.

23. Cicero *Orationes Philippicae* 2.44.112.

24. See Macrobius *Saturnalia* 2.4.18.

25. Cicero *Somnium Scipionis* 16 (=*De republica* 6.16).

26. Suetonius *Caligula* 58.

27. Suetonius *Nero* 47.

28. See Suetonius *Divus Augustus* 99–100.

29. Suetonius *Vespasianus* 24.

30. Suetonius *Titus* 10–11.

31. Suetonius *Domitian* 23.

32. Suetonius *Galba* 20.

33. Suetonius *Vitellius* 17.

34. *Scriptores historiae Augustae* 4.8.3.

35. St. Ambrose, *De obitu Theodosii imperatori*: 26 (=PL 16:1456).

36. Livy *Ab urbe condita* 4.20.

37. Suetonius *Divus Augustus* 28.

38. *Scriptores historiae Augustae* 26.392.

39. An allusion to Erichthonius, the son of Vulcan, king of Athens, who is credited with being the first man to hitch four horses to a chariot; see Vergil *Georgica* 3.113ff.

40. See Justinus *Epitome historiae Philippicae* 6.8.9.33; Cicero *Tusculanae disputationes* 1.2.4; and Valerius Maximus *Factorum et dictorum memorabilium libri IX* 3.7. ext. 5. Petrarch used the same sources in a discussion of Epaminondas in his *Rerum memorandarum libri* 1.7 (Billanovich, pp. 6–7).

41. See Valerius Maximus 3.7. ext. 5.

42. Cf. Vergil *Aeneid* 1.241ff.

43. On this statute, see the essay by G. Tamassia, "Francesco Petrarca e gli statuti di Padova," *Atti della R. Academia di Padova*, n.s. 13 (1896–97): 201ff.

44. An allusion to the cultivation in the Euganean Hills of the grape (the product of Bacchus) and of the liberal arts (represented by Minerva), and emphasizing the lack of cultivation of cereals, such as wheat, barley, or oats (the products of Ceres).

45. Suetonius *Divus Julius* 44.

46. Macrobius *Saturnalia* 2.4.24. The same anecdote is told by Petrarch in *Rerum memorandum libri* 2.71 (Billanovich, p. 93).

47. Aristotle *Politica* 5.9. 1314b40ff., which Petrarch knew only in medieval Latin translation.

48. *Scriptores historiae Augustae* 1.8.3.

49. Suetonius *Divus Augustus* 28.

50. Cicero *De officiis* 1.29.101.

51. Suetonius *Tiberius* 28.

52. Suetonius *Vesparianus* 18.

53. *Scriptores historiae Augustae* 2647.4.

54. Lucan *De bello civili* 3.58.

55. An allusion to a revolt—caused by famine—by the lower classes of Rome against the senatorial families in 1353, just before the return to the city of the demagogic Cola di Rienzo. See F. Gregorovius, *History of the City of Rome in the Middle Ages*, trans. A. Hamilton, 8 vols. (London, 1898), 6:337ff.

56. Suetonius *Divus Augustus* 41.

57. Suetonius *Divus Augustus* 42.

58. See Livy *Ab urbe condita* 26.34.

59. Suetonius *Tiberius* 32.

60. *Scriptores historiae Augustae* 3.6.1.

61. Eutropius *Brevarium ab urbe condita* 10.1.

62. Lucan *De bello civili* 3.152.

63. *Scriptores historiae Augustae* 1.9.7.

64. *Scriptores historiae Augustae* 1.17.1.

65. Ps. 54:22 (Vulgate numbering).

66. Ps. 36.5–6 (Vulgate numbering).

67. An echo from Luke 12:33.

68. Another allusion to the border war fought against Venice in 1372–73.

69. *Scriptores historiae Augustae* 18.65.4.

70. *Scriptores historiae Augustae* 18.66.2.

71. *Scriptores historiae Augustae* 6.8.2.

72. Cf. Seneca *Epistolae* 21.75.

73. See Aristotle *Economica* 2. 1345b5–1553b41.

74. Cf. Cicero *De officiis* 5.5.11.

75. *Scriptores historiae Augustae* 26.43.55.

76. *Scriptores historiae Augustae* 26.432.

77. See Suetonius *Claudius* 28.

78. *Scriptores historiae Augustae* 17.15.1–2.

79. *Scriptores historiae Augustae* 9.9.4.

80. Cf. *Scriptores historiae Augustae* 4.15.2.

81. Prov. 5:9.

82. A reference to Cicero's *De amicitia*, from which Petrarch derived some of the ideas in this section.

83. Quoted in Cicero *De officiis* 1.17.56.

84. Acts 4:32.

85. Cicero *De amicitia* 5.18.

86. Martial *Satirae* 5.81.2.

87. Cicero *De amicitia* 9.31.

88. *Scriptores historiae Augustae* 18.21.2.

89. Cf. Suetonius *Caligula* 22.

90. Cf. *Scriptores historiae Augustae* 7.9.2.

91. Cf. *Scriptores historiae Augustae* 18.17.2–3.

92. Probably an allusion to a French critic of Italy, whom Petrarch had recently inveighed against in his *Invectiva contra eum qui maledixit Italie*.

93. Eutropius 9.26.

94. Suetonius *Divus Augustus* 52.

95. Suetonius *Divus Augustus* 53.

96. *Scriptores historiae Augustae* 18.18.3.

97. *Scriptores historiae Augustae* 17.4–18.1.

98. See Cicero *Tusculanae disputationes* 1.14.34, quoting Ennius.

99. Claudian *De quarto consulatu Honorii Augusti* 299–300.

100. Cicero *De legibus* 3.14.31.

101. Cf. Livy *Ab urbe condita* 21.4.8.

102. Cf. Suetonius *Divus Augustus* 73.

103. Cicero *De officiis* 1.22.74.

104. Cicero *De officiis* 1.22.75–76 provided Petrarch with this list of great leaders from antiquity.

105. Cicero *Orationes Philippicae* 9.5.10.

106. Petrarch derived this list of famous legal experts from the time of the Roman Empire mainly from his reading of the *Scriptores historiae Augustae*, passim.

107. *Scriptores historiae Augustae* 18.34.6.

108. Suetonius *Divus Julius* 42.

109. Acts 22:28.

110. 2 Kings 13:14.

111. Hebrews 9:27.

112. Cf. Cicero *Tusculanae disputationes* 1.48.115.

113. Jeremiah 22:10.

114. Cf. Cicero *Tusculanae disputationes* 1.48.115, quoting Euripides.

Chapter 2. Coluccio Salutati

ON THE TYRANT (1400)

1. The word *superbus* with its variations, *superbia* and *superbe* has been the most difficult one to render into a suitable English equivalent. Its original meaning of "proud," "haughty" seldom meets the precise idea of the author. It shades off into a great variety of grades and distinctions, most of which are covered by our word "tyrannical," yet it is obviously impossible to translate definitions of "tyranny" by the word we are trying to define. The root idea of a person whose actions are governed by a sense of superiority over others and not by a desire to promote their welfare is the most helpful in determining in each case the precise meaning. Not infrequently it has seemed best simply to repeat the Latin word without any attempt at translation.

2. Revised version: "even the number of years that are laid up for the oppressor."

3. *Ecl.* iv, 31–33.

4. *Inf.* xxxiv, 61–67.

Chapter 3. Bartolus of Sassoferrato

DE TYRANNIA (C. 1355)

1. Pope Gregory I (590–604).

2. Henry, Cardinal-Bishop of Ostia (d. 1271). *Commentum meum super decretalibus.*

3. I have been unable to find any work of Plutarch bearing this title. The whole of §28 is an almost literal reproduction of a passage in Aegidius Romanus [Egidio Colonna] *de regimine principum*, book iii, pt. 2, c. x, which is a condensed summary of Aristotle's *Politics*, book v, c. xi. That Bartolus was acquainted with Aegidius is proved by his reference in §44 to the very passage which he here ascribes to Plutarch.

4. The practical quality of Bartolus's reflections is nowhere better shown than here. He accepts all of the articles in "Plutarch's" definitions of tyranny, but his own observation has taught him that most of them need some modification in practice. To apply them to the existing conditions in the Italy of his day would cause as many evils as it would cure. What to do in the given case is, he thinks, sufficiently indicated in the preceding paragraphs. It is always a question of balance between the evils of tyranny and the still worse evils of public disorder. The right of assembly, for example, is precious to a free republic, but if assemblies become nests of sedition they should be suppressed. Proscription of personal enemies is a hideous form of tyranny, but if the case against the proscribed person is founded in justice it may be worthy of approval—and so on through the list. The principle is sound; it is in the application of it that the subtlety of the lawyer finds scope for exercise.

5. As to the validity of the acts of such a "veiled" tyrant, Bartolus makes one important distinction. In general he would apply the same principles which he has laid down in the case of a manifest tyranny. If, however, the alleged tyrant rules the community as a whole justly and wisely, but oppresses his personal enemies, whether these be his fellow-citizens or outsiders, then he is to be judged differently in these two sides of his administration. In other words, it is possible that a man may at the same time be a tyrant and not a tyrant.

6. In this paragraph our jurist allows himself the only departure from a strictly juristic attitude. After all, he says, since no individual is perfect, how can we expect that any government will be solely devoted to the common good with no thought of personal advantage to the rulers? The most we can ask is that the good of the community shall on the whole, prevail. Bartolus is no "idealist."

7. See note to §§27–28.

Chapter 4. Leonardo Bruni

PANEGYRIC TO THE CITY OF FLORENCE (C. 1402)

1. An echo of Homer *Iliad* 12.278–86.

2. An allusion to the recent war with Giangaleazzo Visconti, which Florence eventually won as a result of the dissolution of the Visconti empire following Giangaleazzo's death in September 1402.

3. This description of the feats of the Greek athlete Milo of Croton probably derives from Cicero *De senectute* 3.10.33, and Pliny *Naturalis historia* 7.28.83.

4. Perhaps known from the account of Polydamas, the great Thessalian athlete and victor in the Olympic games of 408 B.C., in Valerius Maximus, *Memorabilia* 9.12.ext.io.

5. Plato *Leges* 704–7, the beginning of book 4.

6. Seneca *Troades* 7–8.

7. Vergil *Aeneid* 2.254–55.

8. Vergil *Aeneid* 2.374–75.

9. From Livy *Ab urbe condita* 28.46.

10. Cicero *Orationes philippicae* 2.44.

11. The following anecdotes about Caligula and Tiberius are derived from Suetonius *Gaius Caligula* 24, 30; and *Tiberius* 43–44.

12. Suetonis *Gaius Caligula* 30.2.

13. Tacitus *Historiae* 1.1.

14. The corruption of Verres, the partisan of Sulla who exploited Sicily during his proconsulship there in 73–71 B.C., was known to Bruni probably from Cicero's famous *Orationes Verrinae*. It seems probable that Bruni is thinking of the Aeolian coward of the *Iliad*, Thersites, who was not an Athenian as Bruni suggests. The precise reference remains obscure.

15. Cicero *De officiis* 3.29.108.

16. A reference to the Emperor Henry VII, who pitched camp before the gate of Florence during his descent into Italy in 1312. See the modern account in F. Schevill, *History of Florence from the Founding of the City through the Renaissance* (New York, 1936), pp. 189–191. Cf. Bruni's later account in his *Historiarum Florentini populi libri* XII, ed. E. Santini, *RIS*, n.e., 19, 3 (Città di Castello, 1914): 107–11.

17. A reference to the *Historiae Florentini populi*, which Bruni later wrote while chancellor of Florence.

18. The campaign against Volterra in 1254 is mentioned in Schevill, p. 122, and in Bruni, *Historiae*, p. 30.

19. An allusion to Florence's defeat of Pisa in 1252 when under the Primo Popolo the Florentines extended their power in Tuscany. See Schevill, *History of Florence*, pp. 120–21, Bruni, *Historiae*, p. 28, and Giovanni Villani, *Cronica*, ed. by F. Dragomanni, 4 vols. (Florence, 1844–45), 1: 274.

20. Another reference to the recent war against Giangaleazzo Visconti, which ended in 1402.

21. The chronology of these events is as follows: Giangaleazzo occupied Pisa early in 1399, Siena during the summer of the same year, Perugia early in 1400, Assisi in May 1400, and Bologna in June 1402. See H. Baron, *From Petrarch to Leonardo Bruni* (Chicago, 1968), pp. 116, n. 257.

22. The defeat of the Florentine Guelf by the Tuscan Ghibellines at the battle of Montaperti in 1260 is discussed in Schevill, pp. 127–30, and the historical situation is described at length by Bruni in his *Historiae*, pp. 34–40.

23. An allusion to the evacuation of Athens in 480 B.C. under the direction of Themistocles.

24. An allusion to Charles of Anjou, whom Pope Urban IV brought to fight against the Hohenstaufens in southern Italy in 1265. See Schevill, *History of Florence*, pp. 135–40.

ORATION FOR THE FUNERAL OF NANNI STROZZI (1428)

25. Estienne *Baluze, Miscellaneorum . . . hoc est, collectio veterum monumentorum*, vol. 3 (Paris, 1681), pp. 266ff.; reprinted by G. D. Mansi in *Stephani Baluzii Tutelensis Miscellanea novo ordine digesta . . . et aucta*, vol. 4 (Lucca, 1764), pp. 2–7. The translation is of the first half (dealing with the city) and omits the second half that is concerned only with the individual career and deeds of Nanni Strozzi.

26. Sallust *Bellum Catilinarium* 7.2.

Chapter 5. Poggio Bracciolini

IN PRAISE OF THE VENETIAN GOVERNMENT (1459)

1. See Aristotle, *Politics* IV.2.

2. Cicero, *De legibus* II.10.23.

3. That is, the doge, who is elected for life by a committee of the Maggio Consiglio, composed of the Venetian nobility.

4. Aristotle, *Politics* III.10 (1286a28–31).

5. *Historia Augusta:* "Alexander Severus" LXV.4. Aelius Lampridius is one of the six authors of the *Historia Augusta*, a collection of biographies of Roman emperors written in the late third and early fourth centuries A.D.

6. George of Trebizond argues that the Venetians modelled their constitution on Plato's *Laws*.

7. Cicero, *Pro Flacco* 63.

8. Cicero, *Pro Balbo* 34.

9. Lucan, *Pharsalia* 1.1.

10. Cicero, *De imperio Cnaei Pompei* 38.

11. Gaius Verres, Publius Clodius and Catiline were all attacked in Cicero's speeches: see the *Verrines, De domo sua* and *Pro Sestio*, and *In Catalinam* respectively.

12. Cicero, *De officiis* II.3.3.

13. The Secession of the Plebs refers to their withdrawal en masse from public life in the middle of the fifth century B.C.

14. According to tradition, the Roman constitution was suspended in 451 B.C., and ten patricians (*decem viri*) were given the power to prepare a new code of laws. A second group of decemvirs was appointed the next year; but the new laws they proposed were considered unfavourable to the plebs, so they were forced to resign and the ancient constitution was restored.

15. Coriolanus, a legendary figure of the fifth century B.C., when charged with tyrannical conduct and with opposition to the distribution of food to the starving plebs, is said to have withdrawn from Rome.

16. According to tradition, Camillus, after being exiled from Rome for appropriating booty, retired to Ardea, where he was appointed dictator at the time of the Gallic invasion of Rome (387/6 B.C.). He raised an army and defeated the Gauls, for which he was regarded as the saviour and second founder of Rome.

17. The sea wall of the Lido of Venice.

18. Plutarch, *Life of Pyrrhus* 19. Cineas was a Thessalian diplomat of the third century B.C.

19. The doge's cabinet was known as the Lesser Council, or Minor Consiglio.

20. Doge Marin Faliero, charged with conspiring against the state, was executed on 17 April 1355.

21. These magistrates were known as the Council of Ten, or Consiglio dei dieci.

22. Members of this magistracy were referred to as the Avogadori di comun.

23. That is, Signori di notte.

24. Reading *caeteros* instead of *caeteris*.

25. Ezekiel 18:20.

26. The condottiere Francesco Bussone, called Carmagnola, was decapitated in May 1432 on a charge of treason in the war against Milan.

27. This paragraph is found as a marginal addition in the original manuscript and evidently represents an afterthought. The text is somewhat garbled.

28. See, e.g., Cicero, *De officiis* I.27.93–6, I.35.126, and *Orator* 21.70.

29. See Cicero, *De senectute* 18.63.

30. Aristotle, *Nicomachean Ethics* X.9 (1180a14–16).

31. Desiderius reigned from 756 to 774; Maurizio Galbaio was doge from 764 to 787.

32. Aristotle, *Nicomachean Ethics* V.1 (1129b18–19).

Chapter 6. Alamanno Rinuccini

LIBERTY (1479)

1. Translated from Francesco Adorno's edition in *Atti Colombaria*, vol. 22 (N. F. 8; 1957), 265–303, previously published by him in E. Grassi, *Colección Tradición y Tarea* (losada), Santiago, Chile, 1952. Notes to classical sources are with one small exception his.

2. Giovanni and Geronimo Andrea seems to refer to two members of the Olgiati family who, in 1476, took part for idealistic reasons in the assassination of Galeazzo Maria Sforza, Duke of Milan. Cf. Jacob Burckhardt, *Civilization of the Renaissance in Italy*, New York, 1950, 37–38.

3. F. Adorno thinks this is a reference to Donato Acciaiuoli's still extant Commentary on the lectures of Argyropoulos. It is even possible that Alitheus may be Rinuccini's fictional name for Donato, and not just for one of his friends.

4. Cicero *Paradoxa* V, I, 34.

5. Cicero *Paradoxa* V.

6. Cicero *Tusc. Queast.* IV, 17–19.

7. Cicero *De finibus* V, 8, 23; V, 29, 87.

8. Aristotle *Ethica Nic.* I, 1097b–1098a.

9. Cicero *Paradoxa* V, I, 34.

10. Aristotle *Politica* III, 1281b, cf. 1279a.

11. The Battle of Benevento in February 1266 ended the Hohenstauffen line in Italy.

12. Florence lay under the interdict from September 1273 till January 1276.

13. Henry VII in September 1312.

14. Uguccione Fagiolano was a Ghibelline leader who became tyrant of Pisa after Henry VII's departure. He defeated Florence at Montecatini in August 1315; he was overthrown by Castruccio in the spring of 1316. Florence warred against Castruccio from 1320 till his death in 1329. Florence took Pisa and could not be dislodged by the Emperor Louis of Bavaria in 1329.

15. Guido Tarlato, appointed Bishop of Arezzo in 1313, led that city in collaboration with his brother, Piero. Arezzo expanded its territory by conquest and Florence responded by conquering Arezzo and its domains in 1336.

16. Cf. note 14.

17. Pisa, rather than Florence, finally took Lucca from Mastino in July 1342.

18. In 1351 Florence repelled the invasion of her territory by Milan, ruled at that time by Archbishop Giovanni Visconti.

19. In the War of the Eight Saints, fought in 1375–78 against Gregory XI, the Florentines sent representatives to papal towns and urged revolt. They carried a banner inscribed with the word, *Libertas.*

20. The wars with Ladislas went on from 1408 till his death in 1414. The purchase of Cortona, according to Schevill, occurred in January 1411, when Florence "abandoned its allies and was rewarded for its treachery by the cession of the town of Cortona." Ferdinand Schevill, *History of Florence*, New York, 1961, 349.

21. 1422–28; 1440.

22. Alfonso's invasion of Tuscany in 1447 provoked a joint Florentine and papal policy of equilibrium in Italy and thus led to the Peace of Lodi of 1454. Peter Partner, "Florence and the Papacy," in Nicolai Rubinstein, *Florentine Studies*, London, 1968, 401.

23. This dates the present dialogue to the period from the summer of 1478 to the end of 1479. It seems unlikely that Rinuccini was writing after Lorenzo had set out for Naples in December 1479, a spectacular mission which did bring peace by February 1480.

24. Rinuccini's attitude to Florentine diplomacy based on calling in foreigners to the peninsula is most unapologetic, compared to the Florentine ambassadors' speech in Bruni's *History*, Book XII. Cf. Schevill (391): "the descent of the French was for many decades suspended like a portent over the peninsula, filling all its states, large and small alike, with alarm, but at the same time exercising a curious, hypnotic fascination." In 1495 Savonarola would convince the Florentines that Charles VIII of France was both a scourge of God falling upon them, and, after negotiations, an ally who would eventually help them regain control of Pisa.

25. Plato *Ep.* IX 358a; Cicero *De Officiis* I, 7, 22.

26. Reference to the Ciompi revolt of 1378 which greatly democratized the government till the counterrevolution of 1382.

27. Aristotle *Ethica Nic.* I, 1098b–1099a.

28. Cicero *De finibus* V, 79; cf. *Acad. Post.* I, 38.

29. Cicero *Oratio pro Murena*, 63.

30. Cicero *De finibus* V, 8, 23; V, 29, 87.

31. Cicero *Pro Cneo Placio oratio* XX, 50.

32. Plato *Ep.* V, 322ab; cf. *Ep.* VII, 325–6, 331d; *Resp.* VI, 496 c–e. Also *Apology* 31d, 32a.

33. Ennius *Scenica* fragm. 409 (Vhalen); Cicero De *Officiis* II, 18, 62.

34. Hesiod *Op.* 238.

Chapter 8. Paolo Vettori

MEMORANDUM TO CARDINAL DE' MEDICI
ABOUT THE AFFAIRS OF FLORENCE (1512)

1. Giovanni de' Medici was absent from Florence for more than two months. Pope Julius II had appointed him papal legate in Bologna and the Romagna in October 1511; and he was charged with recovering Ferrara. He left Florence on 6 November 1512, with papal and Florentine troops, and went to Bologna, where he remained until mid January 1513; he returned to Florence on 19 January. Pope Julius died on 20 February, and on 22 February Giovanni left for Rome, where he was elected pope on 11 March. The dates of his movements are recorded in Luca Landucci, *A Florentine Diary from 1450 to 1516*, ed. Iodoco Del Badia (London, 1927), pp. 263, 265, 266.

2. Cosimo de' Medici (1389–1464); Piero de' Medici (1471–1503). Vettori means the period between 1434 (when Cosimo returned from a year's exile in Padua) and 1494 (when Piero was driven from Florence), and he is referring to four men: Cosimo; his son, Piero (1416–69); Piero's son, Lorenzo the Magnificent (1449–92); and Lorenzo's eldest son, Piero.

3. As the Medici family had done between 1434 and 1494.

4. The Ten of Liberty and Peace (before 1494 called Dieci di Balìa). "The Ten were responsible for conducting wars, procuring supplies and ammunition, hiring soldiers, and conducting diplomatic relations in times of war": M. Domandi's introduction to his translation of F. Guicciardini, *The History of Florence* (New York, 1970), p. xlv.

5. Towards the Medici, who were absent from Florence between 1494 and 1512.

6. The Nine of Ordinanza and Milizia, the body concerned with military organization, founded in 1507.

7. Giuliano de' Medici, Duke of Nemours (1479–1516), third son of Lorenzo the Magnificent. After his brother, Giovanni (1475–1521), was elected Pope Leo X, in March 1513, he lived mostly in Rome.

8. The Palazzo della Signoria, the seat of government; it has been called the Palazzo Vecchio since the late sixteenth century.

9. That is, not through the established political institutions.

10. For the organization and work of the Chancery, see A. Brown, *Bartolomeo Scala, 1430–1497, Chancellor of Florence* (Princeton, N.J., 1979), pp. 135–92, and R. Black, *Benedetto Accolti and the Florentine Renaissance* (Princeton, N.J., 1985), pp. 115–83.

11. Lorenzo the Magnificent (see n. 7); in short, between 1469 (when Lorenzo's father, Piero, died) and 1492.

12. Bartolomeo Scala (1430–97), humanist and first chancellor of Florence, 1465–97. See Brown, *Bartolomeo Scala*.

13. Marcello Virgilio Adriani (1464–1521), humanist and administrator. In 1494 he succeeded Angelo Poliziano in the chair of poetry and rhetoric at the University of Florence. After the death of Scala, in July 1497, Adriani was chosen to succeed him as first chancellor in February 1498 and served until his death.

14. Cristoforo Landino (1424–98), humanist and administrator. After early legal studies, he devoted himself to literature; he began to teach at the University of Florence in 1458 and obtained a chair there in 1471. From the early 1480s, he occupied high posts in the Chancery and became secretary of the Signoria, retiring in 1497 or 1498.

15. Niccolò Machiavelli (1469–1527), head of the Second Chancery and secretary to the Ten of Liberty and Peace, 1498–1512; head of the Nine of Milizia, 1507–1512. Author of *The Prince*, *Discourses on Livy*, etc.

16. Giovanni Guidi (c. 1435–1515), son of Bartolomeo Guidi of Pratovecchio (c. 1400–77), who was head of the office of the Riformagioni from 1458 until 1477. Because of Bartolomeo's age, in 1471 Giovanni was appointed to help his father in his official duties, and on his father's death he was appointed in his place. He was head of the Riformagioni until 1494; he suffered hard times during the popular regime that was then established (*ser* was the title of notaries).

17. This office was concerned with drafting legislation and, after it was passed, transcribing it into the official books.

18. Francesco Ottaviani or Attaviani, born in Arezzo, was head of the office of the Riformagioni from 1499 until December 1514. It is not known whether he died or was dismissed; his successor was appointed on 11 January 1515.

19. Simone Grazzini, born in Staggia c. 1435, died after 1494. He became eligible to hold public office in Florence in 1459. He was head of the office of the Tratte from 1484 until 1494, when he was dismissed.

20. This office was concerned with elections to all public offices, with ensuring that candidates were of the correct age, that they were not disqualified from holding office for any reason, etc.

21. Vespucci was head of the office of the Tratte from 1498 until 1528, when he retired.

22. Francesco Gaddi (c. 1450–1504). After graduating in law, he entered public life in 1476; he held various important posts and undertook several missions in Italy and abroad. He was head of the Second Chancery, 1494–98.

23. Alessandro Braccesi or Bracci (1455–1503), scholar, poet and administrator. He was head of the Second Chancery for a brief period in 1498.

24. Francesco Baroni, also known as ser Ceccone (1451–1503), the son of ser Barone Baron. He was appointed as head of the office of the Eight of Pratica in 1483; he was dismissed in November 1494.

25. Antonio della Valle (1449–1511) held various administrative posts during a long career. In 1509 he was notary of the Signoria, and in 1510 he was civil notary of the Council of Justice.

26. Antonio Guidotti of Colle, notary and clerk in the Chancery; he was entrusted with various missions (to Milan in 1499, to Siena in 1502).

27. He was also known as ser Luca Fabiani; Lorenzo Ficini was an adopted name. He was Bartolomeo Scala's assistant in the Chancery in the 1480s and 1490s. (I owe this information to Alison Brown.)

28. The Nine of Ordinanza and Milizia. The tense used here is different from that in the earlier reference to Machiavelli: the explanation is that when he was appointed to the Nine in January 1507, he retained his other posts as head of the Second Chancery and secretary to the Ten; to Vettori the new position doubtless seemed more important.

29. Biagio Buonaccorsi (1472–c. 1522), a junior colleague and close friend of Niccolò Machiavelli (with whom he corresponded frequently). He lost his administrative post (as did Machiavelli) in November 1512.

30. That is, between 1494 and 1512.

31. Almost certainly Leonardo Guidotti. He was elected a member of the Ten in September 1500. Previously, he had held various offices: he had been a member of the Eight of Pratica (in 1490), and one of the Defenders of the Laws (1493, 1499). According to H. C. Butters, *Governors and Government in Early Sixteenth-Century Florence* (Oxford, 1985), p. 247, at one time he held "the office of depositary." He is mentioned in several letters written by Biagio Buonaccorsi to Machiavelli in 1502: see N. Machiavelli, *Lettere* (Milan, 1961), ed. F. Gaeta, pp. 78–80, 82, 84, 98, 104, 106. He may have still been alive in 1526 (*Lettere*, pp. 392, 394, 483, 488, 498); there are three mentions of "Guidetto" and two of "Guidotto," and Gaeta thinks Leonardo Guidotti is being referred to.

Chapter 9. Niccolò Machiavelli

MEMORANDUM TO THE NEWLY RESTORED MEDICI (1512)

1. Written in November 1512 to "the Palleschi," that is, to the Medici and their partisans. Thanks to Gabriele Pedullà for assistance with the translation.
2. That is, of wishing to wield tyrannical power.
3. That blame for Soderini's ouster and the republic's fall would then fall squarely on the Medici.
4. And who are not necessarily the Medici's friends.
5. That is, the people.
6. Soderini is now beside the point; the people resent the Medici for overturning the republic.
7. That is, partisans of the republic.
8. They prefer a state without either Piero or the Medici.

DISCURSUS ON FLORENTINE MATTERS AFTER THE DEATH
OF LORENZO DE' MEDICI THE YOUNGER (1520–21)

9. Thanks to Gabriele Pedullà for assistance with the translation.
10. A calling of all Florentine citizens to the Palazzo della Signoria to acclaim proclamations put to them by the government.
11. That is, the people.
12. The Eight of Guardia served as a—sometimes temporary, sometimes standing—judicial commission or board; the Balìa was a committee, appointed by the Signoria and ratified by the parlamento, to reform Florence's government in any way they saw fit.
13. Jérémie Barthas points out that Machiavelli refers here not to the maximum size of the Great Council, but rather to the quorum required for it to officially meet. See Barthas, "Il pensiero costituzionale di Machiavelli e la funzione tribunizia nella Firenze del Rinascimento," in Lorenzo Tanzini, ed., *Il laboratorio del Rinascimento: Studi di storia e cultura per Riccardo Fubini* (Florence: Le Lettere, 2015) 239–56 at 242–43n13.
14. Officials charged with selecting from the baggings of eligible citizens the names of individuals who would hold office.
15. The length of time that a citizen must wait, after holding office, before holding office again.

MINUTES OF A PROVISION FOR THE REFORM
OF THE FLORENTINE GOVERNMENT (1522)

16. Thanks to Antonio Ricci for assistance with the translation.
17. Florentine laws were frequently referred to as *provvisioni*.
18. Literally, the chancellors of the "drawings." In the Florentine system, offices were filled by drawing (*tratta*) of names of eligible office holders out of a purse. The Ufficiali delle Tratte was the magistracy charged with supervising the drawings and recording the results.
19. Prior to August 1512.
20. "Operai." Major building projects and maintenance of government and church buildings was entrusted to committees known as *opere*. Many Florentines served on these committees such that their members, or *operai*, could be laypeople with little expertise whose appointment was the result of random sortition or professionals with considerable expertise who were routinely and regularly reappointed to the opere. On this, see John Najemy, *A History of Florence, 1200–1575* (Oxford: Blackwell, 2006), 317.
21. The *Monte*, or mountain, was the city's funded public debt.
22. Machiavelli uses the term "*netti di specchio*." The Florentines recorded the names of public debtors in a volume known as the *specchio*. Only those whose names were not in the specchio could serve on the Great Council.

23. The Councils of the People and the Commune were legislative bodies elected by the Signoria and its two colleges (advisory councils—the Twelve Good Men and the Standard Bearers of the Companies), collectively referred to as the "Tre Maggiori," or Three Major Councils. These councils considered proposals approved by the Signoria and its colleges; two-thirds of the council had to vote in favor for the adoption of the proposal. On this, see Gene Brucker, *Florentine Politics and Society, 1343–1378* (Berkeley: University of California Press, 1962), 61; the Council of One Hundred (*Cento*) was created in 1434 at the beginning of Cosimo de' Medici's rise to power. The one hundred elected officials to the *Monte*, the *Catasto* (census), and to the Otto di Guardia e Balìa, a committee that investigated major crimes and offenses against the state. On this see Najemy, *History of Florence*, 295–96.

24. The Council of Eighty was created in 1494 after the expulsion of the Medici that year. Along with the Signoria, colleges, and Council of Ten, the Council of Eighty elected ambassadors and military commissioners and considered proposals from the Signoria. If approved in the Eighty, the proposal proceeded to the Great Council for approval. See Najemy, *History of Florence*, 387.

25. Machiavelli here means that those with the most black beans go forward, even if they fail to win 50 percent plus one.

26. A parlamento was a general assembly of Florentine citizens, summoned to the main square by the government to grant approval for the creation of *balìe*, special ad hoc emergency councils with powers that superseded the normal government structure. While in theory the assembly could decline to approve the creation of a balìa, it never happened. Machiavelli here and elsewhere opposes extraordinary mechanisms that override normal institutional procedure.

MEMORANDUM TO CARDINAL GIULIO ON THE REFORM OF THE STATE OF FLORENCE (1522)

27. Thanks to Antonio Ricci for assistance with the translation.

SUMMARY OF THE AFFAIRS OF THE CITY OF LUCCA (1520)

28. Thanks to Antonio Ricci for assistance with the translation.

29. The Council of Thirty-Six.

30. Machiavelli uses the Florentine term—*pratiche*—for the body of former office holders who advise sitting councils.

31. The ballot contains the name of the candidate.

32. By "bad choice," Machiavelli means the person is not elected.

33. By "yours," Machiavelli means the Florentine method, given his Florentine audience.

34. Some editions suggest that Machiavelli mistakenly wrote "Florentine" instead of "foreign," on the grounds that Lucca was not subject to Florence and relations between Lucca and Florence were frequently hostile. Given that the Lucchesi often referred to the governors of their subject territories as *podestà*, an entirely different position from the judicial one described here, Machiavelli may have meant a "Florentine-style" podestà to indicate that the office's functions were identical to the Florentine version. Thanks to Daniel Jamison for these details.

35. The Venetian Signoria was a ducal council that represented the republic and that consisted of the doge, six ducal councilors, and the three heads of the Court of Forty (Quarantia), the supreme appeals court for criminal matters. On this, see Robert Finlay, *Politics in Renaissance Venice* (New Brunswick, N.J.: Rutgers University Press, 1980), 21–33.

36. Machiavelli is referring to the Great Council and the Senate (*consiglio dei pregadi*).

37. The text is blank, but Machiavelli is evidently referring to the people or plebs.

38. The necessity of a three-fourths vote.

Chapter 10. Francesco Guicciardini

ON THE METHOD OF ELECTING OFFICES IN THE GREAT COUNCIL (1512)

1. The original reads: "*io non so come il popolo abbia causa a dolersi che gli ufici siano date a chi vuole lui.*" It is the only use of the pronoun *lui* in the text.

2. White and black beans were used as tallies in balloting. A black bean represented a vote in favor of a proposition, while a white bean indicated a vote against.

3. The "fourteen" and the "eleven" were two groups of administrative offices held by Florentines in the major towns and cities of the *contado* and *distretto*. The norms for their election are in the law of 23 December 1494; see G. Cadoni's edition in *Provvisioni concernenti l'ordinamento della Repubblica Fiorentina*, Rome: Nella sede dell'Istituto, 1994 vol. 1, 46–47. Cadoni lists the offices in each group in notes 21 and 22 on the same pages. Thanks to John Najemy for these details.

4. The *mazzocchio* was a large group of lesser administrative offices, both internal and external. The rules for their election can be found in the *provvisione* of 26 November 1495, in G. Cadoni's edition in *Provvisioni concernenti l'ordinamento della Repubblica Fiorentina*, vol. 1, 209–25. On pp. 223–24, in an appendix to the text of the law, Cadoni reconstructs the offices included in the so-called *mazzocchio*. Thanks to John Najemy for these details.

ON THE MODE OF REORDERING THE POPULAR GOVERNMENT (1512)

5. At the time of composition, Louis XII of France was at war with Pope Julius II, the Swiss, the Venetians, and Ferdinand of Aragon, also known as the "Holy League." However, here Guicciardini seems to be referencing the violence initiated in 1494, when Charles VII entered Italy and rendered it a battleground for the other European powers.

6. *Uomini Savi* indicates a category of people who include experts and other men of experience and social standing, who may not necessarily hold office but are consulted to serve the common good. *Uomini savi* and *Uomini da bene* are two distinct categories of men essential to Guicciardini's understanding of Florentine political life. For elaboration on the role of these two categories in his political thought, see Giovani Di Silvano's "Gli uomini da bene' di Francesco Guicciardini: Coscienza aristocratica e repubblica a Firenze nel primo Cinquecento," *Archivio storico italiano* 148.546 (1990): 845–92.

7. *El monte*, Florence's consolidated public debt.

8. The battle of Agnadello was fought 14 May 1509, where the allied forces of the emperor, France, Aragon, and the papacy defeated the Venetians and took all the Venetian territories on the Italian mainland.

9. On the Great Council, see John Najemy, *History of Florence, 1200–1575* (Oxford: Blackwell, 2006), 381–90.

10. The Council of Eighty was created in 1494 after the expulsion of the Medici that year, the same year that the Great Council was established. Along with the Signoria, colleges, and Council of Ten, the Council of Eighty elected ambassadors and military commissioners and considered proposals from the Signoria. If approved in the Eighty, the proposal proceeded to the Great Council for approval. The Signoria needed to consult the Eighty on a weekly basis. See Najemy, *History of Florence*, 387.

11. The Signoria, the traditional ruling body of the republic, consisted of eight magistrates or "priors" and was headed by the gonfalonier. The Signoria governed alongside the colleagues in office, that is, the two colleges of sixteen Gonfalonieri di Compagnia, and the twelve "good men," or *buonuomini*.

12. "*Onori e utili*": The higher offices, or "honors," came without salary while the lesser ones did come with salary because they were filled by men typically in need of the "utility" of compensation.

13. The Ten of War (*Dieci di Guerra*) and the Eight of Ward (*Otto di Guardia*) were powerful executive committees, with broad discretionary powers over, respectively, foreign and domestic affairs.

14. The captains possessed military and penal power in subject cities. In more important subject cities, the captain shared power with the *podestà*, who supervised the more autonomous government of the dependent territory.

15. *Podesterie*, or Florentine citizens who administered the government of subject cities.

16. At the time of writing, the Guelf party still constituted an institution of considerable wealth, and its leaders maintained public influence and recognition.

17. The Six of Commerce, or the Mercanzia, was the judiciary court that regulated economic activity and protected property rights. The Mercanzia was directed by a foreign judge (*ufficiale*) and supported by a small group of counselors who were Florentine merchants. The "Six of the Mercanzia" represented the five major guilds and the fourteen lesser guilds, which together had the right to only one representative. For further reading, see Luca Boschetto, "Writing the Vernacular at the Merchant Court of Florence," in *Textual Cultures of Medieval Italy: Essays from the 41st Conference on Editorial Problems*, edited by William Robins (Toronto: University of Toronto Press, 2011), pp. 217–262; and Najemy, *History of Florence*, 109–12.

18. Established in 1429 to oversee eligibility for office, and to ascertain whether the activity of associations abided by the constitution, the "Conservators of the Laws" also possessed wide police power over political crimes, as they were later empowered to impose sentences of exile and death.

19. *Divieti* were prohibitions that barred close relatives from holding, concurrently or in too close succession, certain offices, and they established the intervals of time between which the same individual could hold posts.

20. "*La può fare con la balìa delle sei fave el tutto*": With eight signori and the gonfalonier, six votes were sufficient for the majority of two-thirds.

21. *Quarantìa*: an extraordinary court established to supervise penal issues.

22. *Consulte*: informal, ad hoc assemblies in which influential elites were invited to discuss important matters of state.

23. *Squittino*, or scrutiny, was the method of determining eligibility of candidates for office by scrutinizing each name on the list, or in the purse. Those charged with such discretion thus played a crucial political role.

24. *Parlemento*: a large assembly with undefined membership who came together in a public square and reached decisions by acclamation, usually determined by the presiding magistrates.

THE GOVERNMENT OF FLORENCE AFTER THE MEDICI RESTORATION (1513)

25. Giuliano de' Medici.

ON THE MODE OF SECURING THE STATE OF THE HOUSE OF MEDICI (1516)

26. Guicciardini intimates here that had all Florentines been more committed to a free and republican way of life, they would have resisted the French invasion, which reveals their weak commitment to republican principles.

27. Borgia and Piccolomini, respectively.

28. On the mercanzia, see above, *On the Mode of Reordering the Popular Government*, note 13.

29. The magistrates allow the people's property to go into foreclosure and then let the *grandi* buy up the property for insignificant sums because they were bribed by these grandi.

Index

Acknowledgments

The editors would like to thank Damon Linker for his support and expert editorial feedback and Noreen O'Connor-Abel, Kathleen Kageff, and Avery Broome for their sharp-eyed and meticulous copy-editing and corrections.